Object-Oriented Languages, Systems and Applications

Edited by
Gordon Blair, John Gallagher,
David Hutchison and Doug Shepherd
University of Lancaster, UK

D0874254

Halsted Press: An Imprint of
John Wiley & Sons, Inc.
New York   Toronto

Published in the USA and Canada by Halsted Press:
An Imprint of John Wiley & Sons, Inc., 605 Third Ave,
New York, NY 10158-0012

Library of Congress Cataloging-in-Publication Data

Object-oriented languages : systems and applications / Gordon Blair
    . . . [et al.].
        p.   cm.
    Includes bibliographical references and index.
    ISBN 0-470-21722-7
    1. Object-oriented programming (Computer science)   I. Blair,
Gordon.
QA76.64.O25   1990
005.1—dc20

© Longman Group UK Limited 1991

First published in Great Britain by
Pitman Publishing, a Division of
Longman Group UK Limited, 1991

Printed and bound in Great Britain by
Biddles Ltd, Guildford and King's Lynn

Contents

Chapter 1

Introduction

Gordon Blair, John Gallagher, David Hutchison, Doug Shepherd
Lancaster University

ABSTRACT *The aim of this chapter is to provide the reader with the necessary background to tackle the rest of the material in this book. The emergence of object-oriented computing is traced and the many fields of application highlighted. The chapter examines the fundamental characteristics of object-oriented computing in terms of the approach to abstraction. Four principles of object-oriented abstraction are presented. Following this, the wide range of techniques associated with object-oriented computing is emphasized. A framework is presented to assist the reader in understanding this range of options. The chapter concludes by describing the overall structure of the book and commenting on the role of each chapter.*

1.1 THE EMERGENCE OF OBJECT-ORIENTED COMPUTING

The emergence of object-oriented computing in the late 1980s is one of the most significant steps in the history of computing. The ideas behind object-oriented computing are now having a profound impact on areas such as languages, databases and artificial intelligence. Indeed, it is now quite rare to find new developments which are not influenced in some way by the ideas behind object-oriented computing.

This recognition of object-oriented computing is a classic example of overnight success after 20 years of painstaking research. The central ideas for object-oriented computing emerged in the late 1960s with the introduction of Simula [Dahl66], a programming language designed for writing simulation packages. The ideas were then developed further with the introduction of the Smalltalk series of languages, starting with Smalltalk-72 [Goldberg76] and culminating in Smalltalk-80 [Goldberg83]. By this time, many of the core ideas behind object-oriented computing were quite mature. However, the use of object-oriented techniques remained restricted to a small but active band of devotees.

It was only around 1986 that interest in object-oriented computing became significantly more widespread. In retrospect, the watershed for the subject may be traced to two classic conferences in the summer and autumn of 1986, namely the Object-

1

Oriented Programming Workshop at IBM, Yorktown Heights [Wegner86] and the 1st International Conference on Object-Oriented Programming Languages, Systems and Applications (OOPSLA'86) at Portland, Oregon [Meyrowitz86]. Both conferences featured a large number of seminal papers on the subject. From the interest in these events, it was clear that many researchers were looking towards object-oriented computing to help solve a wide range of problems. There are many reasons for this phenomenon. But perhaps the biggest influence was the rapid development of workstation technology. The modern workstation has the ability to support a sophisticated personal programming environment and also to provide a graphics-based human computer interface. Both factors provide encouragement to the object-oriented approach. Other reasons for the emergence include the continuing software crisis, the increasing demands placed on computing in terms of complex applications and a general move from quantitative to qualitative aspects of computing.

Since 1986, the renewed interest in object-oriented computing has filtered down from research and development to practical exploitation. It is now commonplace for industry and commerce to adopt object-oriented solutions to their problems. Tools such as Objective-C [Cox86], C++ [Stroustrup86], CLOS [DeMichiel87], MacApp [Schmucker86] and Iris [Fishman87] are now in widespread use. The growth of interest in object-oriented systems is reflected in Figure 1.1 which suggests the total revenue from object-oriented languages in USA and Europe will rise steadily over the next five years. More detailed analyses are available from a number of sources, e.g., Ovum [Jeffcoate89].

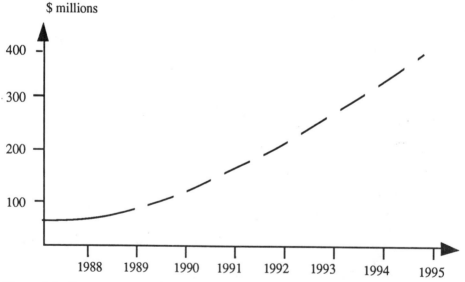

Figure 1.1: Current and projected growth in object-oriented computing

The very success of object-oriented computing, however, is perhaps its biggest problem. Object-oriented ideas are now being used in such diverse fields as programming languages, design methodologies, formal specification, operating systems, distributed computing, artificial intelligence, real time systems, databases, human computer interfaces and even hardware design. With this widespread use, it is inevitable that there will be a divergence in the field. Experience has shown that the relatively simple concepts behind the family of Smalltalk languages will not extend to meet to the requirements of all the above areas. A range of alternative approaches have therefore started to appear. As a consequence, it is no longer a straight-forward task to define precisely what is meant by the term object-oriented computing. This has led to much confusion in the field.

The principal aim of this book is to clarify this confusion and capture the *essence of object-oriented computing*. Despite the divergence, the authors believe that there is still a common bond which identifies exponents of object-oriented computing. In more detail, this book is intended to answer the following questions:-

i)   What are the fundamental *principles* behind object-oriented computing?
ii) What *techniques* are available and how do they relate to one another?
iii) How do object-oriented concepts *manifest* themselves in the various areas of application?
iv) What specific *examples* of object-oriented computing may be found in use?
v)   What are the *future directions* of object-oriented computing?

This chapter provides the necessary background to approach the material in the rest of the book. The chapter is structured as follows. Section 1.2 looks at the importance of abstraction as a general method of problem solving. Section 1.3 then looks at the specific approach to abstraction found in object-oriented computing; four principles of object-oriented abstraction are presented. The result of applying the four principles is considered in section 1.4 and the wide range of techniques is highlighted. A framework to aid the reader in stepping through the various techniques is presented in section 1.5. This framework will be used in subsequent chapters to explain how the various techniques relate to one another. Section 1.6 describes the structure of the book and, finally, section 1.7 describes how the book can be used. The intended readership is defined and various paths through the book illustrated.

1.2 THE ROLE OF ABSTRACTION IN PROBLEM SOLVING

A study of object-oriented computing must inevitably start with a close examination of *abstraction*. As we shall see, it is the particular approach to abstraction which characterises the object-oriented philosophy.

Abstraction is generally defined as 'the process of formulating generalised concepts by extracting common qualities from specific examples'. This process of generalisation is absolutely central to human understanding and reasoning. It is the main tool for handling complexity in two distinct areas:-

i)   in understanding complex issues, and
ii) in solving complex problems.

These two areas are quite distinct; the first is concerned with organising views of the world whereas the second concentrates on the application of these views as a problem solving approach.

As an aid to understanding, abstraction is used to build up conceptual models of the domain of discourse. Generalised concepts are recognised through a process of observation, and identified by association with a label or name. This name is then used to abstract over the various attributes and behaviours of that concept. A prime example of this form of abstraction is provided by the field of biology. Detailed classifications of a range of biological phenomena have been worked out over a period of time and now represent a mature body of knowledge on the subject. For example, the term *carnivores* is now commonly used to represent animals which share certain behaviour or possess certain characteristics, i.e. animals which eat meat. A typical biological classification is shown in Figure 1.2.

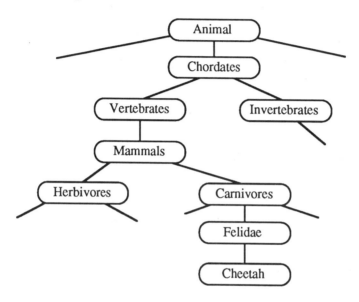

Figure 1.2: Biological classification

Abstraction has also proved to be invaluable as an aid to solving complex problems. The general approach is to decompose complex problems into a number of subsidiary areas and then focus on the individual areas. These areas can then be analysed further until manageable entities have been identified. Abstraction is evident in this process by the identification of sub-problems which correspond to a particular partitioning of the problem domain. The sub-problems are themselves problems which can be tackled in isolation. Once solved, the details of the solution can be abstracted over by the results. As an example of abstraction in problem solving, consider the task of an engineer in designing a new car. Without a methodical approach, the task is daunting. To manage successfully the complexity, the engineer must break down the problem into a number of identifiable sub-domains such as the ignition system, the fuel system, the suspension, etc. This can then be refined down to designing components such as carburettors, coils, and fuel pumps. At this level, the problem appears much easier to solve.

In computing, it is the use of abstraction as a problem-solving tool which is most important. Much of the history of computing has been concerned with providing the right tools and techniques to support a process of abstraction. The use of abstraction in computing is illustrated in Figure 1.3.

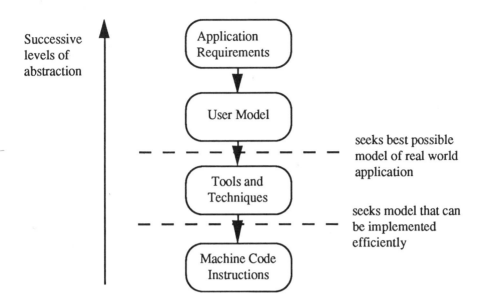

Figure 1.3: The use of abstraction in computing

In computing, the problem facing a programmer is normally one of developing a system to perform a specific task, e.g. managing a company's accounting system. A solution to this problem involves various levels of abstraction corresponding to the stages of a development process. At the highest level, there are certain abstract requirements which the system must attain. Following this, the system developer will have a mental model of components in the solution to the problem. This abstraction must be mapped down on to the abstractions provided by the tools and techniques chosen to solve the problem. Finally, the tools and techniques must themselves be realized as abstractions over the hardware of the underlying computer system.

The most important level as far as the computer scientist is concerned is the provision of suitable tools and techniques. Indeed computing has been pre-occupied by considerations of what are the most suitable tools and techniques at this level. The main difficulty is to resolve two often contradictory sets of criteria:-

i)   the tools and techniques must be well-suited to the specific problem being tackled, and
ii) the tools and techniques must be efficiently implemented on the underlying hardware.

This corresponds to the conflict between the mapping from the user model on to the tools and techniques and the mapping from the tools and techniques on to machine code instructions. It is at the level of the tools and techniques that this conflict must be resolved.

There have been many attempts to define suitable abstractions to support problem solving. Some techniques have been developed specifically for a particular problem domain while others are intended to support general problem solving. However, it is fair to say that computer science has had only limited success in developing tools and techniques to handle complexity.

Historically, most of the abstractions provided by computer systems have been tailored towards underlying machine architectures than to problem domains. Most development work has been carried out using imperative languages such as Fortran, Algol-68 and Pascal. The abstractions provided in such languages are clearly designed for efficient implementation on von Neumann architectures, e.g. variables map on to memory cells, loops map on to branch instructions, etc. The reason for this has purely been one of efficiency; it is crucially important that systems perform reasonably well on existing architectures.

Other approaches to abstraction have been forthcoming though, particularly in the field of Artificial Intelligence. The magnitude of problems tackled in AI are such that tools and techniques must be more supportive of the problem domain. One of the most successful approaches in AI is to provide tools and techniques based on logic. The argument is that logic is more geared towards the way humans tackle complex problems and therefore will support more elegant and expressive solutions. The language Prolog, for example, is based on the abstractions provided by first order logic. Another popular approach is to base tools and techniques on the abstraction of a mathematical function. Again, the rationale is that functions are more geared towards abstract problem solving. A number of functional languages such as Lisp [McCarthy62], Hope [Burstall80] and ML [Gordon79] have been proposed and extensively used.

There is a risk, however, in basing tools and techniques on problem-oriented abstractions, i.e. that it will be extremely difficult to realize efficient implementations on existing hardware. This problem has dogged both logic and functional languages from their inception. The other problem with functional and logic languages are that they tend to be focussed on specific problem domains and hence are not intended to be used in many classes of application.

As with functional and logic programming, object-oriented computing is characterised by its particular approach to providing abstractions. The philosophy of object-oriented computing is to provide tools and techniques which are supportive of problem solving and hence implementation considerations are secondary (in practice however efficient implementations of object-oriented systems have been developed). Unlike functional and logic programming, the abstractions are intended to be more general purpose and hence suitable across a wider range of application domains. To achieve this aim, it is important to capture principles of abstract problem solving which are universal across the spectrum of possible applications. Specific tools and techniques can then be provided which support these principles. The general principles underlying object-oriented computing are presented in the following section.

1.3 FOUR PRINCIPLES OF OBJECT-ORIENTED ABSTRACTION

In this book, we propose four basic principles which define the object-oriented approach to abstraction. These are:-
    i)   data abstraction,
    ii) behaviour sharing,
    iii) evolution, and
    iv) correctness.
These four principles capture the essence of object-oriented computing. Adherence

6

to the general principles defines the scope of the object-oriented community. Each of the four principles is discussed in turn below.

1.3.1 Data Abstraction

The first principle of object-oriented computing is that of *data abstraction*. The essence of data abstraction is that the programmer is presented with a higher level of abstraction over *both* the data *and* the algorithms required to manipulate the data. The user view is that of a number of operations which collectively define the *behaviour* of the abstraction; the user is not necessarily aware of the internal details of implementation. On closer examination, data abstraction actually encompasses two separate but closely related concepts:-

    i)   modularization, and
    ii) information hiding.

Modularization is concerned with the breaking down of complex systems into a number of self-contained entities (or modules). All information relating to a particular entity in the system is held within that module. Thus a module is a self-contained and complete description of a part of the overall system structure. In terms of computing, this means that a module will contain all the data structures and algorithms required to implement that part of the system. This is beneficial as it means that there is an obvious place to go to if changes have to be made or problems occur. More fundamentally, modularization enforces a particular design approach whereby the programmer breaks down the problem domain into a number of recognisable conceptual entities. This design approach forms the essence of object-oriented computing. It also provides the first level of abstraction in our discussion.

Information hiding takes the level of abstraction one stage further by hiding the implementation details of a module from the user. With information hiding, the user must access an object through a protected interface. This interface normally consists of a number of operations which, as mentioned above, collectively define the behaviour of an entity. The user is thus not allowed to see internal details such as local procedures or data structures. This is a major tool in handling complexity as it allows the user to abstract over a level of detail in the system. Information hiding also supports the development of more reliable programs by strictly controlling the entry points to a module. It is not possible to access data structures directly and thus not possible to perform unexpected actions on the data. The only way of accessing data structures is through the operational interface. A thorough testing of the interface operations thus provides a high level of confidence in the correctness of a module. Similarly, in systems which support information hiding, the effects of errors are normally confined within a module. It is therefore not possible for one module to corrupt another, adding to the dependability of a system.

In practice, the behaviour of an entity can be represented in two ways: abstractly in terms of supporting a procedural interface or concretely in terms of an interface and associated implementation. Object-oriented computing actually uses the term behaviour in either sense. It will be seen in later chapters that benefits can be gained by interpreting behaviour in the more abstract sense and thus separating specification from implementation (see chapter 4).

7

Data abstraction is generally recognised as a major step towards more structured programming. The techniques are gaining acceptance and have been incorporated in several important systems and languages, e.g. Cedar and Ada. In terms of this book, the importance of data abstraction is that it provides the starting point of object-oriented computing, i.e. that systems should be decomposed into conceptual entities and that internal details should be hidden. The abstractions provided by this process of modularization and information hiding are at the heart of the object-oriented approach. The first point in realizing an object-oriented approach is to provide techniques to support data abstraction.

1.3.2 Behaviour Sharing

The second principle of object-oriented computing is that systems should support *behaviour sharing*. Data abstraction introduces the important concept of behaviour, i.e. entities can be defined in terms of their external interface. Behaviour sharing takes this concept a stage further by allowing many entities to have the same interface set. This can add greatly to the flexibility of a system. As an example, consider the act of printing an entity. With data abstraction, a *print_yourself* operation would be defined to display a particular representation of the data structures. It would seem natural for this *print_yourself* operation to be defined over a number of objects. This is precisely what is meant by behaviour sharing; the interface for printing is shared across a number of entities in the system (although individual implementations may differ). The alternative would be to define different print operations for each entity in the system, e.g. *print_x* and *print_y*. Note that behaviour sharing adds considerably to the abstraction in a system: *print_yourself* is a much more abstract concept than *print_x*.

Behaviour sharing can be provided in a number of different ways. Two general approaches which are important in object-oriented computing are identified below:-

i) *classification*

The most obvious way of supporting behaviour sharing is to introduce classification into a system. A classification is formed on the basis of the common behaviour of a group of entities. All entities in a particular classification will therefore by definition share common behaviour. As an example, a queue could be classified as an entity which supports insert, delete and print. All queues will therefore share the behaviour of insert, delete and print.

ii) *taxonomies*

Taxonomies are a very popular form of behaviour sharing in object-oriented computing. Indeed, many people would argue that taxonomies represent the most characteristic feature of the object-oriented approach. A taxonomy is a refinement of classification which allows one classification to include another. Inclusion implies a more controlled form of behaviour sharing. Suppose a classification A is included in a classification B. A will exhibit certain behaviour. B will share this behaviour but will have additional behaviour of its own. For example, a stack with behaviour push and pop is included in a new_stack with behaviour push, pop and print. The result of this form of sharing is that a hierarchical structure is built up based on the inclusion relationships.

In general, it is possible for more selective forms of behaviour sharing which are not based on classification. It is perfectly reasonable for two or more entities to share a common item of behaviour without the necessity of being part of a classification. For example, Frank Sinatra and a nightingale both sing but do not otherwise form a sensible classification. In practice, a wide range of alternative approaches to behaviour sharing can be found in object-oriented computing (see chapter 3).

To mirror the discussion in section 1.3.1, behaviour sharing can either be based on sharing of specification or sharing of specification and implementation. Both are valid in object-oriented computing with most flexibility coming from separating the concerns. This issue is dealt with in depth in chapter 4.

Behaviour sharing is a second important principle underlying object-oriented computing systems. One of the biggest tasks in realizing an object-oriented approach is in developing particular techniques for behaviour sharing based on one or more of the categories defined above.

1.3.3 Evolution

The third principle of object-oriented computing is that support should be provided for *evolution*. This is based on the observation that requirements change rapidly in computing environments. Over a period of time, systems change and additional functionality may be required. The object-oriented approach is to support this process of evolution as a fundamental aspect of the computational model. Two aspects of evolution must be considered:-

i)   *requirements evolution*

Once a system has been developed, it is likely that changes will occur which will require modifications or additions. This is particularly the case in dynamic environments where it is difficult to capture a stable set of requirements, e.g. in design environments.

ii)   *solution by evolution*

A more general view of evolution is to develop solutions to problems in an incremental manner from initial experimentation to complete solutions. This approach is particularly attractive where the final goals of a system are not well defined.

The object-oriented philosophy is to provide a single approach which encompasses both aspects. Evolution therefore pervades the entire life-cycle of a system from initial tentative steps through to the ongoing maintenance. The general approach is to evolve towards the complete solution by a series of steps from where the system is now to where it should be going. This evolutionary approach to programming is unique to object-oriented computing. The importance of evolution is recognised by Cox in the title of his book on object-oriented programming: 'Objective-C -- An Evolutionary Approach'.

1.3.4 Correctness

The final principle of object-oriented computing is *correctness*. This is perhaps the most controversial dimension, as historically correctness has not been closely associated with object-oriented computing. Indeed, many object-oriented systems provide little or no support for developing correct applications. However, as applications of object-oriented techniques become more demanding, there is evidence of an upsurge of interest in the topic. Correctness is therefore included because of its perceived future importance as a design principle.

The term correctness has many interpretations in computing, e.g. program correctness, conformance testing, or fault tolerance. In the context of this book, correctness is given a more specific meaning. The term is used to describe *determinant* behaviour of a system. To illustrate this concept, consider a system consisting of a number of inter-working objects. Each object presents a behavioural specification to others in the system. At any point, one object may demand that an operation be carried out on another object. In other words, a particular item of behaviour is requested. A determinant system is one where there is guaranteed to be an interpretation for that behaviour, i.e. the system will never fail due to an inability to respond to an operation. Determinance is an important property in many large and complex systems. For example, in many process control applications it would be unacceptable to have errors due to an inability to react to an external event, e.g. a sudden temperature rise.

System determinance as described above is closely related to the concept of type and in particular type correctness. In effect, guarantees are required that type errors will not occur in a system. However, certain features of object-oriented systems make correctness a much more difficult issue to deal with than in traditional typing systems. In particular, behaviour sharing and evolution add to the complexity of ensuring correctness. Because of this dynamic and flexible environment, it is very difficult to make assertions about the overall behaviour of a system. On closer examination though, it *is* possible to determine whether a particular item of behaviour has an interpretation. It is not possible, however, to determine exactly what this interpretation might be (as this interpretation may change over time). Thus, determinance in object-oriented systems is concerned with the abstract level of specifications and not with particular implementations. The important topic of correctness will be dealt with in chapter 4.

1.4 APPLYING THE PRINCIPLES

The principles described above capture the essence of object-oriented computing. They underpin either explicitly or implicitly the vast majority of developments within the

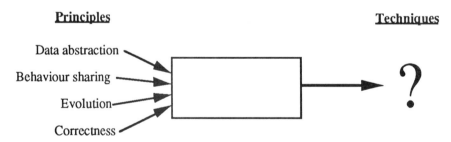

Figure 1.4: From principles to techniques

object-oriented community. Collectively, the principles describe a coherent approach to the problem of handling complexity in computer systems. However, in order to attain the many benefits associated with data abstraction, it is necessary to translate the abstract principles into a set of specific techniques[1]. This process is shown in Figure 1.4.

---

[1] 'Technique' is used as a generic term for an implementation mechanism which contributes to the realization of object-oriented principles.

In the early history of object-oriented computing, there was general consensus over the techniques required to support the object-oriented approach. A number of techniques such as class and inheritance were developed and actually became synonymous with object-oriented computing. More recently, however, the subject has become much more diverse and a much wider range of techniques now exist.

The reason for this divergence is the number of areas in which object-oriented ideas have been applied. Many developers from a range of different disciplines have been attracted by the general benefits associated with data abstraction, behaviour sharing, evolution and correctness. The major areas where object-oriented concepts have been influential are discussed below:-

i)   *Programming languages*

Object-oriented ideas first emerged in the language domain and this has remained the most influential area ever since. Initially attention was focussed on languages such as Simula and Smalltalk. However, a much more diverse range of languages now exist; e.g. Eiffel [Meyer88] BETA [Kristensen83], C++ and ACT-1 [Theriault82].

ii) *Software engineering*

The structuring capabilities of object-oriented computing have also attracted considerable attention from the field of software engineering. Software engineers are interested in extending the object-oriented paradigm from an implementation tool to a range of tools and techniques covering the full software lifecycle. Most work has been carried out on object-oriented design. However, there have also been a number of projects addressing object-oriented specification languages.

iii) *Databases*

Object-oriented databases are now emerging as a valid alternative to the more traditional relational, entity-relational and network models. There is particular interest in object-oriented techniques in databases to support design environments such as computer aided design systems and software engineering environments. Commercially available object-oriented databases include IRIS, Gemstone [Maier86] and ORION [Kim88].

iv) *Artificial intelligence*

Artificial Intelligence researchers are attracted to object-oriented computing principally because of the ability to represent complex bodies of knowledge in a conceptually elegant manner. A number of object-oriented knowledge representation languages have been developed based on the concept of frames. These extend the use of inference systems beyond what is commonly modelled using first order predicate logic.

v)   *Human computer interfaces*

An area that has benefited greatly from object-oriented computing is human computer interfaces. There is now an established harmony between object-oriented ideas and metaphors for visual representation and interaction. Examples of interfaces which benefit from object-oriented approaches include the Smalltalk and Macintosh desktops, and several other designs from the field of office information systems.

vi) *Operating systems*

Operating system designers have always been interested in techniques to impose structuring in the complex environment of systems programming. Many are now attracted to the potential benefits of object-oriented computing. This trend is particularly visible in the distributed operating system community with the emergence of systems such as Clouds [Bernabeu88] and Chorus [Zimmermann81].

vii) *Distributed systems*

As mentioned in vi), there is considerable interest in object-oriented techniques in the distributed operating system community. This interest has also spread to distributed systems in general to the extent that emerging standards for Open Distributed Processing are based on object-oriented concepts [OSN89].

Researchers and developers from all the areas are attracted by the same general principles. Clearly, however, they will all have their own specific requirements which will inevitably affect the techniques adopted. In practice, a wide range of techniques have been proposed under the object-oriented umbrella. For example, techniques such as delegation, conformance, enhancement, actors, prototypical objects and genericity have all been proposed as alternatives to the more traditional techniques. This phenomenon is illustrated in Figure 1.5.

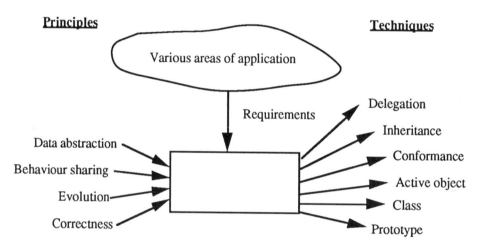

Figure 1.5: Range of techniques

At first sight, this variety of techniques is bewildering. To the newcomer to the field it is often unclear how the various techniques relate to each other. Similarly, it is not clear how the techniques relate back to the fundamental principles described above. The primary aim of this book is to help the reader through the task of understanding the field of object-oriented computing including all the variations shown above. To assist in this process, a framework is introduced in the following section. This framework will be used throughout Part 1 of the book as the various techniques are introduced.

1.5 FRAMEWORK FOR OBJECT-ORIENTED COMPUTING

The main problem in understanding object-oriented computing is to bridge the considerable gap between the abstract principles of object-oriented computing and the concrete techniques that have been introduced. It is very difficult to relate techniques back to the principles. Consequently, it is difficult to see what job a particular technique performs or how two techniques relate to one another. This section therefore introduces a framework to bridge the gap between principles and techniques. This approach is shown in Figure 1.6.

Figure 1.6: Bridging the gap

The framework is based on the observation that it is possible to partition the various techniques into a number of distinct categories with techniques from each category performing a particular role in an object-oriented system. Four categories have been identified:-

   i) encapsulation
   ii) classification
   iii) flexible sharing, and
   iv) interpretation.

The framework introduced in this section is therefore based on four dimensions relating to these four areas. Within this framework, it is relatively easy to see what role a particular technique is performing. Similarly, it is a simple task to relate back the general areas to the four principles introduced earlier. The framework therefore enables connections to be made between the techniques and the principles. It also enables alternative techniques for a particular job to be compared.

The dimensions essentially correspond to particular areas where techniques are required to realize the principles behind object-oriented computing. For each area, most systems tend to choose the appropriate technique (or sometimes techniques) which best fits into the overall system philosophy. This point will become much clearer as specific techniques are introduced in chapters 2, 3 and 4.

The various dimensions within the framework are discussed in more detail below:-

   i)   *Encapsulation*
      Encapsulation is used as a generic term for techniques which realize data abstraction. Encapsulation therefore implies the provision of mechanisms to support both modularity and information hiding. There is therefore a one to one correspondence in this case between the technique of encapsulation and the principle of data abstraction. Encapsulation therefore provides all the benefits associated with data abstraction such as the provision of conceptual building blocks and protection.

   ii)   *Classification*
      Object-oriented systems generally exhibit one or more techniques to support classification of objects with like behaviour. The group of techniques under this heading correspond to the first category of behaviour sharing approaches described in section 1.3.2 (other approaches such as taxonomies are dealt with below). To implement classification, mechanisms are required to support the

formation of groups with the same behaviour in terms of either specification or specification and implementation. This allows the user to reason about the behaviour of an object based on its inclusion in a grouping. Similarly, it is possible to share behaviour (again in terms of specification or specification and implementation) across all objects within a grouping.

iii) *Flexible Sharing*

In object-oriented computing, there is usually a separation between techniques supporting classifications from those supporting a more flexible form of behaviour sharing. The techniques under this category therefore enhance the behaviour sharing techniques of the system. The same techniques also tend to provide support for evolution and thus encompass two of the principles of object-oriented computing. Exactly how this is achieved will become much clearer with specific examples.

iv) *Interpretation*

Given the flexible and evolutionary forms of behaviour sharing in object-oriented systems, it is necessary to provide techniques for resolving the precise interpretation of an item of behaviour. A variety of different techniques have been proposed to support this task of interpretation. They tend to vary according to the timing of this interpretation, i.e. at compile time or run time. Compile time techniques tend to provide more guarantees of the correctness of object-oriented systems (as described in 1.3.4). In contrast, run time techniques tend to be more flexible. It will be seen though that some interesting compromises between the two concerns are now possible in object-oriented systems.

This general framework will be used in the early part of the book as new techniques are introduced. In particular, each of the first few chapters will conclude with a table in the format shown in Figure 1.7. This table will be gradually added to until all the major techniques of object-oriented computing are included. This table will then allow alternative techniques to be placed in perspective.

General Approach	Technique	Description	Xref
Encapsulation	Technique 1	Description of technique 1	
	Technique 2	Description of technique 2	
	etc		
Classification	Technique 1	Description of technique 1	
	Technique 2	Description of technique 2	
	etc		
Flexible sharing	Technique 1	Description of technique 1	
	Technique 2	Description of technique 2	
	etc		
Interpretation	Technique 1	Description of technique 1	
	Technique 2	Description of technique 2	
	etc		

Figure 1.7: Skeletal framework for object-oriented techniques

1.6 THE STRUCTURE OF THIS BOOK

Following the present chapter, the core of this book consists of four main parts, as follows:-

Part 1:   Introducing the Concepts
Part 2:   Objects in Action
Part 3:   Case Studies
Part 4:   Looking Ahead

The first part of the book is important in that it sets the scene for the remaining chapters. The basic concepts and terminology for the subject are established and the basic techniques associated with the object-oriented approach are introduced. The chapters in part 1 follow the framework established above. At the end of each chapter, a summary table is presented showing the full range of techniques introduced so far (as in Figure 1.7). Initially, a small core of techniques is introduced. This is followed by descriptions of alternative approaches until the full range of object-oriented computing has been covered.

The second part of the book parts deals with the object-oriented approach as it manifests itself in different areas of application. The areas covered in this part are programming languages, databases, design, distributed systems and user interfaces. The chapters in this part each present a detailed survey of their particular area and show how the object-oriented approach has been interpreted in that domain.

The third part is concerned with more detailed case studies of particular systems which have been guided by object-oriented principles. The three case studies are as follows. The first to be presented is REKURSIV, an object-oriented hardware design of a processor and its native programming language Lingo. Next, the design principles behind the BETA programming language are introduced and discussed. The third subject is the Iris database and, in particular, the kernel architecture which is designed to support a full object-oriented database model.

Finally, the editors present a chapter which suggests what the future research directions in object-oriented computing could be and perhaps should be. In this chapter, the prospects of object-orientation becoming an integrating factor for computing in general are introduced and assessed.

More detailed descriptions of the various parts of the book are described below.

1.6.1 Part 1: Introducing the Concepts

Part 1 of the book consists of four chapters which incrementally introduce the various techniques associated with object-oriented computing. The basic concepts of object class and inheritance are first introduced. This is followed by more a more detailed examination of techniques to support behaviour sharing and evolution. After this, the issue of typing is examined in considerable detail. The final chapter then presents a more abstract view of what is meant by the term object-oriented. The individual chapters are described in more detail below.

Chapter 2: Basic Concepts I (Objects, Class and Inheritance) *The task of this chapter is to introduce a set of basic techniques which are central to the philosophy of object-*

oriented computing. The chapter therefore provides a platform to enable the reader to explore the more advanced features presented in the rest of part I. The chapter concentrates on the fundamental notions of objects, class and inheritance. Supporting mechanisms such as message passing, object instantiation, specialisation, method binding and polymorphism are also explained. The chapter concludes by assessing the mechanisms that have been introduced and relating them back to the principles of object-oriented computing introduced in chapter 1.

Chapter 3: Basic Concepts II (Variations on a Theme) *This chapter identifies and illustrates the wide variation in design choices and decisions in object-oriented systems. To provide a framework for discussion, the chapter first considers systems that are based on classes as a vehicle for sharing through an inheritance hierarchy. This is followed by discussion of systems that are based on the concept of prototypes and their specific sharing mechanisms. The chapter concludes with a brief examination of systems that support both classes and prototypes. Within these broad categories, policies relating to encapsulation, templates, and binding are discussed. The merits of class and prototype based systems are contrasted. During this discussion a large number of well-known object-oriented concepts are introduced.*

Chapter 4: Basic Concepts III (Types, Abstract Data Types and Polymorphism) *The concept of typing is not normally associated with object-oriented computing. However, there has recently been great interest in the semantics of typing in an object-oriented context. In particular, many language and system designers are investigating the integration of static type checking into object-oriented environments. This chapter surveys the impact of this work on the object-oriented community. The important concepts of type, data abstraction and polymorphism are discussed in depth. Abstract data types are highlighted as a central feature of statically typed object-oriented languages. In addition, several approaches to providing polymorphism in abstract data type based languages are introduced, i.e. subtyping/conformance, genericity and enhancement.*

Chapter 5: What are Object-Oriented Systems? *The first four chapters of this book have introduced most of the fundamental concepts underlying object-oriented computing. It should now be clear that object-oriented computing is a large topic encompassing traditional models based on class and inheritance but also many variations on the basic theme. Techniques such as delegation, conformance and genericity have been introduced to solve problems in a particular area. With all these developments, it is now very difficult to define clearly what it meant by the term object-orientation. This chapter examines the question of what is object-orientation. A model is presented which encompasses all the techniques discussed so far. The model is then used to analyse some of the pertinent questions raised in the object-oriented community. In addition, it is suggested that the model provides a design space for the development of new object-oriented languages and systems. The chapter concludes by examining some formal techniques which might lead to a more precise modelling of the semantics of object-oriented computing in the future.*

1.6.2 Part 2: Objects in Action
There are five chapters in part 2 covering the application domains of programming

languages, databases, object-oriented design, distributed systems and user interfaces. More detailed descriptions of each chapter are presented below.

Chapter 6: Programming Languages Based On Objects *There are many programming languages based on objects, which adopt very different approaches to each of the syntactic, semantic and pragmatic aspects of language design. This chapter illustrates the approaches by describing and comparing some of the more widely-available languages. A framework for comparing and contrasting languages is established and applied to the languages Simula, Smalltalk, CLOS, C++, Objective-C and Eiffel.*

Chapter 7: Object-Oriented Database Systems *This chapter introduces the rationale behind the move towards object-oriented databases (OODBs) through the need for enriched semantics. It also outlines some terminology and describes the model for OODBs. An in depth consideration of the underlying support architecture required for the model, with respect to two particular areas, is given. A brief outline of persistent programming is presented, and the appendix describes the features of a number of OODB programming languages.*

Chapter 8: Object-Oriented Design Methods *Object-oriented design methods have recently begun to gain attention as an alternative to the more traditional ways of structuring large software systems. Much has been claimed of designing software on object-oriented principles, in particular, that it aids maintainability and increases reuse. This chapter views the current state of the art in object-oriented design methods, looking at Booch's OOD, the HOOD method and OOSD as examples of the object-oriented approach.*

Chapter 9: Distributed Systems and Objects *This chapter discusses the application of the object-oriented paradigm to distributed systems. First, we present an overview of the specific problems encountered in programming distributed systems as opposed to centralized systems. Then, in order to alleviate some of the confusion in this particular area, we outline the evolution of object-oriented distributed systems through a discussion of the various distributed systems models which led to its development. This is followed by a discussion of the current application of the object-oriented paradigm to distributed systems and a brief survey of recent distributed object-oriented languages and systems. Finally, the use of objects in distributed systems architectures, and in particular in the international standards work on Open Distributed Processing, is introduced and some of the important aspects of the work emphasized.*

Chapter 10: Interactive User Interfaces *In this chapter, the application of object-oriented ideas and languages to the construction of interactive user-interfaces is described. A discussion of general principles is followed by a description of the Smalltalk-80 Model-View-Controller framework, leading to an overview of more modern window systems and their associated toolboxes. The final section on MacApp shows how object-oriented techniques can be used to build an application framework, capturing the Apple Macintosh user interface guidelines in software.*

1.6.3 Part 3: Case Studies

Part 3 of the book consists of three case studies from the fields of hardware design, programming languages and databases respectively. The REKURSIV hardware design is introduced. This is followed by chapters on the BETA programming language and finally the Iris database architecture. More detailed description of the chapters is given below.

Chapter 11: REKURSIV - Object-Oriented Hardware *The REKURSIV computer architecture is the first processor dedicated uncompromisingly for the object-oriented paradigm to be realised in VLSI technology. This chapter describes its general features and introduces the general design philosophy of Lingo, the systems programming language which exploits its capability to support high level instructions.*

Chapter 12: Basic Principles of the BETA Programming Language *A conceptual framework for object-oriented programming is presented. The framework is independent of specific programming language constructs. It is illustrated how this framework is reflected in the BETA programming language. In addition the language mechanisms are compared with the corresponding elements of other object-oriented languages. Main issues of object-oriented programming are considered on the basis of the framework presented here.*

Chapter 13: An Overview of the Iris Kernel Architecture *We describe an architecture for a database system based on an object/function model. The architecture efficiently supports the evaluation of functional expressions. The goal of the architecture is to provide a database system that is powerful enough to support the definition of procedural functions that implement the semantics of the data model. The architecture has been implemented to support the Iris Database System.*

1.6.4 Part 4: Looking Ahead

The final part of the book consists of one chapter on the future directions of object-oriented computing as described below.

Chapter 14: Future Directions *This chapter discusses future directions of object-oriented computing. The chapter starts by suggesting that object-oriented computing requires a period of consolidation and experimentation in large-scale projects. The discussion then continues with a selection of key areas, namely, software engineering methods, formal methods, sharing and distribution, open distributed processing and finally multimedia objects. In each case, a number of topics are identified as being wothy of further study.*

1.7 USING THE BOOK

1.7.1 The Intended Readership

The main intended readership is the postgraduate Computer Science student and the professional in the field of computing. However, the book is also suitable as the basis of a final-year undergraduate course in universities and colleges.

No previous knowledge of object-oriented concepts is assumed, although a moderately strong background in either programming or computer systems technology is recommended.

1.7.2 Dependencies

The structure of the book is designed with flexibility in mind. People with different backgrounds can used the book in different ways. Many selective paths through the book are possible. To help the reader and course tutor in using this book, a dependency chart is presented (see Figure 1.8). This chart can be used to plan selective reading or to design particular course structures.

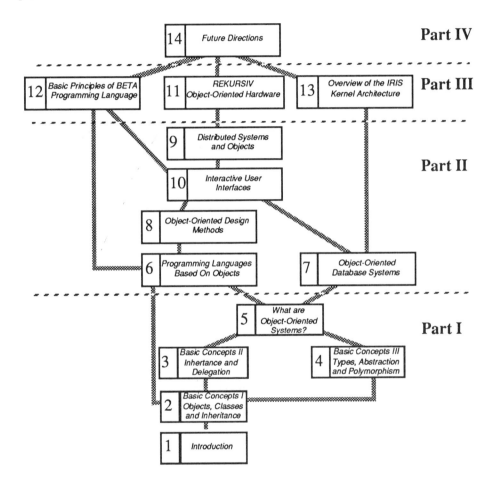

Figure 1.8: Dependency chart for book

The recommended way of using the book is to make several paths through the book at different levels of detail. In the first path, the reader can gain an initial insight into the basic techniques of the object-oriented approach. For example, a computer practitioner interested in learning more about object-oriented programming could read chapters 1 and 2 followed by 6 and 12. This knowledge could be expanded on later either by extending the range of techniques by reading the rest of the chapters in part 1 or by considering other areas of application in part 2. The case studies of part 3 can also be used to supplement the knowledge in a particular area. More specifically, the topic of object-oriented design is highly complementary to object-oriented programming. It is also difficult to appreciate object-oriented programming without studying user interface issues. Similarly, the more advanced topics in chapters 3 and 4 are necessary to fully appreciate the full range of object-oriented languages. Chapter 11 on the REKURSIV processor design also provides an intriguing insight into an approach to supporting efficient implementations of object-oriented languages. Figure 1.9 summarises an approach to to the material in the book from the point of view of somebody principally interested in languages.

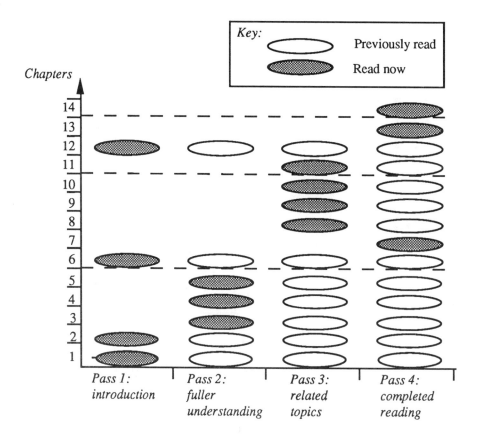

Figure 1.9: Phased reading of book

Similar selective reading can be carried out for people with interests in other areas. For example, for a database specialist, the recommended sequence would be chapters 1, 2, 7 and 13. Again, it would then be helpful to revisit part 1 to investigate alternative approaches and techniques and part 2 to consider issues such as interface design for databases or distribution issues.

It should be stressed though that a full appreciation of object-oriented computing can only be gained by an in-depth understanding of all the many facets of the subject. Readers are therefore encouraged to explore each of the chapters of the book, even those not immediately associated with their areas of interest.

1.8 CONCLUSION

This chapter has set the scene for the rest of the book by explaining the emergence of object-oriented computing and capturing the essential characteristics of the object-oriented approach. The chapter has also established a framework to aid understanding of the many techniques now associated with object-oriented computing. Returning to the objectives of the book (from section 1.1), i.e.

    i)   What are the fundamental *principles* behind object-oriented computing?
    ii) What *techniques* are available and how do they relate to one another?
    iii) How are object-oriented concepts *manifested* in the various areas of application?
    iv) What are specific *examples* of object-oriented computing?
    v) What are the *future directions* of object-oriented computing?

this chapter has answered question i) and has laid the foundation for answering question ii). Responses to questions ii), iii), iv) and v) are given in Part 1, Part 2, Part 3, and Part 4 respectively.

1.9 ACKNOWLEDGEMENTS

The editors would like to take this opportunity to thank the many people who helped in the production of this book. In particular, the following people deserve a special mention:-
John Cushion for his invaluable advice and his considerable patience;
All the individual authors for making the editing task relatively straight-forward;
The various people who commented on draft versions of various chapters, in particular: Mandy Chetwynd, Rodger Lea, Alastair Macartney, John Nicol, Tom Rodden and Ronnie Thompson;
ParcPlace Systems for useful information on trends in object-oriented computing.

REFERENCES

[Bernabeu88] Bernabeu, J., Y.A. Khalidi, M. Ahamad, W.F. Appelbe, P. Dasgupta, R.J. LeBlanc, and U. Ramachandran. "Clouds - A Distributed Object Oriented Operating System: Architecture and Kernel Implementation." *Proceedings of the 88' EUUG Conference*, 1988.

[Burstall80] Burstall, R.M., D.B. McQueen, and D.T. Sannella. "HOPE: An experimental applicative language", Internal Report CSR-62-80, University of Edinburgh. May 1980.

[Cox86] Cox, B.J. *Object-Oriented Programming: An Evolutionary Approach.* Addison-Wesley. Reading, Mass. 1986.

[Dahl66] Dahl, O., and K. Nygaard. "Simula, An Algol-based Simulation Language." *Communications of the ACM* Vol: 9 1966, Pages: 671-678.

[DeMichiel87] DeMichiel, L.G., and R.P. Gabriel. "The Common Lisp Object System: An Overview." Proceedings of the European Conference on Object-Oriented Programming (ECOOP'87). Editor: J. Bézivin, J.-M. Hullot, P. Cointe and H. Lieberman. Springer-Verlag, 1987. Published as: Lecture Notes in Computer Science No. 276 Pages: 151-170.

[Fishman87] Fishman, D.H., D. Beech, H.P. Cate, E.C. Chow, T. Connors, J.W. Davis, N. Derrett, C.G. Hoch, W. Kent, P. Lyngbaek, B. Mahbod, M.A. Neimat, T.A. Ryan, and M.C. Shan. "Iris: An Object-Oriented Database Management System." *ACM Transactions on Office Information Systems* Vol: 5 No.: 1, 1987, Pages: 48-69.

[Goldberg,76] Goldberg, A., and A. Kay. "Smalltalk-72 Instruction Manual", Xerox PARC technical report.

[Goldberg83] Goldberg, A., and D. Robson. *Smalltalk-80: The Language and its Implementation.* Adison-Wesley. Reading, Mass. 1983.

[Gordon79] Gordon, M.J., A.J. Milner, and C.P. Wadsworth. *Edinburgh LCF.* Springer-Verlag. 1979.

[Jeffcoate89] Jeffcoate, J., K. Hales, and V. Downes. "Object-Oriented Systems: the Commercial Benefits." Ovum Reports, UK. 1989,

[Kim88] Kim, W., N. Ballou, J. Banerjee, H.-T. Chou, J.F. Garza, and D. Woelk. "Integrating an object-oriented programming system with a database system", MCC Technical Report ACA-ST-089-88, MCC, Austin, TX. March 1988.

[Kristensen83] Kristensen, B.B., O.L. Madsen, B. Møller-Pedersen, and K. Nygaard. "Abstraction Mechanisms in the Beta Programming Language." *Proceedings of the Tenth ACM Symposium on Principles of Programming Languages,* 1983.

[Maier86] Maier, D., J. Stein, A. Otis, and A. Purdy. "Development of an Object-Oriented DBMS." *Proceedings of the Conference on Object-Oriented Programming Systems, Languages and Applications (OOPSLA '86),* Editor: N. Meyrowitz, Special Issue of SIGPLAN Notices, Vol: 21, Pages: 472-482. 1986.

[McCarthy62] McCarthy, J., P.W. Abrahams, D.J. Edwards, T.P. Hart, and M.I. Levin. *LISP 1.5 Programmer's Manual.* MIT Press. 1962.

[Meyer88] Meyer, B. *Object-Oriented Software Construction.* Prentice-Hall. 1988.

[Meyrowitz86] Meyrowitz, N. "OOPSLA '86 Conference Proceedings." *Special Issue of SIGPLAN Notices* Vol: 21 No.: 11, 1986,

[OSN89] OSN. "Open Systems - Flavour of the Month or the Future of Computing?" *Open Systems Newsletter* Vol: 3 No.: 10, 1989,

[Schmucker86] Schmucker. *Object-Oriented Programming for the Macintosh.* Hayden Book Company. New Jersey. 1986.

[Stroustrup86] Stroustrup, B. *The C++ Programming Language.* Addison-Wesley. Reading, MA. 1986.

[Theriault82] Theriault, D. "A Primer for ACT-1 Language", A.I. Memo No. 672, MIT. April 1982.

[Wegner86] Wegner, P., and B. Shriver. "Special Issue of the SIGPLAN Notices on the Object-Oriented Programming Workshop." Vol: 21 No.: 10, 1986,

[Zimmermann81] Zimmermann, H., J. Banino, A. Caristan, M. Guillemont, and G. Morisset. "Basic Concepts for the Support of Distributed Systems: The CHORUS Approach." *Proceedings 2nd International Conference on Distributed Computer Systems,* Pages: 60-66. April 1981.

Chapter 2

Basic Concepts I (Objects, Classes and Inheritance)

Gordon S. Blair, Howard Bowman and Rodger Lea
Lancaster University

ABSTRACT *The task of this chapter is to introduce a set of basic techniques which are central to the philosophy of object-oriented computing. The chapter therefore provides a platform to enable the reader to explore the more advanced features presented in the rest of part I. The chapter concentrates on the fundamental notions of objects, class and inheritance. Supporting mechanisms such as message passing, object instantiation, specialization, method binding and polymorphism are also explained. The chapter concludes by assessing the mechanisms that have been introduced and relating them back to the principles of object-oriented computing introduced in chapter 1.*

2.1 INTRODUCTION

The first chapter has highlighted the value of the general notion of abstraction to human reasoning and especially to our ability to comprehend and solve complex problems. The chapter also identified a number of principles underlying the object-oriented approach to abstraction, namely:-

   i)   data abstraction,
   ii) behaviour sharing,
   iii) evolution, and
   iv) correctness.

Chapter one also highlighted the myriad of designs that have appeared, based on these four principles. This chapter starts the task of guiding the reader through the various designs by introducing some of the most fundamental concepts of object-oriented computing. The techniques explored in this chapter are very much the traditional techniques associated with object-oriented computing as derived from early work on Simula [Dahl66] and subsequently on the Smalltalk [Goldberg83] series of languages. The approach taken is to consider a simple model of object-oriented computing and then to incrementally introduce the various techniques required for the realisation of this model. The model is derived from a paper by Peter Wegner in the 1986 conference on Object-Oriented Programming Languages, Systems and Applications [Wegner86]. The model considers object-oriented systems as containing three elements, namely objects, class and inheritance (see figure 2.1).

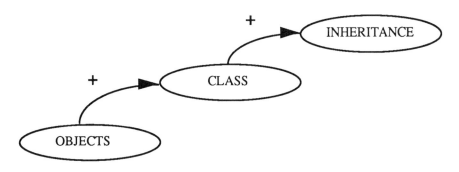

Figure 2.1: Simple model of object-oriented systems

This chapter therefore concentrates on the mechanisms of objects, classes and inheritance; supporting mechanisms such as object instantiation and invocation, overloading and dynamic binding are also described. The technical descriptions are relatively lightweight and often simplify some of the more detailed features of designs. This is deliberate; the aim of this chapter is to give a first order understanding of object-oriented systems. Additional detail is described in later chapters of the book.

The discussion proceeds as follows. Sections 2.2 to 2.4 describe mechanisms to support objects, class and inheritance respectively. This is followed in section 2.5 by a more detailed discussion of the important issue of method binding. Finally, section 2.6 presents some concluding remarks, and places the techniques introduced in the chapter within the framework established in chapter one.

2.2 INTRODUCING OBJECTS

A system based on objects is one whereby a computation is represented by a series of entities (i.e. objects) which interact to achieve the desired effect. In this sub-section, the concept of an object is examined in more depth. Firstly, the concept of an object is described. Following this, the method of object interaction is discussed.

2.2.1 Objects
As mentioned in chapter one, there are many different interpretations of the term 'object-oriented' [Rentsch82]. However, the one thing that unifies everyone in the field is the recognition of objects as the fundamental building block of computations. Curiously though, it is notoriously difficult to capture precisely what is meant by an object. Inquisitive outsiders to the field are often met with the response that 'everything is an object'. This is certainly true in object-oriented computing; however it is less than helpful

in understanding the essence of objects. The question is best answered from two different angles: what is an object at the conceptual level (the user view) and how is an object realised in practical systems (the implementor's view).

At the conceptual level, an object is any *perceived* entity in the system being developed. In constructing a system, programmers will typically analyse the problem and will therefore have a perception of the components required to solve the problem. In a system based on objects, these components are directly represented by objects. It is often stated that objects represent real world entities in the problem domain. As a first approximation, this is true. Objects are representatives for actual entities in the system being modelled. However, it is often also necessary to introduce objects which are necessary to support the environment being developed. As an illustration, consider the implementation of a mailing system. Using an object-oriented approach, the system would be decomposed into a number of 'real world' objects such as customers, letters, mailboxes and receivers. It might also be necessary to have supporting objects such as text storage and linked lists which are necessary to implement the full functionality of the system. The key feature of objects though is that they are geared towards the domain of the problem solver. The abstraction of an object is supportive of the functionality required by the application developer. In contrast, previous approaches (typified by imperative languages such as Pascal and Fortran) have provided a set of abstractions which are more closely related to the underlying hardware architecture and therefore more work is required to produce application programs.

In terms of physical realisation, objects map directly on to the concept of *encapsulation*. In more detail, an object is defined as follows:-

> An object is an encapsulation of a set of operations or methods which can be invoked externally and of a state which remembers the effect of the methods.

This concept of encapsulation is illustrated in figure 2.2.

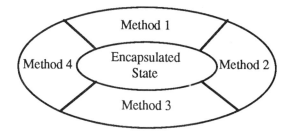

Figure 2.2: Encapsulated objects

The methods are the set of operations which we are allowed to perform within the context of the object. They are the access procedures (the only procedures by which the object can be accessed). The state gives the status of the object at any particular time. This could be defined by the contents and values of the data structures of an object. The external interface will be made up of exactly the information that is required to operate on the object but nothing more. By default this will include a means of executing the access procedures or methods.

The example of a drinks machine is introduced to illustrate the concept of encapsulated objects (this example is developed further in subsequent sections):-

A drinks machine can be considered to be encapsulated as its functionality is sealed inside a metal box.

It has two methods:-

    i)   Make a cup of tea
    ii) Make a cup of coffee

The state of the object is given by the amount of tea, coffee, milk, sugar and water left.

The interface to the object is presented on the front of the box by two buttons marked coffee and tea.The two buttons enable the user to execute the object methods.

The operational interface to an object is restricted to only what is required by the user, with the implementation of the methods externally invisible, i.e. we have *information hiding*. This, as mentioned earlier, is a main objective of encapsulation; it prevents unqualified access since the metal box prevents the user of the machine (who has never studied the intricate mechanisms of drinks machines of course) tampering with it. The other important aspect of the operational interface is that it provides the user view of the behaviour of an object, i.e. it is known that an object provides certain functionality but beyond that no further details are known. This is important in handling complexity in a problem as once an object is implemented it is no longer important to know the internal details of the algorithms and data structures. It is only necessary to know the interface it presents.

2.2.2 Object Interaction

With objects, it is necessary to provide a mechanism to allow one object to interact with another. For example, in the above drinks dispenser the dispenser might have to interact with a water mains system to refresh its supply of water. Following the philosophy of object-oriented computing this interaction should be strictly controlled, i.e. interaction should be limited to the well defined method interface. Thus, object interaction is equivalent to the invocation of methods associated with other objects. In object-oriented computing, invocation is often described as being achieved through *message passing*; whenever an operation is to be invoked, a message is sent to that object with details of the requested operation to be carried out. It should be stressed however that message passing is often purely conceptual. It is not necessarily true that an actual message is sent

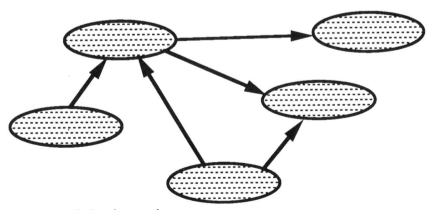

Figure 2.3: Object interaction

to an object; it is equally possible that method invocation will be modelled as a controlled form of procedure call. It is however attractive to visualise an object-oriented system as a set of self-contained objects interacting only through message passing (see figure 2.3).

The syntax for message sending differs from system to system. In general however the following components will be present:-

[receiver_name method_request: any_parameters]

This sends a message from the requester object to the receiver object asking that the specified method be invoked. This method in turn may generate more messages and hence cause the invocation of methods on other objects. One important point is that the quoted method name is declarative in that the requester is not aware whether the object can respond to the request or how the request will be carried out. The requester is simply asking for the object to attempt to fulfil the request. If the receiving object does not know how to respond to the request, it must return a 'method not known' message to the requester (this is actually equivalent to a type error in conventional programming languages).

2.2.3 Self Reference

The mechanism described above for object interaction describes how operations are carried out on remote objects. This leaves the question of how local methods are invoked. It is common in object-oriented systems to provide a uniform approach to invoking methods whether they are local or remote. Thus local method requests are still carried out using the message format described above. This approach demands a form of self reference, whereby a particular object has knowledge of its own identification in the system. Most systems provide a special identifier called self (or me) which maps directly on to the current object. Thus a call of:-

[self print]

would result in the print method being invoked on the local object and hence the contents would be displayed.

2.2.4 Summary

A system supporting objects is characterised by the following features:-
  i)   modularisation -- all details of an object are brought together in one place
  ii) information hiding -- access to an object is controlled through a well-defined interface; all other details of the object are hidden from the user of that object
  iii) behavioural -- the behaviour of an object is captured by the full operational interface presented by that object
  iv) object interaction -- a mechanism is provided to allow an object to invoke methods on another object
  v) self reference -- local operations are accessed in the same way as remote operations by invoking a method on self.

2.3 INTRODUCING CLASSES

The introduction of classes takes the design of systems one step further by introducing a rudimentary form of classification into the system. The mechanisms necessary to achieve this classification are *classes* and *object instantiation*. These are discussed in turn below.

2.3.1 Classes
The motivation in supporting classes is to provide a rudimentary form of classification. Classes support classification by allowing groups of objects to be created which share *identical* behaviour. This is done by providing a number of templates (i.e. classes) for the creation of objects in the system. More precisely, classes can be defined as follows:-

A class is a template from which objects may be created. It contains a definition of the state descriptors and methods for the object.

The class template therefore provides a complete description of a class in terms of its external interface and internal algorithms and data structures. The main advantage of this approach is that the effort of implementing a class need only be carried out once.

A good analogy for a class is provided by a baker's pastry cutter. A pastry cutter defines the precise characteristics of a pastry in terms of size and shape. For example, one particular pastry cutter might define a circular shape of diameter 3 inches. All pastries created from this specific cutter will be guaranteed to have exactly this size and shape.

Returning to the drinks machine example:-

We could define a class of drinks machines as follows:-

Class name:	*Drinks machines*
State descriptors:	Amount of milk
	Amount of sugar
	Amount of water
	Amount of tea
	Amount of coffee
Methods:	Definition of make tea method
	Definition of make coffee method

2.3.2 Object Instantiation
With the introduction of classes, it is necessary to provide a mechanism for creating objects of a particular class. This object creation can be performed dynamically through an *instantiation* mechanism. Instantiation is performed by calling on a class to create a new object based on the template. This object is initialised and then exists in the environment to be accessed by other objects. Objects are aware of which class they belong to; similarly, classes tend to have knowledge of all their instances.

Once we have object instantiation, the uniformity of the object model becomes apparent. Classes are themselves objects in the system and therefore provide one or more methods as an interface. One method which is always provided by a class is the method *new*, which when invoked creates instances of a specific class. Thus object instantiation is modelled by the sending of a message to the appropriate class requesting a new object to be created and initialised. Objects created from a particular class are referred to as *instances* of that class. Note that although all instances of a particular class exhibit common behaviour, they are not identical. They are identical in terms of interface and implementation. However, each object has its own state which can vary over time depending on the previous invocations on that object.

The following example illustrates how an instantiation of a particular instance of a drinks machine would be carried out:-

Machine_A := [Drinks_machine new]

Using this instantiation mechanism, it would also be possible to create other instances, e.g.

Machine_B := [Drinks_machine new]

Machine_C := [Drinks_machine new]

The semantics of object instantiation will guarantee that machines A, B and C will all exhibit common behaviour.

2.3.3 Summary
Classes introduce the following features to a system:-
i)   Classes -- templates which fully define the behaviour of a group of objects
ii) Object instantiation -- the ability to create instances of classes based on the template
iii) Classes as objects -- classes are themselves objects and thus object instantiation is performed by invoking a new method on the class.

2.4 INTRODUCING INHERITANCE

Classes provide a mechanism to declare the structure of a group of objects, in much the same way as types do in traditional programming languages. Classes though go further than types in that classes themselves are objects in the environment and hence can be invoked at any point. This provides an elegant basis for system design. However, the full benefits of object-oriented computing are realised when classes are extended by means of the concept of inheritance. This section examines the concept of inheritance in some detail. The associated concepts of class hierarchies, method binding and polymorphism are also described.

2.4.1 Inheritance
With classes alone, all new classes must be created from scratch, i.e. all the functionality in terms of data structures, algorithms and interface must be described in terms of the base components in the system. In many cases, this can involve unnecessary effort because of the existence of other similar classes in the system. Therefore, it would be attractive to be able to make use of existing classes in specifying new classes. Inheritance provides a systematic way of doing exactly this. A new class can be described in terms of an existing class but with modifications or extensions to meet the requirements of the new class. The new class therefore shares the behaviour of the old class but has modified or additional behaviour. This sharing of behaviour is the essential feature of inheritance:-

Inheritance is the incorporation of the behaviour of one class into another.

A class which inherits from another class inherits all the methods and attributes of that class. It can then add new methods and attributes at will. The new class is said to be a *subclass* of the old class. Similarly, the old class is the *superclass* of the new class.

Inheritance can also be demonstrated through the drinks machine example:-

> Suppose it is necessary to implement a mark 2 class of drinks machine which includes the capability to dispense hot chocolate. Rather than describe a new drinks machine, it would be sensible to inherit from the old design as follows:-

Class name:	*Mark2*
Inherits from:	Drinks machine
State descriptors:	Amount of hot chocolate
Methods:	Definition of make hot chocolate method

> The new mark 2 class of drinks machine will therefore have all the state descriptors and methods from drinks machine but with additional state descriptors for hot chocolate. The above class description is therefore equivalent to:-

Class name:	*Mark2*
State descriptors:	Amount of milk
	Amount of sugar
	Amount of water
	Amount of tea
	Amount of coffee
	Amount of hot chocolate
Methods:	Definition of make tea method
	Definition of make coffee method
	Definition of make hot chocolate method

2.4.2. Forms of Specialization

When creating a new class from an existing class, the user is effectively creating a *specialization* which is a step nearer the requirements of the application domain. There are various ways that a specialization can take place. These are discussed below:-

1. Add new behaviour -- the most common approach is to add new behaviour (in terms of state and methods) to the existing class, i.e. the new class inherits the state and methods from the superclass and adds extra functionality
2. Change behaviour -- a second approach is to re-define the implementation of an existing method; for example, a print method could be re-programmed to give a more sophisticated layout to the presentation of an object
3. Delete behaviour -- less commonly, it might be possible to remove state and methods from the existing class thus creating a new class with less functionality than the superclass
4. Combination of 1-3 -- in general, specialisations will be carried out using a combination of the three approaches.

Object-oriented languages and systems vary in their support for the different forms of specialization. Most will support the first two styles of re-defining classes. However, many systems do not allow behaviour to be deleted from classes. Note that systems which support only the addition of new behaviour are said to have *strict inheritance* whereas those which also allow changing or deletion of behaviour are said to exhibit *non-strict inheritance*.

2.4.3 Class Hierarchies

As an object-oriented system develops, subclasses are constructed out of existing classes until the appropriate functionality is developed. As a result, a class hierarchy is formed with nodes representing classes and arcs representing subclass relationships. The hierarchy is normally rooted by a special class, often referred to as *object*, which contains a minimal set of behaviour common to all classes.

As an illustration of a class hierarchy, consider the drinks dispenser analogy. Further versions could be created over a period of time with mark 3 produced from the original version and mark 4 later developed from mark 3. The resultant class hierarchy is shown in figure 2.5.

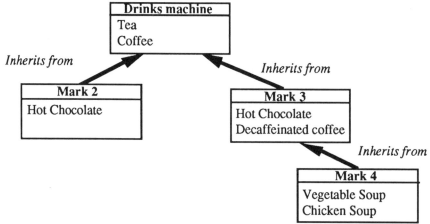

Figure 2.5: Example class hierarchy

In the literature on object-oriented systems, subclass relationships are often described as *is-a links*. Thus if an object A is a subclass of an object B, then A is-a B. This interpretation stems from the fact that a subclass can always be used in place of its superclass because it has at least the behaviour of the superclass (it may of course have additional functionality). Thus, as far as the user is concerned, the subclass is effectively an example of the superclass. It should be stressed at this point that considering subclass relationships as is-a links is only partially true. In precise terms, a subclass relationship states that one class shares the behaviour of another class or in other words one class is composed out of another class. This is only one interpretation of the term 'is-a'. Several other interpretations of is-a links can also exist in an object-oriented environment [Brachman83].

In practice, object-oriented systems tend to have a library of existing classes arranged in a class hierarchy. These are particular abstractions which are seen as useful and hence have been added to the system over a period of time. This encourages the style of programming where classes are built out of existing classes in a bottom-up manner until the appropriate functionality of a system is reached. Classes near the root of the hierarchy tend to be generic services applicable to a range of applications whereas classes near the leaves tend to be more application specific. For example, a linked list class is likely to be found at the top of a hierarchy and an account class near the leaves. A typical segment of a class hierarchy is shown in figure 2.6.

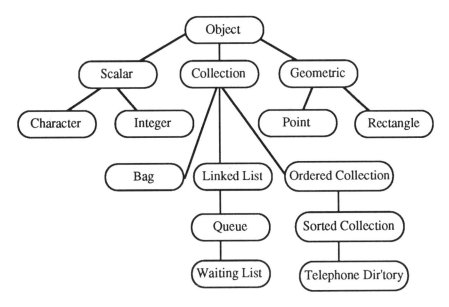

Figure 2.6: Typical class hierarchy

In many object-oriented environments, the class hierarchy will be quite large. As an example, the basic Smalltalk-80 library consists of approximately 250 classes. It is therefore very important that a support is provided to help the user manoeuvre round the set of available classes. Therefore, class *browsers* are usually central elements of an object-oriented programming environment. Many systems invest great effort in providing browsers which are easy to use and help the user to trace existing classes which are appropriate in a given context. Indeed, the existence of powerful browsing facilities has contributed to the popularity of the Smalltalk-80 environment.

2.4.4 Method Binding

One consequence of class hierarchies is that the complete knowledge of an object's behaviour is no longer held in a central place. Classes inherit behaviour from superclasses which in turn inherit behaviour from their superclasses and so on, and of course modifications or additions may have been made. Thus the complete behaviour of an object of a particular class is determined by the definitions in the class and in the subsequent line of superclasses. In practice, this means that a particular method may exist at any point in this search path. Thus it is necessary to carry out a binding from method name to implementation of a method whenever a method is invoked. A simple example should clarify the need for method binding:-

Consider the class hierarchy shown in figure 2.7. This figure shows a class *Linked List* with methods *insert*, *delete*, *next* and *print*. From this, the class is specialised to produce class *Queue* which provides a more specialised implementation of *insert* and *delete* (to reflect the particular semantics of a queue). Finally, another class is produced

(*Waiting List*) by re-implementing the *print* method to provide more sophisticated layout and providing an extra method, *length,* to provide the current length of the waiting list.

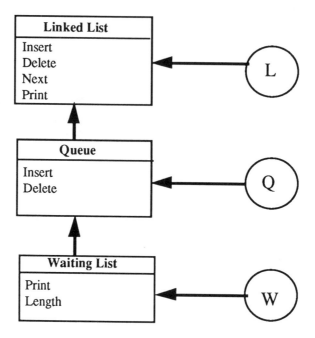

Figure 2.7: Need for method binding

Suppose now three objects are created called L, Q and W which are instances of *Linked List, Queue* and *Waiting List* respectively. Now, consider the following scenarios:-

i) the method *print* is invoked on object Q

In this case, the class *queue* will be searched for the method *print.* It will not be found, so the superclass *linked list* will then be searched. This time the appropriate method will be found and applied to produce a printed list of elements in the queue.

ii) the method *print* is invoked on object W

This time, the method will immediately be found in the class *waiting list* and will be applied to give the more specialised form of layout.

iii) the method *insert* is invoked on object W

In this final example, class *waiting list* and then class *queue* will be searched before the correct method implementation is found. Note that the *insert* for *queue* will be invoked in preference to the *insert* from *linked list,* thus ensuring that the correct semantics of queueing are maintained.

It is therefore necessary to carry out a binding of method name to implementation for every single method invocation in the system. In general, the system will select the most specific method, i.e. the first method found in an upward search of the class hierarchy. The binding mechanism is one of the key features of object-oriented environments and will be examined in more depth in section 2.5. More specifically, section 2.5 will consider the timing of this binding and whether mappings should be carried out statically when programs are created or dynamically as programs are executed. It will be seen that dynamic binding is particularly attractive in object-oriented environments.

2.4.5 Polymorphism

Another repercussion of a class hierarchy is that it is possible to have a limited form of *polymorphism* in the system. Polymorphism is informally defined as the ability of behaviour to have an interpretation over more than one class. For example, it is common for the method *print* to be defined on most classes in an object-oriented system. Polymorphism can actually be introduced in two ways in an object-oriented environment:-

    i)   through sub-classing
           -- a method defined on one particular class is automatically defined on all its sub-classes
    ii)   through overloading
           -- it is also possible to use the same name for methods in independent parts of a class hierarchy and hence to overload the meaning of the term

In the example in section 2.4.4, the method *print* is polymorphic because it is defined over classes *linked list*, *queue* and *waiting list* It is also perfectly possible that another class somewhere else in the class hierarchy also has a definition for this method.

Polymorphism is one of the most characteristic features of object-oriented systems. It represents a shift in programming towards the abstract behaviour an object presents rather than how this behaviour is implemented. It is a recognition that there may be a one to many mapping of a method name on to implementations. Note that the need for method binding is a consequence of polymorphism. Without polymorphism, method binding is a straight-forward one to one mapping.

This concern with what an object will do and not how it is done provides a framework in which great flexibility can be offered. This flexibility is a direct result of polymorphism and is best illustrated by a further example.

> Consider a class, *bag*, that is designed to represent a simple sack. The sack is used for putting miscellaneous objects into and storing them until required. The operations that we would like to be applicable to the class *bag* are: store an item, give up an item and display the contents. Note here that we wish our sack to contain objects of many different types and not to be constrained to only holding one type of object.

> Each object is referenced by an object identifier whose format is identical for all objects in the system. This provides the basis for the message passing system because all messages are sent to an object uniquely defined by a standard format identifier. Thus we can define a class that holds an array or linked list of object identifiers. What those identifiers point to is of little concern to the *bag* object; all it needs to know is the identifier. Thus the definition of the add and remove element methods would be trivial and in most object-oriented systems would be provided by inheriting a class responsible for handling groups of objects, for example a class that implements a linked list. The display method is potentially more complex; we need some means of iterating over all elements in the *bag* and displaying them. However, for each different type of object in the *bag*, its

display message is potentially different; displaying an integer is different from displaying a string, and certainly very different from displaying a picture. In a traditional language we would need to determine the type of object referenced by the *bag* and then call the correct display routine for objects of that type, e.g. display_integer or display_picture. However, in object-oriented systems, all objects are responsible for their own internal details. All we have to work with is the interface they present to the rest of the system. Therefore we only need to ensure that all objects respond to a generic message, say, display_yourself, and our problem becomes straight-forward. The method display would look a little like this:-

```
class bag is
    inherit from linked list
    method display is
        begin
            for all elements in my linked list
                message each one with 'display_yourself'
        end method display
end class bag
```

The key concept here is the overloading of the message display_yourself across many classes. As long as each object that is placed in the *bag* supports a method display_yourself then we have no problems. What is actually happening is that the method request display_yourself is being bound to the correct method implementation for each object that receives it.

Thus, because object orientation supports a model of 'what can you do' as opposed to 'how do you do it' the problems of displaying complex representations is abstracted over and hidden outside that object.

Note: In a traditional programming language we would have been running up against difficulties very early in the development of this sack example since traditional languages find it difficult to support structures with different and potentially unknown elements. For example consider the implementation of our bag using an array. Firstly, it would need to be potentially infinite in length, and secondly its elements would need to be pointers to objects. However, each pointer may be different so that we would need meta-pointers, each of which could potentially point to any object. In a language such as C it would be possible to exploit the knowledge that pointers are 4 bytes long, as are integers and thus we could use an array of integers. However, we still have problems because we have no way of knowing what each pointer actually points at. We could tag each array element, or provide an operation on each data element that returned its type. Nevertheless, the solution would be clumsy.

Polymorphism is a very important concept in object-oriented computing and is revisited in depth in chapter 4.

2.4.6 Summary
Inheritance adds the following features to object-oriented systems:-

    i)   Inheritance -- the ability to create new classes as specialisations of existing classes

ii) Various forms of specialization -- new classes created out of old classes by the addition, re-definition or deletion of behaviour

iii) Class hierarchies -- classes formed into hierarchies as a result of class specialization

iv) Method binding -- mapping carried out from method names onto implementations by searching the class hierarchy

v) Polymorphism -- methods defined over more than one class either through inheritance or by name overloading.

2.5 BINDING REVISITED

The concept of method binding was briefly introduced in section 2.4.4. This section takes a more detailed look at method binding and in particular how method binding can be supported in object-oriented environments. The alternative approaches of static and dynamic binding are presented; the advantages and disadvantages of each approach are also debated.

2.5.1 Static Binding

The simplest approach to method binding is to resolve all mappings at compile time. With this approach, the compiler must build a table of classes and associated method implementations and then determine the subclass relationships between classes. With this information, it is possible to determine the appropriate bindings from method name to implementation. The actual calls to implementations would then be embedded in the code produced.

The advantage of static binding is that there is no run time overhead in accessing methods. The binding of method names to implementations is carried out once, before the execution phase of an object-oriented program, and thus invocation of a method may be no more expensive than a traditional procedure call. A secondary advantage is that failed bindings are caught at compile time and therefore there is no need to respond to 'method not found' messages at run time.

However, there are several significant limitations of static binding. The major limitation is that bindings cannot change without re-compilation. This is against the spirit of object-oriented computing in that there is little support for the evolution of code. A related problem is that many object-oriented environments are interpreted and hence it is not possible to support compile time activity. Consequently, the vast majority of object-oriented environments have opted for dynamic binding as described below.

2.5.2 Dynamic Binding

With dynamic binding, the mapping of method name to implementation is carried out on every method invocation. Each time a method is invoked, the class hierarchy will be searched to find the appropriate implementation. In practice, a (conceptual) message will be sent to the object requesting that a method be applied to the object. This will result in a search of the object's class, then its superclass, etc. until a method is found. If the search reaches the root of the class hierarchy, then a 'method not found' message must be sent back to the requesting object. This is exactly equivalent to a typing error in traditional programming languages, i.e. the requesting object has asked for an invalid operation.

The rationale for dynamic binding is that bindings can change from invocation to invocation. Thus, if the class hierarchy changes between invocations, this will be reflected in the final binding. Consequently, dynamic binding supports evolution of a program without requiring re-compilation and hence is suitable for an interpreted environment.

The great drawback of dynamic binding is the cost incurred at run time. It is expensive to search the class hierarchy for every method invocation in the system. In addition, it is often the case that this expense is not necessary because bindings have not changed in the interim. The other disadvantage is that the system must handle 'method not found' messages at run-time, adding to the complexity of user code. If failed bindings are not anticipated by the programmer, erroneous behaviour can result (for a further discussion of this issue, refer to chapter 4).

Despite these drawbacks, dynamic binding has been favoured in nearly all implementations of object-oriented languages and systems. Indeed, dynamic binding has become synonymous with object-oriented programming. The flexibility provided by dynamic binding is one of the key characteristics expected of an object-oriented environment. The ability to accommodate change is central to the object-oriented philosophy.

2.6 SUMMARY

2.6.1 Techniques Introduced in Chapter 2

The important techniques introduced in this chapter are summarised in Figure 2.8. The purpose of the table is to show how the various techniques map on to the framework established in chapter 1 (section 1.5). The table will be gradually built up in subsequent chapters of part one as new techniques are introduced. This will enable the various techniques to be studied within an overall context.

The concept of an *object* was introduced as the fundamental unit of encapsulation in object-oriented systems. *Class* was then introduced as a template for creating objects with a given specification and implementation. Classes thus provide a mechanism for grouping objects according to their abstract behaviour *and* the realisation of this behaviour. Two techniques for flexible sharing were identified. The first technique is the important concept of *subclassing* or *inheritance* whereby one class can include the implementation of another class but can specialise the class with various refinements. This enables an implementation hierarchy to be established. A second technique for sharing behaviour across classes is to use a particular method name across two or more classes (*overloading*) in different parts of the class hierarchy. Thus the behaviour denoted by the method name will have a different interpretation in the different contexts. Finally, two alternative techniques were introduced for resolving the interpretation of behaviour within a class hierarchy. The choice available is either to bind behaviour to the correct implementation at compile time (*static binding*) or leave this binding until run time (*dynamic binding*). The relative merits of the two approaches were discussed in section 2.5.

2.6.2 Rationale for Techniques

The purpose of this section is to relate the techniques introduced in this chapter to the guiding principles of object-oriented computing introduced in chapter 1 (section 1.3). Each of the four principles is considered in turn.

General Approach	Technique	Description	Xref
Encapsulation	Object	encapsulation of data and interface	2.2.1
Classification	Classes	groupings based on common specification and implementation	2.3.1
Flexible sharing	Subclassing (inheritance)	inclusion of specification and implementation of one class in another	2.4.1
	Overloading	sharing of method names across specific objects or classes	2.4.5
Interpretation	Static binding	compile time resolution of names in subclass hierarchy	2.5.1
	Dynamic binding	run time resolution of names in subclass hierarchy	2.5.2

Figure 2.8: Summary of techniques

Data Abstraction The introduction of objects is a significant step in its own right. The concept of an object effectively provides data abstraction as discussed in chapter one and hence leads to the many well known advantages of data abstraction. In particular, objects have the following benefits:-

i)   *modularity*

With the introduction of objects, a system has a natural modular structure consisting of a number of objects interacting via message passing. Each object represents a conceptual entity in the problem domain and is the single place to look for algorithms or data structures related to that conceptual entity. This makes the task of understanding or debugging large programs much easier. With this approach, it is also possible to test fully a particular object in isolation before integrating its behaviour into the rest of the system.

ii)   *abstract behaviour*

The other major advantage of objects is that it is possible to abstract over the details of implementation and consider an object solely in terms of its interface (or behaviour). It is sufficient to know that an object will respond to a particular message without knowing how the message will be interpreted. This process of abstraction is invaluable in dealing with complex systems. A secondary advantage is that it is possible to change the internal details of an object without affecting the overall behaviour of the system. This behavioural view of objects is central to the philosophy of object-oriented computing.

Behaviour sharing Various mechanisms have been introduced which support behaviour sharing in object-oriented systems, namely classes, subclassing and overloading.

Classes introduce a crude form of behaviour sharing by guaranteeing that all instances of a class will share the same behaviour in terms of specification *and* implementation. This is a useful structuring technique as it means that all objects of a particular class will respond in a certain way to a given method. In addition, if the implementation of a class changes, all the instances will reflect this change in behaviour.

A more refined form of behaviour sharing is provided by subclassing. This allows a new class to share the specification and implementation of another class; however, the programmer is free to specialise this behaviour to meet particular requirements. Thus, the behaviour of the superclass is included in the behaviour of the subclass. A major benefit of this approach is that it encourages *re-use* of existing classes. The subject of software re-use has attracted much attention recently because of the huge investment of industry in the software process. The advantage of the object-oriented approach to re-use is that it is not necessary to find exactly the required behaviour. Rather, the programmer can find a class which provides most of the required functionality and then specialise the class to meet the full requirements.

Overloading provides a further (ad-hoc) mechanism for introducing behaviour sharing in object-oriented systems. By re-using method names, it is possible to allow a particular behaviour to be implemented in classes not related in the subclass hierarchy.

Note that overloading is concerned with the sharing of behaviour in terms of specification and does not imply a sharing of implementation. This point causes much confusion in object-oriented computing. There is a clear distinction between the two concepts:-

i)   sharing of specification
     -- concerned with behaviour having an interpretation over different objects or groupings of objects.

ii) sharing of implementation
     -- concerned with the re-use of code between different objects or groupings of objects

This distinction is important and will be revisited in later chapters of the book (particularly chapter 4). The sharing of specification leads to benefits in terms of dealing abstractly in terms of behaviour across different contexts. In contrast, the benefits of sharing implementation are more pragmatic (e.g. code re-use).

Evolution Inheritance has a dual role in object-oriented systems. As well as supporting behaviour sharing between classes, inheritance supports an evolutionary style of programming. By allowing classes to be refined, the programmer is encouraged to develop systems in a bottom-up manner by browsing the class hierarchy for suitable classes and then developing new classes based on existing classes eventually moving towards a solution to the complete problem. This approach is often referred to as *programming by differences* because of the emphasis on the difference between what exists at present and what is required.

This style of programming also supports experimental developments and *rapid prototyping* solutions. Experience of object-oriented programming suggests that solutions can be developed very rapidly once the requirements of a system are known. This is principally because of the wide range of software already available in the class hierarchy.

Subclassing therefore supports *evolutionary programming* from the initial conception of a project to the final deliverable product. By the same mechanism, support is also provided for the maintenance of software. As requirements change, it is possible to specialise existing classes to meet the new requirements. For example, it is relatively easy to add new methods to provide extra functionality to a class.

The introduction of dynamic binding takes support for evolution one stage further by allowing systems to evolve without re-compilation. If systems are statically bound, then it would be necessary to generate new code for the whole system to ensure that all method invocations map on to the correct implementation. However, with dynamic binding this is not necessary. The system will adapt dynamically to additions or changes in behaviour. This aspect of object-oriented computing is particularly attractive in applications such as process control environments where the cost of a system shut-down may be high.

Correctness The mechanisms introduced so far provide little or no assistance for the development of correct software. Indeed, with systems which support dynamic binding there are no guarantees that the system will be able to respond to every message generated. The programmer will therefore have to deal explicitly with exceptions resulting from failed bindings. This is one of the major problems faced by object-oriented systems. However, other techniques have been developed to deal with this problem (see chapter 4).

REFERENCES

[**Brachman83**] Brachman, R.J. "What IS-A Is and Isn't: An Analysis of Taxonomic Links in Semantic Networks." *IEEE Computer* 1983, Pages: 30-36.

[**Dahl66**] Dahl, O., and K. Nygaard. "Simula, An Algol-based Simulation Language." *Communications of the ACM Vol:* 9 1966, Pages: 671-678.

[**Goldberg83**] Goldberg, A., and D. Robson. *Smalltalk-80: The Language and its Implementation.* Adison-Wesley. Reading, Mass. 1983.

[**Rentsch82**] Rentsch, T. "Object Oriented Programming." *SIGPLAN Notices Vol:* 17 No.: 9, 1982, Pages: 51-57.

[**Wegner86**] Wegner, P. "Classification in Object-Oriented Systems." *Proceedings of the Object-Oriented Programming Workshop,* Editor: P. Wegner and B. Shriver, Special Issue of SIGPLAN Notices, Vol: 21 No:10, Pages: 173-182. 1986.

Chapter 3

Basic Concepts II (Variations on a Theme)

John Gallagher
Lancaster University

ABSTRACT *This chapter identifies and illustrates the wide variation in design choices and decisions in object-oriented systems. To provide a framework for discussion, the chapter first considers systems that are based on classes as a vehicle for sharing through an inheritance hierarchy. This is followed by discussion of systems that are based on the concept of prototypes and their specific sharing mechanisms. The chapter concludes with a brief examination of systems that support both classes and prototypes. Within these broad categories, policies relating to encapsulation, templates, and binding are discussed. The merits of class and prototype based systems are contrasted. During this discussion a large number of well-known object-oriented concepts are introduced.*

3.1 INTRODUCTION

The first two chapters have introduced the basic concepts and terminology of object-oriented computing. Chapter 1 presented a general discussion on the object-oriented approach to abstraction; four principles of object-oriented abstraction were introduced: namely data abstraction, behaviour sharing, evolution and correctness. Chapter 2 then gave an overview of a simple model of object-oriented computing. In particular, the concepts of object, class and inheritance were introduced. However, the discussion did not dwell on the intricacies of a real implementation; nor did it consider the many variations which now exist in contemporary object-oriented environments.

This chapter will take a closer look at object-oriented systems and will describe the rich variation that exists amongst many implementations in their approach to meeting these basic principles. In particular, it is the intention of this chapter to focus on the techniques related to the first three principles (data abstraction, behaviour sharing and evolution) whilst leaving the treatment of correctness to chapter 4.

The chapter is laid out as follows: Section 3.2 takes the three aspects (encapsulation, behaviour sharing and evolution) and prepares the reader for the wide variation in implementations. Class-based systems are examined first in Section 3.3, as historically they have enjoyed greater prominence through systems such as the Smalltalk language and environment. The characteristics of inheritance are outlined and the variations listed. An interpretive view of such systems reveals that on the whole they have statically defined patterns of sharing. Section 3.4 deals with the other group of systems that do not rely on the class concept and which in general exhibit more dynamic patterns of sharing. This section introduces, amongst other things, the actor model of computation and its associated mechanism of delegation that supports sharing. Following this, section 3.5 focuses on the debate surrounding the respective merits of classes and prototypes. Section 3.6 briefly looks at the advantages to be gained from systems that offer an integration of classes and prototypes, and section 3.7 summarizes the techniques introduced in this chapter.

3.2 THE ISSUES: A PREVIEW

There is significant variation in the techniques that have been developed to support data abstraction, behaviour sharing and evolution. There is an equally wide range of their effectiveness in implementation. A few simple questions will serve to highlight this variation.

Do all object-oriented systems provide strict encapsulation for objects?   This first issue is concerned with the concept of the object itself. In this we have *encapsulation*, or *data abstraction*: data structures are hidden behind a set of operations that form the interface to the object. All access to the data is forced to pass through this interface, an interface whose implementation code is not visible or accessible to the user. Whilst it may seem self-evident that all objects observe this principle, we will see later in the chapter (section 3.3.5) that often this principle is broken in the implementation of inheritance.

There are other questions associated with this principle of encapsulation such as where the implementation code for the methods should reside. Should it reside locally with the object or can it reside elsewhere? Should there be one implementation or can there be many?

Is classification necessary to support behaviour sharing?   We now focus on the issue of *classification*. Classification at its most basic allows objects to be categorized; all objects in a category, or class, have a common structure and thus share common behaviour or attributes as in Simula [Dahl66] for example. As a consequence, changes made to methods and structure in a class can automatically be passed on to all instances of that class. This implicit mechanism allows systems to be updated on a 'per group' basis. A class, in this sense, provides the template or schema for all similar objects: change the schema and all the created instances reflect the change after recompilation.

Such is the variation in object implementations that in fact not all objects have a class/instance structure. Such objects, however, can still share behaviour with other objects, without having recourse to the class/instance model. Further, this sharing can be either implicitly supported by the language or left to the explicit instruction of the programmer. When we examine object creation, we will see that again the Smalltalk class concept is but one way of creating objects; in some classless languages objects carry templates from which to clone new objects directly.

Do all systems support an inheritance hierarchy? Classification in its most general sense holds the key to organization of knowledge. Each group of objects, or class, can be considered a node. Each node can be related to one or more nodes by a binary relation. A typical relation, for example, is the 'is-a' link between classes along which inheritance paths are defined. The resulting abstraction, be it a taxonomic hierarchy or a general graph, has great expressive power and brings significant leverage to the programmer. The links in general provide the means to share code, interface or policy between nodes.

Those classless systems that do have techniques for sharing at the level of individual objects, do not refer to the map of linkages as an inheritance hierarchy. In that sense, they do not have inheritance. Equally, there are some systems that have *both* class based sharing and instance based sharing. Such systems have inheritance, and something else besides. These distinct hierarchies can be used to enforce different policies; e.g., perhaps a subtype hierarchy on one and code sharing on another. Furthermore, in the context of databases, the semantics of the links can be complex. Such links generalize to 'has attribute' and 'has-part' semantics, for example.

Are all inheritance hierarchies fixed at compile time? Classification hierarchies are rarely static - they allow incremental modification and/or extension to encourage the creation of new nodes that are related to existing nodes in the hierarchy. In this we have a further aspect, namely *evolution*, which is concerned with how and when these inter-nodal links are allowed to change.

This extra *interpretive* dimension raises the possibility of *static* or *dynamic* patterns of sharing between nodes. In general, class based systems have a static pattern of sharing; i.e. once an instance is created from a class then its pattern of sharing is fixed. Truly dynamic systems can decide on sharing patterns at message receipt time. As a generalization, instance-based sharing can allow greater opportunity for implementing dynamic changes than can class-based sharing.

Each scheme has advantages and drawbacks, depending on the application domain. For example, the creation of new types of object by modification or extension of existing types at compile time allows type checking policies to be imposed; on the other hand, the flexibility of creating new object types 'on the fly' without recompiling the system can sometimes outweigh the benefits of compile time type checking.

The security of compile time creation of classes versus the flexibility of creating new objects 'on the fly' is a central issue in the design of object-oriented systems. The implementation of mechanisms for code and behaviour sharing depends on your chosen policy. There has been lively debate in the object-oriented community on the relative merits of sharing mechanisms.

All three elements in this section have been subject to much attention. Perhaps the most frequently raised issues have been those associated with the *mechanisms* for behaviour sharing and for evolution. In particular, their implications for sharing have received most attention. Early attention focused on inheritance as the basic code and behaviour sharing mechanism. Originally introduced in Simula, it was popularized by the Smalltalk [Goldberg83] series of language/environment implementations. At one time, it was held that a language needed inheritance in order to be considered object-oriented. Latterly, a more permissive view of language classification holds, although such languages should still support the concept of type extension by some notion of sharing. Some form of type evolution by sharing is germane to object-oriented programming. We now look at the main strands of development in these aspects and their variations.

Discussion will first focus on systems that rely on the 'class' feature to implement inheritance and mechanisms for type evolution, followed by discussion of those systems that do not have a class construct but use 'prototypes' for these purposes. Systems that offer both classes and prototypes are then examined. In the discussion, frequent reference will be made to the Smalltalk80 language and environment. In part, this is in recognition of the impact it has had on the development of object-oriented programming and its associated terminology. The specific points of illustration, however, have general application.

3.3 BEHAVIOUR SHARING AND EVOLUTION: CLASS BASED SYSTEMS

In this section we briefly recap on some of the concepts introduced in chapter 2, and then go on to describe their implementation in greater detail.

3.3.1 Classes and Metaclasses

A *class* is a description of what is common to each of the elements in a class grouping. These elements are referred to as *instances*. All instances of a class have the same structure and share common behaviour. What is *not* shared is their individual state values, which are held separately in each instance. The class provides a repository for the shared behaviour code and, additionally, provides the structural template with which to create each new and distinct instance. (The previous chapter indicates how they are created and initialized.) Schematically, the relationship between a class and its instances is as shown in Figure 3.1.

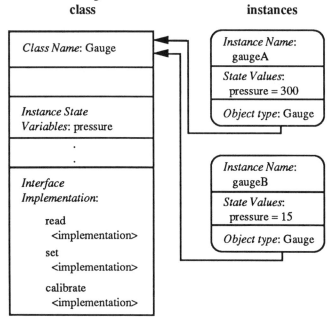

Figure 3.1: Classes and instances

The objects' state values are held individually in each instance, whilst the code modules that implement the methods are held in the class. On receiving a message, the instance looks in its class for the method. The principle of encapsulation holds as each instance will respond only to one of these interface methods that are held in the class: only through these methods can the instance variables be changed.

In the Smalltalk implementations, *class variables* are initialized when the class is created. The values of these variables are seen by every instance; that is, these values are available to the methods held in that class. Like instance variables, they are inherited along the class hierarchy and are visible to subclasses. Unlike instance variables, the initialized values (i.e., not just their declarations) are visible to subclasses.

Since the class is an object in its own right, the class too must have a class that describes it. Just as a class holds the description of its instances, so a *metaclass*[1] holds the description of its single instance; i.e., the description of the class. As such it provides the protocol for initializing the class variables, and also holds the protocol for creating an initialized instance of itself - that instance is the class.

So, we have seen, for example, that all classes have the ability to create new instances. The *class methods* for doing this are held in the metaclass. There is (in Smalltalk, for example) a distinct metaclass for each class. This allows classes to have different methods to customize the initialization of instances in each class. Schematically[2], this looks like Figure 3.2.

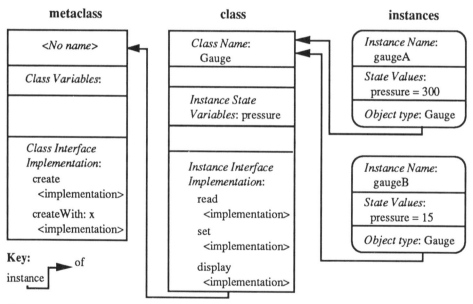

Figure 3.2: Relationship of instances, class and metaclass

In some systems, these distinct structures are merged and it is merely implied that

---

[1]the metaclass concept is just one way of achieving this, and is the Smalltalk solution. See, for example, CommonObjects in Section 3.3.5 for an alternative way of creating classes.

[2]the examples used in parts of this chapter refer to the implementations of types of gauge. These have variables to hold state values, such as pressure, range, etc and methods to manipulate that state, such as read, set, display, and so on.

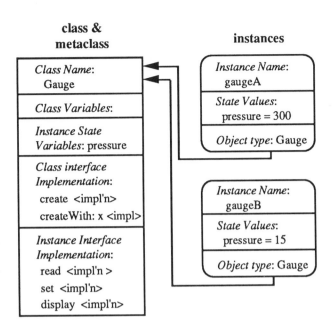

class &
metaclass

instances

| Class Name: Gauge |
| Class Variables: |
| Instance State Variables: pressure |
| Class interface Implementation: create \<impl'n> createWith: x \<impl> |
| Instance Interface Implementation: read \<impl'n > set \<impl'n> display \<impl'n> |

| Instance Name: gaugeA |
| State Values: pressure = 300 |
| Object type: Gauge |

| Instance Name: gaugeB |
| State Values: pressure = 15 |
| Object type: Gauge |

Figure 3.3: Aggregated form of Figure 3.2

instance methods reside in the class, and that class methods reside in the metaclass. Thus we have the aggregated form of Figure 3.3.

It is worth remarking that a class, in fact, holds metadata that applies to each of its instances. So, in this sense, a class can be considered to be the metaclass of its instances. The terminology is not often used in this sense, however.

In the type of systems described in this subsection, all the instances are identical. Once they have been formed from the template held in the class they can not be structurally changed. In other words the template is *strict*. This is in contrast to systems to be discussed later in section 3.4.4 that allow objects to mutate after creation and initialization.

Abstract classes It should be apparent, after some reflection, that not all classes need to have instances! In some situations, the class still acts as a repository for shared code and behaviour, but it just does not make sense to create instances of it. Take the class Collection in Smalltalk, for example. It does not make sense to create a plain instance of Collection.: rather, a particular type of collection having specific properties will be required and thus, quite rightly, a new subclass with these specific properties will be created before making the instances. The class Collection, however, still serves a useful role in holding the general properties of all types of collections. The class Collection, in this case, is a superclass and since it never has instances of its own, it is referred to as an *abstract class*.

3.3.2 Behaviour Sharing and Evolution in Class/Metaclass Systems: Inheritance
A new class is created by making it a *sub-class* of some existing class (classes are "rooted' in a base class that is usually called 'Root' or 'Object' or equivalent). This process

can be described as *differential programming*. The existing class has most, but not all of the behaviour that is required in the new setting, so a subclass is created that specifies only what *extra* behaviour and structure is required. In effect, this is a process of successively specializing the class hierarchy. Classes defined in this manner share behaviour across class/subclass links.

The newly created class shares, or *inherits*, the structure and code of the existing class, which is referred to as its direct *superclass*. In the types of implementations covered in this section (for example: Smalltalk80, ObjectiveC [Cox84]), the methods that operate on the instance objects are inherited along the class hierarchy whilst the class methods that operate on classes (typically to create new objects) are inherited along the metaclass hierarchy, as illustrated in Figure 3.4.

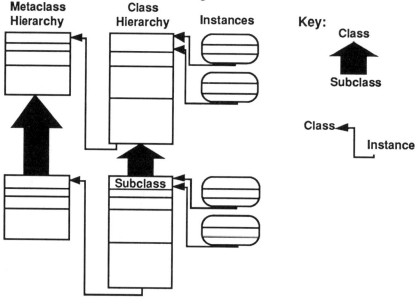

Figure 3.4: Sub-classing

The inheritance mechanism causes the new class that is created to merge the existing instance variable declarations of its superclasses with extra declarations that are made in the new class. In this way, the state of each instance of the class will be held wholly local to that instance. Note that in the Smalltalk type of implementation, methods access state values via implicit lexical variables. It is, therefore, an error to have two variables of the same name occur in an upward closure to the root of the class hierarchy. Any attempt to declare two variables of the same name in that closure will be caught at compile time. There is no requirement for variable names to be unique in any wider context. This inheritance of the representation of the existing class occurs at class creation time - a once and for all event. Classes in this type of system are thus statically defined and can not change at runtime.

Metaclasses and inheritance At this point, it is worth a brief digression to examine the behaviour of the inheritance mechanism in the metaclass hierarchy, as implemented in Smalltalk80. It is implementation specific, and has no general application outside this language. Whilst a full description is available in [Goldberg83], a summary is presented now to give an indication of the design.

As a starting point, observe that the metaclass hierarchy parallels the class hierarchy, as illustrated in Figure 3.4. The class hierarchy terminates in Object as the ultimate superclass; i.e., all classes are subclasses of Object. However, the metaclass structure beyond Object's metaclass follows a complex path back to the root class, Object.

All metaclasses share similar behaviour as they all hold the protocols to create classes and initialize class variables. This common behaviour is held in the superclass of Object's metaclass. This superclass is **not** a metaclass, but a class. The class is called Class (with a capital letter to distinguish it!) and yes, Class has a metaclass too.

All metaclasses are instances of some class. This class is Metaclass (again with a capital letter to distinguish it). The metaclass of Metaclass is itself, and it is here that the infinite recursion ends. However, the story does not quite end here.

Class and Metaclass are classes in their own right. They are both subclasses of the abstract class called ClassDescription, which in turn is a subclass of the class Behaviour, which is a subclass of Object. Thus *all* classes are subclasses of Object. The metaclass of Class is no different to any other metaclass, so it appears in the metaclass hierarchy below ClassDescription's metaclass and so on.

The significance of this scheme lies in the way the designers adhere to consistent principles throughout. For example, the new method that each metaclass must customize to produce an initialized class is inherited from the metaclasses' superclass, i.e., from Class. Since Class is a subclass of ClassDescription, which is a subclass of class Behaviour, which is a subclass of Object, all default behaviour is ultimately inherited from Object.

The metaclass concept is not without criticism, as will be discussed in section 3.3.5.

Method binding A method is invoked on an object as a result of sending that object a message. In Smalltalk-like systems, the message usually comprises: the name of the *receiver*, and a *selector*. The selector carries the method name and appropriate arguments. The binding of the method code to the method call on the object is thus made at run time - so to that extent the system is dynamic. The pattern of sharing is *static* in that the run time search for method code will always traverse the superclasses in the same order. In other words, an instance of a class in this type of system, on receipt of a message will *always* follow the same search path through its superclasses for a desired method. The pattern of sharing is thus fixed. This, of course, is a highly desirable characteristic in a language that is used for large static systems in which type security is needed. In this type of object system, to change the behaviour or *specification*[3] of an object, the class is edited and the code passed again through the interpreter or compiler to recreate a new object that has the new specification. This is a cumbersome, but secure, task.

Should a method call be unable to bind to a code module in the receiver, the program halts and an exception is raised. This typically takes some default form such as a

---

[3]This chapter will not go into typing aspects in any depth. That is left to chapter 4. However, to have an informal concept of type it is useful to consider the type of an object to be specified by the set of operations that denotes the object's behaviour and forms its visible interface. More sophisticated typing schemes make implementation-independent demands on the operands of the operations and on the results returned by the operations.

"message not understood" notification that is returned to the programmer at run time. More complex exception control structures can usually be built from basic language features. In section 3.3.4, we shall examine a more explicit approach to the handling of exceptions.

Single inheritance search paths Let us examine these search paths more closely. What, for example, do we do when a method is invoked on an object and more than one method of that name exists in the upward closure of the hierarchy, as shown for example in Figure 3.5.

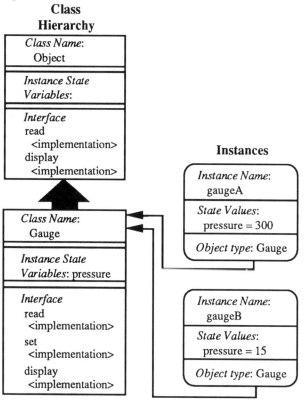

Figure 3.5: Single inheritance: conflicting method names

In the type of inheritance hierarchy in which a class only ever has one direct superclass, the conflict resolution rule is to invoke the 'closest' method of that name. If the method is defined in the class of the receiver, then it is invoked; otherwise an upward search is made through the class hierarchy and the first method of that name which is found is chosen. For example, the read method when invoked on gaugeB will cause Gauge's version to be executed. Failure to locate any method of that name would be flagged as a runtime error. The exception to this search rule occurs in some systems when a method is invoked not on the pseudo variable "self", but on "super", in which case the search starts in that object's superclass. Some languages, such as Trellis/Owl [Schaffert86], CommonObjects [Snyder86a], and C++ [Stroustrup86] go further and allow the user to specify explicitly the search start point, by specifying the superclass and operation as a single compound name.

Most languages offer only single inheritance and users are prepared to tolerate the restrictions imposed by the single hierarchy, in a trade-off between greater modelling power and greater problems of handling the conflicts in a more general inheritance scheme.

3.3.3 Extensions to Inheritance: Multiple Inheritance

Conceptually, multiple inheritance is a tool for structuring knowledge. At an implementation level, multiple inheritance is also a mechanism to promote the sharing of common nodal attributes on separate hierarchies. As such, it can be seen as a mechanism for creating *polygenetic* objects; that is, objects that have several distinct ancestors. The new object inherits from each ancestor. The resulting graph of links is no longer tree-like, as it is with simple inheritance, but is more general. On the question of utility, there is a division of opinion. In knowledge representation and associated applications, there is a self evident demand for the modeling power it brings. The general experience of users in the Smalltalk community [Borning87] suggests that the complexities introduced by multiple inheritance, coupled with the lack of adequate support tools, may deter many users.

So, what complications does this extension introduce for the inheritance mechanism? The response must be intimately linked with the particular implementation of the mechanism. It should be noted, moreover, that in general the problems are similar for many different sorts of semantic links that can exist in graph-like structures of nodes. In this sub-section we will consider systems with mechanisms operating through class/metaclass hierarchies, although analogous solutions exist for systems using inheritance based on instances (see section 3.4.2). Section 3.3.4 examines systems that tackle such problems at a more fundamental level.

A class that is derived from more than one direct superclass inherits structure and behaviour from each. In a class based system, the class Clock (Figure 3.7) usually receives a full copy of the structures of Gauge and Timer. Additionally, Clock inherits both Gauge's and Timer's interfaces. It is readily apparent that name conflicts are potentially present in both elements. In the example of Figure 3.7, the state variable range is declared in both Timer and Gauge. Clock, which could be a timer with a gauge interface, will inherit two conflicting declarations of range. Similarly, Clock will inherit two conflicting display methods. Which one should it choose? How should it resolve the conflict? Should it invoke both?

Conflict resolution Conflicts in the naming of state variables can be resolved at class creation time by renaming conflicting variables in the new object, e.g. Gauge.range, Timer.range . A method start invoked on an instance of Clock would be found in the Timer arm of the hierarchy and would use the Timer.x variables where such values are required. Note that it is the clear sight of Gauge's internal structure given to Clock (by the process of copying) that wholly defeats the concept of encapsulation. As a result, state variable names *must* be unique in all superclasses of Clock. Through the inheritance mechanism, this requires that the uniqueness extends through all Gauge's and Timer's superclasses, and so on.

There is greater variation in the ways of resolving conflicting method names. In some implementations, e.g. [Schaffert86], [Borning81] where multiple inheritance is modeled as a general graph, it is even acceptable for two different sets of subclass/superclass links coming from a subclass to reach the same ancestor class, as shown in Figure 3.6.

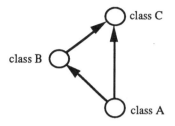

Figure 3.6: Closed path in the inheritance hierarchy

In these implementations, the attempt to inherit duplicate operations may not signal an error; this, however, is only on condition that the conflicting names refer to the *same* operations. Convenient though this solution may be, such implementations will compromise the principle of encapsulation, as the inherited representations are now part of the inheritance contract. This is discussed in full in [Snyder86b]

However, there is still the problem of identifying and resolving the conflicts arising from the multiple distinct declarations of identically named methods in the hierarchy or graph. For example, consider what should be done when a method display is called on an instance of Clock, as in Figure 3.7. The method display is not defined locally but is defined in both direct superclasses Gauge and Timer. Thus the simple rule of choosing the 'closest' definition of the method finds two copies of the method at the same

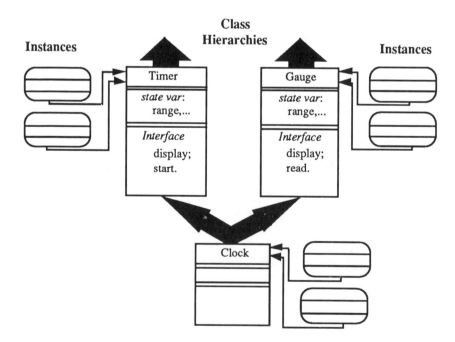

Figure 3.7: Inheritance from more than one superclass

'distance' from the object. Which copy should be invoked? Two options exist: either remove the conflicts by renaming, or define a more appropriate traversing algorithm for the inheritance graph.

Taking the first course of action: at Clock's creation time, all conflicts are identified and removed by creating a new, distinctly named operation in Clock's class. If the semantics of the inheritance implementation require it, this method can call both display operations on its parents and in addition perform some local computation to complete the operation. This is the safest course of action and is that proposed, for example, in the implementation of multiple inheritance in Smalltalk variants. It can be argued that an enforced default conflict resolution rule, or *precedence rule*, is not appropriate in all cases and that resolution must be made by the programmer explicitly.

Following the second line of thought, a rule for traversing the inheritance graph (as it is no longer a simple tree-like structure) can be devised or, alternatively, the inheritance graph can be flattened into a linear chain and duplicate operation names eliminated. There are a number of graph traversal algorithms that could be specified. Most common is the 'depth-first' search of the graph [Bobrow86], whilst occasionally some systems employ 'breadth-first' search patterns [Ferber83]. Within the depth-first schemes, there are many variations [Ducournau87]. The traversal algorithm specifies an order in which the search should proceed. For example, in a simple depth-first search following a rule such as

"Clock inherits from Timer *and then from* Gauge"

i.e., the local superclasses of Clock are given by

Clock : Timer Gauge

In this case, a call for display locates Timer's copy of display first. The example given above suggests a traversal of the left branch followed by a traversal of the classes on the right branch. If the general inheritance graph meets in a *join*, the *join* class is then traversed in search of the method, and so on.

This latter example is equivalent to flattening the inheritance graph into a linear chain and removing the duplicates. The linear inheritance graph for Figure 3.7 would then be as shown in Figure 3.8.

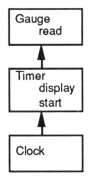

Figure 3.8: Linearized inheritance graph

Different implementations have different policies on which duplicates (all but first, all but last) to remove. There are other variations. In CommonLoops [Bobrow86], for example, the metaclasses have the protocols for determining the class precedence lists.

These transformations of the inheritance graph may have subtle side effects. For example, note that linearization in Figure 3.8 has the effect of making Timer the effective parent of Clock, a consequence which may be neither wholly appropriate nor expected. Whilst the use of *super* in a single inheritance tree is well defined, the consequences of linearizing the multiple inheritance graph may produce unexpected results. As a result of the linearizing transformation, the effective parent of a subclass may change so allowing *super* to access an unexpected interface. The apparently straightforward simplification has been bought at the cost of increased conceptual complexity. Later in this chapter, when we consider alternative implementations of inheritance that link instances rather than classes, we shall examine a more radical approach to conflict resolution.

Method specialization It should be apparent that there is wide variation in the implementation of inheritance mechanisms. The discussion so far has focused on mechanisms having granularity of change at the level of methods. That is, if an existing method in a class does not do what is required, a new subclass is created and the method redefined in it. Some implementations, e.g., Loops [Bobrow81], allow the incremental specialization of methods. For example, in Figure 3.7, the method display could be implemented as

display
      (some specialized local action
           invoke the inherited method in the superclass
)

This has the benefit of allowing code in the superclass to be reused, rather than having to copy large tracts of it into the declaration of the new method.

Further, the Flavors implementation allows the combination of methods at compile time. The method combination forms three parts: a primary or main part, a part that is executed *before* the primary part, and a part that is executed *after* the primary part. A more detailed description is available in [Moon86], and in [Stefik86].

Mixins Multiply inheriting from several distinct class hierarchies achieves the desired effect of importing specific functionality from these classes. It can also import undesired functionality as, in general, the default inheritance mechanism does not include 'inheritance with exclusions'. In other words, it is not easy to selectively inherit only the characteristics and functionality that is desired. An example of an implementation that does allow this is given in [Snyder86a]

One variant that is used to good effect in Flavors and LOOPS, is the use of *mixins*: packages of operations in classes that can be 'mixed in' to other classes. Schematically, the mixin appears as in Figure 3.9.

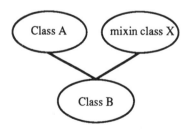

Figure 3.9: Mixins

Mixins are abstract classes in that they do not have any instances; they exist only to add functionality to existing classes. For example, the class Timer could be augmented with some accounting attributes. If all the devices in the class are considered to be company assets, then the class could be augmented as follows:

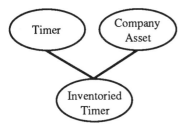

Figure 3.10: Example: inventoried assets

A method called value that is invoked on a particular timer would find its implementation in the Company Asset mixin class, and would return a value for the timer based on its initial cost and on the company's depreciation policy. An alternative mixin class Personal Possession could have been employed which could value all timers at replacement value for personal possession insurance purposes.

One problem is that this approach, if used indiscriminantly, can lead to the creation of an exponentially large number of new classes for each original class of objects, according to the number of mixins that can be invented! Every variation in functionality needs a distinct class before the instance can be created. The flexibility, in effect, can lead to a loss in programmer control of the class evolution hierarchy. Note again that the templates used are strict, in that once an instance has been created it can not mutate.

One approach suggested by Hendler [Hendler86] proposes that instead of using mixins at the level of *classes*, they could be used at the level of *instances*. For example, given a particular instance myTimer of class Timer, should it be upgraded, for example with an electronic mechanism, then the added functionality is simply added as a package to that *instance*, as in Figure 3.11.

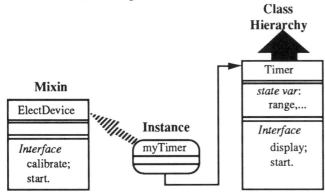

Figure 3.11: Mixins at level of instances

Hendler describes this process as one of *enhancement*. Note that enhancement does not alter the type of the instance: myTimer is still a Timer. Since the enhanced instance does not form a new type, it can have no descendants; although this limits the use of the mechanism, it does point the way to a different notion of inheritance - inheritance based on instances. There are still name conflicts to handle as before; the usual rule is that the 'up to the joins' search protocol ensures that mixins are accessed before the root class.

To conclude this section, therefore, we have seen that there are significant difficulties in designing, implementing, and not least of all, in using systems that have multiple inheritance. The advantages of increased expressive power are countered by the implementation difficulties of managing such systems.

3.3.4 Class Based Systems: Fundamental Improvements

The previous section discussed the practical difficulties of resolving conflicts in inheritance hierarchies. The problems encountered have their roots, at least partly, in the language designers' breaking of encapsulation in the implementation of the inheritance mechanism. Consider, however, the fundamentally different view taken, for example, by the implementors of Trellis/Owl, a language that has multiple type inheritance and strict, compile time type checking. It is an important landmark in the history of object-oriented language design. For the purposes of the present chapter, however, discussion of the role of type checking aspects in general and their implementation in Trellis/Owl in particular, is left to chapter 4. In this chapter, we mention the concept only in passing reference, preferring to concentrate on the Trellis/Owl model of code and behaviour sharing.

Encapsulation in Trellis/Owl: operation visibility In Trellis/Owl, the term *class* and *type* are used interchangeably. A *class* or *type* is a grouping of instances with similar *behaviour*, where *behaviour* is considered to be the list of *operations* that can manipulate the objects. Thus objects with the same type have the same operations. As before, there are instance operations that operate on instances and class operations that apply to classes. Consider, by way of example, the syntax of Figure 3.12 in which an increment operation is invoked on a particular gauge.

```
operation increment (me: gauge; value: real)
returns(gauge)
is
    Begin
        * implementation *
    end;
```

Figure 3.12: Trellis/Owl operations

The interface of this operation includes the operation name, the number and types of its arguments, the type that the operation returns, and the exceptions that can be signalled. The reserved word me in this illustration, indicates that push is an instance method. By comparison, the appearance of aType as in the following fragment

```
operation create (aType)
returns(aType);
```

indicates that create is a class operation. The set of operations that make up the external interface form the *specification* of the class; whilst the internal representation, which may include internal operations, is the *implementation* of the class. Operations are analogous to methods in the Smalltalk-like implementations. However, there are significant differences in the visibility of these operations. Specifically, operations can be declared *public*, in which case they will form part of the external interface, or *private* in which case they will be visible only within the type. In other words, public operations are available to the *clients* of the type, whereas private operations are only available to *implementors* of the type. There is an additional category of operation which is called *sub-type visible*. This, as you would expect, makes the operation visible to all of that type's subtypes. Note that in Trellis/Owl, whilst public operations in a supertype can be redeclared in a subtype, they can not be excluded. Further discussion on the rationale for this is given in chapter 4 when *typing* is discussed in detail.

Encapsulation in Trellis/Owl: state values as operations More significant in the design of Trellis/Owl is its consistent view of state in terms of the operations that access it. The equivalent in Trellis/Owl to an instance variable is a *component*. So, for example, the value shown on an instance myGauge of type gauge could be

```
myGauge.value
```
which is shorthand for the equivalent operation
```
get_value(myGauge)
```
whilst
```
myGauge.value:= 200
```
is equivalent to the operation
```
put_value(myGauge, 200.00)
```
These put_ and get_ operations are created specially for each component.

Components are defined, for example on myGauge, as
```
component me.value: Real;
```
which generates automatically the get_ and put_ operations as
```
operation get_value(me)
returns(Real);

put_value(me, value: Real)
returns(Real);
```
The component itself can be declared as a *field*, in which case it is stored, or it can be *computed* from other components or operations when called. Furthermore, to prevent clients from writing to a particular component, the component is simply declared as *private*. Just as there are instance operations and class operations, so there are instance components (as in the examples above) and class components. A class component declared as private ensures that all instances of the class will have that component declared as private, for example:
```
component gauge.count: Integer
put private
is field
```
In this way, clients can not alter the field gauge.count of gauge. With this consistent view of state and operations, Trellis/Owl achieves rigorous encapsulation: *no-one* can access the state values directly, *all* must go through a well defined procedural interface.

What are the benefits for inheritance? Simply these:

- the implementation of rigorous encapsulation that forces access to variables through an operational interface makes the implementation of these state value holders invisible to clients. Components can be implemented as *field* or *computed* without affecting the external view of the type.
- the facility to declare operations as *private* makes them invisible to clients of the type. This extends to inheritance. Private operations are not inherited, thus reducing complexity in the interface. Inherited public operations that call private operations will still access these private operations, without the need for these private operations to be visible in the subtype.

Exception handling techniques A further interesting feature of the Trellis/Owl implementation which has significance for this chapter is its explicit handling of exceptions. When an operation is invoked and it is unable to complete, the interface of the operation has a list of *exceptions* that the operation can signal. This gives optional control to the programmer in handling run time error conditions. Note that the error "message not found" (a familiar runtime error when programming in an untyped language) could not occur in the strict compile time type checked Trellis/Owl programs. A typical example of this implementation is given below in the declaration of an operation called opName, where opName will perform a range check during the course of its execution:

```
operation opName(me, value: Integer)
returns (Integer)
signals (OutofRange)
is
Begin
.
if (condition) then signal OutofRange;
.
end;
```

This would be called during the course of the program, for example, as:

```
begin
.
i := opName(thisNumber, 5);
.
except on OutofRange do
        <implementation>
end;
```

There are explicit exception handling routines in a number of object-oriented programming languages, e.g., C++, and Eiffel [Meyer88]. The role of exceptions in the implementation of information systems is given in [Borgida86]. The reader is referred forward to chapter 6 for further discussion of these features.

3.3.5 Class/Metaclass Based Inheritance Hierarchies - Cause for Thought

Class-based systems are popular and have great utility. It would be a mistake, however, to think that they are free from criticism. The following subsections indicate some consequences of design decisions and their implementations. For further discussion of such concerns, see [Raj89]

Implementation vs logical hierarchies Object-oriented programming assists in the production of reusable code. As such it can be a valuable tool for industry. In class based language implementations, large libraries of hierarchically ordered classes are supplied. In the Smalltalk80 environment there are of the order of two hundred and fifty classes supplied, each with a protocol (or interface) to be learned. Whilst this provides an excellent springboard for fast programming, it has a number of drawbacks: firstly, it is necessary to become proficient in the use of the libraries. Secondly, the designers of classes see them from an implementor's viewpoint, that is they see the classes as they fit into an inheritance hierarchy that encourages code sharing. The class designers see the potential of providing classes that users may want to use, if the users classify their concepts in the same way as did the designers in the outset. So, as long as users follow the same lines of reasoning, they can build on the *implementation* hierarchies that are supplied with the language. However, the categorization of these implementation classes may conflict with a *logical* hierarchy that may appear more obvious. Thus the static and rigid nature of class categorization may lead to an unnatural style of programming.

Implementation vs specification hierarchies Following on from the previous point, an implementation hierarchy has limited scope in abstract reasoning. There are significant benefits to be gained for program correctness and for abstract reasoning by having type checked specification hierarchies based on behaviour, i.e., based on interface specification. Smalltalk has no type checking and thus does not have a specification hierarchy. Trellis/Owl does have a specification hierarchy but this parallels the class (implementation) hierarchy. In other systems, (see section 3.6.2) the class hierarchy and the specification hierarchy are decoupled, thereby gaining the benefits of type checking and efficient implementation.

Extending the system One dilemma that faces class designers is the handling of small variations in the desired behaviour of instances. What should be done if an existing class requires a small change in its definition? A number of solutions have been suggested. These include:

- redefining the class to include the extra structure and behaviour;
- defining a new class (a subclass) that specifies the additional structure and behaviour;
- defining exceptions *at the level of instances*, which if sufficient in number could be promoted to form a new subclass.

The first solution will lead to ever bigger, monolithic class definitions, which are unnecessarily cumbersome. The second solution is the instinctive response to the problem but, expedient though this solution may be, such practice leads to a proliferation of branches in the class tree, especially when a class has to be created to support a single instance. The third solution is efficient and borrows from conventional programming practices. However, it is somewhat restricted in a class based environment in that the 'exception instance' cannot be used to create new sets of such instances until it has been promoted to the status of a class. This latter solution leads the way for inheritance systems to be developed that do not rely on the class concept. This aspect is covered more fully in section 3.4.

Breaking the principle of encapsulation Throughout the development of class-based object systems, the benefits of abstraction are apparent. Successive levels of abstraction serve to hide implementation details at each level. Subclasses are defined in a class-superclass hierarchy; each new subclass is an abstraction with more specialized behaviour than its superclasses. However, it is interesting to look more closely at one of the consequences of this type of sharing: the impact of class inheritance hierarchies on the concept of encapsulation.

In defining a new subclass in these class based systems, instance variable names have to be unique. The reason for this is that whilst the method code is held in the class hierarchy and is shared, the instance variable declarations are copied into each instance. An instance thus holds *all* the instance variables declared in *every* superclass in the upward closure to the root class! The result is that encapsulation, the protection of state behind a procedural interface, is broken. A subclasses, instead of being reliant only on the external interface of its superclasses, is now wholly dependent on the internal representation of each and every superclass as well. In other words, any subclass has explicit and unqualified access to any variable in any of its superclasses. Thus, whilst many object-oriented languages promote the concept of encapsulation as a protection and abstraction mechanism, in that its state may be only accessed via its protocol, these languages disregard the constraints of encapsulation within the class/superclass hierarchy. Thus any changes to the implementation of any instance variable in a superclass will have an immediate side-effect throughout all instances of the hierarchy beneath it [Snyder86b].

Restrictions on multiple users Programming in the large calls for the concurrent working of many programmers on interacting parts of the system. The traditional class based programming system, however, is essentially a single user workspace and namespace. In its simplest form, the traditional class based language environments do not help users with their own workspace image to share code. Global naming conventions are an immediate pre-requisite for such systems. The task of controlling the growth of classes, some with perhaps significant commonalty, is non-trivial.

Inheritance and distribution Systems that use conventional class based inheritance mechanisms are not suitable for use in a fully distributed system. The problems of handling multiple users is now compounded by the problems of simultaneous shared use on many machines. There are immediate problems in maintaining consistency amongst the many nodes, and at the same time providing adequate response times in allowing all users to see the effect of changes. Particular problems to be faced are associated with migration, leading to the separation of classes and instances across nodes, as well as the problems of class hierarchy distribution across many nodes. Equally, the usual problems of distributed debugging and distributed garbage collection are compounded by the class convention. [Bennett87] highlights a number of design decisions and restrictions imposed in an implementation of distributed Smalltalk. The role of objects in distributed systems is discussed in Chapter 9.

Conceptual difficulties The metaclass concept has been considered an obstacle to newcomers to this style of programming [O'Shea86] This naturally leads one to question whether the concept is essential. The metaclass is there to allow class variables and class methods to be declared. Class variables are accessible to any method defined in the class;

these variables are shared. The class methods typically provide customized object instance creation and initialization. Can this be achieved in any other way?

CommonObjects, an object extension to Common Lisp, uses a single function to create new classes. This is achieved through the define-type construct that declares:
- the state variables that each instance of the type will hold;
- any initialization values;
- any routines to be called on initialization; and
- the visibility of each each element; (i.e., can it be seen and accessed by users, or is it private to the type?)

Note that the operations or methods are not defined in this construct.

Unlike Smalltalk, the type (i.e. class) is not an object. The syntax of this define-type construct is similar for all types. Instances of any type are created by a single function make-instance. This function takes the name of the class as a required argument, and initialization arguments as keyword parameters. An operation or method is declared separately and is bound to its type in a define-method construct. Methods can be declared *private* to achieve encapsulation. The significance of the separate method definition routine is that new methods can be dynamically added or reimplemented without recompiling the type definition (i.e. class structure).

Static systems With the exception of CommonObjects, all of the implementations considered in this section are *static*. That is, the pattern of sharing is determined at class creation time. Each subclass knows which superclass link it will traverse in its search for method code each time. Any changes require a redefinition of the class hierarchy and a recompilation of the system. In experimental programming, a significant feature is a need to dynamically create and amend types and instances without recompilation. Systems supporting such practices are discussed in the next section.

3.4 BEHAVIOUR SHARING AND EVOLUTION: SYSTEMS WITHOUT CLASSES

The concept of sharing code and behaviour, even when the patterns of sharing are static as described in the last section, is without doubt a significant benefit. What then is the mechanism for dynamically changing patterns of sharing? What are the significant advantages, if any, of this over the static systems? What are the architectural differences of such systems compared with the static systems? What implementations exist?

In examining these questions, we take a different conceptual model of arranging knowledge. In the previous sections we had assumed a class-based system. Classes were repositories for information that is shared; that is, for information that is common to all instances in the class. To encourage the evolution of classes, a specialization mechanism allowed new classes (subclasses) to be defined as extensions or modifications of existing classes. Linkages to the ancestor classes (superclasses) formed the lines along which the subclass inherited structure and behaviour. These links were fixed at object creation time which precluded any dynamic changes to the type system.

The use of inheritance to encourage differential programming, to reduce storage overheads by sharing common code, and additionally to provide a conceptual classification tool to assist in reasoning in the problem space is a tall order for a single mechanism. Inevitably, as it is applied in an ever widening range of applications, it is found to be less than ideal.

The use of the class concept, for example, produces a very simple classification system that is not universally useful in the real world. For example, when trying to fit a class-based taxonomy to real world entities, how easy is it to specify a rule that will encompass all the potential members of the class, and exclude all those who should not belong to the class? The set of integers that form the Fibonacci series can be specified by an all-embracing rule, but the set of "calculators" is less easy to describe. Their range of functionality and design makes comprehensive specification difficult; a single taxonomic hierarchy may not be sufficient to describe all calculators. Furthermore, with innovation in design, a static taxonomy may not even be appropriate.

When considering modelling the calculator, it may be necessary for the calculator to dynamically alter its behaviour to give optimal performance at the time of calculation. In other words, in the model of the calculator, when it receives a message it may *dynamically* determine which behaviour it wishes to borrow to give the best answer. It may indeed wish to borrow behaviour from objects which were not in existence when the object was created. In a static system this would not be possible as the patterns of sharing would be fixed at the time of object creation. An alternative view is needed.

3.4.1 Actors and Prototypes

In contrast to the class-based languages, typified by Smalltalk, are the 'actor' languages [Hewitt77], [Agha86]. Whereas the class based object-oriented languages emphasize structural abstraction in that they are concerned with the structural organization of data, actor languages are primarily concerned with the communication structure of interacting process. Actors are active objects. Each actor consists of an *acquaintance vector* which holds its state and a *script* which holds the computational elements of the actor. In an actor system, everything is an actor. Actors are basically computational agents: they are active processes that communicate by message passing. These messages are themselves actors. Actors support an object-oriented style of programming. All actor languages offer encapsulation: their private state is accessible only through a public interface, or protocol.

There is no class/instance distinction in pure actor languages. There is no natural grouping of instances to form a class of identically structured entities. There is no shared repository of behaviour, a role filled by the class in traditional class based systems. There is no special place that holds a template for instance generation. And, of course, as there are no classes there are no metaclasses! Such objects, on the whole, are smaller than class based objects as they are not hardwired into a class inheritance hierarchy; they trade a reduction in size for an increase in message traffic at run time.

Basic actors, as typified by the implementation in the language Act1, for instance, have a very simple protocol that is executed on message receipt: the receiving actor creates a new actor to handle the next incoming call, performs the required computation, passes the result on to another named actor, and dies. There is no updating of state in pure actor systems. Instead, a process of *replacement* is used, where the replacement actor with the new state is put in place and the old actor dies. This model provides a very powerful primitive for distributed and concurrent applications.

We now consider additional features that may be created around this simple object model that can offer familiar object-oriented benefits, such as code sharing and differential programming.

3.4.2 Delegation

Higher-level actor languages take the concept of computational agents and add to them mechanisms for *delegation*. Delegation is a mechanism for sharing which, in contrast to inheritance, does not limit itself to creating a logical structuring in the data. Instead, more flexibly, it allows a less constrained form of sharing. As indicated, each object or *prototype* as it can also be called, defines its own type. To illustrate the features of delegation and to examine the characteristics of prototypes, we refer to their implementation in Lieberman's language DELEGATION [Lieberman85].

Method objects Everything in this type of object system is an object. Thus state and interface methods can both be considered objects in their own right. Consider methods first. The messages that an object receives are handled by a set of methods. Each method has a *name* and a *response*. Thus on receipt of a message, an object sends a *delegate message* to each of its methods. This message carries the name of the client (i.e. the original sender of the delegate message) as an argument. The value of the first method to accept the message is returned.

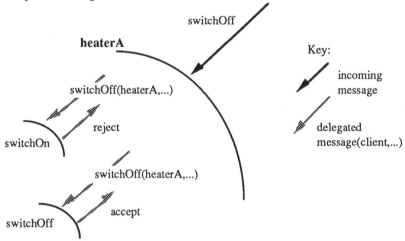

Figure 3.13: Delegated messages to method objects

Referring to the example in Figure 3.13, heaterA on receiving a switchOff message delegates the message to each of its method objects. Each method object checks that the type of the message matches its own name. If identical, the method object accepts the message and invokes its response. Contrast this protocol with the equivalent in class based systems where methods are located by table look up and executed by binding to the code with the *client* holding the thread of control.

Now consider state variables and their values. They too are objects that have names and values. When a read access is required on a state variable, just as with methods the client delegates the message. The object of that name responds by accepting the message and returning its value. Equally, when write access is required to a state variable, all state variables get a delegate message to *set a new value*. The object named in the message responds by changing its value to the new value. So, variables are accessed by message sends. The significant advantage of this is that the representation of the state variable object (i.e., how it is implemented behind its procedural interface) is not visible to clients and thus adheres strictly to the principle of encapsulation. Contrast this with the way in which methods have unrestricted, direct access to the representation of the state variables in many class based languages and use this knowledge in their procedures. Thus changes made to the representation in that case will inevitably cause the breakdown of existing method code.

Extension objects In class based systems, a subclass defines some specialised structure and behaviour and inherits default structure and behaviour from its superclasses. How are such elements shared in classless systems? Simply, an *extension object* can be created that can share with one or more original prototypes. These objects, declared as shared from the view point of the extension object, act as surrogates or proxies to which the extension object will turn for assistance. More specifically, extension objects do not just share behaviour; they can share knowledge contained in their prototypes in a more general way; that is, the value of state variables (which are isomorphic to methods) can be shared between objects. An extension object, therefore, consists of two parts: a *personal* part and a *shared* part. The personal part holds what is unique to the new object, whilst the shared part holds a list of prototypes which are under contract to share certain state and behaviour with the new object.

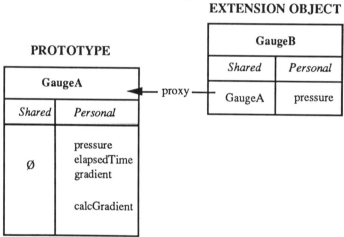

Figure 3.14: Shared and personal parts

Consider, for example, Figures 3.14 and 3.15 in which a metering system has, amongst other things, a gauge that records changes in pressure over time. The original gauge (GaugeA) is our prototype pressure gradient gauge. Should another pressure gradient gauge (GaugeB) be required in a different chamber, it is a simple matter to create a new extension object that declares separate pressure readings, but shares the elapsedTime value of the prototype gauge by naming it as a proxy. In listing GaugeA as a proxy, the extension object can thereby share all the method objects of the prototype. So, when a pressure gradient is required for the new chamber, the calculateGradient message to GaugeB (Fig. 3.15) is delegated to a method of that name locally. As none is found (as we have only declared pressure objects), the message is delegated to its proxies in turn, with the new gauge (GaugeB) named as client. The only proxy named is the original prototype, so GaugeA receives the delegated message and its method object of that name accepts it. When the method calculateGradient requires a pressure value it delegates a message 'pressure' back to the *client* for the value, which is returned. When the elapsedTime value is required, again the message 'elapsedTime' is delegated back to the client. However, in this case the elapsedTime variable (object) was not declared in the client, so the message is delegated to the proxy and value held in the GaugeA is returned. In this way, the elapsedTime value is shared between two objects.

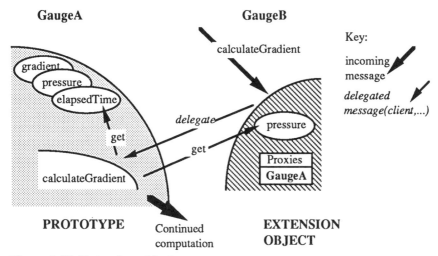

Figure 3.15: Extension object

One criticism made of the implementation of traditional class based systems is that the size of the instances can get large as the depth of the inheritance tree increases. This is due to the instances receiving a full copy of every instance variable declaration from every one of its superclasses, whether it uses them or not. Extension objects can reduce this growth by delaying local declaration of a variable until it is written to. This is a direct consequence of the delegation protocol to access variables. The delegated message 'X' is for read access to X, whilst the delegated message 'X set:arg' writes a value to X. So, returning to Figure 3.15, should calculateGradient require to write a value to gradient in GaugeB, the delegated message 'gradient set:arg' is not delegated to GaugeA (to avoid corrupting GaugeA's last gradient value!) but causes the new variable (object) gradient to be created locally in GaugeB and given set's argument.

Finally, we have seen that an extension object can share behaviour and values with other objects; it can also specialise its behaviour by defining new methods in its personal part. For example, GaugeB may define a new method, digitalDisplay, that specializes its behaviour; i.e., by giving it a method that is not available to the prototype. Equally, GaugeB may choose to reimplement calculateGradient which would always pick up delegated messages of that name and prevent them being passed to the old implementation in GaugeA.

New objects, of course, can list many proxies in their shared part and thereby have opportunity to delegate to many surrogates. This is analogous to the concept of multiple inheritance that was discussed in class based systems. Delegated messages run into similar problems as method calls do in multiple inheritance. Unless the user is prepared

65

to accept non-deterministic program behaviour, there needs to be a protocol for delegating messages to objects in the shared list. Usually, the first object listed in the shared part is messaged, which recursively messages *its* shared list of objects before passing on to the next object in the shared list, and so on until a method object accepts the delegated message. Such delegation lists support implicit sharing and to that extent may appear static. In general, the delegation mechanism can explicitly name the receiver at message dispatch time and is thus intrinsically dynamic.

3.4.3 Delegation - a More General View

The underlying basic actor model is highly dynamic and relies on delegation in its most general sense to achieve large scale, fine grained concurrent activity amongst its active objects. The actor protocol requires that an actor communicates by messaging, that an actor can dynamically create new actors, and that it must specify a replacement actor to receive the next message. Actors in general do not have an assignment command, but instead allow an actor to specify a replacement. This feature is exploited in the use of continuations to carry forward both the thread of control and object state in the process of computation. An actor performs what computation it can, then passes on the remainder of the computation in a message to a named actor. These messages are themselves objects. They can be manipulated, therefore, as first class objects in their own right. They can be suspended, and reactivated, by messaging them; this feature can be used to significant advantage in a dynamic environment.

3.4.4 Classless Systems - Cause for Thought

Efficiency concerns As there is no class in which to store a single copy of the shared code, there could be a loss of space/speed efficiency when a new prototype, copied from an existing prototype, is required. This would arise when a new, distinct prototype is needed that will not share with an existing prototype. In such a situation, the whole prototype is copied even though what may only be different is its state values.

No group-update mechanism Delegation is a mechanism that fits well into the dynamic category of object-oriented languages. The ability to make new objects, on the fly, with patterns of sharing that are not fixed until message receipt time gives extraordinary flexibility for exploratory programming. Gaining this flexibility means foregoing some of the useful features of class based languages. For example, the class holds the template for all instances of its type. Make a change to the template and, upon recompilation, all instances automatically reflect the change. The prototype based systems as described above do not have templates. The best we can do is to make a change to the prototype and all objects that quote that prototype in their shared lists will see the change. However, you still have to change each distinct occurrence of prototype individually. There is no way to reason about and to manipulate *groups* of similar objects.

There are systems that are not class based, yet do have templates. For example, objects are prototypes in the language SELF [Ungar87] yet they carry templates with which to clone new objects. The instances produced can be altered to produce prototypes of a new type. The templates are thus non-strict in that not all instances produced from a given template are guaranteed to look the same. The templates themselves do not define a type or class. Sharing is achieved by the new object implicitly delegating messages to its named parent as before. The sharing is dynamic in that objects can change their structure dynamically and thus influence the delegation mechanism.

Erroneous modification of a prototype   As there is a uniform protocol for prototypes, it is possible to modify a prototype by mistake. This will then have an immediate effect on all extension objects that are connected to it. The fundamental distinction between class and instance protocols in class based languages does prevent this to some extent in that type of system. In a prototype system, it would be up to the implementor to arrange for some extra protection for prototype modification.

Appropriate model   At a knowledge modelling level, is it appropriate to model everything in terms of prototypes? When considering a general concept, it is usual to consider its abstract qualities. It is less usual to consider a specific, known example and then decide how your needs vary from it.   To take a concrete example, how do you describe characters and integers? Must every integer be related to the prototypical 0 and 1? [Borning86] provides a detailed discussion of these aspects.

3.5 CLASSES vs PROTOTYPES

Inevitably, the different models for sharing have been tested against each other with their respective advantages and disadvantages aired. In 1987, however, at the OOPSLA Conference in Orlando, Florida, three of the protagonists in this good humoured debate drew up a joint statement [Stein89] on what they considered to be common amongst implementations, and further, they identified the major axes of the variations along which they differed. What was common was their recognition of the distinct roles played by *empathy* and *templates* in object-oriented systems. Empathy concerns the sharing of state and behaviour between objects, whilst a template provides at least a minimal guarantee for the structure of objects created from it.

The independent dimensions along which they differed are identified as follows:
- are patterns of sharing *STATIC* or are they *DYNAMIC*? Are the patterns of sharing fixed at the time that the object is created, or are the patterns of sharing only fixed when the object receives the message?
- are the mechanisms for sharing *EXPLICIT* or are they *IMPLICIT*? Does the compiler automatically and uniformly locate the shared code, or does the programmer need to explicitly state where it is located?
- are objects manipulated on a *PER OBJECT* basis or on a *PER GROUP* basis? Is behaviour specified for a whole group of objects or can individual objects be given specific behaviour? Equally, given that an object is a member of a group, can it be guaranteed to have specific behaviour?

The treaty recognises the need for differences in strategies according to the needs of particular application domains. So, for example, some applications may need the flexibility of dynamic, per object sharing with such sharing explicitly controlled by the programmer, whilst others need the security and support of static languages where the sharing mechanisms are implicit and apply uniformly to all members of a group.

3.5.1 "Delegation *is* inheritance"
Earlier sections have discussed the two mechanisms of inheritance and delegation; and

the previous paragraphs overviewed significant variations between systems based on these mechanisms. There is a fundamental similarity in the two mechanisms which was demonstrated formally in [Stein87]. Using limited models for delegation and inheritance, specifically: *single inheritance and single parent delegation*, and omitting discussion of the complications introduced by allowing cancellation of attributes, Stein showed that "...there is a 'natural' model of inheritance that captures all the properties of delegation". Additionally for systems in which objects are either classes or instances, but not both, she identified some constraints under which delegation could operate to model inheritance. Without going into the formal aspects of the paper, but taking its main points, consider the following line of reasoning taken from that paper.

Delegation systems have only one type of object. There is no class/instance distinction. There is no template that defines abstract attributes for an object. Any object can be defined in terms of any other; both methods and values can be shared when an object delegates these to a prototype. A change in a stored value in the prototype is immediately seen in all other objects that share that value.

A class holds the *template* for its instances, and all instances created from it are guaranteed to be identical in structure. All instances from the template share common attribute definitions. Whilst definitions are shared, inheritance does not allow one instance to share a value with another instance.

A class is also an object; it is an instance of its metaclass. To that extent, it is like any other instance. However, inheritance allows a class to share not only common attribute definitions but also attribute values with another class - its superclass. That is, whilst each class could keep its own copy of all class variables, to meet the needs of the Axiom of Upward Compatibility[4] it must use the values of attributes in its superclass unless it redefines them locally. So, any changes to these values in a superclass must be immediately reflected in all subclasses. Values are thus shared. When considering inheritance at the level of *classes*, therefore, the inheritance mechanism behaves in an identical manner to delegation.

Delegation, on the other hand, uses no template. Delegation does not allow attributes to be defined in one object and values stored in another. In modelling inheritance for an object (i.e. where that instance of a class inherits from its superclass), a system supporting delegation must create two parent objects: one to model the class and one to model the superclass. This multiple parent requirement exceeds the terms (for single parenthood) laid down in the opening paragraph of this subsection. In other words, delegation can model single inheritance at the level of classes, provided that the requirement for single parenthood is relaxed. This proof countered earlier claims in [Lieberman86] that delegation was fundamentally more powerful than inheritance, and thus led to the peace treaty described in the previous sub-section!

Stein goes on to list a number of ways in which delegation and inheritance do differ: In her view, these differences all fundamentally depend on classes holding templates for their instances, whilst prototypes do not. The advantage for each type of system is respectively that with a template there is a guarantee that all instances of a class are, at least in part, identically structured, whilst without a template there is much greater flexibility and freedom for prototypes. The differences can be tabulated as follows:

---

[4]Axiom of Upward Compatibility: (informally) if A *is-a* B, then anything that is true of B must also be true of A.

	Inheritance allows:	Delegation allows:
Incremental Definition	only on classes	on all objects
Sharing of Attributes	sharing of class attributes sharing of instance methods	sharing of all attributes of all objects
Dependence of Instances	no	yes
Grouping of Instances	required	not required

3.6 BEHAVIOUR SHARING AND EVOLUTION: SYSTEMS THAT USE BOTH PROTOTYPES *AND* CLASSES

A significant benefit of a class hierarchy lies in its ability to describe the behaviour of large groups of objects, whilst an equally significant benefit of prototypes lies in their ability to share state and behaviour between instances directly. The hallmark of a class based systems lies in encoding the inheritance mechanism in the class hierarchy, whilst the prototype based system implements that mechanism over the prototypes themselves. The obvious question is: how do we reconcile these two distinct views?

In the discussions so far, it has been assumed that systems support sharing at either the level of instances (as in the prototype based languages) or at the level of classes (as in the class based languages). However, there is a half-way house. A number of systems support sharing at both levels. The language Hybrid [Mercado87], for example, allows instances to create new instances that are exceptions - they differ in some way. Yet, to avoid proliferation of unstructured instances, Hybrid offers a mechanism that allows at run time the promotion of a group of such exceptions into a template. Hybrid combines the dynamism of delegation with the structuring capabilities of template (or class) driven systems. In a different manner, exemplars [LaLonde86], [LaLonde87] allow one type of sharing based on instances with another, independent type of sharing, based on classes. These are now briefly discussed.

3.6.1 Hybrid
Hybrid grew out of a desire to combine the advantages of class based and prototype based systems in a single model that would allow the user to select the required mix of characteristics for a given application.

Hybrid does this by providing classes that have templates that carry a minimal guarantee. That is, every instance is guaranteed to have at least the structure of the template. However, it is possible to create new instances by augmenting any existing *instance* with extra variables or methods. Delegate links connect the new instance to the existing instance. In this sense, the instance is behaving like a prototype - it is the instance that is being extended to share state and behaviour. However, should sufficient extended instances warrant the creation of a new class, then as a group these instances can be promoted to be instances of a new class defined with the new common structure. The instances now adopt the characteristics of class-based instances (i.e., no shared state) and the delegate links become standard instance links.

3.6.2 Exemplars
[LaLonde89] uses the synonym *exemplar* for *prototypical object*. In general, an exemplar is described by: a superexemplar, a class, state, and methods. There are two types of

exemplar: a class exemplar and an instance exemplar. Class exemplars inherit from other class exemplars, and instance exemplars inherit from other instance exemplars - thus producing two distinct hierarchies! Note that the inheritance hierarchy is encoded in the exemplars, and not in the class. A class, therefore, is an exemplar that has class operations. Lalonde views a class, in fact, as "...an abstract specification that might apply to many exemplars". A class hierarchy is an inheritance hierarchy that parallels the subtype hierarchy, as in Trellis/Owl. As such the class hierarchy forms an intuitive, logical hierarchy for the user. There is no need to force unnecessary superclasses into a chain just to share their code. It is wholly uncoupled from the implementation hierarchy.

An instance exemplar does not necessarily need a class; however, a class in order to exist must contain at least one instance exemplar - it may have more. In other words, if a class has multiple instance exemplars, the class may have instances of different representations. Since the instance exemplars can share representation and code, independently of their class exemplars, the implementor is free to ignore the logical hierarchy and have a code sharing hierarchy that is different from the class hierarchy. There is no need to have distinct subclass hierarchies, just because instances with specialized methods or different representations are needed. It is now simply a matter of defining a new instance exemplar for the class that will meet the new requirements.

The code sharing hierarchy and the logical conceptual hierarchy are thus decoupled, bringing with it greater freedom and flexibility for behaviour sharing, yet still retaining the benefits of compile time type checking for programme correctness.

3.7 SUMMARY

3.7.1 Techniques Introduced in Chapter 3
This chapter introduced the concepts of active objects and prototypes, and revisited the concepts of encapsulation., class and inheritance. The composite table of techniques is shown in Figure 3.14.

3.7.2 Rationale for Techniques
The chapter focussed on specific examples of techniques for data abstraction, behaviour sharing and evolution to give a flavour of the variations that exist in contemporary systems.

The systems can be segregated into those whose implementation of behaviour sharing is based on classes, those whose behaviour sharing is based on instances, and those which exhibit behaviour sharing on both class and instance hierarchies.

With class based systems, it was shown that encapsulation was often compromized by the implementation of inheritance. The effects of this problem were seen to be greater when multiple inheritance was considered. The merging of distinct hierarchies inevitably produces lexical conflicts in variable and method names, which in turn requires an examination of conflict resolution rules. Alternative ways of incorporating behaviour from different object hierarchies were discussed. The use of mixins, for example, provides an ad-hoc technique for doing this.

Examples showing fundamental improvements to circumvent these shortcomings were indicated, particularly with respect to supporting purer forms of encapsulation.

On a more general level, some shortcomings of class based systems were listed; their

General Approach	Technique	Description	Xref
Encapsulation	Object	encapsulation of data and interface	2.2.1 3.3.4
	Active object	encapsulation of data, interface and autonomous thread(s) of control	3.4
Classification	Classes	groupings based on common specification and implementation	2.3.1 3.3.1
	Prototypes	rejection of classification as structuring philosophy	3.4.1
Flexible sharing	Subclassing (inheritance)	inclusion of specification and implementation of one class in another	2.4.1 3.3.2 3.3.3
	Overloading	sharing of method names across specific objects or classes	2.4.5
	Prototyping	inclusion of implementation of one object instance in another	3.4.2
Interpretation	Static binding	compile time resolution of names in subclass hierarchy	2.5.1
	Dynamic binding	run time resolution of names in subclass hierarchy	2.5.2 3.3.2
	Delegation	resolution along delegation paths	3.4.2

Figure 3.14: Summary of techniques

shortcomings prepare the ground for considering the actor model of computation. Behaviour sharing is made more flexible by its incorporation at the level of instances. Introduction of the technique of delegation illustrated how it could be achieved.

These contrasting implementations were compared and found to be similar in many respects. If a restricted view is taken, it becomes possible to suggest that delegation is the same as inheritance.

The respective merits of both types of system suggested that there could be much utility in those systems that support sharing at the levels of both classes and instances. This is borne out by the experience of Hybrid and by the exemplar based systems discussed towards the end of the chapter. These hybrid systems combine the benefits of flexibility in instance based sharing with the benefits of correctness in type checked class based systems, and were introduced in section 3.6. This latter element holds the key to determinance in program execution and forms the main topic of the next chapter.

REFERENCES

[Agha86] Agha, G.A. *ACTORS: A Model of Concurrent Computation in Distributed Systems*, Cambridge, MA: The MIT Press, 1986.

[Bennett87] Bennett, J.K. "The Design and Implementation of Distributed Smalltalk." *Proceedings of the Conference on Object-Oriented Programming Systems, Languages, and Applications (OOPSLA '87)*, 1987: Editor: N. Meyrowitz, Special Issue of ACM SIGPLAN Notices, Vol: 22, Pages: 318-330.

[Bobrow86] Bobrow, D.G., K. Kahn, G. Kiczales, L. Masinter, M. Stefik, and F. Zdybel. "CommonLoops: Merging Lisp and Object-Oriented Programming." *Proceedings of the Conference on Object-Oriented Programming Systems, Languages and Applications (OOPSLA '86)*, 1986: Editor: N. Meyrowitz, Special Issue of ACM SIGPLAN Notices, Vol: 21, Pages: 17-29.

[Bobrow81] Bobrow, D.G., and M. Stefik. "The LOOPS Manual", Technical Report KB-VLSI-81-13. Xerox Parc, Palo Alto, CA, 1981.

[Borgida86] Borgida, A. "Exceptions in Object-Oriented Languages." *Proceedings of the Object-Oriented Programming Workshop*, 1986: Editor: P. Wegner and B. Shriver, ACM SIGPLAN Notices, October 1986, Vol: 21, No.10, Pages: 107-119.

[Borning86] Borning, A. "Classes versus prototypes in object-oriented languages." *Proceedings of the ACM/IEEE Fall Joint Computer Conference*, 1986. Pages: 36-40.

[Borning81] Borning, A. "The Programming Aspects of Thinglab, a Constraint Oriented Simulation Laboratory." *ACM TOPLAS* Vol:3 No. 4 1981) Pages: 353-387.

[Borning87] Borning, A., and T. O'Shea. "Deltatalk: An Empirically and Aesthetically Motivated Simplification of the Smalltalk80 Language." *Proceedings of the European Conference on Object-Oriented Programming*. Editors: J. Bézivin, J-M. Hullot, P. Cointe and H. Lieberman. Published as: Lecture Notes in Computer Science No.276. Springer-Verlag, Pages: 1-10. 1987.

[Cox84] Cox, B.J. "Message/Object Programming: An Evolutionary Change in Programming Technology." *IEEE Software* Vol.1. (1) 1984. Pages: 50-61.

[Dahl66] Dahl, O., and K. Nygaard. "Simula, An Algol-based Simulation Language." *Communications of the ACM* Vol.9 1966. Pages: 671-678.

[Ducournau87] Ducournau, R., and M. Habib. "On Some Algorithms for Multiple Inheritance in Object-Oriented Programming." *Proceedings of European Conference on Object-Oriented Programming (ECOOP 87)*, Editor: J. Bézivin, J-M. Hullot, P. Cointe and H. Lieberman. Published as: Lecture Notes in Computer ScienceVol: 276, Springer-Verlag, Pages: 243-252.

[Ferber83] Ferber, J. "MERING: un lagage d'acteur pour la représentation et la manipulation des connaissances". These de Docteur Ingeniéur, Université Paris VI, 1983.

[Goldberg83] Goldberg, A., and D. Robson. *Smalltalk-80: The Language and its Implementation*. Adison-Wesley, Reading, Mass. 1983.

[**Hendler86**] Hendler, J. "Enhancement for multiple inheritance." *Proceedings of the Object-Oriented Programming Workshop,* 1986: Editor: P. Wegner and B. Shriver, ACM SIGPLAN Notices, October 1986, Vol: 21, No.10, Pages: 98-106.

[**Hewitt77**] Hewitt, C. "Viewing Control Structures as Patterns of Passing Messages." *Journal of Artificial Intelligence* 8 (3) 1977. Pages: 323-364.

[**LaLonde87**] LaLonde, W.R. "Designing Families of Data Types Using Exemplars", Tech. Report No.: K1S 5B6, School of Computer Science, Carleton Univ., Ottawa, Ontario, Canada. 1987.

[**LaLonde89**] LaLonde, W.R. "Designing Families of Data Types Using Exemplars." *ACM TOPLAS* 11 (2) 1989. Pages: 212-248.

[**LaLonde86**] LaLonde, W.R. "Why Exemplars are Better than Classes", Tech. Report No.: SCS-TR-93. School of Computer Science, Carleton Univ., Ottawa, Canada. 1986.

[**Lieberman85**] Lieberman, H. "Delegation and Inheritance: Two Mechanisms for Sharing Knowledge in Object-Oriented Systems." *Journées d'Etudes Langages Orientés Objet,* AFCET, Paris. 1985. Pages: 79-89.

[**Lieberman86**] Lieberman, H. "Using Prototypical Objects to Implement Shared Behavior in Object-Oriented Systems." *Proceedings of the Conference on Object-Oriented Programming Systems, Languages and Applications (OOPSLA '86),* 1986: Editor: N. Meyrowitz, Special Issue of ACM SIGPLAN Notices, Vol: 21, Pages: 214-223.

[**Mercado87**] Mercado Jr., A. "Hybrid: Implementing Classes with Prototypes", Technical Report CS-88-12, Department of Computer Science, Brown University, 1987.

[**Meyer88**] Meyer, B. *Object-Oriented Software Construction,* Prentice-Hall, 1988.

[**Moon86**] Moon, D.A. "Object-Oriented Programming with Flavors." *Proceedings of the Conference on Object-Oriented Programming Systems, Languages and Applications (OOPSLA '86),* 1986: Editor: N. Meyrowitz, Special Issue of ACM SIGPLAN Notices, Vol: 21, Pages: 1-8.

[**O'Shea86**] O'Shea, T. "The Learnability of Object-Oriented Programming Systems." *ACM Conference on Object-Oriented Programming Systems, Languages and Applications,* 1986: Editor: N. Meyorwitz, Vol: 21; No.11, Pages: 502-504.

[**Raj89**] Raj, R.K., and H.M. Levy. "A Compositional Model for Software Reuse." *Proceedings of the Third European Conference on Object-Oriented Programming (ECOOP '89),* 1989: Editor: S. Cook, Cambridge University Press, UK., Pages: 3-24.

[**Schaffert86**] Schaffert, C., T. Cooper, B. Bullis, M. Kilian, and C. Wilpolt. "An Introduction to Trellis/Owl." *Proceedings of the Conference on Object-oriented Programming Systems, Languages and Applications (OOPSLA '86),* 1986: Editor: N.

Meyrowitz, Special Issue of SIGPLAN Notices, Vol: 21, Pages: 9-16.

[Snyder86a] Snyder, A. "CommonObjects: An Overview." *Proceedings of the Object-Oriented Programming Workshop,* 1986: Editor: P. Wegner and B. Shriver, ACM SIGPLAN Notices, October 1986, Vol: 21, No.10, Pages: 19-28.

[Snyder86b] Snyder, A. "Encapsulation and Inheritance in Object-Oriented Programming Languages." *Proceedings of the Conference on Object-Oriented Programming Systems, Languages and Applications (OOPSLA '86),* 1986: Editor: N. Meyrowitz, Special Issue of ACM SIGPLAN Notices, Vol: 21, Pages: 38-45.

[Stefik86] Stefik, M., and D.G. Bobrow. "Object-Oriented Programming: Themes and Variations." *The AI Magazine* Vol:6 (4) 1986. Pages: 40-62.

[Stein87] Stein, L.A. "Delegation Is Inheritance." *Proceedings of the Conference on Object-Oriented Programming Systems, Languages, and Applications (OOPSLA '87),* 1987: Editor: N. Meyrowitz, Special Issue of ACM SIGPLAN Notices, Vol: 22 no. 10, Pages: 138-146.

[Stein89] Stein, L.A., H. Lieberman, and D. Ungar. "A Shared View of Sharing: The Treaty of Orlando." In: Object-Oriented Concepts, Databases, and Applications. Editors: W. Kim and F.H. Lochovsky. ACM Press, New York. 1989. Pages: 31-48.

[Stroustrup86] Stroustrup, B. *The C++ Programming Language,* Addison-Wesley, Reading, MA. 1986.

[Ungar87] Ungar, D., and R.B. Smith. "Self: The Power of Simplicity." *Proceedings of the Conference on Object-Oriented Programming Systems, Languages, and Applications (OOPSLA '87),* 1987: Editor: N. Meyrowitz, Special Issue of ACM SIGPLAN Notices, Vol: 22 (no.10), Pages: 227-242.

Chapter 4

Basic Concepts III (Types, Abstract Data Types and Polymorphism)

Gordon S. Blair
Lancaster University

ABSTRACT *The concept of typing is not normally associated with object-oriented computing. However, there has recently been great interest in the semantics of typing in an object-oriented context. In particular, many language and system designers are investigating the integration of static type checking into object-oriented environments. This chapter surveys the impact of this work on the object-oriented community. The important concepts of type, data abstraction and polymorphism are discussed in depth. Abstract data types are highlighted as a central feature of statically typed object-oriented languages. In addition, several approaches to providing polymorphism in abstract data type based languages are introduced, i.e. subtyping/ conformance, genericity and enhancement.*

4.1 INTRODUCTION

The first three chapters of this book have introduced the fundamental concepts underlying most work in object-oriented computing. However, there is one major area not yet explored, namely the role of typing in object-oriented languages and systems. Object-oriented concepts have recently been applied to certain areas such as real-time systems which have stringent demands in terms of the correctness of applications. It is normally expected that languages for such environments should at the very least provide a guarantee of type correctness in programs. Consequently, there is a current interest in providing static type checking in object-oriented languages.

Object-oriented languages are traditionally not statically type checked. Rather, typing errors are detected at run time when dynamic binding is attempted. For example, consider the simple class hierarchy shown in Figure 4.1.

Now suppose there exists an object *source* which is an instance of the class *Pascal* and a second object *document* which is an instance of the class *Text*. An attempt to *print source* will be dynamically bound to the print method of the *Text* document. However, an attempt to *compile document* will clearly fail and will result in a run-time error. This is

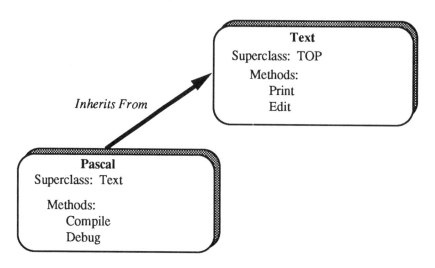

Figure 4.1: Simple class hierarchy

not as serious as it might seem because most object-oriented languages will not abort the program. Rather, they will send a message back to the caller carrying the information 'method not known'. The caller is then free to act on this message in an appropriate way. For many fields of application, this approach is unacceptable especially when you move away from simple, single user environments. As systems grow larger, or when different people are working on different aspects of the development, or when the interaction between objects is complex, it becomes important to have more confidence in the 'correctness' of existing code and that new code is compatible with what is already in place. Similarly, for many real-time, critical applications run time detection of typing errors is not appropriate. Imagine sending an emergency shutdown message in a nuclear power station only to find out that the method is not known.

The notion of type is not normally associated with object-oriented computing. However, it must be stressed that the above problems are precisely problems of typing and type checking. Many workers in the field have now realized the existence of this problem and are examining the role that typing should have in object-oriented languages. This work has led to many interesting developments and a great deal of clarification about the semantics of object-oriented languages. The work has been particularly interesting because of the apparent tension between the demand for correctness through typing and the demand for flexibility through dynamic binding. The resolution of this tension has been one of the successes of recent work in object-oriented computing and arguably has moved the subject into a new generation, thus opening the door to many more fields of application.

This chapter surveys the impact of typing in object-oriented computing and discusses in depth the important concepts of type, abstract data type and polymorphism. Section 4.2 examines more closely the meaning of typing and surveys some important developments in the history of typed systems. Section 4.3 then examines the interpretation of typing in an object-oriented context. The relationship between type and class and between subtyping and subclasses is examined. The important class of languages based on abstract data types is then introduced in Section 4.4. This section includes an examination of extensions to abstract data types which attempt to mirror the benefits of object-oriented languages.

4.2 THE CONCEPT OF TYPING

This section examines in some detail the concept of typing, concentrating on the various manifestations of typing in language and system design. Polymorphism emerges as important concept, especially in the context of object-oriented computing. Type checking is also highlighted as an important issue. The section concludes by examining the nature of type checking in polymorphic environments.

4.2.1 What is a Type?

Typing is a fundamental concept in computing and indeed a study of the history of typing teaches a lot about the major developments in computing over the past thirty years. It is relatively easy to understand the meaning of the word type in a computing context and yet, strangely, it is notoriously difficult to give a precise, formal definition of type. A fairly intuitive description of typing now follows. Consider a computer system consisting of a series of values requiring manipulation. It is convenient to group related values into types in order to reason about their properties. A type is therefore a description in the abstract of a related group of entities. For example, the type *integer* is commonly understood to denote entities which exhibit properties similar to the mathematical concept of whole numbers.

   Types are essentially about abstraction. In an untyped world it would be impossible to reason about individual values as they would all appear different and unconnected. Typing allows like values to be grouped together in such a way that similarities can be promoted and differences ignored. In scientific disciplines, abstraction has become a central tool in understanding complex systems. Similarly, in computing, typing is the major mechanism for constructing large programs.

4.2.2 The Different Roles of Type

Types deal with several different aspects of abstraction in a programming language. Three different roles for a typing system can be identified: types abstract away from the underlying properties of entities in the system, they allow higher level abstractions to be developed and, finally, they provide a level of protection. Each role is now examined in more detail:-

   i) Abstraction over underlying properties
      Values in programming languages can be complex entities consisting of a particular *structure* and an associated set of *semantics*. The structure defines the representation of the value both internally in the computer memory and externally as viewed by the programmer. The semantics define the way in which this value can be interpreted, the operations that can be performed on the value, and possibly the algorithms for implementing these operations. Both the structure and semantics can be thought of as being *properties* of the value. Types provide a shorthand way of signifying a value with appropriate properties. It can then be assumed that all values of that type share these properties; they may have other differences, but the properties will remain

invariant. For example, all values of type integer in Pascal will be stored within a computer word and can be manipulated with the usual arithmetic operations with the expected results. Note that different typing systems will specify the properties in different ways. For example, some will fully define internal structure, algorithms, etc; others will only specify the external behaviour. As we shall see later, this is an important distinction in object-oriented languages.

ii) Type composition

As well as abstracting away from underlying properties, a typing system will provide mechanisms for creating higher level abstractions from existing abstractions (types). This process is the very essence of programming. Most programming languages provide a set of primitive types such as boolean, character, integer and real, and a set of aggregate types such as arrays, records and sets. The aggregate types can be used to construct more complex data structures from existing types. Furthermore, aggregate types can be defined over aggregate types to implement higher levels of abstraction. For example, a personal profile can be modeled as a record consisting of various primitive fields (age, salary, etc). A filing system can then be modeled as an array of this new record type. This is a classic example of the traditional method of abstraction in programming languages. The concepts of class and inheritance in object-oriented languages has added a new dimension to abstraction in languages. The exact relationship between the concepts of class/inheritance and typing will be explored shortly (see section 4.3).

iii) Protection

A type system also provides a level of protection in the system against incorrect or undesirable actions. Type checking can be incorporated in a language to ensure that invalid operations are not carried out on values. Cardelli and Wegner [Cardelli85] provides a strong metaphor for the protective role of typing as follows: '*A type may be viewed as a set of clothes (or a suit of armour) that protects an underlying untyped representation fro ʌ arbitrary or unintended use. It provides a protective covering that hides th underlying representation and constrains the way objects may interact with ⸗ .her objects. In an untyped system untyped objects are naked in that the underlying representation is exposed for all to see. Violating the type system involves removing the protective set of clothing and operating directly on the naked representation*'.

4.2.3 Type Checking

Attention is now focussed on the latter role of a type system, i.e. type checking. Type checking is concerned with preventing typing inconsistencies in a language through the elimination of type errors where a *type error* is defined to be an action in a programming language which results or may result in an application of an invalid operation to a value. There are two possible sources for a type error in a programming language:-

i)   Parameter passing - it is important that the actual parameter passed to a procedure or function is compatible with the formal parameter defined in its description.

ii) Assignment - similarly, it is important that the resultant type of an expression on the right hand side of an assignment is *compatible* with the type of the left hand side.

It will be assumed in this chapter that the semantics of type checking is the same for both parameter passing and assignment.

Type compatibility is an interesting topic in type checking. In the simplest case, two types being compared will be the same, e.g. integer and integer, and hence there is no difficulty in determining equivalence. However, the situation may arise that two types being compared are different: does this automatically imply a type error? It may be that two different types are perfectly compatible with each other. For example, consider the following program fragment taken from Cleaveland [Cleaveland86]:-

```
type BLACK is INTEGER;
type WHITE is INTEGER

B: BLACK;
W: WHITE;
I: INTEGER;

begin
      W := 5;
      B := W;
      I := B + 3;
      etc....
```

Different languages take a different view of whether these types are compatible. This general problem is referred to as *type equivalencing*. Two main approaches can be identified: *name equivalencing* and *structural equivalencing*. In name equivalencing, two types are equivalent if and only if they have the same name. Therefore in the above example a type error would be notified. Name equivalencing is very straightforward to implement but leads to a great deal of inflexibility in the language. For example, name equivalencing is used in Pascal and leads to many of the irritating features of the design. Structure equivalencing, in contrast, states that two types are equivalent if their underlying structure is the same. Thus, the above example would be passed as correctly typed. Structure equivalence therefore provides much more flexibility than name equivalence but can be very difficult to implement.

The most important characteristic of the type checking mechanism is the *timing* of the detection of type errors. There are two possible timings of detection: compile time/ link time or run time giving *static type checking* and *dynamic type checking* respectively. In static type checking, type errors are determined from a static program analysis. Thus, all type errors can be caught at compile time or when separately compiled modules are linked together. There is no question of type errors occurring during the execution of the program. This approach requires that all variables and expressions are bound to a particular type at compile time which imposes a restriction on the language. However, in terms of protection the programmer does not have to be concerned with the possibility of typing errors occurring during execution.

The alternative is to adopt dynamic type checking whereby type errors are detected at run-time. Type errors are not allowed to develop into type inconsistencies; rather, the type errors are detected as the program executes and a notification is given of the typing violation. Notification is normally through an *exception* mechanism, i.e. typing errors are treated in the same way as divide by zero errors, etc. Dynamic type checking tends to be more flexible than static type checking as there is no requirement for types to be resolved at compile time. However, extra complexity is introduced as the programmer must make allowances for the possibility of type errors.

Dynamic type checking is precisely the policy adopted in most object-oriented languages. Type errors are notified by the 'method not known' messages mentioned at the start of this chapter. Both dynamic and static type checking have a place in object-oriented programming. It is a question of balancing the advantages and disadvantages of each approach for a particular application domain. Dynamic type checking is fairly well understood in object-oriented languages. This chapter focuses on the less well understood area of static type checking.

Type checking, it should be stressed, is primarily concerned with deciding whether a particular action is valid and whether it will lead to type inconsistencies. Type checking does not define how operations will be carried out, or more specifically, what code will perform the necessary operation. This is the task of *binding*.

There is a very close relationship between type checking and binding in object-oriented computing. Both issues become considerably more complex and inter-dependent than in traditional language environments. The relationship between type checking and binding will be revisited later (in section 4.2.5) after the important concept of polymorphism has been discussed.

4.2.4 Polymorphism

Typing systems in most programming languages are largely *monomorphic* in that values are deemed to have a single type. Type checking is then performed on the basis of this typing information. However, in many instances, this can be overly restrictive in a programming language. Therefore, language designers have looked towards polymorphism as a means of providing more flexible typing disciplines. *Polymorphism* is defined to be the ability for a value to have more than one type. The values can therefore be used in several contexts (parameter passing or assignment) demanding different types. Simple set diagrams provides a good visual means of denoting polymorphism. In programming languages, the concept of a type mirrors closely the concept of a set[1]. Consider an environment E consisting of the set of all possible values in a particular language. In monomorphic languages, all data items must be of one unique type; this is equivalent to data items belonging to disjoint sets (see Figure 4.2).

If, however, sets can intersect then an element of polymorphism is introduced, i.e. data items can have more than one type. This is shown in Figure 4.3.

Polymorphism should be applicable to all types in a well designed language. In particular, given that functions are types, then a language should support *polymorphic functions*. A polymorphic function is a function which can have different types. For example, consider a function add which is of type *integer × integer → integer*. This function would be monomorphic if it only supported integer addition. However, if the function add could also be of type *real × real → real*, then the function is polymorphic. This example illustrates the inflexibility in truly monomorphic languages. It would be completely unacceptable to have a range of different add functions declared, each with

---

[1] In strict terms, it can be shown that sets are not necessarily equivalent to types. However, the intuitive approximation will suffice for this discussion. A fuller analysis of the relationship between sets and types will be presented in Chapter 5.

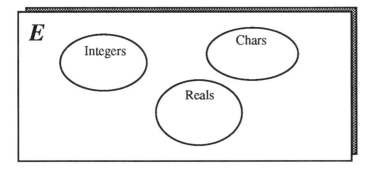

Figure 4.2: Monomorphic types

their own name, for different combinations of types. Note also that well designed languages should also support *polymorphic procedures* and *polymorphic operations* if they are to be truly orthogonal.

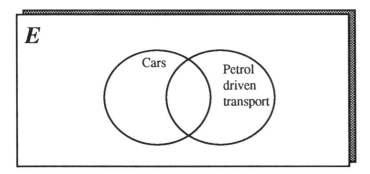

Figure 4.3: Polymorphic types

Polymorphism is not a new idea. Forms of polymorphism have been around since the early days of programming languages. Indeed, it is almost impossible to imagine a programming language which is completely monomorphic. The stringent type checking and rigidity would make such languages unusable. *Coercions* and *overloading* are two early forms of polymorphism which many languages support:-

i)   Coercions provide a simple way of circumventing the rigidity of monomorphic languages and provide a limited form of polymorphism. Languages supporting coercion have certain in-built mappings (coercions) between types. If a particular context demands one type and a different type is provided, then the language will look to see if there is an appropriate coercion. For example, if add is defined on two reals and an integer and a real are provided as parameters then the integer will be coerced on to a real value in the obvious manner.

ii) Overloading allows a function name to be used more than once with different types of parameter. For example, the add function could be overloaded to operate on both integers and reals as above. The typing information of the parameters will then be used to select the appropriate function.

Overloading together with coercions provide a satisfactory solution to the inflexibility of strict monomorphism and are to be found in most programming languages. In particular, the two techniques are often applied to operations in programming languages. Polymorphism, however, can be a much more powerful technique with more general application. Recently, several polymorphic programming languages have been developed exhibiting more fundamental forms of polymorphism than coercions or overloading, e.g. ML [Gordon79], Miranda [Turner85] and Russell [Demers80].

The topic of polymorphism is examined in depth in a classic paper by Cardelli and Wegner [Cardelli85]. In this paper, a taxonomy of polymorphic techniques is developed. This taxonomy is shown in Figure 4.4.

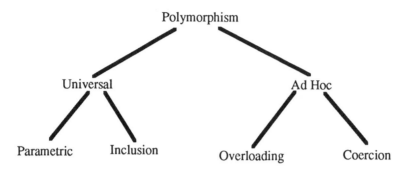

Figure 4.4: Cardelli and Wegner's taxonomy

The paper refers to coercions and overloading as *ad hoc polymorphism* in that the techniques work only on a specific number of types in an unprincipled way. This is distinguished from *universal polymorphism* which will work uniformly on a potential infinite set of types in a principled manner (it is normally expected that the types will exhibit some common structure). It is interesting to consider the meaning on universal polymorphism as applied to functions. This implies that functions can operate on *more than one type*. There is an interesting contrast between universal polymorphic functions and overloaded functions. In the former case, it is expected that the function will execute the same code for different typed parameters whereas overloaded functions will execute different code. This illustrates the principled approach of universal polymorphism whereby functions will retain similar semantics irrespective of parameter type whereas ad hoc techniques may have completely different semantics from one type to another The following example should make this distinction clear.

> Consider the provision of a size of function which will return the size in bytes of a particular data structure. In a universal polymorphic language, this would be specified once in a general manner and would operate on all types. Using ad-hoc techniques (in this case, overloading), the function could be written N times for N different types. However, size of will not work for types other than that set of N types.

Cardelli and Wegner distinguish between two types of universal polymorphism: *parametric polymorphism* and *inclusion polymorphism*. Each technique is now discussed in turn:-

i) Parametric polymorphism

> In parametric polymorphism, a single function (coded once) will work uniformly on a range of types. It is possible that the function will operate on all

types but more likely the types will be required to exhibit some common structure. A function will have an explicit or implicit type parameter which determines the the type of the argument for each application of that function. Parametric functions are also sometimes called *generic functions*, i.e. the function works generically on a range of types. This style of polymorphism is re-visited in section 4.4.3.

ii) Inclusion polymorphism

Inclusion polymorphism also allows a function to operate on a range of types. However, the range of types is determined by *subtyping* relationships. With inclusion polymorphism, a function defined on a particular type can also operate on any subtypes.

Subtyping is a fundamental concept in statically typed, object-oriented languages and will be examined in depth in section 4.3.3. For now, an intuitive understanding will suffice. Consider the set diagrams introduced earlier. If one set is completely enclosed in another (i.e. is a subset), then every value in the subset is also in the larger set. This corresponds to a value of one type also being a value of the supertype. This is precisely what is meant by inclusion polymorphism. For example, in Figure 4.5 all Fiat cars are also considered to be cars. Hence, any function defined on cars (e.g. a function providing mileage figures) is also applicable to Fiat cars.

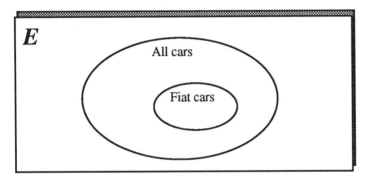

Figure 4.5: Inclusion polymorphism

Polymorphic languages have several important advantages over their monomorphic or mostly monomorphic counterparts:-

i) Flexibility - it is possible for polymorphic languages to be rigidly typed checked whilst retaining a great deal of flexibility.

ii) Abstraction - polymorphism enhances abstraction by allowing abstract operations to be defined over many types. Thus, polymorphic languages can be thought of as higher level languages.

iii) Behaviour sharing - similarly, polymorphism allows different types to share common behaviour, i.e. the same operations can be defined over multiple types.

iv) Code sharing - universal polymorphic languages provide a level of code sharing in that code is only specified once for a range of types.

Polymorphic languages are also important in that they provide the key to understanding typed, object-oriented languages. Polymorphism will therefore feature heavily in the rest of this chapter. The following sub-section examines the nature of type checking in a polymorphic environment. The important interplay between type checking and binding is highlighted.

4.2.5 Polymorphic Type Checking and Binding

At a first glance, there is an apparent conflict between the flexibility of polymorphic languages and the requirement for correctness through type checking. It is however possible to support a flexible interpretation of a piece of code and yet still guarantee correct behaviour (in terms of absence of type errors). To fully appreciate how this conflict can be resolved, it is important to examine closely the relationship between type checking and binding in a polymorphic environment.

Binding is a general concept which applies to all levels of a system. For example, traditionally binding is concerned with the mappings between textual names and virtual addresses, virtual addresses and physical addresses, etc. The task of binding is to resolve such mappings at a particular layer of abstraction. In short, binding has the task of resolving abstraction. As with type checking, binding can be carried out statically or dynamically. Static binding implies that mappings are resolved at compile time, whereas dynamic binding resolves them at run-time. It is quite possible in a particular system for static binding to operate at one level of abstraction and dynamic binding to operate at another. The major advantage of dynamic binding is that bindings can change over time. Thus, the system can adapt to changing circumstances. For example, in memory management it is common for the mapping from virtual to physical address to be performed dynamically. This allows segments/pages to be re-allocated to a different physical address during execution. The major problem is that dynamic binding carries a substantial overhead in terms of run-time table look-ups, etc. Often, system support is provided to enhance performance. For example, memory management bindings are often carried out in hardware.

In terms of object-oriented programming, binding is normally concerned with the mapping from method name to implementation (see chapter 2). Usually, that this binding will be carried out dynamically. One of the major benefits of object-oriented languages is that they support evolution of code, e.g. a new method can easily be added to perform a particular function. Without dynamic binding, this would require a complete re-compilation of the system.

Now, consider the case of a procedure applied to an actual parameter:-

```
Procedure X (param: some_type);
Begin
    . . .
End;

Begin
    . . .

    X (some_actual)
```

In monomorphic languages, the interpretation of this procedure call is straightforward. The procedure X can only take one possible parameter type as defined by the formal parameter. In other words, there can only be one possible procedure with that name defined in the system. Type checking is therefore a case of checking the actual parameter against the formal parameter (either by name or structural equivalence). Similarly, it can be deduced that there will be a strict one to one mapping from procedure name to code body. Thus binding is simply concerned with finding the corresponding code body. This is a trivial binding at the level of abstraction of the typing system. The only complexity might be at lower levels of abstraction, e.g. if virtual addresses are mapped on to physical addresses. It is only at the lower levels that issues of dynamic versus static binding, etc become important.

However, in polymorphic languages, the relationship between type checking and binding becomes much more interesting. The procedure X may support a range of parameter types with each type possibly demanding a different interpretation of the procedure. It is precisely this feature which introduces flexibility into polymorphic languages. Type checking then provides a guarantee that an interpretation exists for a given type. In contrast, binding resolves the exact interpretation for that type.

Type checking and binding are entirely complementary. It is possible to determine whether an interpretation exists for a type without binding to a specific implementation. It is therefore possible for a particular type checking policy to co-exist with a particular binding policy. In particular, static or dynamic type checking can co-exist with static or dynamic binding in various combinations. The possible permutations are examined below:-

i) Static type checking with static binding

The question of whether an interpretation exists for a particular fragment of code and the exact interpretation of the code can both be resolved by the compiler. This provides guarantees of correctness at compile time and provides a level of flexibility in that there is not a strict interpretation of code. However, the interpretation of code is fixed during execution.

ii) Dynamic type checking with dynamic binding

The interpretation of a program is fully determined at run time. Type checking then corresponds to a failed binding. This is the approach found in many object-oriented languages, e.g. Smalltalk. The advantage of a dynamic environment is that interpretations can change over time and hence *evolutionary* programming is supported.

iii) Static type checking with dynamic binding

Guarantees of type correctness can be given at compile time whilst leaving the exact interpretation until run-time. This is the most interesting combination of policies as it allows the evolutionary nature of dynamic binding to co-exist with the benefits of static type checking.

iv) Dynamic type checking with static binding

This combination is perfectly possible but is not very sensible. Static binding implies that an interpretation for the code is found at compile time. However, this guarantees that an interpretation for the code exists and hence dynamic type checking is completely wasteful.

The various combinations are summarised in Figure 4.6.

The last permutation illustrates the inter-relationship between type checking and binding in polymorphic languages. The functionality of binding encompasses the functionality of type checking but with extra steps to find the exact interpretation of the code.

The focus of this chapter is very much on languages and systems which support

	Static Type Checking	Dynamic Type Checking
Static Binding	Guarantee of correctness Inflexible interpretation	Invalid combination
Dynamic Binding	Guarantee of correctness Flexible interpretation	No guarantee of correctness Flexible interpretation

Figure 4.6: Combinations of type checking and binding policies

static type checking with either static or dynamic binding.

4.3 TYPES AND OBJECT ORIENTED SYSTEMS

Object-oriented computing is often portrayed as a separate branch of computing which is completely independent of any developments in more mainstream language design. However, the discussion above highlights the astonishing parallel between developments and rationale in typing and the concepts and motivations behind object-oriented computing. This is perhaps understandable because all language designers can agree on the general requirements for languages. Most disputes centre on mechanisms for achieving such benefits. For example, it is now recognized that languages should provide greater modularity and abstraction, more flexibility, behaviour and code sharing, etc. It is also recognized that languages should be based on a small number of orthogonal concepts. This is the motivation behind the object/class/inheritance model. The strive for orthogonality also leads to classes being considered as objects. Similar developments in typing systems have been expounded above.

In examining the semantics of typing in object-oriented languages, it is tempting to equate directly the mechanisms developed in each area. For example, there appears to be a strong correlation between type and the concept of class. The question therefore arises of whether class provides a framework for a typing system in object-oriented languages. Similarly, there seems to be strong relationship between the concepts of subclass and subtype. More generally, it must be considered whether inheritance and polymorphism are performing the same function.

The aim of the following sub-sections is to demonstrate that a simple mapping from the typing dimension to classes and inheritance would be a mistake. It is not so much that this approach would be wrong; rather, it would be very limiting. It can be shown that type is a more general concept that class and subtyping is more general than subclassing. It is therefore important to distinguish between the two concepts.

4.3.1 Types
Before examining the relationship between type and class, it is important to reflect on the precise interpretation of type in an object-oriented world. In section 4.2.2, the three roles of typing were highlighted as being abstraction over underlying properties, a means of implementing higher level abstractions and a means of implementing protection (through type checking). The same roles apply in the context of object-oriented languages. However, it is possible to be more specific with respect to object-orientation. In terms of the first role, types provide abstractions away from the underlying properties in terms of the structure and semantics of values. In object-oriented languages, it can be assumed

that all properties will be encapsulated within an object and furthermore this encapsulation will be protected behind an abstract interface. The term *behaviour* is introduced to denote this abstract interface. Type is then denotable solely in terms of this behaviour. Two types are then the same if they *provide the same behaviour*. Note that this is irrespective of the underlying implementation or data structures. The second and third roles also become more focussed dealing with the use of existing behaviour in creating higher levels of behaviour and checking the behaviour of objects respectively. This general interpretation of typing is completely within the spirit of object-oriented languages and indeed any language claiming to provide encapsulation and abstraction.

4.3.2 Type is not Class
From the above definition of type, it is very easy to see that type is not the same as class. Class is fundamentally about implementation whereas type is concerned with abstract behaviour. Two objects of the same class will be of the same type. However, it is not necessarily the case that two objects of the same type will be of the same class. There may be other ways of providing that abstract behaviour.

To illustrate this important point, consider the following example:-

A particular class *my_stack* is implemented as a specialization of a linked list class. In addition, a second class called *your_stack* is implemented as a specialization of an ordered bag. Both implement push and pop operations and are thus clearly of the same type. However, they are not of the same class because they are *implemented in different ways*.

It would be possible to use class as an approximation to type and to type check accordingly. This would prevent type errors from occurring but would be overly restrictive. For example, in the above example it would not be allowed to use an object of type *my_stack* in place of an object of type *your_stack*. Thus, there are benefits to be gained from separating the concepts of type and class in a statically typed object-oriented language.

Note that there is a potential problem in this separation. Because *my_stack* and *your_stack* are implemented in different ways, there is no guarantee that they have the same semantics. One of the programmers may have completely misunderstood the concept of a stack and may actually have implemented a queue. There is no protection from this source of errors if type checking is based on the interface alone. It would be necessary to define behaviour in terms of the interface and the associated semantics. This is a major problem in statically typed, object-oriented languages and will be discussed again in section 4.4.

4.3.3 Subtypes
The intuitive description of subtyping presented in section 4.2.5 is insufficient to explain the proper interpretation of the term in object-oriented models. A more precise definition therefore follows.

In 4.3.1, typing was defined in terms of the behaviour of an object. Similarly, subtyping is concerned with *behaviour sharing*. A particular type T is a subtype of T' if and only if T provides at least the behaviour of T'. This is written as $T \leq T'$. An object of type T can thus be used *as if* it is of type T' because it is guaranteed to provide at least the operations of T'. This is sometimes also referred to as conformance, i.e. type T conforms to type T'.

As an example, consider the following types:-

```
i)  Array  providing the following operations:-
        Print
        Set_element
        Get_element
ii) Vector providing the following operations:-
        Print
        Set_element
        Get_element
        Add
        Multiply
```

Clearly, *Vector* is a subtype of *Array* and an object of type *Vector* can be used wherever the context demands an object of type *Array*. Therefore, in a static type checking analysis, assignments and parameter passing can be checked to ensure that the object provided is either of the correct type or is a valid subtype. For example, the following fragment of code is correctly typed:-

```
V: Vector;
A: Array;

Begin
    . . .
    A := V;
    Print (A);
```

Note that subtyping provides the flexibility expected of a polymorphic type checking system.

Subtyping has a well defined semantics based on the mathematics of *partial orders*. Indeed, subtyping defines a partial order over the set of all types in the system (see Chapter 5). Therefore, the following properties hold for subtyping:-

Consider the set of all types S.

i) $X \leq X$ for all X in S (reflexive)
ii) $X \leq Y$ and $Y \leq Z$ implies that $X \leq Z$ (transitive)
iii) $X \leq Y$ and $Y \leq X$ implies that $X = Y$ (antisymmetric)

These rules have a straightforward interpretation in typing systems. The first rule implies that all types conform to themselves. The second rule states that if one type is a subtype of a second type and that second type is a subtype of a third type, then the first type must also be a subtype of the third type. Finally, the third rule defines equality in subtyping. Two types are equal if they are both subtypes of each other.

Within a particular typing system, it is necessary to derive rules which define the subtyping relationships in the system. The rules for an object-oriented environment are complex and are deferred until section 4.4. However, rules are given below for the simpler cases of subranges, records and functions.

i) Subranges

Subranges, as found in languages like Pascal, provide a simple example of the concept of subtyping. A subrange is specified as X..Y, with the semantics that a value must be an integer greater than or equal to X and less than or equal to Y. The conformance rule for subtyping is straightforward:-

Rule: A..B ≤ C..D ⇔ C ≤ A and B ≤ D

i.e. a subrange A..B is a subtype of a subrange C..D if and only if A is numerically greater than or equal to C and B is numerically less than or equal to D. Thus 2..4, 2..6, 1..2 and 1..6 are all subtypes of 1..6.

ii) Records

For the purposes of this discussion, a record is defined to be a finite association of values to labels, e.g. {maker : ford; model : escort; year_of_make : 1986}. Furthermore, the order of labels is not significant. Given this definition, Bruce and Wegner [Bruce86] describe the following subtyping rules for records:-

Rule 1: $\{A_1:T_1; \dots ; A_n:T_n\} \leq \{A_1:U_1; \dots ; A_n:U_n\} \Leftrightarrow T_i \leq U_i \ \forall i : 1 \leq i \leq n$

Rule 2: $\{A_1 : T_1; \dots ; A_n : T_n ; A_{n+1} : T_{n+1}\} \leq \{A_1 : T_1; \dots ; A_n : T_n\}$

Rule 1 states that the values of the common fields in the two records must be in a subtype relationship and rule 2 states that the subtype must have at least the fields of the supertype. Thus, {maker : string; model : string; year_of_make: 1900..1990; registration: string} is a subtype of {maker : string; model : string; year_of_make: 1900..2000}. It is always possible to use a record of the first type in place of a record of the second type.

iii) Functions

Consider the simple case of a function F taking a value from a specified domain X and returning a value from a specified range Y. The type of such a function can be written as F: X -> Y. The rule for subtyping between two functions is then given by:-

Rule: $F_i: B \rightarrow C \leq F_j: A \rightarrow D \Leftrightarrow A \leq B \ and \ C \leq D$

i.e. a function F_i is a subtype of F_j if and only if the type of the result of F_i is a subtype of the type of the result of F_j and type of the parameter of F_i is a *supertype* of the type of the parameter of F_j. Thus a function F_1: 2..7 → 10..15 is a subtype of F_2: 3..6 → 7..20. The latter requirement for parameters of functions is rather surprising but it can be shown be be correct [MacQueen82]. Consider first the subrule for results. Clearly function type F_1 can be used in place of F_2 above because the result would be in the range 10..15 which is completely compatible with a result in the range 7..20. For parameters, however, if F_1 is to be used in place of F_2 then F_1 must be able to handle any parameter given to F_2. Therefore, the type must be 3..6 or a supertype of 3..6 and hence 2..7 is acceptable. It can therefore be confirmed that F_1 is a subtype of F_2. This property for parameters is referred to as *antimonotonicity* [Danforth88] and has major repercussions for typing systems in object-oriented languages (see 4.4.2).

4.3.4 Subtype is not Subclass

In a similar way that type is not the same as class, it can easily be shown that subtyping is a different concept from subclassing. Subtyping is a very general concept concerned with whether two types share common behaviour, i.e. a subtype will share all the behaviour of the parent type. In contrast, subclassing is concerned with how a class is implemented, i.e. a new class is constructed from a parent class or classes by specialization re-using some or all of the parent's methods. It is normally the case that a subclass will be a subtype but the opposite may not be true, i.e. a subtype is not necessarily a subclass. Two types can share common behaviour independent of their position in a class hierarchy. Consider the following example:-

> In section 4.4.3, two types were introduced, namely *Vector* and *Array*. It was shown that *Vector* is a valid subtype of *Array*. However, it might be in implementation that *Array* is implemented as a specialization of an ordered bag whereas *Vector* is implemented as a specialization of a linked list. If this was the case, then there is certainly no subclassing relationship between *Vector* and *Array*. However, this would not affect the subtyping relationship.

It is also important to realize that a subclass may not be a subtype. This depends very much on the style of specialization used in creating the subclass. A subclass may be specialized in a number of ways[2]:-

i)   *Extension* - add a new method
ii)   *Redefinition* - retain the same interface but re-code a particular method
iii) *Alteration* - similar to above except new method re-uses code from the previous method
iv)   *Restriction* - inherit a subset of methods

Each of these actions will have a different effect on the subtyping relationship. For example, extension will create a valid subtype. Changing a method, however, by either redefinition or alteration will not change the type; both types will be subtypes of each other and hence they are equivalent. Finally, restriction will actually create a supertype.

Combinations of the above are also possible. For example, consider the class template shown below:-

```
class Deque
inherits linked_list (* say*)
methods
        Push_left (Integer)
        begin
                <Implementation of Push_left>
        end;
        Pop_left () Integer
        begin
                <Implementation of Pop_left>
        end;
        Push_right (Integer)
        begin
                <Implementation of Push_right>
        end;
        Pop_right () Integer
        begin
                <Implementation of Pop_right>
        end;
```

---

[2] Note that in actual object-oriented languages, not all of the listed options will be available. For example, few languages support restricted inheritance. There are however some notable exceptions, e.g. CommonObjects [Snyder86].

This class implements a double ended queue, i.e. a queue where elements can be added or removed at either end. A programmer wishing to implement a stack might be tempted to base the implementation on Deque by excluding two of the operations. Furthermore, the programmer might want to extend the class to include an operation to report if the stack is empty. This would result in the following subclass:-

```
class Stack
inherits Pop_left, Push_left from Deque
methods
        Stack_empty () Boolean
        begin
                <Implementation of Stack_empty>
        end;
end class;
```

There is actually no subtyping relationship between this class and its subclass. Note that the distinction between strict and non-strict inheritance is important in this context. Remember, that strict inheritance does not allow methods to be altered or deleted whereas non-strict inheritance has no such restrictions (see chapter 2). Strict inheritance will always result, therefore, in a subtype being created. The relationship between subclassing and subtyping is summarized in the following table (Figure 4.7):-

Specialisation by	Class Relationship	Type Relationship
Extension	Subclass	Subtype
Redefinition	Subclass	Same type
Alteration	Subclass	Same type
Restriction	Subclass	Supertype

Figure 4.7: Subtyping vs subclassing

Several projects have started to take note of this distinction between subclass and subtype including Pool [America87], Trellis/Owl [Halbert87] and Guide [Decouchant88]. Some of the most significant work in this area has been carried out by Black et al [Black86] in the Emerald project. The distinction between subclassing and subtyping (conformance) is captured nicely by Black [Black87] as follows:- *'In Smalltalk, a subclass does not necessarily conform to its superclass; for example, it may override some of the operations of the superclass so that they expect different classes of argument. Moreover, one class may conform to another without a subclass relationship existing between them. What a subclass and its superclass do have in common is part of their representation and some of their methods. In short, inheritance is a relationship between implementations, while conformance is a relationship between interfaces'*

4.4 APPROACHES BASED ON ABSTRACT DATA TYPES

The previous section highlighted the important distinction between type and class and between subtype and subclass. Both distinctions are a consequence of the separation of concerns between the specification of behaviour and the implementation of behaviour. In providing statically typed, object-oriented languages it is therefore almost inevitable that this separation will be a feature of the language design. It is no surprise then that abstract data types have attracted a great deal of attention in the object-oriented world. Abstract data types were introduced as an explicit recognition of the distinction between specification and implementation. This section reviews the impact of abstract data types in object-oriented community.

4.4.1 Abstract Data Types

Abstract data types are a development of the principle of *data abstraction* which emerged in the 1970's as a major technique in handling complexity. Data abstraction is concerned with providing an abstraction over data structures in terms of a well defined procedural (or functional) interface. The roots of data abstraction can, curiously enough, be traced back to the language Simula-67 [Dahl66] which is also the root of all object-oriented languages. Until recently, languages using data abstraction and object-oriented languages have followed parallel development paths. It may be that with the interest in statically typed, object-oriented languages that the two paths will merge.

There are two requirements for data abstraction facilities in a language:-
i)   the data structures and operations are described in a single syntactic unit, and
ii) the data structures and internal representation of the data abstraction are not visible to the programmer; rather, the programmer is presented with a well-defined procedural interface.

The advantages of data abstraction are well recorded. For example, there are major benefits to be gained from all code and data structures concerned with a particular abstraction being recorded in a single place. This leads to well structured, understandable code which can easily be modified. In addition, the information hiding aspect provides a level of protection against unexpected or undesired access to data structures. These are precisely the advantages claimed for object-oriented languages; there are obviously strong parallels between data abstraction and the concept of class.

Abstract data types extend the principle of data abstraction by separating the specification of a data abstraction from its implementation. This is an important step because the abstraction gained from abstract data types is reflected directly in the syntax and semantics of the language. To use an abstract data type, it is only necessary to know the specification. There is absolutely no need to know about the implementation. Abstract data types were first pioneered in languages such as Clu [Liskov78] and Modula [Wirth77]. More recently, abstract data types have attracted considerable attention with their adoption as a central feature of Ada [Booch83].

Abstract data types can be considered to consist of two parts, namely the *specification part* and the *implementation part*. In addition, each part can be further subdivided with the specification being denoted by the syntax (signature) of the specification together with the desired semantics and the implementation part given by the representation (data structures) and the associated algorithms. This structure is summarized in Figure 4.8.

The specification and implementation parts of abstract data types are now discussed in turn.

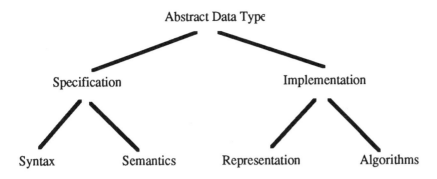

Figure 4.8: Structure of abstract data types

Specification part As mentioned above, the specification part of an abstract data type should specify the syntax of the abstract data type and its associated semantics. The syntax is normally referred to as the *signature* of the abstract data type and fully defines the procedural interface. This must include a complete statement of the type of each procedure in terms of parameters and results. For example, the following is a possible signature for a queue (the notation is loosely based on the abstract data type specification language ACT-ONE [Ehrig85]):-

```
type Queue[Item] is
opns
        Qnew   :                     →      Queue
        Qpush  : Queue,  Item        →      Queue
        Qpop   : Queue               →      Queue
        Qread  : Queue               →      Item U Error
        Qempty: Queue                →      Boolean
    endtype Queue;
```

However, this syntactical specification alone is not sufficient to describe the behaviour of a queue. For example, there is no indication of what each operation does or what constraints are associated with each operation. Therefore, many abstract data type languages support a mechanism for specifying (in varying amounts of detail) the semantics of the data type. This is an attempt to coerce programmers into considering the semantics of their data abstractions before embarking on an implementation. Thus, the specification enforces a discipline on the programmer. In addition, specifications provide a means for checking the semantic correctness of a particular implementation.

There are several alternative ways of writing a specification for an abstract data type. Unfortunately, one of the most common approaches is to use the English language. This is a compromise technique which reflects the current state of the art in specification. More formal techniques include *operational specifications* which describe the semantics in terms of an underlying abstract machine and *logical specifications* which describe input and output predicates for each operation. One of the most successful techniques is called *algebraic specification* [Ehrig85]. This technique interprets an abstract data type as an algebra and requires the programmer to define a set of axioms for the abstract data type. As an example, the following algebraic specification for a queue completes the abstract data type specification started above. Again, the notation is based on ACT-ONE:-

```
type Queue[Item] is
opns
      <as above>
eqns
for all q in Queue, i in Item:
      Qempty(Qnew) = True;
      Qempty(Qpush(q,i) ) = False;
      Qpop(Qnew) = Qnew;
      Qpop(Qpush(q,i) = if Qempty (q)
                              then Qnew
                              else Qpush (Qpop(q),i);
      Qread(Qnew) = error;
      Qread(Qpush(q,i)) = if Qempty (q)
                              then i
                              else Qread(q);
endtype Queue;
```

It should be stressed that most programming languages do not yet make much use of semantic specifications. In fact many only require the programmer to specify the syntax.

Implementation part The implementation part of an abstract data type is much more straightforward than the specification and has a conventional module-like structure. The first part of the implementation describes the realization of the abstract data type in terms of more primitive data structures. For example, a queue could be implemented as an array or as a linked list. The second part of the implementation then describes the algorithms for each of the operations. It is important that there is an exact match between the operations described and the specification of the abstract data type. This match should at least be in terms of the syntax in the specification and hopefully also in terms of the semantics.

It is possible for an abstract data type to have several implementations and for implementations to change dynamically. This has several important benefits. For example, a queue implementation based on bounded arrays may prove to be too restrictive in that there is a fixed upper bound on the size of queues. This could be rectified by implementing a queue of unlimited size based on linked lists. To programmers using the queue abstract data type, this change would be invisible. Similarly, there may be occasions when two implementations of an abstract data type can usefully co-exist. For example, one implementation may be optimized for speed and a second one for space efficiency.

The following example shows a complete abstract data type description, including both the specification and implementation parts, for a simple stack of integers. The example is written in Ada and is taken from Barnes [Barnes84]:-

```
package STACKS is
type STACK is private;
procedure PUSH (S: in out STACK; X: in INTEGER);
```

```
procedure POP (S: in out STACK; X: out INTEGER);
private
        MAX: constant:= 100;
        type INTEGER_VECTOR is
                array (INTEGER range <>) of INTEGER;
        type STACK is
                record
                        S: INTEGER_VECTOR (1..MAX);
                        TOP: INTEGER range 0..MAX:= 0;
                end record;
end;

package body STACKS is
procedure PUSH(S: in out STACK; X: in INTEGER) is
        begin
                S.TOP := S.TOP + 1;
                S.S (S.TOP) := X;
        end PUSH;
procedure POP (S: in out STACK; X: out INTEGER) is
        begin
                X := S.S (S.TOP);
                S.TOP := S.TOP-1;
        end POP;
end STACKS;
```

Note that it is not necessary to understand Ada fully to appreciate this example. The intention is merely to give a flavour of the use of abstract data types in practice.

4.4.2 Subtyping in Abstract Data Types

One of the main motivations for adopting abstract data types as the basis for a language is that they naturally support static type checking. For this reason, many projects which are addressing the problems of statically typed, object-oriented languages have looked to abstract data types as a starting point. It is then necessary to extend abstract data types with facilities to provide full object-oriented features. One of the most common approaches is to provide a flexible, polymorphic type checking mechanism based on subtyping. This approach provides many of the advantages expected of an object-oriented language including encapsulation, abstraction and behaviour sharing but with the added bonus of static type checking. However, there is some debate as to whether such languages are really object-oriented. Such questions are deferred until chapter 5.

Static type checking in languages based on abstract data types use structural equivalence with the structure being uniquely determined by the specification of the abstract data type, i.e. there is no interest in the implementation of the type. Two types are therefore the same if they have the same specification. The notion of equality of two types is usually replaced by subtyping to provide more flexibility, i.e. a particular context will require a subtype which provides at least the functionality of the target type. Two types are then deemed to be equal if they are both subtypes of each other, i.e.

$adt_1 \le adt_2$ and $adt_2 \le adt_1$ implies $adt_1=adt_2$.

Subtyping in abstract data types is no different in principle from subtyping in other type constructs (see section 4.3.3). Therefore, one abstract data type T is a subtype of another abstract data type T' if T provides at least the behaviour of T'. If this is the case, then T can safely be used as if it is a T' because anything that is attempted on T' is guaranteed to be provided by T. This is the basic principle behind extensions of abstract data types to include subtyping.

Note that rules for type checking are normally based on the syntax of the specification alone. For example, two types which provide the same operations must be considered to be the same type irrespective of the semantics of the operations. Similarly, rules for subtyping must be based solely on the interface provided. This is a major weakness of many abstract data type based languages and is an area for future research. To implement subtyping, it is necessary to derive conformance rules for abstract data types. This has been done successfully in several projects. As an example, the conformance rules derived for the Emerald programming language are described below. The rules are more complex than for the simple cases presented in section 4.3.3. They can be seen however to be an amalgamation of the rules for functions and for records.

Conformance Rules for Abstract Data Types (Emerald) Work on conformance rules for abstract data types was pioneered in the development of the Emerald programming language. Emerald is an object-based language for programming distributed subsystems and applications. They were motivated to incorporate static type checking for two main reasons. First, static type checking provides better detection and notification of errors. This was felt to be important in the complex distributed applications and systems which would be developed with Emerald. Second, static type checking avoids the need to explicitly handle run time type errors.

The conformance rules developed in Emerald are now largely accepted and have been adopted in several other projects, e.g. ANSA [ANSA89]. The rules allow assignments and procedure invocations to be checked for legality at compile time. If a particular context expects a particular type, then it is assumed that any valid operations on that type may be invoked later. Thus, the actual type must be checked to see if it can provide at least the operations of the expected type. In effect, the type checker must ensure that the actual type is a subtype of the expected type. Rules must also be provided to check the parameters and results of the operations defined on the abstract data type. The full set of rules for conformance are given below.

An abstract data type P is a subtype of an abstract data Q if and only if the following rules are satisfied:-

Rule 1:   P provides at least the operations of Q (P may have more operations),
Rule 2:   for each operation in Q, the corresponding operation in P has the same number of arguments and results,
Rule 3:   the abstract data types of the results of P's operations conform to the abstract types of the results of Q's operations, and
Rule 4:   the abstract data types of the arguments of Q's operations must conform to the abstract types of the arguments of P's operations (i.e. arguments must conform in the opposite direction).

It is not difficult to understand the reasons for each rule. They collectively ensure that an abstract data type P can be used as if it is a Q in any context. Consider the following fragment of code:-

```
P₁ : P;
Q₁ : Q;

Procedure Proc₁ (Formal : Q);
Begin
        ...
        Result = Formal.operation (parameter);
        ...
End;

Begin
        ...
        if <boolean condition>
                then Proc₁ (P₁)
                else Proc₁ (Q₁);
```

As far as the compiler is concerned, the formal parameter of *Proc₁* is of type Q and will behave as a type Q. However, with the boolean condition, it is possible that *Proc₁* will be called with a parameter of type P. Thus, the program would only be legal if the variable of type P will behave exactly like a Q. Rule 1 guarantees that the assigned variable will have at least the same behaviour. Rule 2 then extends this to guarantee that the number of arguments and results are the same. It then remains to check that the parameters and results are compatible.

To explain rules 3 and 4, focus on the body of *Proc₁*. Within this body, an operation is invoked on the object given by *Formal*. Furthermore, this operation takes one parameter and returns one result. It must be assumed that *Formal* is of type Q at this point. Hence, the parameter and result will be checked to see if they are valid for the operation as defined for Q. However, it must be remembered that *Formal* might actually be of type P. In this case, the parameter will be *passed to* an object of type P and hence the parameter type for P must be able to handle the parameter type for Q. In other words, the parameter for Q must be a subtype of the parameter for P. In contrast, the result from the operation is expected to be of the type specified for Q's operation. However, it might have *come from* an object of type P. Therefore, the result from P must be able to replace the result from Q. Consequently the result from P's operation must be a subtype of the results from Q's operation. This corresponds to the rules for subtyping defined for functions (see section 4.3.3). Rule 4 actually mirrors the antimonotonicity property described for functions.

This example also illustrates the need for dynamic binding. It is not known at compile time whether the parameter to *Proc₁* is of type P or Q. However, this does not prejudice static type checking.

The conformance rules of Emerald ensure that type errors will not occur at run time. However, the rules are now recognized as being overly restrictive. This results from the rather conservative nature of rule 1 which demands that a subtype provides at least the operations of the target type even though some operations of the target type will not be invoked in a given context.

Similar restrictions are introduced by the antimonotonicity reflected in rule 4. This rule can lead to many intuitive notions of subtyping breaking down. For example:-

```
type Integer is
opns
        "+"    :        Integer, Integer   →        Integer
        "*"    :        Integer, Integer   →        Integer
        "-"    :        Integer, Integer   →        Integer
endtype Integer;
type New_Int is
opns
        "+"    :        New_Int, New_Int   →        New_Int
        "*"    :        New_Int, New_Int   →        New_Int
        "-"    :        New_Int, New_Int   →        New_Int
        mod    :        New_Int, New_Int   →        New_Int
endtype New_Int;

I  :    Integer;
N  :    New_Int;
Begin
        . . .
        I := N;
```

It might be expected that a New_Int would be a valid subtype of an Integer and hence the above assignment would be legal. Intuitively, this is certainly the case. However, rule 4 would disallow the relationship between Integers and New_Ints. The parameters of each operation do not conform in the opposite direction. This is a curious result but is absolutely correct. To appreciate this, consider the semantics of the assignment statement. After the assignment, N and I refer to the same object. Now if I is subsequently called with a '+' operation and an Integer parameter, the actual object invoked will be a New_Int which takes a New_Int parameter. This would be a type error

The other problem with conformance is that it is based entirely on the syntax of an abstract data type. Therefore, abstract data types which share common interfaces must be assumed to provide common behaviour. This may not be a valid assumption.

The rules described above, however, provide a workable means of incorporating static type checking in a polymorphic language and as such represent a major step forward. Resolution of the difficulties described above remain fruitful avenues for research.

4.4.3 Other Approaches to Polymorphism

There have been several other notable attempts to introduce polymorphism into abstract data type languages. In this sub-section, two approaches are described: *genericity* [Meyer86] as found in Ada and *enhancement* [Horn86a] as developed in the Comandos project [Horn87]. In both cases, the flexibility of polymorphism is combined with the correctness guarantees of static type checking.

Genericity This technique evolved principally in the development of the Ada programming language but has featured in several other designs, e.g. Clu. Genericity can be defined as the ability to parameterize a software element (in Ada, a package or sub-program) with one or more types. For example, a generic swap program could operate on several different type parameters. Similarly, a generic stack could be written independently of the type of the item on the stack. Therefore, genericity is a form of parametric polymorphism.

Ada distinguishes between *constrained* and *unconstrained* genericity. In constrained genericity, a restriction is placed on the actual type of the generic parameter(s) whereas in unconstrained genericity there are no such restrictions. In practice, restrictions are given by the operations which a type must support. The two forms of genericity are examined in more detail below. Most of the examples are taken from Meyer [Meyer86].

Unconstrained genericity is the simplest form of genericity and is used in Ada to overcome the restrictions of static type checking. It is applicable for algorithms whose description is truly generic and is completely independent of the type of the argument(s). There is an implicit assumption that any operations used in the body of the algorithm will be defined for all types. This generally implies that only assignment and equality can be used in the code body.

A swap routine is an excellent example of a generic piece of software and could be written in Ada as follows:-

```
generic
      type T is private;
procedure swap (x, y: in out T) is
      t : T
begin
      t := x; x := y; y := t
end swap;
```

The code is completely generic because assignment is meaningful for all possible types in the system. Type T acts as a placeholder in the generic description of the algorithm. T can be replaced by any valid type to give a procedure to swap two values of that type.

It is important to realize that the above Ada code does not actually establish any procedures. Rather, the generic description acts as a template for the later establishment of one or more procedures of different types. Actual procedures are *instantiated* as follows:-

```
procedure int_swap is new swap (INTEGER);
procedure string_swap is new swap (STRING);
```

The effect of this is to establish two *separate* code bodies, one for swapping integers and one for swapping strings. INTEGER and STRING will replace T in *int_swap* and *string_swap* respectively.

The main advantage of genericity is that the programmer only writes the template once for all types. Consequently, Ada's use of generics has been compared to macro expansion in that generic procedures provide a short hand way of writing code. The explicit instantiation of procedures allows the compiler to statically type check an Ada program. In addition, because of the underlying macro expansion, the actual interpretation of Ada generics is also determined at compile time (static binding).

Constrained genericity is a more restricted form of genericity. In more complicated generic algorithms, it is likely that certain operations will be used which are not defined for all types in the language. Thus some restrictions must be placed on the types of actual parameters. Constrained genericity allows the programmer to specify which operations must be defined on a type. For example, a minimum function must have a comparison operator, say <=, defined on parameter types. A generic minimum function can be written in Ada as follows:-

```
generic
        type T is private;
        with function "<=" (a,b : T)
                return (BOOLEAN is <>;
function minimum (x, y: T) return T is
begin
        if x <= y   then return x
                    else return y
        end if;
end swap;
```

The keyword **with** defines the constraints for a legal type. Actual procedures can then be instantiated as before, e.g.:-

```
function string_minimum is new minimum (STRING);
```

The compiler can check at this point whether the constraints are met by the given types.

The real power of genericity becomes apparent when it is used in conjunction with Ada's package construct. Packages implement a form of abstract data type in Ada. Thus generic packages combine data abstraction with polymorphism giving a functionality which is comparable to the type system of Emerald (exact comparisons are deferred to the next chapter). An example of a generic package in Ada is given below without further commentary. The example shows the outline specification for a generic stack package:-

```
generic
        type T is private;
package STACKS is
type STACK is private;
procedure PUSH (S: in out STACK; X: in T);
procedure POP (S: in out STACK; X: out T);
private
        MAX: constant:= 100;
        type STACK is
        record
                S: array (1..MAX) of T;
                TOP: INTEGER range 0..MAX:= 0;
        end record;
end;
```

Note that a similar form of constrained genericity is provided in Clu through the use of a **where** clause.

The main difference between the two forms of genericity is that with unconstrained genericity, a generic type is effectively parameterized with the formal type *top* (i.e. the supertype of all types) whereas with constrained genericity, the parameterized type provides more specific constraints on the structure of a valid type.

Enhancement This technique was developed by researchers at Trinity College, Dublin during work on the Esprit-funded Comandos project. Enhancement is an interesting hybrid approach to providing polymorphism in abstract data type based languages and combines aspects of genericity, conformance and standard inheritance.

In the typing model for Comandos, a rich algebra of types is defined including a number of base types, enumerated types, records, lists, sequences and sets. A catalogue of conformance rules are then defined to determine subtyping relationships between various types. The conformance rules are similar to Emerald and are described in detail in the literature [Horn86b]. As usual, a value of type T can be used as if it is of type T' if T is a valid subtype of T'. The designers of the type model however recognized the restrictive nature of conformance. In their model, if T is not a subtype of T' it may still be possible to use values of T as if they are of type T' through *enhancement*.

Enhancement is best understood as a combination of genericity (constrained and unconstrained) and traditional inheritance. The technique allows types to be parameterized; the new parameterized type can then be viewed as *enhancive* because it extends the behaviour of the actual type parameter. Any valid type can be used as a parameter to an enhancive type. In addition, this type can then appear anywhere in the construction of the new type. For example, the following are both enhancive types:-

i) Stack

```
type Stack (Item as top) = module is
        Push    :       procedure (Item) → ();
        Pop     :       procedure () → Item;
        private part is
                Data    :       array[0..N] of Item;
                ToS     :       [0..N];
end;
```

This example corresponds to unconstrained genericity. A stack is defined in terms of a parameterized type *top*. The actual parameter must then be compatible with *top*. *Top* actually corresponds to the top element in the type lattice and hence every type in the system conforms to *top*.

ii) Matrix

```
type Matrix (R as Ring) = module is
        "+"     :       procedure (Matrix) → (Matrix);
        "*"     :       procedure (Matrix) → (Matrix);
        private part is
                Me      :       array [1..N][1..M] of R;
end;

type Ring= (     Zero :: Ring;
                 Unity :: Ring;
```

101

```
                              "+" : procedure (Ring) → (Ring);
                              "*" : procedure (Ring) → Ring);
                )
```

In this example, a matrix is defined generically for elements of type ring. This is
equivalent to constrained genericity as rings must have certain properties,
namely an interpretation of zero and unity as well as operations to add and
multiply individual elements.

Furthermore, if the parameter is of certain types, then the type can be directly *implanted*
into the new type. Thus the type supplied as parameter provides some of the behaviour of
the new type directly. The following example illustrates the use of implantation.

```
        type Person=(    Name : String;
                         Age : Cardinal;
                )

        type Student (P as Person) = (
                         <P>;                    (* Implant P*)
                         College : String;
                         IdNo : Cardinal;
                )
```

Implantation provides a similar functionality to inheritance. Indeed, multiple
inheritance can be modeled by implantation. It is also possible to model restricted
inheritance. For example, returning to the example in section 4.3.4, it is possible to
implement a stack in terms of a double ended queue as follows:-

```
        type Stack (R as Deque(only Push_left, Pop_left)) is
              <R>
        end Stack;
```

Any type which is a valid subtype of Deque can be used for Stack. However,
only Push_left and Pop_left will be available from Stack.
It is also possible to rename the operations within stack as follows:-

```
        type Stack (R as Deque(only Push <= Push_left,
                                    Pop <= Pop_left)) is
              <R>
        end Stack;
```

Enhancement therefore attempts to combine the best features of various approaches
to polymorphism. It can model both constrained and unconstrained genericity as well as
multiple inheritance. It also provides a less restrictive form of subtyping. As mentioned
above, a type T can be used in place of a type T' even though it is not strictly a subtype.
Abstract data type descriptions can be enhanced with a concrete implementation of an
operation; a type must then only conform to the base type (pre-enhancement) of the
abstract data type but gains access to the added concrete operation.

Other languages have also taken a hybrid approach to polymorphism. For example, Eiffel [Meyer88] features conformance, genericity and inheritance in the design. Similarly, Guide [Decouchant88] employs both conformance and inheritance. Other hybrid languages include Trellis/Owl [Schaffert86], Pool [America87] and Kitara [Guffick89].

Other Polymorphic Languages In a separate strand of development, type theorists have designed several languages based on universal, parametric polymorphism. Leading examples of this category of languages include Miranda [Turner85], ML [Gordon79], Russell [Demers80], and Hope [Burstall80]. Many of these languages also support a form of data abstraction and hence can legitimately be compared to the languages described in this section. The big advantages of these languages is that interpretation of polymorphic code is resolved at run-time, i.e. dynamic binding is employed. This contrasts with Ada which supports parametric polymorphism but interpretations are fixed at compile time. This distinction is often referred to as a *syntactic* versus a *semantic* view of polymorphism. The syntactic view corresponds to the macro expansion treatment of polymorphism as found in Ada (see above). This approach has many problems because it does not really capture the true semantics of polymorphism. For example, polymorphic functions are very quickly mapped on to several monomorphic functions, one for each type. Each monomorphic function is then compiled and executed as a separate entity. With a semantic interpretation of polymorphism, the polymorphic nature of code is preserved right through to execution. There will only be one code body for a function and the true interpretation of the code body is resolved dynamically. This has several advantages. For example, there will only be one instance of a code body thereby saving space. Similarly, less type checking is required because there is only one description to examine. Inevitably, however, dynamic binding will incur a certain amount of run-time overhead.

It can be anticipated that this category of languages will have a major impact on future developments in language design. The repercussions for object-oriented languages, however, remain a matter for speculation.

4.5 SUMMARY

4.5.1 Techniques introduced in Chapter 4
Several new techniques have been introduced in this chapter giving the composite table of techniques as shown in Figure 4.9.

The major additions have been the introduction of the concepts of *type*, *abstract data type* and *polymorphism*. Specific techniques for implementing polymorphic types in object-oriented languages have also been presented (*subtyping*, *genericity* and *enhancement*). The chapter also examined closely the related issues of *type checking* and *binding* in polymorphic environments.

4.5.2 Rationale for Techniques
As with previous chapters, the techniques introduced in this chapter are related back to the four principles of object-oriented computing. Each of the four principles is now discussed in turn.

General Approach	Technique	Description	Xref
Encapsulation	Object	encapsulation of data and interface	2.2.1 3.3.4
	Active object	encapsulation of data, interface and autonomous thread(s) of control	3.4
Classification	Classes	groupings based on common specification and implementation	2.3.1 3.3.1
	Prototypes	rejection of classification as structuring philosophy	3.4.1
	Types	groupings based on common specification	4.2 4.3
	Abstract Data Types	groupings based on common operational interfaces	4.4
Flexible sharing	Subclassing (inheritance)	inclusion of specification and implementation of one class in another	2.4.1 3.3.2 3.3.3
	Overloading	sharing of method names across specific objects or classes	2.4.5 4.2.4
	Prototyping	inclusion of implementation of one object instance in another	3.4.2
	Polymorphism	sharing of behaviour across multiple objects, classes or types	4.2.4
	Subtyping	inclusion of specification of one type in another type	4.2.4 4.3.3 4.4.2
	Genericity	sharing of implementation across *parameterized* data types	4.4.3
	Enhancement	hybrid approach to sharing	4.4.3
Interpretation	Static binding	compile time resolution of names in subclass hierarchy	2.5.1 4.2
	Dynamic binding	run time resolution of names in subclass hierarchy	2.5.2 3.3.2 4.2
	Delegation	resolution along delegation paths	3.4.2
	Static typing	compile time resolution of types	4.2
	Dynamic typing	run time resolution of types	4.2

Table 4.9: Summary of techniques

Data Abstraction The introduction of abstract data types adds considerably to the expressive power of a system or language. In particular, abstract data types provide a clean separation between the abstract behaviour of an object and its implementation in terms of data structures and algorithms. This separation encourages the system developer to think abstractly about the functionality of an object before considering how this functionality might be realised.

Behaviour Sharing Abstract data types and polymorphism both introduce forms of behaviour sharing in object-oriented systems. Each technique is considered in turn below.

Abstract data types introduce a form of classification (in a similar way to classes). All implementations of a particular abstract data type are guaranteed to share the behaviour as defined by the abstract data type. However, unlike classes, the behaviour sharing is at the level of specifications and does not necessarily involve sharing of implementations.

Finer control over the level of behaviour sharing is introduced by polymorphism. The various styles of polymorphism discussed in the chapter all allow particular items of behaviour to span a number of different abstract data types. At the simplest level, overloading allows particular operation names to be re-used in different contexts. More structured approaches to behaviour sharing are also provided by subtyping, genericity and enhancement. Again, polymorphism is concerned with the sharing of specifications and does not imply sharing of implementations. This clean separation adds considerably to the flexibility of a system. In particular, it is no longer necessary for two objects to be implemented in the same way to share behaviour.

Evolution The techniques introduced in this chapter do not directly contribute to evolution. In object-oriented computing, most support for evolution is provided by inheritance. Nevertheless, the design approach of separating specifications from implementations makes the task of modifying existing code much easier.

Correctness This chapter has been primarily concerned with techniques to introduce correctness in object-oriented computing. It has been shown that it is possible to retain the flexibility of the object-oriented approach and also give guarantees of type correctness. This is made possible by the separation of type checking and binding. Type checking mechanisms can guarantee that there exists an interpretation for every item of behaviour in the system and binding can then resolve this behaviour. The combination of static type checking with dynamic binding can therefore allow interpretations to evolve over time but without prejudicing the overall correctness of a system.

4.6 ACKNOWLEDGEMENTS

The author would like to thank the following people for comments on early drafts of this chapter: Tom Rodden, Ronnie Thompson, Mandy Chetwynd and Alastair Macartney. Special thanks also to Chris Horn and Alexis Donnelly from Trinity College, Dublin for their helpful comments on conformance and enhancement.

REFERENCES

[**America.87**] America, P. "Inheritance and Subtyping in a Parallel Object-Oriented Language." *Proceedings of The European Conference on Object-Oriented Programming,* Pages: 281-289. 1987.

[ANSA89] ANSA. *Introduction to ANSA*, ANSA 24 Hills Road, Cambridge, U.K. March 1989.

[Barnes84] Barnes, J.G.P. *Programming in Ada (Second Edition)*. Addison-Wesley. London. 1984.

[Black86] Black, A., N. Hutchinson, E. Jul, and H. Levy. "Object Structure in the Emerald System." *Proceedings of the Conference on Object-Oriented Programming Systems, Languages and Applications (OOPSLA '86)*, Editor: N. Meyrowitz, Special Issue of ACM SIGPLAN Notices, Vol: 21, Pages: 78-86. 1986.

[Black87] Black, A., N. Hutchinson, E. Jul, H. Levy, and L. Carter. "Distribution and Abstract Types in Emerald." *IEEE Transactions on Software Engineering Vol:* SE-13 No.: 1, 1987, Pages: 65-76.

[Booch83] Booch, G. *Software Engineering with Ada*. Benjamin Cummings. 1983.

[Bruce86] Bruce, K.M., and P. Wegner. "An Algebraic Model of Subtypes in Object-oriented Languages." *SIGPLAN Notices Vol:* 21 No.: 10, 1986,

[Burstall80] Burstall, R.M., D.B. McQueen, and D.T. Sannella. "HOPE: An Experimental Applicative Language", Internal Report CSR-62-80, University of Edinburgh. May 1980.

[Cardelli85] Cardelli, L., and P. Wegner. "On Understanding Types, Data Abstraction, and Polymorphism." *Computing Surveys Vol:* 17 No.: 4, 1985, Pages: 471-522.

[Cleaveland86] Cleaveland, J.C. *An Introduction to Data Types*. Addison-Wesley. 1986.

[Dahl66] Dahl, O., and K. Nygaard. "Simula, An Algol-based Simulation Language." *Communications of the ACM Vol:* 9 1966, Pages: 671-678.

[Danforth88] Danforth, S., Tomlinson, C. "Type Theories in Object-Oriented Programming." *ACM Computing Surveys Vol:* 20 No.: 1, 1988, Pages: 29-72.

[Decouchant88] Decouchant, D., A. Duda, A. Freyssinet, M. Riveill, X.R.d. Pina, G. Vandome, and R. Scioville. "Guide: An Implementation of the COMANDOS Object Oriented Distributed System Architecture on Unix." *Proceedings of the '88 EUUG Conference*, 1988.

[Demers80] Demers, A.J., Donahue, J.E. "Data Types, Parameters and Type Checking." *Conference Record of the 7th Annual ACM Symposium on Principles of Programming Languages*, Pages: 12-23. 1980.

[Ehrig85] Ehrig, H., Mahr, B. *Fundamentals of Algebraic Specification*. Springer-Verlag. 1985.

[Gordon79] Gordon, M.J., A.J. Milner, and C.P. Wadsworth. *Edinburgh LCF*. Lecture

Notes in Computer Science. Vol: 78. Springer-Verlag. 1979.

[**Guffick89**] Guffick, I.M., Blair, G.S. "Kitara: A Parallel Object-Oriented Language for Distributed Applications." *Proceedings of Parallel Computing '89*, Leiden, The Netherlands, 1989.

[**Halbert87**] Halbert, D.C., and P.D. O'Brien. "Using Types and Inheritance in Object-Oriented Languages." *Proceedings of the European Conference on Object-Oriented Programming*, Pages: 23-34. 1987.

[**Horn86a**] Horn, C., and L. White. "Type Model", TCD-d2-T2.1-080487b, Department of Computer Science, Trinity College Dublin, Ireland.

[**Horn86b**] Horn, C. "Conformance, Genericity, Inheritance and Enhancement", Technical Report, Department of Computer Science, Trinity College Dublin, Ireland.

[**Horn87**] Horn, C., Krakowiak, S. "Object-Oriented Architecture for Distributed Office Systems." *Proceedings of ESPRIT '87*, North-Holland, 1987.

[**Liskov78**] Liskov, B.H., and et al. "The CLU Reference Manual", CSG Memo #161, M. I. T. Laboratory for Computer Science. 1978.

[**MacQueen82**] MacQueen, D.B., Sethi, R. "A Semantic Model for the Types of Applicative Languages." *Proceedings of the 1982 ACM Symposium on LISP and Functional Programming*, Pages: 243-252. 1982.

[**Meyer86**] Meyer, B. "Genericity versus Inheritance." *Proceedings of the Conference on Object-Oriented Programming Systems, Languages and Applications (OOPSLA '86)*, Editor: N. Meyrowitz, Special Issue of ACM SIGPLAN Notices, Vol: 21, Pages: 391-405. 1986.

[**Meyer88**] Meyer, B. *Object-Oriented Software Construction*. Prentice-Hall. 1988.

[**Schaffert86**] Schaffert, C., T. Cooper, B. Bullis, M. Kilian, and C. Wilpolt. "An Introduction to Trellis/Owl." *Proceedings of the Conference on Object-oriented Programming Systems, Languages and Applications (OOPSLA '86)*, Editor: N. Meyrowitz, Special Issue of SIGPLAN Notices, Vol: 21, Pages: 9-16. 1986.

[**Turner85**] Turner, D.A. "Miranda: A Non-strict Functional Language with Polymorphic Types'." *Proceedings of the IFIP International Conference on Functional Programming Languages and Computer Architecture*, 1985.

[**Wirth77**] Wirth, N. "MODULA: A Language for Modular Multiprogramming." *Software Practice and Experience* No.: 7, 1977, Pages: 3-35.

Chapter 5

What *are* Object-Oriented Systems?

Gordon S. Blair
Lancaster University

ABSTRACT *The first four chapters of this book have introduced most of the fundamental concepts underlying object-oriented computing. It should now be clear that object-oriented computing is a large topic encompassing not only traditional models based on class and inheritance but also many variations on the basic theme. Techniques such as delegation, conformance and genericity have been introduced to solve problems in a particular area. With all these developments, it is now very difficult to define concisely what it meant by the term object-orientation. This chapter examines the question of what is object-orientation. A model is presented which encompasses all the techniques discussed so far. The model is then used to analyse some of the pertinent questions raised in the object-oriented community. In addition, it is suggested that the model provides a design space for the development of new object-oriented languages and systems. The chapter concludes by examining some formal techniques which might lead to a more precise modeling of the semantics of object-oriented computing in the future.*

5.1 INTRODUCTION

As mentioned in chapter one, there is now considerable interest in object-oriented computing from such diverse areas as language design, artificial intelligence, databases, parallel and distributed systems, software engineering and operating systems. All are attracted by the general benefits of object-oriented computing in terms of modularity, abstraction, code re-use, flexibility etc. However, the requirements of each of these areas are often very different, e.g. in terms of granularity of objects, performance or semantic modeling capabilities. It is simply not possible for one set of *techniques* to solve all the problems in each of these areas. Consequently, developers have experimented with various alternatives or variations of the basic object-model in an attempt to tailor systems for their own needs. This trend is especially apparent in the area of statically typed object-oriented computing as discussed in the previous chapter. Many new techniques have emerged in this work including conformance [Black87], genericity [Meyer86] and enhancement [Horn86]. The trend is also visible in other areas, e.g. delegation [Lieberman86] was designed as a more flexible strategy for concurrent object models (see chapter 3). Similarly, techniques of multiple inheritance [Ducournau87] and the modeling of exceptions [Borgida86] have emerged in the field of artificial intelligence. This situation is shown pictorially in Figure 5.1.

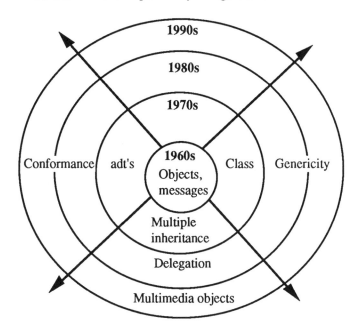

Figure 5.1: Variations in object-oriented computing

The range of techniques encompassed by the term *object-oriented* is therefore vast. There is general agreement that all the above techniques are within the domain of object-oriented computing and yet, curiously, there is no accepted definition of object-orientation. This is not necessarily a major problem. After all, a labeling exercise does not necessarily add to the understanding of a subject. However, a more serious problem is the lack of an agreed semantics of object-oriented computing. There is a real requirement for a model for discussing object-orientation which captures all the variations mentioned above and which allows reasoned debate about the relative merits of adopting one approach over another. Ideally, there should exist a design space for object-oriented computing which would allow designers to choose certain features in order to meet the requirements from their own specific areas.

This chapter presents such a model. This model is based closely on the framework established in chapter one. In more detail, the objectives of the model are:-

i) to highlight various design options, and

ii) to provide a framework for reasoned debate about object-oriented techniques.

The chapter is organized as follows. Section 5.2 presents the prevalent view of object-oriented computing as described in chapter 2. This view highlights the concepts of object, class and inheritance as central to object-oriented computing. A more complete view is presented in section 5.3. It is proposed that encapsulation, classification, polymorphism and interpretation provide a set of orthogonal dimensions for object-oriented computing. The four dimensions are then examined in depth and alternative techniques for each dimension are explored. The definition is evaluated in section 5.4 with respect to the two objectives. It is argued that the definition creates a *design space* for object-oriented systems. In addition, a number of key questions are analysed using the model. In the long term, it must be hoped that a more formal basis for object-oriented computing will be established. Some preliminary work in this area is thus presented in section 5.5. Work on type theory and the typed lambda calculus is presented. It should be stressed, however, that there is still a gap between the informal model presented in this chapter and general formalism for object-oriented computing. Finally, some conclusions are presented in section 5.6.

5.2 TRADITIONAL VIEW OF OBJECT-ORIENTED COMPUTING

Most work on object-orientation has been carried out in the language domain. Consequently, it is not surprising that the most widely accepted interpretation of the term *object-oriented* arose out of this field of study. This view was covered in detail in chapter two. Briefly, however, object-orientation consists of a series of steps leading to full object-oriented systems (as illustrated in Figure 5.2).

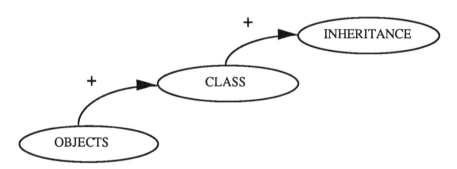

Figure 5.2: Traditional view of object-orientation

The first step is that languages must include the notion of *objects*, where an object is an encapsulation of a set of operations with state which remembers the effect of operations. Languages which meet this criterion are deemed to be *object-based*. The second step is that languages should feature the concept of *class*, i.e. a template defining behaviour (in terms of interface and implementation) from which objects may be created by a *new* operation. Languages which exhibit objects and class are then referred to as *class-based*. Finally, the third step is that languages should support *inheritance*, i.e. the ability to create subclasses from existing classes, hence establishing a class lattice. Languages which support all three features can then be described as *object-oriented*. The model therefore provides a framework for discussing various languages which feature aspects of object-oriented computing. For example Ada is an example of an object-based language, Clu is class-based and Simula and Smalltalk are full object-oriented languages.

This view of object-oriented computing is clear and precise and provides a good framework for discussing most of the traditional work in object-oriented languages. However, limitations become apparent when the classification is applied to some of the recent developments in object-oriented computing. This is especially true in the area of statically typed object-oriented languages, i.e. there is no explanation of the role of conformance, genericity and enhancement in object-oriented computing. Similarly, there is no mention of alternative approaches to behaviour sharing and evolution as discussed in chapter 3.

The main restriction of this classification is that it is based on a specific set of *mechanisms* which object-oriented languages should support. Languages which do not feature these mechanisms or which adopt alternative mechanisms are therefore not considered to be object-oriented. This is rather unsatisfactory especially as new mechanisms for object-oriented computing are emerging all the time. In addition, the more interesting issues are concerned with what a particular system offers to the user rather than how it is implemented. This chapter presents the thesis that a more general view of object-orientation is required. An alternative model is therefore proposed based on the more general *dimensions* of an object-oriented environment.

5.3 A MODEL OF OBJECT-ORIENTED COMPUTING

The model of object-orientation proposed in this chapter is based closely on the framework established in chapter one (section 1.6). Chapter one described four dimensions of object-oriented computing, i.e. encapsulation, classification, flexible sharing and interpretation. The model described in this chapter retains the same four dimensions with one subtle change: the term *flexible sharing* is replaced by *polymorphism*. Polymorphism is normally associated with typed systems. However, it will be argued that the concept of polymorphism is equally applicable to other forms of classification, e.g. classes. With this general interpretation, polymorphism is a more descriptive term than flexible sharing.

The dimensions were discussed briefly in chapter one. However, for completeness, short definitions are presented below.

The first dimension of an object oriented system is encapsulation.:-

Encapsulation:

> Encapsulation is defined as the grouping together of various properties associated with an identifiable entity in the system in a lexical and logical unit, i.e. the object. Furthermore, access to the object should be restricted to a well-defined interface.

The second dimension of an object-oriented system is classification, as defined below:-

Classification:

> Classification is the ability to group associated objects according to common properties. Various classifications can be formed representing different groupings in the system. All objects within a particular grouping will share all the common properties for that grouping but may have other differences.

The third dimension of object-orientation is polymorphism. Polymorphism is given a general interpretation as follows:-

Polymorphism:

> Polymorphism implies that objects can belong to more than one classification. Classifications can therefore overlap and intersect. Thus it is possible for two different classifications to share common behaviour.

The fourth dimension of object-oriented computing is interpretation, as defined below:-
Interpretation:

> Interpretation is defined as the resolution of polymorphism. In polymorphic environments, it is possible for a particular item of behaviour to have several different meanings depending on the context. It is therefore the task of interpretation to resolve this ambiguity and to determine the precise interpretation of an item of behaviour.

The four dimensions described above constitute a model of object-oriented systems. The author believes that this model captures the very essence of object-oriented computing in all its manifestations. Encapsulation is completely fundamental to object-oriented computing and is the reason for many of the benefits of object-orientation, e.g. modularity and maintainability. Classification then adds to the benefits by allowing groupings to be formed over the body of encapsulated objects. It is thus possible to reason about such groupings by highlighting their shared behaviour and ignoring the differences. In addition, different classifications can be formed to meet different needs, e.g. both class and abstract data types are valid classifications. Polymorphism then injects a degree of flexibility into a system by allowing different interpretations of objects to co-exist. Again, various forms of polymorphism can be supported, e.g. overloading, parametric and inclusion polymorphism (as discussed in depth in chapter 4). It will also be shown in section 5.3.2 that inheritance can also be thought of as a form of polymorphism. Finally, interpretation is necessary to determine the exact semantics of an operation in an object-oriented environment. The key issue is whether this interpretation should be performed statically (at compile time) or dynamically (at run time).

The complete model of object-orientation is illustrated in Figure 5.3.

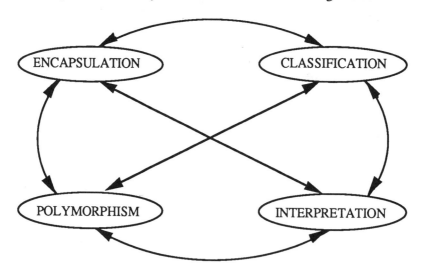

Figure 5.3: Model of object-oriented computing

It should be stressed that the model is not intended to be a definition of object-orientation.. It is important to move away from the view that there exist absolute definitions of terms in this field. It is now virtually impossible and probably not very rewarding to give a precise definition of object-orientation. Rather, the model should be viewed as a framework for debating various alternative implementation strategies for each dimension. All languages and systems which fill the dimension space described above can legitimately be discussed within the object-oriented community. The discussions though should centre on the relative merits of different strategies and not on whether a particular language is object-oriented.

The following sub-sections now consider each dimension in more detail. The exact nature of each dimension is explored in depth and various implementation strategies examined.

5.3.1 Encapsulation Dimension

As mentioned above, encapsulation is the grouping together of various properties associated with an identifiable entity in the system in a lexical and logical unit, i.e. the object. Furthermore, access to the object should be restricted to a well-defined interface. All fields of object-oriented computing start with the basic concept that it is possible to describe the universe as a series of fairly autonomous, encapsulated objects which then access each other through a protected interface. This notion is captured nicely by Snyder [Snyder86] who states that *'encapsulation is a technique for minimizing inter-dependencies among separately-written modules by defining strict external interfaces. The external interface of a module serves as a contract between the module and its clients, and thus between the designer of the module and other designers. If clients depend only on the external interface, the module can be re-implemented without affecting any clients, so long as the new implementation supports the same (or upward compatible) external interface. Thus the effects of compatible changes can be confined'.*

The term *property* is used in the above definition of encapsulation in a general sense to convey any information pertaining to the object. Different systems vary in the range of properties they support. The following is a fairly comprehensive list of possible properties of an object:-

i) Representation

The representation of an object is the internal data structures used to model and record the state of that object. For example, the representation of a stack might be a linked list data structure.

ii) Operations

The operations of an object are the interfaces to the procedures and functions which manipulate the internal state of the object. For example, the stack object might support push, pop and is_empty operations.

iii) Algorithms

The algorithms are then the implementation of the procedures and functions defined on an object.

iv) Attributes

Attributes are name to value pairs which enhance the description of an object. For example, a stack might have an attribute defining the maximum size of the stack.

v) Constraints

Several object models also encapsulate constraints with objects. Constraints impose limitations on the behaviour of an object, e.g. to prevent pop operations on an empty stack. One approach to implement constraints is to place assertions at the start and finish of operations to check their consistency [Meyer88].

vi) Triggers

More recently, several implementations have associated triggers [Weiser89] with objects. A trigger is an asynchronous action which is fired as a result of a change in state. For example, a trigger might be associated with a change of address in order to update mailing lists managed by other objects. Triggers are useful for modeling behaviour of objects not directly related to individual operations.

It is therefore necessary in designing an object-oriented system to decide what properties should be associated with objects. This will inevitably vary from application to application. For example, it is common in object-oriented databases to limit the range of properties to attributes and constraints. However, in programming languages it is inevitable that representation, operations and algorithms will be encapsulated (although perhaps not attributes). Office information systems, on the other hand, place great emphasis on features such as triggers to provide support for various office procedures.

Once the properties of an object are defined, it is then necessary to decide on the visibility of the properties, i.e. which properties are to be visible to the outside world and which are to represent internal state. It is at this stage that the interface to an object is defined. Normally, direct access to the actual representation of an object would be prevented; rather, the programmer would access the object through the operational interface. This property is usually referred to as *information hiding*. The visibility of other properties is not so clear cut. A discussion of the issues concerned with the visibility of attributes can be found in Snyder [Snyder86]. In the rest of this chapter, the visible interface of an object is referred to as the *(external) behaviour* of that object.

5.3.2 Classification Dimension

In systems supporting encapsulation, the environment is represented by a finite set of objects with each object exhibiting certain behaviour, i.e. external properties. It is very natural to extend this model to include classification. As defined above, classification is the ability to group associated objects according to common behaviour. All objects within a particular grouping will share all the common properties for that grouping but may have other differences. Classification is a very powerful tool and is absolutely central to most scientific and engineering disciplines.

In general, a classification is defined by a *predicate* over the environment of objects. For example, one valid classification would be all objects with an attribute colour = red. All objects within this grouping are guaranteed to meet this predicate but may have many other differences. A particular classification also has an *intent* and an *extent*. The intent of a classification is the description of the behaviour of that classification. The intent denotes all the possible objects which exhibit a certain behaviour and is therefore potentially infinite. In contrast, the extent of a classification is the finite set of objects in the current environment which feature such behaviour. The intent of a classification is therefore specified by a particular predicate whereas the extent is obtained by applying the predicate to a specific environment.

For example, consider an environment consisting of the following values:-

```
46
"Gordon"
-10
True
```

12

"Blair"

and a predicate defined as follows:-

$$\{ x : x \in N \} \qquad \text{(where N is the set of all Natural numbers)}$$

The intent of this predicate is the set of all Natural numbers, i.e. $\{1, 2, 3, 4, 5, ...\}$

The extent however is the set containing 46 and 12.

Both the intensional and extensional aspects of classification are important in object-oriented computing. This is particularly true in the object-oriented database community where it is vital to be able to represent both intensional and extensional concepts (see chapter 7).

Various classifications can be formed representing different groupings in the system. The important question is which classifications should be represented in a particular system. The example above is a general classification described in terms of attributes of objects. Another possibility is to specify classifications in terms of the operations provided by objects, e.g. one useful classification would be the set of objects which support open, read, write and close operations. The choice of how to model classifications in a particular object-oriented system is absolutely central to the design process. The most significant choices are discussed below:-

i) Sets

The most general way of representing classifications in a system is through sets. Sets are sufficiently powerful to model any possible classification required in a system. After all, the result of any predicate is a set of objects fulfilling that predicate. It is very uncommon to find sets in object-oriented languages. However, they are used more frequently in the area of object-oriented databases. For example, the Semantic Data Model is based on simple set theory (see chapter 7). The advantage of using sets is that there is an associated body of knowledge and a well understood semantics from the field of mathematics. The intent of a set is given by a particular predicate or query. The extent is then given by all the objects answering that predicate or query. Note that in the database community it is quite common to denote the extent of a query by the term class. This illustrates the need for an agreed terminology for object-oriented computing.

ii) Abstract Data Types

As mentioned in chapter 4, types are essentially forms of classification. However, they are more specific classifications than sets in that they are purely concerned with the external interface to an object. A type is a set of objects which share common behaviour. Thus, all types are sets but not all sets are types (this distinction between set and type will be revisited in section 5.5.1). An abstract data type is then the template which defines a particular classification. In effect the predicate is given by the set of objects which meet the syntax and possibly semantics of the abstract data type. The intent of the classification is therefore the abstract data type description whereas the extent is the set of all objects which are deemed to be of this abstract data type (this distinction is also discussed in chapter 4, section 4.2.1).

iii) Classes (Concrete Data Types)

The most restricted form of classification found in object-oriented computing is the class. Ironically, many people would consider this to be the only classification compatible with object-oriented computing. A class is a template which fully defines the behaviour of a group of objects in terms of the operations, representation and algorithms (more generally, the complete internal and external behaviour). A class can therefore be considered to be a concrete data type where the specification and implementation has been fully described. The intent of a class is given by the class template. In addition, the extent is the instances of a particular class.

iv)   *Objects (Prototypes)*

In order to be complete, it is necessary to consider the individual object as a degenerate form of classification. This is needed to model the approaches based on prototypes as described in chapter 3. The designers of such systems take the view that every object defines a new classification with only one element, i.e. a prototype.

Classification is therefore a sufficiently general concept to encompass sets, abstract data types, classes and objects, i.e. all the actual techniques found in object-oriented computing. The list above also defines classifications in decreasing order of generality. In chapter 4, it was argued that type (or abstract data types) is a more general concept than class. It can also now be seen that set is a more general concept than type. This presents the designer of an object-oriented system with a spectrum of possibilities (ignoring the degenerate case):-

Set > Abstract Data type > Class

It is important to realize that the choice of one classification does not exclude the choice of a second classification. For example, chapter 4 highlighted several languages where abstract data types and classes co-exist. Similarly, there are several database models where set and class co-exist. It would also be possible to design a system or language which features all three concepts.

5.3.3 Polymorphism Dimension

Polymorphism was discussed in detail in chapter 4 in the context of typing systems. In that context, polymorphism is defined to be the ability for an object to have more than one type. Consequently, objects can be used in different contexts demanding different typed values. In this chapter, polymorphism is extended to take on a more general meaning. In terms of the model, polymorphism implies that an object can belong to more than one classification. This can be interpreted as meaning that objects can have more than one type. Equally, polymorphism can apply to other classifications and therefore objects can belong to more than one set or class. Thus, polymorphism is an orthogonal concept to classification.

The power of polymorphism is that it supports a more flexible model of computing. In non-polymorphic (i.e. monomorphic systems) objects can only belong to one classification. Hence, it is not possible for different classifications to share common behaviour. Therefore, classifications become protective walls which isolate objects into various disjoint categories. In polymorphic environments, however, classifications can overlap and intersect. Therefore, it is possible for two classifications to share some common behaviour. Similarly, it is possible for one classification to have a subset of the behaviour of a second classification.

Cardelli and Wegner's taxonomy of polymorphism was introduced in chapter 4. This distinguished between ad-hoc polymorphism which works on a limited, finite number of

116

types in an unprincipled manner and universal polymorphism which will work uniformly for a potentially infinite set of types in a principled manner. Coercions and overloading were introduced as examples of ad-hoc polymorphism. In addition, parametric and inclusion polymorphism were described as universal polymorphism techniques.

All styles of polymorphism are possible in an object-oriented language. However, it is *inclusion polymorphism* which really typifies this style of programming. Inclusion polymorphism supports a style of interaction where one classification can be used in place of another because it exhibits all the behaviour of the target classification. Classifications therefore do not exist in isolation. Rather, they are inter-related through a series of is-a relationships, i.e. classification C_1 is-a C_2 if C_1 exhibits all the behaviour of C_2. This form of polymorphism was discussed in chapter 4 in the context of typing. However, it must be stressed that inclusion polymorphism is equally applicable to other classifications, in particular set and class. In typing, the is-a relationships are often referred to as subtyping relationships. Similarly, in set and class classifications, the is-a relationships are referred to as subset and subclass respectively. In all cases, the is-a relationships provide a partial order over the environment and hence establish a lattice of classifications. This general interpretation of inclusion polymorphism is summarized in Figure 5.4[1].

Abstraction	Is-a Relationship	Resultant Lattice
SETS	SUBSET	SET LATTICE
ADT's	SUBTYPE	TYPE LATTICE
CLASSES	SUBCLASS	CLASS LATTICE

Figure 5.4: Inclusion polymorphism and classification

It is normally expected that object-oriented languages and systems should feature inclusion polymorphism. However, one major question remains, i.e. *how are the relationships between classifications established?* There is a clear choice in object-oriented computing between the following options:-

i) Implicit approach

In this approach the relationships between classifications is implicitly determined from the structure of classifications. Therefore, relationships exist between classifications because they share common behaviour.

ii) Explicit approach

In this approach, the relationships between classifications is specified explicitly by the programmer. Therefore, classifications share common behaviour because they are explicitly created this way.

In both cases, the net result is the same, i.e. one classification can be used in place of another because they are related.

There are advantages and disadvantages to both approaches. With the implicit style of polymorphism, the programmer makes a clear and full statement of the behaviour of a classification and leaves the system to determine inter-relationships. In contrast, in the explicit approach, the programmer makes a statement about the inter-relationships and leaves the system to determine the full behaviour. The former technique has the

---

[1] This interpretation of polymorphism is similar to the generalised view of inheritance described in [Canning89].

advantage that there is an explicit statement of how a classification should behave and this is visible within the program. The latter technique has the advantage that classifications are constructed out of other classifications and hence an element of re-use is possible.

It must be remembered that the above discussion applies to all classifications, i.e. set, abstract data type and class. It may well be that one technique might be used with abstract data types and a second technique with classes. For example, conformance rules illustrate the use of an implicit technique to determine relationships between abstract data types. In contrast, inheritance is an example of an explicit statement of relationships between classes.

One interesting observation is that the implicit approach has similarities with top down design of computer systems whereas the explicit approach mirrors a bottom up approach. In top down design methodologies, it is common that designers describe in full the behaviour of objects without consideration of the implementation. Abstract data types are often used for this process. In bottom up methodologies, however, classifications are created out of existing classifications until a target environment is established. Classes and inheritance are often proposed as an ideal vehicle for bottom up design. Therefore, by implementing both abstract data types and classes in an object-oriented language, it is possible to marry the advantages of top down and bottom up design. An implicit style of polymorphism can be used with abstract data types to preserve the full specification of objects and an explicit approach can be used with classes to introduce an element of re-use. This approach is featured in the language Kitara [Guffick89].

It is also possible to introduce other styles of polymorphism in object-oriented languages and systems. This might be used to enhance inclusion polymorphism or might be implemented as an alternative to inclusion polymorphism. The main alternatives are overloading and parametric polymorphism. These are briefly discussed below (see chapter 4 for more details):-

i) Overloading

With this technique, names can be overloaded to signify different properties, e.g. attributes or operations, in different contexts. Contextual information is then used to resolve the conflict. Overloading is an ad-hoc technique, i.e. it is introduced in an unprincipled way by the programmer. It can actually be shown that most inheritance systems support overloading in conjunction with inclusion polymorphism [Blair89].

ii) Parametric polymorphism

The form of parametric polymorphism most commonly found in object-oriented models is genericity. Briefly, genericity is the ability to parameterize a piece of software with one or more types. The parameterized types can then be used in the construction of the software element. Languages such as Ada and Clu support this form of polymorphism alone. Several other languages use genericity in conjunction with inclusion polymorphism. It should be stressed that genericity is not a replacement for inclusion polymorphism. They both provide different and complementary styles of polymorphism. Genericity provides a short hand way of representing a number of different classifications which share a generic description. In effect, genericity saves the programmer from writing the same descriptor for various uses of a common algorithm, e.g. to represent a stack of integers, a stack of characters, etc. Inclusion polymorphism, in contrast, provides a more general mechanism for expressing relationships between classifications. It is therefore perfectly reasonable to employ both approaches in a particular design [Meyer88].

5.3.3 Interpretation Dimension

The final aspect of object-oriented computing to be discussed is the interpretation dimension. This dimension is responsible for the resolution of polymorphic behaviour. In polymorphic environments, it is possible for an item of behaviour to span many classifications. For example, a *print* operation is likely to have many interpretations in a system.

It is the task of this dimension to determine the precise interpretation of an operation in a specific context. It is therefore necessary to resolve the ambiguity which can exist in a polymorphic environment. On closer examination, this can involve two discrete steps:-

    i)   determine whether an operation is valid in the specific context, and

    ii) determine the precise implementation to be invoked.

The two steps correspond to type checking and binding respectively. Type checking determines whether operations are supported by a particular object and binding locates the correct implementation of the operation.

In both cases, the issue remains of when this interpretation procedure is carried out. Two possible choices exist: the polymorphic behaviour can either be resolved at compile time or run time. This choice applies equally to type checking and binding giving rise to the following decisions:-

    i)   static type checking vs dynamic type checking, and

    ii) static binding vs dynamic binding.

The various combinations of static and dynamic type checking and binding have been discussed in considerable depth in earlier chapters (particularly chapters two and four). Rather than repeat the discussion , we summarise the findings of previous chapters by revisiting the table developed in chapter four (section 4.2.5). This table is shown in Figure 5.5.

	Static Type Checking	*Dynamic Type Checking*
Static Binding	Guarantee of correctness Inflexible interpretation	Invalid combination
Dynamic Binding	Guarantee of correctness Flexible interpretation	No guarantee of correctness Flexible interpretation

Figure 5.5: Combinations of type checking and binding policies

The decisions made at this level can therefore have a significant impact on the characteristics of a system in terms of flexibility and correctness.

5.4 APPLYING THIS DEFINITION

In the introduction, two objectives were set for our definition of object-oriented computing:-

    i) to highlight various design options, and

ii) to provide a framework for reasoned debate about object-oriented techniques.
This section evaluates the model by looking at each objective in turn.

5.4.1 A Design Space for Object-Oriented Computing?

An interesting feature of this definition of object-oriented computing is that it defines a design space consisting of the four dimensions: encapsulation, classification, polymorphism and interpretation. All three dimensions are orthogonal[2] in that independent design decisions can be made in each dimension. It is therefore possible to use this design space in the development of a new object-oriented system or language. This was the approach taken in the design of the Kitara language mentioned above. This view of the definition as a design space is illustrated in Figure 5.5.

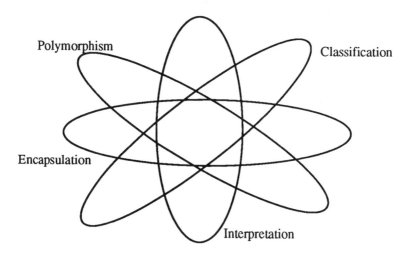

Figure 5.5: Design space for object-oriented computing

The first decision to be made is the range of properties to be supported. This is a case of selecting from the list given in section 5.3.1. Within the same dimension (i.e. encapsulation), it is then necessary to decide on the visibility of the properties and hence determine the external behaviour of objects.

Moving into the classification dimension, the major decision to be made is which classifications should be modeled in the system, i.e. set, type or class. Following this, it remains to decide whether to model both the intent and extent of each classification.

It is then necessary to inject some flexibility into the model by layering polymorphism on top of the various classifications. There are several decisions to be made for each classification, for example:-

i)   what style(s) of polymorphism should be supported?
ii)   if inclusion polymorphism is selected, should the relationships be implicitly or

---

[2] The dimensions may not be completely orthogonal in a mathematical sense. A decision in one dimension is likely to influence decisions in other dimensions. For example, a decision to support abstract data types might suggest the adoption of conformance rules.

explicitly determined?

Finally, there are some crucial decisions to be made in the interpretation dimension. Firstly, it is necessary to decide whether guarantees of type correctness are important and hence whether to support static or dynamic type checking. Subsequently, it must be decided whether to have static or dynamic binding.

Within the design space, there are many significant decisions which can greatly influence the resultant system. Consequently, a huge variety of quite different designs can emerge from this model. Each potential design will exhibit a particular set of properties which can then be matched against the requirements of a particular application area. Therefore, it should be possible to design a model with a specific set of requirements in mind.

Note that all systems which emerge from this process should be considered to be within the domain of interest of the object-oriented community. It is this design space which really provides our definition of object-oriented computing.

5.4.2 Analysis of Existing Systems

The second real test of the definition is whether it supports constructive statements about some of the difficult semantic problems faced in object-oriented computing. It should be stressed at this point that definitive statements on some of these problems is still beyond the state of the art and will await a more complete semantics for object-orientation. However, the definition presented above does provide a framework to clarify many of the confusions in object-oriented computing. This is demonstrated in an informal way by considering twenty questions commonly asked about object-oriented computing.

Twenty Questions

1. *What is object-oriented computing?*
    This chapter proposes that object-oriented computing is best understood as an aggregation of techniques which fit within the design space outlined above. Furthermore, the temptation to place a more rigid interpretation on object-orientation ought to be resisted.
2. *What are the benefits of object-oriented computing?*
    The benefits commonly claimed for object-oriented computing all tend to be manifestations of the benefits of encapsulation, classification, polymorphism and interpretation. These benefits all relate back to the principles of object-oriented computing introduced in chapter one.
3. *Is object-oriented computing a certain frame of mind?*
    The question is often raised of whether object-oriented computing is a completely new model of programming. It is probably more accurate to say that object-oriented programming is a recognition of the benefits of encapsulation, classification, polymorphism and interpretation.
4. *What is an object?*
    An object is any identifiable encapsulation in the system which probably represents a concept in the world being modeled. The task of identifying objects in a particular application of object-oriented computing is fraught with difficulties and is addressed further in chapter 8.
5. *Is message passing fundamental to object-oriented languages?*
    No. Message passing is one possible technique for implementing object-oriented

systems. It is equally possible to adopt other solutions. However, message passing is conceptually a very good way of viewing object-oriented programs.

6. *Is dynamic binding essential?*

Dynamic binding (or the dynamic interpretation of polymorphism) is not essential to object-oriented environments. However, the benefits to be gained from dynamic binding should not be under-estimated (see the discussion in chapter 4).

7. *Is inheritance fundamental to object-oriented computing?*

Again, inheritance is not essential within the proposed definition. Other methods of obtaining polymorphism may be used. However, inheritance has proven to be a very useful technique in many environments and should not be overlooked lightly.

8. *What is the relationship between class and type?*

Class and type are alternative techniques for modeling classification in object-oriented systems. The distinction is that type is solely concerned with the external behaviour of objects whereas class is also concerned with how this behaviour is implemented. Both concepts can co-exist in the same system.

9. *Is static type checking possible in object-oriented languages?*

Yes. It was demonstrated in chapter 4 that it is possible to statically type check object-oriented languages. This can be most satisfactorily achieved by having a clean separation between the concepts of class and type.

10. *What does conformance provide?*

Conformance provides an alternative technique for achieving polymorphism in languages. In contrast with inheritance, conformance is concerned only with the type of an object. Conformance uses this typing information to implicitly derive the subtyping relationships between types. Further details of conformance can be found in chapter 4, section 4.4.2.

11. *What about genericity?*

Similarly, genericity provides a mechanism for implementing polymorphic types. Essentially, genericity allows generic algorithms which can operate across a range of types to be written only once. The same description can then be re-used in several different situations. Again refer to chapter 4 (section 4.4.3) for more information on genericity.

12. *Is Ada object-oriented?*

This is one of the most frequent questions in the object-oriented community, partly because of the interest in Ada in the field of object-oriented design. In short, this is the wrong question to ask. For one thing, it can only have a yes/ no answer which is not particularly helpful. The more interesting questions are concerned with the properties which Ada possesses in comparison with say Smalltalk or Eiffel. Ada certainly provides encapsulation and classification through the package mechanism. In addition, polymorphism is supported through genericity. Therefore, it is right that Ada should be compared with other languages within the object-oriented community. However, there are some limitations to Ada which ought to be pointed out. Firstly, genericity is not a replacement for inheritance or conformance; it is a specific style of polymorphism which helps with the construction of generic modules. Secondly, the resolution of this polymorphism is carried out at compile-time in Ada. This decision sacrifices many of the benefits associated with dynamic binding (see chapter 4). An entertaining discussion of this issue can be found in [Touati87].

13. *Is genericity compatible with inheritance?*

Yes. As mentioned above, inheritance and genericity are different styles of polymorphism which perform different jobs. Inheritance establishes code and behaviour sharing between classes whereas genericity provides a short-hand way of specifying the same algorithm on different types. It would therefore be possible (and probably very sensible) to use both styles in the same language. Similar comments apply to the question of whether genericity is compatible with conformance.

14. *What does enhancement provide?*

Enhancement is an example of a mixing of styles of polymorphism. Enhancement combines aspects of inheritance, conformance and genericity thus combining the benefits from each technique. Enhancement is described in detail in chapter 4, section 4.4.3.

15. *What is delegation?*

In systems with delegation, objects are encapsulated entities as in any object-oriented model. However, objects do not belong to classifications; neither are they created from classifications. Instead, objects exist as self-standing entities and are created using other objects as prototypes (this corresponds to the degenerate form of classification mentioned in section 5.3.2). The technique of delegation is used in such an environment to implement behaviour sharing, but at the level of individual objects (see chapter 3).

16. *How are languages such as Miranda and Hope related to object-oriented computing?*

The answer to this question is that there is a whole range of polymorphic programming languages such as Miranda and Hope which ought to be considered within the object-oriented community. Often the style of polymorphism is different, e.g. Miranda and Hope support parametric polymorphism. However, a lot can be learned from studying such languages. It should also be mentioned that most of these languages also support classification.

17. *What is the relationship between class and set?*

Class and set are alternative ways of modeling classification in an object-oriented system. As mentioned above, a class represents a set of objects which share common behaviour and a common implementation. In contrast, a set is a collection of objects which share some common properties. Set is therefore a much more general concept than class. Sets are commonly used in the object-oriented database community where confusingly they are often referred to as classes (see chapter 7).

18. *What is the semantic data model?*

The semantic data model is a leading data model to emerge from the object-oriented database community. It is based on sets as the unit of classification and exploits set operations such as intersection and union (again, see chapter 7).

19. *Can object-oriented languages be used in a parallel or distributed environment?*

There has been some doubt about whether some object-oriented techniques translate into a parallel or distributed environment. For example, Wegner has stated that inheritance is incompatible with distribution [Wegner87]. However, taking a more general view of object-oriented computing allows other techniques to be explored which might be more suitable than traditional techniques such as class and inheritance. This issue is addressed in detail in chapter 9.

20. *How generally applicable are object-oriented techniques?*

In general, a wider view of object-oriented computing increases the suitability of the techniques for other fields of application. Particular techniques can be employed to meet the needs of a particular application area. The concepts underlying object-oriented computing are more important than specific mechanisms.

5.5 STEPS TOWARDS A THEORY OF OBJECT-ORIENTATION

As mentioned above, a complete understanding of object-oriented computing will only emerge when a full semantic theory of objects is developed. A useful parallel can be drawn from developments in traditional language design. It was only when formal techniques such as denotational semantics [Stoy77] and type theory [Danforth88] emerged that poor design features became apparent and more consistent designs emerged. It is only from a more formal understanding that contradictions and unnecessary constraints can be avoided. Similarly, formal studies often lead to clean and simple constructs and language features.

Object-oriented computing is an area which desperately requires such a formal grounding. Many researchers acknowledge this fact; indeed, there are several significant projects addressing the need for such a formalism [Cardelli84][Cook89]. At present, there are various formal methods which offer promise in this area. However, a complete formalism for object-oriented computing is still several years away. Most of the techniques adopted to date arise from a study of typing. In this section, two such areas are presented. Firstly, *algebraic approaches* to describing the semantics of types are introduced. Some elementary type theory is presented. It is then shown how this can be extended to incorporate object-oriented concepts. Secondly, an extension to lambda calculus, namely *typed lambda calculus* is described. This calculus has proved useful in the study of polymorphism. A more comprehensive study of this area is beyond the scope of this chapter. The interested reader is directed towards the excellent survey by Danforth and Tomlinson [Danforth88].

5.5.1 Algebraic approaches

Most of the formal approaches to describing object-oriented computing have centred on the area of *type theory*. Type theory is an established field of computer science which has made significant advances in describing the semantics of types in programming languages. This section concentrates on one particular algebraic approach to type theory which has been used extensively in explaining object-oriented concepts and terminology.

Basic concepts Intuitively, types can be considered to be *sets* with the set being defined by a particular *predicate* over the environment. For example, the type integer can be considered to be the set of Integers as defined in mathematics. This is an attractive proposition because a theory of types could then be based on the well understood area of set theory. Unfortunately, though, it is incorrect to equate types directly with sets. It is certainly the case that all types define sets of values. In addition, many sets are valid types. However, not all sets can be considered to be types. It is normally expected that types will share a common structure. However, many sets contain elements of completely heterogeneous structure, e.g. the set of objects sitting on a desk. This analysis is reflected in the model introduced in section 5.3. Within that model, sets were described as the most general form of classification with types being defined as particular classifications which *share common behaviour*. It is also incorrect to equate a subset with a subtype [Bruce86]. Again, there is an intuitive appeal to this analogy. However, again, the equation falls down under closer scrutiny. For similar reasons, many subsetting relationships also define subtyping relationships. However, it is incorrect to state that all subsets are subtypes.

It is therefore necessary to provide a more precise definition of type (and subtype). One theory which has been proposed is the view of types as *ideals*. In simple terms, an ideal is a set which exhibits a particular structure. A more formal definition of ideals is given below. First, however, it is necessary to define some terminology.

Definition: Partial Orders

A partial order, $\leq$, satisfies the following on a set S:-

PO_1: $X \leq X \; \forall \; X \in S$ (reflexive)

PO_2: $X \leq Y$ and $Y \leq Z \Rightarrow X \leq Z$ (transitive)

PO_3: $X \leq Y$ and $Y \leq X \Rightarrow X = Y$ (antisymmetric)

$(S, \leq)$ is then called a *partially ordered set* or *poset*.

Note that this is exactly the set of properties described for subtyping in chapter 4. In effect, subtyping provides one example of a partial order over the set of types. The set of integers, Z, together with the usual partial order, $\leq$ (less than or equal to) also forms a poset as does Z together with the partial order 'is a divisor of' (i.e. a $\leq$ b iff a is a divisor of b).

It is now possible to define several important elements in a poset $(S, \leq)$.

Definition: Upper bound and lower bound

An upper bound of the poset $(S, \leq)$ is an element x_u which satisfies the following:-

UB_1: $x \leq x_u \quad \forall \; x \in S$

Similarly, a lower bound of $(S, \leq)$ is an element x_l such that:-

LB_1: $x_l \leq x \quad \forall \; x \in S$

It is important to realize that a set can have more than one upper bound and more than one lower bound. Thus it is important to introduce the concepts of the least upper bound (l.u.b.) and the greatest lower bound (g.l.b.) of a poset. Informally, the least upper bound of a poset is simply the 'smallest' of all the upper bounds. Similarly, the greatest lower bound is the 'biggest' of all the lower bounds. More formal definitions are given below:-

Definitions: Least upper bound and greatest lower bound

Consider all upper bounds of S.

LUB_1: x_{lu} is the least upper bound of a poset $(S, \leq)$ if, whenever x_u is any upper bound of $(S, \leq)$, then $x_{lu} \leq x_u$.

The least upper bound may not exist but if it does it is guaranteed to be unique.

It is also possible to define a greatest lower bound of S as follows:-

GLB$_1$: x_{gl} is the greatest lower bound of a poset $(S, \leq)$ if $x_{gl} \leq x_l$ for all lower bounds x_l.

It only remains now to introduce two very important elements in a poset, namely bottom and top.

Definitions: Bottom and Top

The bottom (or least) element, $\bot$, of a poset $(S, \leq)$ is an element which satisfies:-

B$_1$: $\bot \leq x$ $\forall\, x \in S$

Similarly, the top (or greatest) element, T, of a poset $(S, \leq)$ is an element which satisfies:-

T$_1$: $T \geq x$ $\forall\, x \in S$

The definitions above now lead to the following definition of a *complete partial order*.

Definition: Complete partial order

A complete partial order (c.p.o.) is a poset $(S, \leq)$ such that:-

CPO$_1$: $\bot$ exists

CPO$_2$:   every ascending chain $x_1 \leq x_2 \leq \ldots$ has a least upper bound.

Given the definitions of a complete partial order and least upper bounds, it is now possible to present a definition for an ideal.

Definition: Ideals

An ideal I of a complete partial order D is a subset of D such that:-

I$_1$:   if $x \in I$ and $y \leq x$ then $y \in I$

I$_2$:   for any increasing sequence in I $x_1 \leq x_2 \leq \ldots \leq x_n$,
then the lowest upper bound of $\{x_1, x_2, \ldots, x_n\}$ is in I

Rule I$_1$ introduces the requirement that the complete partial order is *downwardly closed* under $\leq$. In addition, rule I$_2$ checks that the complete partial order has *upward completeness*. The rule for downward closure ensures that approximations of individual elements of a type are also in the type. In addition, the rule for upward completeness ensures that the least upper bound of a subset of a type is also in the type.

As an example, consider the set P which contains $\{1, 2, 3\}$. The following elements form an ideal of P:-

$\{\}, \{1\}, \{2\}, \{1, 2\}$

and hence would be a valid type in this environment. However, if the element $\{1\}$ was removed, then this would not be an ideal because property I$_1$ of ideals would be violated.

Finally, it is important to introduce the concepts of lattice and complete lattice which play an important role in type theory.

Definition : Lattice and complete lattice

A lattice is a poset $(S, \leq)$ such that:-

L$_1$: $\forall\, x, y \in S$ the l.u.b (x, y) and the g.l.b. (x, y) exist.

A complete lattice is then a lattice such that:-

CL$_1$:   T and $\bot$ exist.

Application to Types The concept of ideals is very important in type theory. It leads nicely to the following definition of a type. Consider the set V which is the set of all possible denotable values and a complete partial order $\leq$ defined over V. This defines a complete poset $(V, \leq)$.

Definition : Type

    A particular subset T of V is a type $\Leftrightarrow T$ is an ideal of V.

This leads to the important result that the set of all types (i.e. the set of all ideals of V) becomes a *complete lattice* under the partial ordering of subsetting [MacQueen82]. This finally provides a precise formulation of the concept of subtype:-

Definition: Subtype

    S' is a subtype of T' $\Leftrightarrow$ S' is a subset of T' and both S' and T' *are ideals.*

The theory of types as ideals therefore provides a satisfying formal model of a typing system which closely mirrors the intuitive descriptions provided earlier in this chapter. Types *are* sets of values; however, not all sets are valid types. A set which represents a type must also exhibit the properties of an ideal as defined above. This corresponds to the view that only certain sets with certain structures can legitimately be considered as types. The set of all ideals then form a lattice which denotes the set of all valid types and their inter-relationships (in terms of the partial order). Between ideals, the concept of subtype and subset can be considered to be the same. Note that a type lattice denotes all possible types. In a particular language or system, not all types will have a representation. Thus there is a separation between the abstract world of types as lattices and the concrete world of a particular type system. Further details on the theory of ideals can be found in [Scott76].

Cusack's Model Elspeth Cusack from British Telecom Research Labs used similar algebraic concepts to develop a language-independent model of inheritance [Cusack89]. The work was motivated by the requirements of the International Standards Organization (ISO) in their attempts to develop a general model for Open Distributed Processing (ODP). In the work on ODP, there is a real need for a common framework to explain the various concepts required to model a distributed system. More specifically, there is a growing need to understand fully the concepts underlying object-oriented computing (work on ODP will be discussed further in chapter 9).

    In Cusack's model, objects are considered to be members of a set C. Behavioural relationships between objects are then modeled by the concept of *refinement*, as defined below:-

Definition: Refinement

    A refinement is a relationship between two components in which the first
    component is in some sense behaviouraly compatible with the second.

This definition is deliberately vague and is intended to encompass such notions as specialization, abstract implementation and conformance. In contrast with partial orders, refinement relationships are always reflexive but *need not be* transitive.

    Cusack's model is then as follows:-

    Let T be a non-empty subset of C and let $>$ denote a preorder on T (preorder is
    used in place of partial order because the order need not be reflexive). In
    addition, let $\sim$ denote the equivalence relation induced on T by $>$ (i.e. if $r, t \in T$
    with $r > t$ and $t > r$, then $r \sim t$). Finally, let ref (refinement) denote a reflexive
    relation on C with the property that whenever $a \in C$ and $r, s \in T$ then a ref r and
    $r > s$ together imply that a ref s (1).
    It is now possible to associate with each element t in T a subset class(t) of C:-

class(t) = { c ∈ *C* | for some s ∈ *T*, c ref s and s ~ t }.

It follows that if r, t ∈ *T* with r > t, then class(r) ⊆ class(t) (2).

Condition (1) also ensures that an instance of a class is an instance of each superclass, and that instances of classes can be further refined to produce more instances.

In terms of object-oriented computing, the set *T* is the set of class templates and *C* is the set of all objects. The membership of class(t) is then given by a type statement (class predicate) expressed in terms of a refinement relationship on *C* (ref) and a subtyping relationship on *T* (>) satisfying the condition (1) above. The statement (2) establishes that if one class predicate implies (is a subtype of) a second, then the first class is a subclass of the second class. However, the reverse implication does not necessarily follow. This corresponds to the relationship between class and type discussed above and in chapter 4.

5.5.2 Typed lambda calculus

The lambda calculus was invented in the 1930s by a logician called Alonzo Church [Church41]. However, no real use was found for lambda calculus until the advent of theoretical computer science where it was found to be a valuable tool for describing mathematically the semantics of languages and processes. The lambda calculus can also be considered to be the most basic of all programming languages. Indeed, some programming languages are just 'sugared up' versions of the lambda calculus, e.g. ML [Gordon79] and Lisp [McCarthy62].

Basic Concepts The lambda calculus is based on a generalized interpretation of *functions*. In lambda calculus, a function is interpreted to be some process which receives an input and produces an output. Functions differ significantly from mathematical functions in that:-

i) the arguments to a function can be from any domain, e.g. numbers, characters, booleans or even other functions, and

ii) it is not necessary for all arguments to be present to compute a function.

The basic concepts of the lambda calculus are introduced by a couple of examples.

Example 1: The Identity Function

Consider the identity function, ID, where the output is exactly the same as the input. In lambda calculus, this would be written as:-

$$ID \quad = \lambda x.x$$

In this notation, λ introduces a function. The following symbols (in this case x) then represent *function variables*. The dot then acts as a separator between the input variable and the output expression. Thus, in this example, the output expression is exactly the function variable.

Once a function is established, it is possible to invoke an *application* of the function. For this, it is necessary to supply an *argument*:-

$$ID(6) \quad = (\lambda x.x) \ (6)$$
$$= 6$$

Alternatively, the same function could be applied to a string expression:-

$$ID('Hi') \quad = (\lambda x.x) \ ('Hi')$$
$$= 'Hi'$$

Thus, the basic lambda calculus is *untyped*.

This simple formalism can also be used to capture the semantics of more complex processes. The following example illustrates the use of lambda calculus to formalize data structures (in this case a linked list).

Example 2: Formal description of CONS

It is possible to view the adding of an item (or items) to a list as a function which takes two lists as arguments and produces a new joint list as a result. For example, a CONS function can be defined as follows:-

$$CONS [L_1] [L_2] = [L_1, L_2]$$

where L_1 and L_2 are lists (items can be thought of as lists with length one).

In lambda calculus, this would be expressed as:-

CONS = λhead.λtail.λc.c head tail

This can then be applied as follows:-

CONS [2, 3, Nil] [1]   = (λhead.λtail.λc.c head tail) [2] [3, Nil] [1]
                         = (λtail.λc.c 2 tail) [3, Nil] [1]
                         = [λc.c 2 3 Nil) [1]
                         = [1, 2, 3, Nil]

Introducing Type The untyped nature of basic lambda calculus is a potential drawback. There are many examples of functions which should have restrictions on valid inputs. For example, the function

$$SQUARE = λx.x^2$$

is only valid for types real and integer. Therefore, a typed lambda calculus has been introduced to provide more control over expressions. In typed lambda calculus, the above function could be re-written as:-

$$SQUARE_{int} = λ x^{int}.x^{2(int)}$$

This function is then said to have type *int* → *int* and belongs to the set of all functions of that particular type. In general, a set of *atomic types* are provided, i.e. int, real, bool, etc. New types can be constructed out of existing types via functions. For example, the following are valid types:-

int → bool

int → (int → bool)

(int → char) → (char → (char → bool))

Polymorphic Types Polymorphic types have also been introduced into typed lambda calculus. This greatly extends the usefulness of typed lambda calculus. For example, consider the ID function defined in example 1. In typed lambda calculus, it would be unreasonable to require a new ID function to be declared for each input type. ID can act on all types and produce an output of that type. This can be written in lambda calculus as:-

$$ID_α = λx^α.x^α$$

Therefore, ID takes an input of any type α and returns an output of type α. Strictly, $ID_α$ is said to have type:-

$$ID_α : ∀ α.α → α$$ (for all types α, ID has type α → α)

The above use of the *for all* statement is known as *universal quantification*.

Other forms of polymorphism are also supported. For example, consider the following definition of a function F:-

$$F_{real} = \lambda x.x^2$$

$$F_{char} = \lambda x. \text{ CODE } (x)$$

i.e. if the input is a real number, then the output is its square. Otherwise, if the input is a character, then the output is its ascii code.

In the first case we say F has type

$$F: \exists \alpha . \alpha \rightarrow \alpha \quad \text{(there exists an } \alpha \text{ such that F } can \text{ have type } \alpha \rightarrow \alpha)$$

In this particular case, α is the type real.

Similarly, in the second case, F has the type:-

$$F: \exists \beta \sigma.\beta \rightarrow \sigma$$

i.e. there exist types β and σ such that F can have type $\beta \rightarrow \sigma$. In this example, β is the type char and σ is the type int.

The use of the terminology *there exists* signifies the use of *existential quantification*. Note that in this case, existential quantification models the overloading style of polymorphism.

It is important to appreciate the difference between universal and existential quantification. In universal polymorphism, a function is valid for *all* types. However, in existential polymorphism, the function is valid for one or more *specific* types.

Therefore, polymorphic lambda calculus allows the user to specify which types are applicable in a given context. This is in contrast with untyped lambda calculus where it must be assumed that all types are applicable. However, as described so far, there is still one major limitation: it is not possible to constrain the *range* of types which are applicable. At the moment it is only possible to specify 'for all' types or 'for at least one' type. In order to provide more control, a technique called *bounded quantification* is introduced.

Bounded quantification is very similar to the concept of subtyping and is used to place restrictions on the set of valid types. For example, consider the ID function introduced earlier. It might be that it would be necessary to restrict ID to be valid for integers and respective subtypes of integers. To do this, it is necessary to restrict the 'for all' statement in some way. This is represented in typed lambda calculus as follows:-

$$ID : \forall \alpha < \text{restriction} > . \alpha'$$

This is interpreted as 'for all types α , *such that α satisfies the restriction*, ID has type α'. Therefore, this indicates that the function is valid for all types subject to the restriction. This technique is known as bounded universal quantification, i.e. the universal quantification is bounded or restricted in some way. The restriction can be stated in terms of subtyping. For example, α could be restricted so that only subtypes of integers are considered:-

$$ID: \forall \alpha \leq INT. \alpha'$$

It is also possible to use this technique on the existential quantifier to produce statements like:-

$$G : \exists \alpha \leq INT . \alpha'$$

i.e there is a type α *which is* a subtype of INT such that G has type α' . This is an example of *bounded existential quantification*.

Therefore, polymorphism can be introduced into the lambda calculus using basic universal and existential quantification. Both techniques can be enhanced by bounding the range of types. One of the real benefits of the polymorphic lambda calculus is that it encourages a pure view of polymorphism which is not corrupted by any particular programming language syntax or semantics. Therefore, it is possible to study the semantics of polymorphism in isolation. It can be shown that universal quantification corresponds to parametric polymorphism and that bounded universal quantification corresponds to subtyping. Similarly, it was mentioned above that existential quantification can model overloading. More significantly, it can also be demonstrated that existential quantification can be used to describe abstract data types and information hiding (i.e. it is possible to state that there exists a type such that it has a certain type signature). Bounded existential quantification can then be used to achieve a fusion of data classification and subtyping (for further details of this topic, refer to Cardelli and Wegner [Cardelli85]). Thus, the polymorphic lambda calculus provides a promising technique for describing the semantics of various object-oriented models.

5.6 SUMMARY

5.6.1 General Comments
This chapter has presented a model of object-oriented computing which is intended to encompass all the techniques discussed in the first part of the book. The important feature of this model is that it is based on a design space for object-oriented systems rather than on specific implementation mechanisms. In particular, the model consists of four dimensions, namely encapsulation, classification, polymorphism and interpretation. This more general interpretation widens the scope of object-orientation and includes alternative techniques such as delegation, conformance and genericity. In addition, such a definition encourages debate on the relative merits of different techniques and allows system designers to select appropriate techniques for particular application domains. Such flexibility is crucial if object-oriented computing is to adapt to the many new fields of application.

Object-oriented computing is still a relatively immature and fast developing subject. There is inevitably still a lot of confusion about the merits of different techniques. This chapter has attempted to resolve some of the confusion by discussing some pertinent questions in the light of our definition. In so doing, we hope that we have made some progress towards answering the sorts of questions raised at the end of chapter 4. However, in the long term it is essential that object-oriented computing is given a more formal foundation. It is only then that rich and consistent object-oriented models will emerge. Work on formal models of computing is therefore of the utmost importance. Some important work in this direction was summarized in this chapter. This work has already had an impact on object-oriented computing. For example, the theoretical distinction between set and type and between type and class has certainly contributed to language designs and indeed has heavily influenced the model presented in this chapter. In addition, the typed lambda calculus provides an excellent language-independent framework for studying the semantics of polymorphism. It can only be hoped that further work on formal methods will have similar spin-offs in terms of an understanding of object-oriented computing.

5.6.2 Final Range of Techniques
We conclude part one of the book by presenting the final table of techniques (see table

of the concept of set and subset.

General Approach	Technique	Description	Xref
Encapsulation	Object	encapsulation of data and interface	2.2.1 3.3.4
	Active object	encapsulation of data, interface and autonomous thread(s) of control	3.4
Classification	Classes	groupings based on common specification and implementation	2.3.1 3.3.1
	Prototypes	rejection of classification as structuring philosophy	3.4.1
	Types	groupings based on common specification	4.2 4.3
	Abstract Data Types	groupings based on common operational interfaces	4.4
	Sets	groupings based on common properties	5.3.2
Flexible sharing	Subclassing (inheritance)	inclusion of specification and implementation of one class in another	2.4.1 3.3.2 3.3.3
	Overloading	sharing of method names across specific objects or classes	2.4.5 4.2.4
	Prototyping	inclusion of implementation of one object instance in another	3.4.2
	Polymorphism	sharing of behaviour across multiple objects, classes or types	4.2.4
	Subtyping	inclusion of specification of one type in another type	4.2.4 4.3.3 4.4.2
	Genericity	sharing of implementation across *parameterized* data types	4.4.3
	Enhancement	hybrid approach to sharing	4.4.3
	Subset	inclusion of properties of one set in another set	5.3.3
Interpretation	Static binding	compile time resolution of names in subclass hierarchy	2.5.1 4.2
	Dynamic binding	run time resolution of names in subclass hierarchy	2.5.2 3.3.2 4.2
	Delegation	resolution along delegation paths	3.4.2
	Static typing	compile time resolution of types	4.2
	Dynamic typing	run time resolution of types	4.2

Figure 5.6: Final table of techniques

5.7 ACKNOWLEDGEMENTS

The author would like to thank the John Nicol, Mandy Chetwynd and Alastair Macartney for commenting on early versions of this chapter. Special thanks are also due to Alastair Macartney for help in writing the formal section of the chapter.

REFERENCES

[**Black87**] Black, A., N. Hutchinson, E. Jul, H. Levy, and L. Carter. "Distribution and Abstract Types in Emerald." *IEEE Transactions on Software Engineering Vol:* SE-13 No.: 1, 1987, Pages: 65-76.

[**Blair89**] Blair, G.S., J.J. Gallagher, and J. Malik. "Genericity vs Inheritance vs Delegation vs Conformance vs. . . (Towards a Unifying Understanding of Objects)." *Journal of Object-Oriented Programming* 1989,

[**Borgida86**] Borgida, A. "Exceptions in Object-Oriented Languages." *Proceedings of the Object-Oriented Programming Workshop,* Editor: P. Wegner and B. Shriver, ACM SIGPLAN Notices, October 1986, Vol: 21, No.10, Pages: 107-119. 1986.

[**Bruce86**] Bruce, K.M., and P. Wegner. "An Algebraic Model of Subtypes in Object-oriented Languages." *SIGPLAN Notices Vol:* 21 No.: 10, 1986,

[**Canning89**] Canning, P.S., W.R. Cook, W.L. Hill, and W.G. Olthoff. "Interfaces for Strongly-Typed Object-Oriented Programming." *Proceedings of OOPSLA '89,* Pages: 457-467. 1989.

[**Cardelli84**] Cardelli, L. "A Semantics of Multiple Inheritance." *Proc. Semantics of Data Types International Symposium,* Springer-Verlag, Berlin, 1984.

[**Cardelli85**] Cardelli, L., and P. Wegner. "On Understanding Types, Data Abstraction, and Polymorphism." *Computing Surveys Vol:* 17 No.: 4, 1985, Pages: 471-522.

[**Church41**] Church, A. *The Calculi of Lambda Conversion.* Princeton University Press. Princeton, N.J. 1941.

[**Cook89**] Cook, W. A Denotational Semantics of Inheritance, PhD, Brown University. 1989.

[**Cusack89**] Cusack, E. "Refinement, Conformance and Inheritance." *Workshop on the Theory and Practice of Refinement,* 1989.

[**Danforth88**] Danforth, S., and C. Tomlinson. "Type Theories in Object-Oriented Programming." *ACM Computing Surveys Vol:* 20 No.: 1, 1988, Pages: 29-72.

[**Ducournau87**] Ducournau, R., and M. Habib. "On some algorithms for multiple inheritance in object-oriented programming." *Proceedings of European Conference on*

Object-)riented Programming (ECOOP 87), Editor: J. Bézivin, J-M. Hullot, P. Cointe and H. Lieberman, Springer-Verlag, Vol: 276, Pages: 243-252. 1987.

[Gordon79] Gordon, M.J., A.J. Milner, and C.P. Wadsworth. *Edinburgh LCF*. Springer-Verlag. 1979.

[Guffick89] Guffick, I.M., and G.S. Blair. "Kitara: A Parallel Object-Oriented Language for Distributed Applications." *Proceedings of Conference on Parallel Computing '89*, 1989.

[Horn86] Horn, C. "Conformance, Genericity, Inheritance and Enhancement", Technical Report, Department of Computer Science, Trinity College Dublin, Ireland.

[Lieberman86] Lieberman, H. "Using Prototypical Objects to Implement Shared Behavior in Object-Oriented Systems." *Proceedings of the Conference on Object-Oriented Programming Systems, Languages and Applications (OOPSLA '86)*, Editor: N. Meyrowitz, Special Issue of ACM SIGPLAN Notices, Vol: 21, Pages: 214-223. 1986.

[MacQueen82] MacQueen, D.B., Sethi, R. "A Semantic Model for the Types of Applicative Languages." *Proceedings of the 1982 ACM Symposium on LISP and Functional Programming*, Pages: 243-252. 1982.

[McCarthy62] McCarthy, J., P.W. Abrahams, D.J. Edwards, T.P. Hart, and M.I. Levin. *LISP 1.5 Programmer's Manual*. MIT Press. 1962.

[Meyer86] Meyer, B. "Genericity versus Inheritance." *Proceedings of the Conference on Object-Oriented Programming Systems, Languages and Applications (OOPSLA '86)*, Editor: N. Meyrowitz, Special Issue of ACM SIGPLAN Notices, Vol: 21, Pages: 391-405. 1986.

[Meyer88] Meyer, B. *Object-Oriented Software Construction*. Prentice-Hall. 1988.

[Scott76] Scott, D. "Data Types as Lattices." *SIAM J. Comput. Vol:* 5 No.: 3, 1976, Pages: 522-587.

[Snyder86] Snyder, A. "Encapsulation and Inheritance in Object-Oriented Programming Languages." *Proceedings of the Conference on Object-Oriented Programming Systems, Languages and Applications (OOPSLA '86)*, Editor: N. Meyrowitz, Special Issue of ACM SIGPLAN Notices, Vol: 21, Pages: 38-45. 1986.

[Stoy77] Stoy, J. *Denotational Semantics: The Scott-Strachey Approach to Programming Language Theory*. MIT Press. Cambridge, Mass. 1977.

[Touati87] Touati, H. "Is Ada an Object Oriented Programming Language?" *SIGPLAN Notices Vol:* 22 No.: 5, 1987, Pages: 23-26.

[Wegner87] Wegner, P. "Dimensions of Object-Based Language Design." *Proceedings of the Conference on Object-Oriented Programming Systems, Languages, and*

Applications (OOPSLA '87), Editor: N. Meyrowitz, Special Issue of ACM SIGPLAN Notices, Vol: 22, Pages: 168-182. 1987.

[Weiser89] Weiser, S.P., and F.H. Lochovsky. "OZ+: An Object-Oriented Database System." Object-Oriented Concepts, Databases, and Applications. Editor: W. Kim and F.H. Lochovsky. ACM Press, 1989. Pages: 309-337.

Chapter 6

Programming Languages Based On Objects

Stephen J. Cook
Queen Mary College, University of London.

ABSTRACT *There are many programming languages based on objects, which adopt very different approaches to each of the syntactic, semantic and pragmatic aspects of language design. This chapter illustrates the approaches by describing and comparing some of the more widely-available languages. A framework for comparing and contrasting languages is established and applied to the languages Simula, Smalltalk, CLOS, C++, Objective-C and Eiffel.*

6.1 INTRODUCTION

A variety of programming languages have emerged in both the academic and commercial communities which are said to be object-oriented or object-based languages. The purpose of this chapter is to illustrate the choices which underlie the design of these languages, and thereby to enable the reader to assess them.

An exhaustive and complete comparison of languages based on objects would be a huge undertaking. To make the illustration manageable, this chapter restricts its focus to languages which are readily available in the commercial marketplace and which are intended for widespread use. It assumes that the reader already has sufficient knowledge of programming languages to be able to look at a program in an unfamiliar language and to grasp its structure and general flavour: to be able to recognise the comments, the assignment statements, and the type declarations, for example. It also assumes a basic knowledge of object-oriented programming concepts, which are introduced in the earlier chapters in this book. Many detailed aspects of each language will not be explained, and the reader is referred to the source material for accurate details. The intention is to give a framework within which each language can be set, and to give the reader the context to ask and answer more specific questions.

Section 6.2 establishes the basic framework which will be used to compare the languages. Section 6.3 introduces each language briefly, using the same programming example for each one, and section 6.4 makes a comparison using the framework set up in 6.2. Section 6.5 completes the overview by giving a brief history of the development of the languages, and stating the primary sources of reference.

6.2 FRAMEWORK FOR COMPARISON

It is traditional in language descriptions to deal separately with the form of a language (*syntax*), its meaning (*semantics*), and the origins, uses, effects and environment of a language (*pragmatics*).

6.2.1 Syntax

An important syntactic distinction which is unique to object-based languages is the form of expression used to denote the application of an operation to an object. Some languages adopt a conventional-looking procedure call or function application syntax with an object-oriented interpretation, while other languages turn the expression round the other way, putting the name of the operation after the name of its argument. In this chapter, details of the syntactic differences between the languages being compared are not discussed any further, and the reader is asked to infer an idea of the syntax of each language by studying the programs presented in section 6.3.

6.2.2 Semantics

The semantic aspects of the languages are compared on 11 dimensions, which lay out a space of possibilities within which object-oriented languages may be located. The comparison is categorized by the following sets of questions:

Objects and Values. Do some expressions in the language denote objects and other expressions denote other kinds of values (e.g.numbers, Booleans, functions or records), or do all expressions uniformly denote objects?

Classes and Instances. Do all objects belong to a class? Is the behaviour of each object fully specified by its class, or can instances have behaviour independently of their class? Are classes themselves objects?

Inheritance. What kind of inheritance is provided? How are conflicts resolved?

Self reference. How does the language provide for making reference to the current object?

Type System. Does the language have a type system? Does type-checking take place prior to execution? How expressive is the type system - does it have parameterized types, subtypes, polymorphism? How does the type system deal with inheritance? Does the language distinguish between classes and types?

Object Initialization. What facilities are provided for initializing the state of objects when they are created?

Encapsulation, Scoping and Hiding. Which textual contexts can variables and methods be accessed from? Does the language provide mechanisms for explicitly controlling scope?

Methods, Binding and Polymorphism. Are methods regarded as part of objects, or separate entities? Can methods be overridden when inherited, and what are the rules for doing this? Does the language have virtual methods to enable type-checking?

Control Structure. Are (sequential) control structures built into the language or constructed from lower-level primitives? What facilities for creating control structures are there?

Concurrency. Are objects concurrent? Do they have autonomous action sequences? What is the granularity of concurrency? How is it controlled?

Metalevel Programming. To what extent are the language's features programmed in the language itself? Does it have metaclasses or other kinds of metaobjects?

6.2.3 Pragmatics

The pragmatic dimensions of language design are as varied as the semantic dimensions, although they are generally less precisely defined. For lack of space, this comparison limits itself to touching on the following issues:

Environment. What environments does the language require for development and delivery of code?

Implementation. Is the language interpreted or compiled? How efficient is the implementation? Is there an automatic garbage collector?

Modularity. What unit of modularity is provided? What checking occurs when units are put together?

Error handling. How are run-time errors dealt with?

Methodology. What, if any, kinds of applications is the language specifically aimed at? How is it intended to be learnt, understood and applied?

6.3 THE LANGUAGES

The languages chosen for description and comparison are Simula, Smalltalk, the Common Lisp Object System (CLOS) , C++, Objective-C, and Eiffel. These languages are all commercially available and represent a wide range of design approaches. In this section each language is briefly introduced by means of a small example to illustrate its form, showing how classes and their attributes are written, and how subclasses are created. The example (which is intended to be illustrative, rather than useful or complete) is similar in each case and shows the creation and use of a class of abstract rectangles which can be scaled in size, and a subclass of drawable-rectangles which use a pen object, held as part of the state of the drawable-rectangle, to do the drawing. The example illustrates some of the basic aspects of each language, including class inheritance, object invocation and object initialization.

6.3.1 Simula

Simula is a programming language developed in the late 1960s and intended for system description, simulation and modelling. Simula is a superset of Algol-60, adding the ideas of *class* and *inheritance* to produce a hybrid language which if it were invented today would probably be called Object Algol.

All Simula objects belong to *classes*, and consist of three parts:
- an *identifier* indicating the class of the object;

- a set of *attributes*, which are either *variables* or *procedures*;
- an *action sequence*, executed when the object is created.

Objects are created at run time by a new statement which produces a reference to the new object. Before the new statement completes, the action sequence of the new object is run until it either terminates or relinquishes control. The action sequence part of a Simula object gives it some of the characteristics of an independent active process, while the attribute part gives it the characteristics of a passive data object. Simula objects can be used to fulfil either or both of these roles.

The following Simula code declares a class `Rectangle`, assuming the existence of a class `Point` with real attributes x and y:

```
class Rectangle(origin, corner);
        ref(Point) origin, corner;
begin
    real width, height;
    procedure scale(n); real n;
    begin
        width := width * n;
        height := height * n;
        corner.x := origin.x + width;
        corner.y := origin.y + height;
    end scale;

    comment this part is the action sequence;
    width := corner.x - origin.x;
    height := corner.y - origin.y;
end Rectangle;
```

The attributes of this class are `origin`, `corner`, `width`, `height` and `scale`. The action sequence initializes the local variables `width` and `height` for each new instance of the class. Subsequently the attribute `scale` can be used to change the size of the rectangle.

A subclass of `Rectangle` called `DrawableRectangle` may be created as shown below. This inherits all of the attributes of the class `Rectangle` and adds a `draw` procedure enabling the rectangle to be drawn, using an instance of class `Pen` (whose definition is not shown) which is created in the action sequence.

```
Rectangle class DrawableRectangle(borderwidth);
        integer borderwidth;
begin
    ref(Pen) p;
    procedure draw;
    begin
        p.up; p.moveto(origin);
        p.north; p.down;
        p.turn(90); p.forward(width);
        p.turn(90); p.forward(height);
        p.turn(90); p.forward(width);
```

```
        p.turn(90); p.forward(height);
    end draw;


    p :- new Pen(borderwidth);
end DrawableRectangle;
```

The following program fragment creates and uses instances of the classes `Point` and `DrawableRectangle`:

```
ref(Point) p1, p2;
ref(DrawableRectangle) R;
p1 :- new Point(10.0,10.0);
p2 :- new Point(80.0,80.0);
R :- new DrawableRectangle(p1,p2,4);
R.scale(1.35);
R.draw;
```

6.3.2 Smalltalk

There are two different versions of Smalltalk available commercially, called Smalltalk-80 and Smalltalk/V. The description here relates equally to both of these and the generic name Smalltalk will be used in this chapter unless it is necessary to distinguish between versions.

A running Smalltalk system consists of a set of objects which possess *instance variables* and communicate by sending *messages*. When an object receives a message it executes a *method*. A method is a routine associated with an object which can access and change the object's instance variables, and send messages to other objects. A method always returns a result to the sender of the original message, and this result forms the value of the expression which caused the message to be sent. The ^ sign is used to denote the expression whose value will be returned as the result of a method.

Smalltalk is not a language designed to be written on paper. On the contrary, it is intended to be used in the context of a comprehensive programming environment which provides a wide range of tools for manipulating and understanding programs. Hence any attempt to give the flavour of the language on paper will inevitably miss the point to some extent. However it is necessary for this description to give some paper representation of the language, and the format chosen for the purpose is derived from that which the Smalltalk-80 environment itself uses when creating files. The example shows how a class `Rectangle` is created as a subclass of `Object`, with methods for accessing its `width`, `height` and `origin`, and to `scale` it by a real number; a further subclass `DrawableRectangle` uses an instance of class `Pen` to implement a `draw` method.

```
Object subclass: #Rectangle
    instanceVariableNames: 'origin corner'
    classVariableNames: ''
    poolDictionaries: ''
    category: 'Shapes'
Rectangle methodsFor: 'initialization'
```

```
origin: originPoint corner: cornerPoint
    origin <- originPoint.
    corner <- cornerPoint
```

Rectangle methodsFor: 'accessing'
```
height
    ^corner y - origin y
origin
    ^origin
width
    ^corner x - origin x
```

Rectangle methodsFor: 'scaling'
```
scale: n
    corner <- origin + ((self width*n)@(self height*n))
```

Rectangle class methodsFor: 'instance creation'
```
origin: originPoint corner: cornerPoint
    ^super new origin: originPoint corner: cornerPoint
```

Rectangle subclass: #DrawableRectangle
    instanceVariableNames: 'pen'
    classVariableNames: ''
    poolDictionaries: ''
    category: 'Shapes'

DrawableRectangle methodsFor: 'initialization'
```
borderWidth: anInteger
    pen <- Pen new defaultNib: anInteger
```

DrawableRectangle methodsFor: 'drawing'
```
draw
    pen up. pen goto: self origin.
    pen north. pen down.
    pen turn: 90. pen go: self width.
    pen turn: 90. pen go: self height.
    pen turn: 90. pen go: self width.
    pen turn: 90. pen go: self height
```

The following fragment of Smalltalk code creates and uses an instance of the class DrawableRectangle:

```
| r |
r <- (DrawableRectangle origin:10@10 corner:80@80)
            borderWidth:4.
r scale: 1.35.
r draw
```

141

6.3.3 CLOS

CLOS, the Common Lisp Object System, is an object-oriented extension to Common Lisp. It builds on top of Common Lisp to provide support for object-oriented programming, and is intended to be a standard.

CLOS objects contain slots (another name for instance variables). Methods to act on objects are defined separately from the objects and are accessed by a functional syntax: (f a) denotes applying the function called f to the object called a. To allow different methods to be associated with different objects, CLOS introduces *generic functions*. Each generic function provides an interface to a number of distinct methods, and the method to be invoked is determined by the classes of the arguments to the function. The definition of a method implicitly causes the definition of a corresponding generic function if one does not already exist; however if one does already exist, the new method definition must correspond to the existing function in the form of its arguments.

The following CLOS fragment, which defines a class of rectangles, is exactly analogous to the corresponding Smalltalk fragment in 6.3.2.

```
(defclass rectangle ()
    ((origin :initarg :origin :accessor origin)
     (corner :initarg :corner :accessor corner)))

(defmethod height ((r rectangle))
    (- (y (corner r)) (y (origin r))))

(defmethod width ((r rectangle))
    (- (x (corner r)) (x (origin r))))

(defmethod scale ((r rectangle) (n number))
    (setf (corner r) (make-instance 'point
                          :x (+ (x (origin r)) (* n (width r)))
                          :y (+ (y (origin r)) (* n (height r)))))
       r)
```

The rectangle class declares slots called origin and corner. The :initarg option generates a way to initialize the corresponding slot on instance creation, and the :accessor option generates functions to access the slot for reading and writing. The methods height, width and scale assume the presence of a class point declared as follows:

```
(defclass point ()
    ((x :initarg :x :accessor x)
     (y :initarg :y :accessor y)))
```

The rectangle class is again used as a superclass for a drawable-rectangle class which uses a pen to implement its draw method. The new class has a slot p which can be accessed for reading, using the name pen. This slot is initialized with an instance of the class pen by a special method initialize-instance, which is declared so that it is automatically called by the CLOS framework during the creation of an instance of the class drawable-rectangle. The definition of the pen class is not given.

142

```
(defclass drawable-rectangle (rectangle)
   ((p :reader pen)))

(defmethod initialize-instance :after ((dr drawable-rectangle)
        &key pen-width)
   (setf (slot-value dr 'p)
         (make-instance 'pen :nibwidth pen-width)))

(defmethod drawrect ((r drawable-rectangle))
   (let* ((p (pen r)))
   ;;; which binds p to the value (pen r) for the following
   (penup p) (moveto p (origin r))
   (north p) (pendown p)
   (turn p 90) (forward p (width r))
   (turn p 90) (forward p (height r))
   (turn p 90) (forward p (width r))
   (turn p 90) (forward p (height r)))))
```

After the drawable-rectangle class has been defined, the following expressions may be typed to the CLOS interpreter to create instances p1 and p2 of class point, followed by an instance r of class drawable-rectangle, which is then scaled and drawn.

```
(setf p1 (make-instance 'point :x 10 :y 10))
(setf p2 (make-instance 'point :x 80 :y 80))
(setf r (make-instance 'drawable-rectangle
                  :origin p1 :corner p2 :pen-width 4))
(scale r 1.35)
(drawrect r)
```

6.3.4 Objective-C and C++
Objective-C and C++ are hybrid languages which add object-oriented programming ideas to C, taking very different approaches. C itself is a relatively low-level general-purpose programming language which deals with pointers, integers, and characters, and provides facilities for the definition of higher-level types based on these primitive types and arrays and structures of them. It has a type-checking scheme, but is not strongly-typed in the sense of Pascal or Algol; a C type can be freely converted to another type which has a similar machine representation. C is a small and easily portable language, and produces efficient code for a wide variety of machines. For these reasons, it has become very popular.

Objective-C
Objective-C can be thought of as a cross between C and Smalltalk. It comes in the form of a pre-compiler which takes the Objective-C language as input and produces standard C as output. It introduces one new data type to the C language, the *id* or object identifier. An id is a handle for referring to an object in a *message expression*. Message expressions are adapted from Smalltalk-80. They are enclosed in square brackets, to

143

distinguish them from normal C expressions. Message expressions and normal C expressions can appear interchangeably in an Objective-C program. The resulting ability to program in either style gives the language its particular hybrid quality. The value of a message expression is the value returned by the method invoked, and this can have any type, including all normal C types and type id.

The example program below is the equivalent in Objective-C to the Smalltalk example in section 6.3.2. The similarities between the two languages should be very apparent. In Objective-C, *class declarations* appear after a = sign, *instance methods* after a − sign and *class methods* after a + sign. The points in the example are implemented by a normal C structure, rather than a class, to illustrate the hybrid nature of the language. As with the Smalltalk example, the existence of a Pen class with appropriate behaviour is assumed.

```
typedef struct {float x, y; } point;

= Rectangle : Object {point origin, corner; }

- origin: (point)originPoint corner: (point)cornerPoint
    { origin = originPoint;
      corner = cornerPoint;
      return self; }

- (float)height
    { return corner.y - origin.y; }

- (float)width
    { return corner.x - origin.x; }

- (point)origin
    { return origin; }

- scale: (float)n
    { corner.x = origin.x + ([self width]*n);
      corner.y = origin.y + ([self height]*n);
      return self; }

+ origin: (point)originPoint corner: (point)cornerPoint
    { return ([super new] origin: originPoint
                          corner: cornerPoint); }


= DrawableRectangle : Rectangle { id pen; }

- borderWidth: (int)anInteger
    { pen = [[Pen new] defaultNib: anInteger];
      return self; }
```

```
- (void)draw
    { [pen up]; [pen goto:[self origin]];
      [pen north]; [pen down];
      [pen turn: 90]; [pen go:[self width]];
      [pen turn: 90]; [pen go:[self height]];
      [pen turn: 90]; [pen go:[self width]];
      [pen turn: 90]; [pen go:[self height]];
    }
```

Objective-C, in contrast to Smalltalk and CLOS, is a compiled language and so the definitions in this example would need to be exercised from a complete compiled and linked program with a main body such as the one below.

```
main(argc, argv)
    char *argv[];
{
    id r;
    point p1, p2;

    p1.x = 10.0; p1.y = 10.0;
    p2.x = 80.0; p2.y = 80.0;
    r = [[DrawableRectangle origin:p1 corner:p2]
                            borderWidth:4];
    [r scale: 1.35];
    [r draw];
}
```

C++

C++ is designed to be almost a superset of C, with the addition of facilities for data abstraction and object-oriented programming. C++ allows for the definition of *structures* containing *members*, which may be data items or functions. Structures may be called *classes*, in which case they have both *private* and *public* parts. Member functions may be declared *inline* (possibly causing faster code to be generated), or separately from the class A class may have *constructors*: members having the same name as the class in which they are declared. These provide a concise way of initializing instances.

A program for the rectangle example is given below. In this example an interface to the class pen has been declared, because in C++ it might be difficult to infer from context.

```
struct point
{
    float x, y;
    point(float nx=0.0, ny=0.0){x = nx; y = ny; }
};

class pen
{
    point location;
```

145

```
       float direction;
       int position;
       int nibwidth;
   public:
       pen(int);        //constructor: parameter is nibwidth
       void up();
       void down();
       void north();
       void turn(float);
       void moveto(point);
       void forward(float);
   };


   /* implementations of members for the class pen are omitted */

   class rectangle
   {
       point orig;
       point corn;
   public:
       rectangle(point o, point c)  { orig = o; corn = c;}
                                    // inline constructor
       float height()               { return corn.y - orig.y;}
       float width()                { return corn.x - orig.x;}
       point origin()               { return orig;}
                                    // inline member functions
       void scale(float);           // not inline: defined below
   };


   void rectangle::scale(float n)
   {
       corn.x = orig.x + (n*width());
       corn.y = orig.y + (n*height());
   }


   class drawable_rectangle : public rectangle
   {
       pen p;
   public:
       drawable_rectangle(point, point, int);
       void draw();
   };


   /* using the following syntax, the drawable_rectangle constructor
   forwards its arguments to its parent constructor and to the member p
   */
```

```
drawable_rectangle::drawable_rectangle
    (point o, point c, int borderwidth) : (o, c), p(borderwidth)
{
/* having initialized orig, corn and pen, there is nothing else to
do */
}

void drawable_rectangle::draw()
{
    p.up(); p.moveto(origin());
    p.north(); p.down();
    p.turn(90.0); p.forward(width());
    p.turn(90.0); p.forward(height());
    p.turn(90.0); p.forward(width());
    p.turn(90.0); p.forward(height());
}

main(int argc, char *argv[])
{
    point p1(10,10);
    point p2(80,80);
    drawable_rectangle r(p1,p2,4);
    r.scale(1.35);
    r.draw();
}
```

6.3.5 Eiffel

Eiffel is a compiled object-oriented programming language which provides both multiple
inheritance and static type-checking. Each class has a number of *features*, which may be
attributes or *routines*. Routines may be functions or procedures. All references in Eiffel
have a *type*, and at any time a reference is either *void* or refers to an object of a
compatible type. Each class may define a routine called Create to initialize its
instances.

Once again a program for the example is presented. The interface to the class PEN is
omitted, as it can readily be inferred from the context.

```
class POINT
export
    x, y, add
feature
    x, y: REAL;

    Create(nx, ny: REAL) is
            -- initialize new point
        do x := nx; y := ny end;
```

```
        add(p:POINT):POINT is
        do
                Result.Create(x + p.x, y + p.y)
        end     -- add
end;        -- class POINT


class RECTANGLE
export
    origin, height, width, scale
feature
    origin, corner: POINT;

    Create(o,c: POINT) is
            -- initialize new rectangle
    require
            o.x <= c.x;
            o.y <= c.y
    do
            origin := o;
            corner := c
    end;    -- Create

    height: REAL is
    do
            Result := corner.y - origin.y
    end;    -- height

    width: REAL is
    do
            Result := corner.x - origin.x
    end;    -- width

    scale(n: REAL) is
    require
            n >= 0
    local
            extent: POINT
    do
            extent.Create(n*width, n*height);
            corner := origin.add(extent)
    end     -- scale

invariant
    height >= 0; width >= 0
end;        -- class RECTANGLE
```

```
class DRAWABLE_RECTANGLE
export
    origin, height, width, scale, draw
inherit
    RECTANGLE rename Create as rect_Create
feature
    p: PEN;        -- not exported

    Create(o,c: POINT; borderwidth: INTEGER) is
    do
            rect_Create(o,c);
            p.Create(borderwidth)
    end;    -- Create

    draw is
    do
            p.up; p.moveto(origin);
            p.north; p.down;
            p.turn(90.0); p.forward(width);
            p.turn(90.0); p.forward(height);
            p.turn(90.0); p.forward(width);
            p.turn(90.0); p.forward(height)
    end     -- draw
end;        -- class DRAWABLE_RECTANGLE
```

As Eiffel is a compiled language it is necessary to create a complete program in order to exercise the class definitions. Unlike the compiled languages so far, Eiffel provides no separate concept of a procedure, and the only construct which can be used is a class. The following class MAIN provides what is required. The run-time environment will be told that MAIN is the *root class* of the system and will automatically instantiate it, thereby running the example.

```
class MAIN
feature
    Create is
    local
            r: DRAWABLE_RECTANGLE;
            p1, p2: POINT
    do
            p1.Create(10.0,10.0);
            p2.Create(80.0,80.0);
            r.Create(p1,p2);
            r.scale(1.35);
            r.draw
    end     -- Create
end         -- class MAIN
```

6.4 COMPARISON

6.4.1 Objects and Values. *Do some expressions in the language denote objects and other expressions denote other kinds of values (e.g.numbers, Booleans, functions or records), or do all expressions uniformly denote objects?*

Simula has two kinds of values: firstly references to objects, and secondly those values such as integers, reals, Booleans and Arrays which are supported in the Algol-60 substrate. Smalltalk, on the other hand, has only one kind of value: objects are used to represent every value in the system including numbers, Booleans, control structures and processes, as well as classes. CLOS integrates the object system as far as possible with the Common Lisp substrate, and most values can be treated uniformly as objects. Objective-C and C++ both support all of the values provided by C in addition to a new and separate domain of objects. However in Objective-C there is just one type in this domain, while in C++ the domain of objects is very rich (see 6.4.5). In Eiffel as in Simula, all values are objects except for a limited number of primitive kinds of value (Integers, Characters, Reals and Booleans) which are treated in a more traditional way.

6.4.2 Classes and Instances. *Do all objects belong to a class? Is the behaviour of each object fully specified by its class, or can instances have behaviour independently of their class? Are classes themselves objects?*

In each of the languages being compared all objects belong to a class. Object-based languages in which this is not the case do exist: an example is Object Logo.

Only CLOS allows specific instances to have behaviour independently of their class. This is programmed by defining a method which specializes one or more of its parameters to be a specific object. For example the following code (taken from [Keene89]) defines a method `divide` for use with pairs of numbers, and a more specific method which will be used only if the second number is zero.

```
(defmethod divide ((dividend number) (divisor number))
   (/ dividend divisor))
(defmethod divide ((dividend number) (zero (eql 0)))
   (error "cannot divide by zero"))
```

In Simula, C++ and Eiffel, classes are compile-time entities which act as templates for the creation of objects. In these languages classes have no explicit representation as objects at run time; this means they cannot be passed as parameters or assigned to variables, and they cannot be created dynamically. In Smalltalk and CLOS, classes are first-class objects and can be treated just like any other object, including being dynamically created. Objective-C classes are objects in principle, in the sense that they have a run-time representation, and respond to messages in a very similar way to Smalltalk classes. However, this representation is created statically by the compiler, and Objective-C classes cannot be dynamically created.

6.4.3 Inheritance. *What kind of inheritance is provided? How are conflicts resolved?*
Simula was the first language to provide class inheritance. In Simula the *prefix class* construct allows a class definition to be prefixed with the name of another class,

indicating that the attributes of the prefixed class are to be inherited. Only one class can be prefixed, so Simula provides single class inheritance.

Smalltalk and Objective-C also provide single class inheritance. In these languages, every class has a superclass except class `Object`, which is directly or indirectly the superclass of all other classes. (Smalltalk-80 does provide a simple multiple inheritance system, but this is not well integrated with the environment, contains semantic inconsistencies and is not very effective).

CLOS is a multiple inheritance system, and a class can have several direct superclasses. For each class, all of its superclasses, their superclasses and so on are ordered into a *class precedence list* according to two rules: a class always has precedence over its superclasses; and each class specifies the precedence order of its direct superclasses by the order in which it declares them. If CLOS fails to produce an overall class precedence list according to these rules, it signals an error. If more than one class precedence list is valid, the one which keeps *family trees* of classes adjacent on the list is chosen. When the optimal class precedence list has been computed, it is used to determine the order of specificity of methods, i.e. which methods take precedence when CLOS is computing how to respond to the call of a generic function with particular arguments. CLOS provides various ways of combining methods from the classes on the precedence list (see 6.4.8).

C++ at the time of writing provides single class inheritance, in a manner very similar to Simula. In C++, inheriting classes are called *derived* classes, and the classes they inherit from are called *base* classes. C++ is a rapidly evolving language, and proposals for multiple inheritance are being developed [Stroustrup87].

Eiffel provides multiple inheritance; however, it adopts a different philosophy from that of CLOS. In CLOS, all of the ancestor classes of a given class are ordered into a sequential *list*, and that list is used to decide which methods are applicable in any given case. In Eiffel, the ancestors of a class form a *directed acyclic graph*. Conflicts caused by different inheritable features with the same names are prohibited, causing a compile-time error. An Eiffel class may rename or redefine the features it inherits, and if a different feature with the same name appears in more than one ancestor class, it must be renamed to eliminate the conflict. A feature inherited by more than one path may be inherited many times, by renaming it on one of the inheritance paths. This is impossible in CLOS, which has no concept of an inheritance path.

6.4.4 Self reference. *How does the language provide for making reference to the current object?*

In Simula, Smalltalk, C++, Objective-C and Eiffel there is a mechanism for referring to the object on behalf of which the current method or routine is being executed. In Smalltalk and Objective-C this object is the receiver of the message, and is called `self`. In Simula it is the object possessing the routine, and is called `this`. All Simula references are qualified, and `this` must be followed by the name of the qualifying class, which should be the class of the current object or one of its superclasses. C++ also uses the keyword `this`, but no explicit qualification is needed. Eiffel calls the current object `Current`. In Simula, Smalltalk and Eiffel the name of the current object is a special keyword and does not denote a variable; in particular it cannot be the target of an assignment. In C++ and Objective-C, the name of the current object is simply a special variable, and can be used as the target of an assignment.

151

In CLOS there is no concept of a current object. A method call which in Smalltalk or Objective-C would be written as `obj1 doSomething:obj2`, or in Simula, Eiffel or C++ as `obj1.doSomething(obj2)`, would be written in CLOS as `(doSomething obj1 obj2)`. The status of the object `obj1` in CLOS is simply the first argument to the generic function `doSomething`, and no special mechanism is needed to access it.

6.4.5 Type System. *Does the language have a type system? Does type-checking take place prior to execution? How expressive is the type system - does it have parameterized types, subtypes, polymorphism? Does the language distinguish between classes and types?*

Smalltalk has no static type system at all. As long as a method has no syntax errors and no undeclared variables it will compile, and if there are any type errors they will occur at run time, where Smalltalk provides comprehensive facilities for dealing with errors.

Objective-C does not have any type system for objects. Although C is a typed language, all of the objects added by Objective-C have the single type `id`, and the only type checking that occurs for message expressions is to check that the message recipient is of this type. A major aspect of the Objective-C philosophy is to emphasize in the hybrid nature of the language the distinction between loosely-coupled collections of objects for which no type is known at compile-time, and tightly-coupled collections where the type is known beforehand. Objects are intended to be used for the former, while the latter can be coded up in the C language substrate for additional efficiency.

Simula, C++ and Eiffel are all statically-typed languages, a major design aim of these languages being to be able to pick up type errors at compile-time and eliminate run-time errors as far as possible. Each of these languages identifies the concept of *class* with that of *type*, and *subclass* with *subtype*. If a variable is of a type A, then it may only refer to objects of class A or its subclasses. When a subclass is declared, those of its attributes which redefine attributes declared in a superclass must be declared in a way consistent with the existing declaration. In Simula and C++, this means the overriding declarations must have exactly the same type. In Eiffel, they must have *conformant* types, where *conformance* is a more flexible relationship between types which still allows compile-time checking to prevent run-time type errors.

Of the three statically-typed languages, Eiffel is the only one which provides the kind of parameterized or generic types which are found in languages such as Ada and CLU. An Eiffel class can be declared with type parameters and the parameters subsequently instantiated with any type. Proposals have been made to extend C++ to provide parameterized types [Stroustrup89], although at the time of writing this has not been done.

In Common Lisp all objects have a dynamic type, which can be checked at run-time. It is possible to make type declarations which may be used by the compiler to generate optimal code, but in general no static type-checking is carried out by Common Lisp. In CLOS, a built-in class is provided corresponding to each of the simple Common Lisp types, providing integration between the Common Lisp substrate and the CLOS extensions. However the concepts of class and type are not unified, and declaration of a new class does not create a new type.

Assertions In addition to its type system, Eiffel introduces a framework of assertions: logical statements about the pre- and post-conditions for each routine, overall invariants for classes, and invariants for loops. These assertions provide highly-formalized documentation on the interfaces presented by each component of the program. For example, when a subclass is created, the programmer should be satisfied that it does not violate the class invariant of its superclass, that each of its routines satisfies the pre- and post-conditions of any corresponding routine in the superclass, and that new assertions are made to document fully the interfaces presented by the new class. There is no mechanical checking that the assertions are satisfied; this would require the power of automatic theorem-proving, which is not provided.

6.4.6 Object Initialization. *What facilities are provided for initializing the state of objects when they are created?*

One of the uses of the Simula action sequence is to initialize instances of classes. i.e. to give each of the attributes an appropriate initial value. In Eiffel, instances are created by invoking the `Create` feature of a class. Each Eiffel class has just one `Create` feature, and for object initialization the `Create` feature performs a similar role to the Simula action sequence. However instance initialization is not the only purpose of action sequences in Simula, another being to provide coroutine facilities (see 6.4.10).

In Smalltalk and Objective-C it is normal to provide for each class one or more *class methods* for the purpose of creating initialized instances (the class method `origin:corner:` does this in the example). These class methods send messages to the newly-created instance to ensure it is correctly initialized. The use of class methods allows the provision of several different ways of initializing instances of a class, if this is desirable; this contrasts with the Simula and Eiffel approaches, which provide a single fixed way to initialize instances of any class.

CLOS adopts a different approach. For initializing slots, each slot is declared with certain options, including the ability to initialize the slot with a value either automatically or by means of a keyword parameter to the `make-instance` function. For running more complex code on object creation it is possible to declare an *after method* for the `initialize-instance` generic function. The combination of keyword and default parameters to `make-instance` makes it possible to provide different kinds of initialization for different circumstances.

C++ adopts yet another approach. In a C++ class definition, a member with the same name as the class is a *constructor*: a function which is called automatically whenever an instance of the class is created. For any class, a number of constructor functions may be declared, each taking different types of arguments, providing different ways of initializing instances.

6.4.7 Encapsulation, Scoping and Hiding. *Which textual contexts can variables and methods be accessed from? Does the language provide mechanisms for explicitly controlling scope?*

In Simula there is no distinction between public or private attributes of an objects. If an object a has an attribute x, where x is a variable or routine, the expression $a.x$ can be used to access the attribute regardless of where the expression occurs.

Smalltalk and Objective-C distinguish strongly between the scope of *variables*, which can only be accessed from methods of the object possessing the variable, and the scope of *methods*, which can be accessed from anywhere. Access methods must be explicitly provided to enable variables to be accessed from outside an object. However, variables are equally accessible from methods in the class where the variables are declared, and in its subclasses.

In CLOS, objects are declared as possessing *slots*, another name for instance variables. Slots are normally only accessed by means of *accessors*, methods which are explicitly generated by the options with which the slot is declared. A slot may be given an accessor to read it only, to read and write it, or (rarely) only to write it. Once an accessor for the slot has been declared, it may be accessed from anywhere. There is no way of limiting access to slots to a particular set of methods.

Eiffel controls the scope of access to features by an *export* clause included in the header to class declarations. All features which are to be accessed from outside the class must appear in this clause, which may optionally restrict exports to specific named classes. When an Eiffel class inherits from another, it automatically inherits access to all of the features defined in the inherited class. These may be renamed or redefined in the inheriting class, by means of explicit `rename` and `redefine` clauses in the class header.

C++ provides a number of facilities for controlling in detail the scope of access to attributes of classes from different parts of the program. A C++ class is declared with private and public parts, where the private parts can only be accessed by the *member* functions belonging to the class, while the public parts can be accessed from anywhere. In addition, specified non-member functions may be given access to private parts of classes. These functions are called *friend* functions, and may be globally defined functions or members of other classes. Whole classes may be declared as friends of another class, in which case every member of the friend class can access the private attributes of the befriended class.

Privacy in C++ extends to subclasses as well as client classes. Members of derived classes in C++ do not have access to the private members of their base classes, in contrast to the other languages, which allow full access to inherited variables. Public members of a C++ base class do not automatically become public members of the derived class; the base class must be explicitly declared as public to make this be so.

In most languages it is possible for the experienced programmer to get around the scoping rules by using knowledge of the run-time implementation of objects to access their variables from anywhere in the program, but this is regarded as very poor style except when writing tools like debuggers and inspectors. Smalltalk and CLOS provide facilities to support this type of access in the language itself, while in the other languages it would be necessary to delve more deeply into the implementation.

6.4.8 Methods, Binding and Polymorphism. *Are methods regarded as part of objects, or separate entities? Can methods be overridden when inherited, and what are the rules for doing this? Does the language have virtual methods to enable type-checking?*

In each of the languages Simula, Smalltalk, Objective-C, C++ and Eiffel, attributes (methods, variables, features, routines, procedures and functions) are regarded as *belonging to* objects and their classes, and accessed via the objects they belong to using either message-sending notation or dot-notation. In contrast, as noted in 6.4.4, CLOS methods exist independently of objects, and each CLOS method is regarded as *belonging to* a generic function, which gathers together all of the methods with the same name. All of the methods of a CLOS generic function must have the same parameter-pattern. When a generic function is called, the class precedence list (see 6.4.3) is used to select from its methods those which are applicable to its particular arguments. The rules for method selection are complex and this is not the place to go into great detail. Basically CLOS provides *primary* and *auxiliary* methods. The most specific applicable primary method is used, and a variety of mechanisms are provided to call *auxiliary* methods *before*, *after* or *around* the primary method, as well as providing access to less specific primary methods. The way methods are called for a generic function depends on its *method combination type*, which may be standard, one of a set of provided alternatives, or even user-defined.

In Smalltalk and Objective-C, methods can simply be overriden by methods in subclasses with the same name. Overriden methods can be accessed from the overriding method by using the keyword `super` to stand for the recipient of the message. `Super` is a *pseudo-variable*: a syntactic device which causes method lookup to start in the superclass of the class of the current method.

In each of the statically-typed languages Simula, C++ and Eiffel , it is important to keep in mind the distinction between the *static type* of a reference and the *dynamic type* of the object it refers to, which are not necessarily the same. The rule is that the dynamic type must be a descendant of the static type. With this rule, by inspecting the static type a compiler can determine the legality of access to attributes of the object, as long as the language also enforces suitable restrictions on how subclasses may be declared.

Simula and Eiffel introduce the *virtual* concept (in Eiffel called *deferred*). This feature provides the ability to declare the existence of an attribute in a class, for the purposes of typechecking, but to defer the implementation to a subclass. An example would be the declaration of an abstract class `shape`, intended for use as the superclass for a number of classes representing concrete geometrical shapes such as polygons, rectangles, circles etc. The class `shape` declares a number of *virtual* attributes such as `rotate` and `draw`, with types but no implementations. The *virtual* declarations ensure that these operations can be applied to variables of type `shape` without type errors. Once an attribute has been declared as virtual it can be overriden in subclasses, subject to the type conformance rules (see 6.4.5).

C++ also has virtual members, but their purpose is different. In C++ a member declared as virtual must still be given an effective implementation; the purpose of the virtual declaration is simply to declare that this member is capable of being redefined in a subclass. This makes it easier for the compiler to generate optimal code, because calls on members which will never be redefined can be statically bound, saving some run-time overhead.

6.4.9 Control Structure. *Are (sequential) control structures built into the language or constructed from lower-level primitives? What facilities for creating control structures are there?*

Simula adopts the straightforward conventional control structure of Algol-60, with `if`, `for` and `while` statements. Objective-C and C++ adopt their control structure from the C substrate. Eiffel provides simply `if` statements and a `loop` construct. None of these languages provide facilities other than the conventional ones for creating and encapsulating new control structures.

CLOS adopts its control structure from its parent Common Lisp. In this case the

155

parent language itself provides facilities for packaging control structures, because LISP can be used as a functional programming language in which higher-order functions such as iterators and maps can be programmed. However the ability to create control structures is not related to the object-oriented nature of the language and does not concern us further here.

Smalltalk control structures are created as a fundamental aspect of the object-oriented nature of the language, by sending messages to objects called *blocks*. A block is created by an expression enclosed in square brackets. Once created, the block is available for future evaluation, which occurs whenever it is sent the `value` message. So, for example, the expression

```
incrementBlock <- [i <- i+1].
```

creates a block object containing code to add 1 to the variable `i`. At this stage, the variable `i` itself remains unchanged. Each subsequent evaluation of the expression

```
incrementBlock value.
```

adds 1 to `i`.

Smalltalk block objects are used in conjunction with other objects, notably `true`, `false` and objects representing *collections* of various kinds, to create a wide variety of control structures. For example conditional execution, which in a conventional language would be represented by an if-statement, is implemented in Smalltalk by the message `ifTrue:ifFalse:` sent to the objects `true` or `false` with blocks as arguments.

The Smalltalk class hierarchy has a number of related classes which all inherit from the abstract class `Collection`, and represent various kinds of collection, including `Set`, `OrderedCollection`, `Interval` and `Dictionary`. Each of these is a useful abstraction and is heavily used in the construction of the environment (see 6.4.12). They all inherit a set of methods which take blocks as arguments and which implement various kinds of iteration and mapping. Central to these methods is `do: aBlock`, which is implemented in all subclasses of `Collection` and causes the one-argument block `aBlock` to be evaluated for each element in the collection. So, for example,

```
totalWeight <- 0.
basket do: [:each | totalWeight <- totalWeight+each weight]
```

adds up the weights of the items in `basket`, where `basket` is an instance of some subclass of `Collection`..

New Smalltalk control structures can be created by the programmer and packaged so they can be used with exactly the same status as the structures provided. An article in the August 1981 Byte magazine [Deutsch81] shows how case statements, generators, exceptions, dynamic binding, coroutines and monitors can be programmed using these facilities.

6.4.10 Concurrency. *Are objects concurrent? Do they have autonomous action sequences? What is the granularity of concurrency? How is it controlled?*

In Simula, each object starts life with its own sequence of actions, and continues to run in parallel with other objects until the action sequence terminates, whereupon it becomes simply a data object. As noted in 6.4.6, a simple use of the action sequence is for initializing the state of the object. However Simula was particularly developed with the requirements of discrete event simulation in mind, and for this purpose the action sequence takes on a further significant role. Primitive procedures detach and resume, which suspend the current object and resume a named object respectively, provide the basis for a *coroutine* scheme. A prefix class simulation provides a complete discrete-event simulation framework, with simulated time.

None of the other languages have concurrent action sequences as part of the basic structure of objects. In Smalltalk, C++, Objective-C, CLOS and Eiffel, objects and their methods or routines are essentially passive. In Smalltalk, a class Process provides a way of starting and controlling concurrent processes. These processes all operate in the same space of objects. Any concurrent access to data must be explicitly programmed, and a class Semaphore provides the low-level mechanism for this. As with sequential control structures it is possible to construct and encapsulate high-level concurrent structures in Smalltalk. The work by Bézivin [Bézivin87] shows how this can be accomplished for creating simulations.

None of CLOS, C++, Objective-C or Eiffel define processes as part of the language itself. In each case, processes may be available in the operating environment of the language, in which case the object structure of the languages can be used to encapsulate concurrent mechanisms.

6.4.11 Metalevel Programming. *To what extent are the language's fundamental features accessible from programs? Does it have metaclasses or other kinds of metaobjects?*

Only Smalltalk and CLOS provide systematic metalevel facilities of any kind. Each of the other languages is strongly isolated from its own implementation, and it is not practical in these languages to alter dynamically the interpretation of basic language statements, the inheritance scheme or the behaviour of classes.

In Smalltalk, classes are objects like any other and are created and modified from a running program. The entire Smalltalk philosophy is based on the notion of modifying a running system on the fly, rather than creating a description of a new system and subsequently installing it in a separate environment by means of tools like compilers and loaders. Classes are created, installed and modified dynamically by sending messages to the compiler object. It is feasible to install a modified compiler dynamically, or to create specialized compilers by subclassing. Each Smalltalk class has a *metaclass*; the purpose of these is to provide a place to define methods for the class object itself, for purposes such as object creation and initialization.

Like Smalltalk, CLOS is a dynamic system, and classes, generic functions and methods can be defined on the fly by using defclass, defgeneric and defmethod. CLOS provides specific support for the dynamic redefinition of classes, with a generic function update-instance-for-redefined-class which is called when a class is redefined and its instances need updating. The programmer can supply additional methods for this generic function to specialize it for particular cases.

CLOS provides a level of programming, the *metaobject level*, at which the fundamental behaviour of the language elements themselves can be redefined, for the exploration of entirely new paradigms. There are metaobjects for all of the entities of the system, including classes, methods, generic functions and slots. The behaviour of each of these entities is determined by the appropriate metaobject. Predefined

157

metaobjects include `class`, `standard-class`, `built-in-class`, `structure-class`, `slot-description`, `standard-slot-description`, `method`, `standard-method`, `generic-function` and `standard-generic-function`.

6.4.12 Environment. *What environments does the language require for development and delivery of code?*

Most traditional languages are defined quite independently of the environment in which they are going to be used. The language definition includes the syntax and semantics, but leaves quite open such questions as the nature of the editor, the kind of debugger to be used, or the way of managing dependencies between modules.

In contrast, Smalltalk is a tightly integrated language and environment which has demonstrated many advantages in defining the system as a whole. In the Smalltalk environment there are extensive facilities for classifying, finding, displaying and explaining the code, finding all of the senders or implementors of a particular message, displaying all of the instance variables inherited by a given class, dynamically inspecting individual objects, source-level debugging, and many more. These facilities are essential in understanding the considerable complexities of the system. The Smalltalk language without its environment would be an impoverished tool.

Even though such an integrated environment confers many advantages, none of the other languages are *defined* with one. Eiffel, Objective-C and C++ are currently normally supplied in the context of the UNIX environment, which provides generic tools for many purposes including editing, building, searching through, profiling and debugging programs. Eiffel and Objective-C also come with a limited range of specialized tools; in the case of Eiffel tools for configuration management, debugging, documentation and optimizing; in the case of Objective-C an interpreter and symbolic debugger.

CLOS is a recent development and its definition says nothing about its environment, although it is clearly expected to have one. Present CLOS implementations will adopt the environment from the version of Common Lisp in which they are embedded.

Simula was first developed in the days of batch program development, before programming environments emerged. Recently the Mjølner environment [Hedin88] has been developed, which provides window-based incremental program development facilities for dealing with the Simula language.

6.4.13 Implementation. *Is the language interpreted or compiled? How efficient is the implementation? Is there an automatic garbage collector?*

Simula, Eiffel, Objective-C and C++ are compiled languages, a source text being submitted to a compiler to produce an object module for subsequent execution. Smalltalk lies midway between the conventional concepts of compiled and interpreted, with compilation occurring at the level of methods. Each method, when added to the system, is compiled into a representation which can be dynamically accessed by the dispatch mechanism invoked on each message send. This compilation normally takes a very few seconds and Smalltalk consequently has the *feel* of an interpreted system. CLOS is not defined to be either compiled or interpreted; it adopts the implementation of the Common Lisp system in which it is embedded, which is likely to contain facilities for both compilation and interpretation.

Efficiency and performance are complex questions. One issue which is clear is the ability of a compiler to use static type information to optimize the generated code. The statically typed languages (Simula, Eiffel and C++) are therefore likely to have higher performance for the same algorithms on the same target hardware as the untyped languages (Smalltalk, CLOS and Objective-C). On the other hand this run-time performance is gained at the cost of a greater amount of computation at compile-time, to do the necessary checking and optimization. Overall efficiency, considering all factors from design and conception through to final implementation, is not simply a question of code optimization and many tradeoffs must be taken into account depending on the nature of the overall problem.

Automatic garbage collection, that is the reclamation of storage occupied by objects which no longer have references, is provided by Simula, Smalltalk, CLOS and Eiffel. This facility relieves the programmer from the need to keep track of references within the program and to release the storage space explicitly. Efficient garbage collection schemes for object based languages have developed along with the languages themselves, and the technique of *generation scavenging* [Ungar84] can produce very good results while absorbing only a small percentage of the overall computational load. Objective-C and C++ do not provide automatic garbage collection, and the programmer must take care of storage management explicitly. C++ *constructor* and *destructor* functions, called whenever objects are created and destroyed, can assist with the management of resources.

6.4.14 Modularity. *What unit of modularity is provided? What checking occurs when units are put together?*

In both Eiffel and Objective-C, the unit of modularity is the class. Each class definition occupies a file and is compiled separately. In both cases the compiler checks the interfaces between classes, before producing as output a C file which is then processed using the normal C compilation, linking and loading mechanism.

In C++, the principles of modularity are adopted from C. The division of parts of the program between files is flexible, and governed by a set of practical conventions. The C linker does not do any type-checking, so the conventions are designed to ensure that references between modules are type-consistent, normally by including in each file identical header files containing declarations of shared structures, and allowing the compiler to detect inconsistencies between the included header and the body of the file.

CLOS follows Common Lisp, which provides *packages* for modularizing programs. Packages define bundles of exported symbols which can be accessed from elsewhere by explicitly naming the exporting package. Packages are orthogonal to both files and classes, and provide a separate mechanism for program modularity.

Smalltalk development occurs in the context of a Smalltalk *image*. The image is a memory image of all of the objects and classes in a running program. Each image is progressively modified as the programmer works, eventually converging on the desired behaviour. Parts of images can be shared by means of files ("fileOuts") containing the source code for making changes to the image. However controlling these files is a difficult problem, because such a file makes many assumptions about the image it came from and will only work successfully in an image for which these assumptions are true. Smalltalk provides no mechanism for declaring or checking these assumptions, and this can be a serious bottleneck when using Smalltalk in projects involving more than one programmer.

Simula provides separate compilation either of complete classes or of libraries of procedures. In the base language, predefined modules `SIMSET` and `SIMULATION` provide list handling and discrete event simulation features.

6.4.15 Error handling. *How are run-time errors dealt with?*

The statically typed languages Simula, Eiffel and C++ are designed with the specific intention that run-time errors should not occur. If one does occur, the result is an abnormal termination of the program, probably with the production of a memory image file for debugging, and the programmer is expected to find and correct the error in the source code of the program, using tools provided by the operating system.

In the case of Eiffel, an exception mechanism is included which allows exceptions generated by the underlying system and by the programmer to be handled within the program. Exceptions may be generated in a number of situations, including the invocation of invalid attributes, the violation of assertions, and abnormal conditions in the hardware or run-time system. *Rescue clauses* can be defined to intercept exceptions, and typically will attempt to amend the state of the computation before retrying the routine which caused the exception.

Objective-C follows in the tradition of C, and compiled programs with errors will terminate abnormally. An interpreter for Objective-C is available, and running under this interpreter allows program development to occur in an environment where run-time errors can be handled dynamically.

In the Smalltalk environment, most run-time errors occur when a message for which no method exists arrives at an object. In this case, the run-time system sends a special message `doesNotUnderstand:` to the object receiving the offending message. A method for this message is supplied in class `Object` and understood by all objects; it causes a *notifier* to appear on the screen giving some information about the error, and providing the ability to invoke the debugger. The error can then be found and corrected dynamically.

6.4.16 Methodology. *What, if any, kinds of applications is the language specificau. aimed at?*

Simula was developed particularly to meet requirements for discrete event simulation, and libraries for simulation are an integral part of the language support. It can also be used as a general-purpose programming language, and indeed its object-oriented basis make it quite appropriate for that purpose. However it has been in existence for considerably longer than the other languages described here, and lacks some of the more powerful facilities contained in those later languages.

Smalltalk was developed as the language for the Dynabook, Alan Kay's vision of a hand-held interactive graphics-oriented computer, particularly intended for use by children as a tool for learning. Smalltalk has become too complex for children to understand, but still retains its focus on interactive graphical applications, personal computing and the use of software as a way of exploring concepts. Smalltalk is excellent for individuals working with half-formed ideas, gradually refining and moulding them until they become clear and precise. It does not provide a very suitable environment for the delivery of production versions of the refined ideas.

In contrast, Eiffel is a language specifically designed for the production and delivery of engineered software. The assertions and static type-checking provide redundancy and interface documentation intended to enable the development and reuse of tightly engineered modules. An underlying notion in the language design is *software contracting* - the ability to state accurately the interface of a software module, and to promise that the module will satisfy its interface.

CLOS is a system more in the spirit of Smalltalk, designed for exploratory programming; its roots are in the LISP tradition, and concerned with applications in AI (artificial intelligence). However CLOS does not provide any specific mechanisms for AI applications, and directs itself more to the world of general-purpose programming, this also being the world addressed by C++ and Objective-C.

6.5 HISTORY AND BIBLIOGRAPHY

The history of object-based programming languages started in the late 1960s as Simula was designed by Dahl, Myhrhaug and Nygaard at the Norwegian Computing Centre with the requirements of discrete-event simulation programming in mind. Simula was the first mainstream language to shift the emphasis from what the program is to *calculate* onto what it is to *model*. A good introduction to Simula is the book "Simula Begin" [Birtwhistle79].

Simula was not called an object-oriented programming language by its creators. This terminology appeared in the early 1970s with the development of Smalltalk at the Learning Research Group, Xerox Palo Alto Research Center (PARC). The motivation behind the LRG research was the development of a software system for the *Dynabook*, a personal hand-held graphics-oriented computer proposed by Alan Kay. Smalltalk-72 was the first in a sequence of languages of which the most recent is Smalltalk-80. The latter came to wide notice with the publication in August 1981 of a special Smalltalk-80 issue of Byte Magazine, and in 1983 a set of Smalltalk-80 books appeared [Goldberg83] [Goldberg84] [Krasner83], followed by two commercially-available implementations of the language [Deutsch84] [Caudill86]. Smalltalk-80 is now marketed by the company ParcPlace Systems.

Smalltalk/V, developed by Digitalk Inc, is based on Smalltalk-80 in its conception but has been completely re-implemented and optimized to run on small personal computers, and is now a successful product. The Smalltalk/V programmers manual [Digitalk88] is a good introduction to object-oriented programming in its own right.

Simula also influenced another major development in programming languages, the *abstract data type* languages. Simula, with Algol-68, were the first programming languages to have a general mechanism for the programming of user-defined types, and these ideas were built on in the 70s by Barbara Liskov's group at MIT in their development of CLU [Liskov81]. CLU focussed on the ability to define new abstract data types and to use them in just the same way as the built-in types of the language. It is debatable whether CLU is an object-oriented language; however it is interesting because it was among the first languages to introduce parameterized types and user-defined abstract data types. CLU was one of the primary influences in the development of ADA, the language developed by the US Department of Defense for use in embedded systems. The other main influence on ADA was the procedural language Pascal.

Lisp was introduced by McCarthy in the 1950s, as a very simple language based on

Church's lambda-calculus. Since then there have been many different dialects of Lisp, incorporating a wide variety of programming ideas. Lisp itself could be called a meta-language rather than a language, for this reason. Common Lisp [Steele84] was developed in the early 1980s with the goal of focusing the work of several Lisp implementation groups and producing a common dialect.

Several *object-oriented* Lisp dialects have evolved since 1980. The first major ones were *LOOPS* (Lisp-based Object Oriented Programming System) developed around 1980 at Xerox PARC [Bobrow83], and *Flavors* developed around the same time at the MIT Lisp Machine Group and subsequently at Symbolics Inc. Each of these systems added objects to Lisp with a somewhat different syntax, philosophy and mechanism. LOOPS evolved in 1985 into *CommonLoops*, based on Common Lisp and providing greater integration between the basic Lisp facilities and the added object facilities [Bobrow86]. Meanwhile Flavors was also redesigned to produce *New Flavors* [Moon86]. During 1986 the two groups met to explore combining their designs to produce an object-oriented extension for submission to the working group responsible for the ANSI standard for Common Lisp. The result of this collaboration is CLOS. CLOS is fully documented in the "Common Lisp Object System Specification" [Bobrow88], and a very readable introduction is the book "Object-Oriented Programming in Common Lisp" [Keene89].

From the late 1970s a system of increasing importance was the UNIX operating system, coupled with the C programming language. C was designed and implemented by Dennis Ritchie at Bell Laboratories during the mid 1970s, and has become an enormously popular programming language, falling squarely into the procedural programming tradition. Objective-C was developed around 1983 by Brad Cox at the company Productivity Products International, Inc., now called The Stepstone Corporation. The language and its design rationale, together with many interesting insights into object-oriented programming, are presented in "Object Oriented Programming - An Evolutionary Approach" [Cox86]. C++ was designed between 1980 and 1983 by Bjarne Stroustrup at Bell Laboratories. C++ is fully described in "The C++ Programming Language" [Stroustrup86].

Objective-C and C++ are the two main object-oriented successors to C; there are a few similar developments which have made much less impact. Object-oriented hybrids based on other procedural languages have also been developed, Object Pascal from Apple being notable.

In the mid-1980s two separate streams of development, both rooted in Simula, have intersected again in Eiffel and similar languages like Trellis/Owl [Schaffert86], which couple the expressive modelling power of classes and inheritance (adopted in Smalltalk and pursued in the Lisp-based languages) with the strong type-declaration and type-checking power of abstract data type technology (adopted in CLU and pursued in Ada, and also in functional languages like ML). Eiffel was developed by Bertrand Meyer of Interactive Software Engineering in Santa Barbara, California and is fully described in his book "Object-Oriented Software Construction" [Meyer88], which contains many insights into language design and software engineering.

Simula itself has a natural successor, the language Beta, developed at the Norwegian Computing Center, Oslo and Aarhus University [Kristensen83]. Beta provides a construct called the *pattern* which may be instantiated into objects which possess both attributes and action sequences. Beta has single inheritance, and supports concurrency in various forms.

There is one other main historical stream of development in the object paradigm. In 1977 Carl Hewitt of MIT published a number of papers which introduced "actor systems", a very general model of computation viewed as the concurrent execution of autonomous agents communicating by the passing of messages. This work has its roots in Artificial Intelligence research and is more concerned with the properties of the computational model than with programming language development. It has however impacted programming languages in introducing the ideas of prototypes and delegation as an alternative to classes and inheritance, and in providing an important framework for the investigation of concurrency in the object paradigm. The book by Gul Agha [Agha86] covers the Actor approach. The question of how concurrency and object-orientation co-exist in a language is a fertile research area.

ACKNOWLEDGMENTS

Thanks to Bruce Anderson and Gillian Lovegrove for their comments on earlier versions of this chapter.

REFERENCES

[Agha86] G.Agha, *Actors: a Model of Concurrent Computation in Distributed Systems*, MIT Press 1986.

[Bézivin87] J. Bézivin, "Some Experiments in Object-Oriented Simulation", in OOPSLA'87, *ACM SIGPLAN Notices*, Vol. 22 No. 12, pp. 394-405, Dec. 1987.

[Birtwistle79] G.M.Birtwistle, O-J. Dahl, B.Myhrhaug, K.Nygaard, *Simula Begin*, 2nd Edition, Van Nostrand Reinhold, New York 1979.

[Bobrow83] D.G.Bobrow and M.Stefik, *The Loops Manual*, Intelligent Systems Laboratory, Xerox Corporation, 1983.

[Bobrow86] D.G.Bobrow et al, "CommonLoops: Merging Lisp and Object-Oriented Programmng", OOPSLA'86, *ACM SIGPLAN Notices*, Vol. 21 No. 11, pp. 17-29, Nov. 1986.

[Bobrow88] D.G.Bobrow et al, *Common Lisp Object System Specification*, X3J13 Document 88-002R, June 1988.

[Caudill86] P.J.Caudill and A.Wirfs-Brock, "A Third Generation Smalltalk-80 Implementation", OOPSLA'86, *ACM SIGPLAN Notices*, Vol. 21 No. 11, pp. 119-130, Nov. 1986.

[Cox86] B.J.Cox, *Object Oriented Programming: an Evolutionary Approach*, Addison-Wesley 1986.

[Deutsch81] L.P.Deutsch, "Building Control Structures in the Smalltalk-80 System", *BYTE Magazine*, Vol. 6 No. 8, pp. 322-346, August 1981.

[Deutsch84] L.P.Deutsch and A.Schiffman, "Efficient Implementation of the Smalltalk-80 System", *11th Annual ACM Symposium on Principles of Programming Languages*, pp. 297-302, Jan. 1984.

[Digitalk88] *Smalltalk/V Manual*, Digitalk, Los Angeles.

[Goldberg83] A.Goldberg and J.Robson, *Smalltalk-80: The Language and its Implementation*, Addison-Wesley, 1983.

[Goldberg84] A.Goldberg, *Smalltalk-80: The Interactive Programming Environment*, Addison-Wesley, 1984.

[Hedin88] G.Hedin and B.Magnusson, "The Mjølner Environment: Direct Interaction with Abstractions", *Proceedings of ECOOP'88*, Lecture Notes in Computer Science No. 322, Springer-Verlag, 1988.

[Keene89] S.E.Keene, *Object-Oriented Programming in COMMON LISP*, Addison-Wesley 1989.

[Krasner83] G.Krasner (editor), *Smalltalk-80: Bits of History, Words of Advice*, Addison-Wesley, 1983.

[Kristensen83] B.B.Kristensen, O.L.Madsen, B.Møller-Pedersen and K.Nygaard, "Abstraction Mechanisms in the Beta Programming Language", *Proceedings of the Tenth ACM Symposium on Principles of Programming Languages*, Austin, Texas, 1983.

[Liskov81] B.Liskov et al, *CLU Reference Manual*, Lecture Notes in Computer Science No. 114, Springer Verlag, 1981.

[Meyer88] B.Meyer, *Object-Oriented Software Construction*, Prentice-Hall, 1988.

[Moon86] D.A.Moon, "Object-Oriented Programming with Flavors", OOPSLA'86, *ACM SIGPLAN Notices*, Vol. 21 No. 11, pp. 1-8, Nov. 1986.

[Schaffert86] C.Schaffert et al, "An Introduction to Trellis/Owl", OOPSLA'86, *ACM SIGPLAN Notices*, Vol. 21 No. 11, pp. 9-16, Nov. 1986.

[Steele84] G.L.Steele Jr, *Common Lisp: the Language*, Digital Press, 1984.

[Stroustrup86] B.Stroustrup, *The C++ Programming Language*, Addison-Wesley, 1986.

[Stroustrup87] B.Stroustrup, "Multiple Inheritance for C++", *Proceedings of the EUUG Spring Conference*, Helsinki, May 1987.

[Stroustrup89] B.Stroustrup, "Parameterized Types in C++", *Journal of Object-Oriented Programming*, Vol. 1 No. 5, pp. 5-16, Jan. 1989.

[Ungar84] D.Ungar, "Generation Scavenging: A Non-disruptive High Performance Storage Reclamation Algorithm", *ACM SIGSOFT/SIGPLAN Practical Programming Environments Conference*, pp. 157-167, April 1984.

Chapter 7

Object-Oriented Database Systems

John A. Mariani
Lancaster University

ABSTRACT *This chapter introduces the rationale behind the move towards object-oriented databases (OODBS) through the need for enriched semantics. It also outlines some terminology and describes the model for OODBs. An in depth consideration of the underlying support architecture required for the model, with respect to two particular areas, is given. A brief outline of persistent programming is presented, and the appendix describes the features of a number of OODB programming languages.*

7.1 INTRODUCTION

Object-oriented databases (OODBs) are systems which allow the storage, retrieval and manipulation of objects. Objects consist of attributes (or instance variables as they are referred to in object-oriented programming languages (OOPLs)) and methods, and can be interrelated through relationships. It is possible to build complex objects. In this chapter, we aim to give a comprehensive introduction to OODBs, including their terminology, underlying architectural support, and what is meant by persistent programming. The growth of interest and research activity in this single area of object-oriented computing is so vast, it is quite impossible to provide full coverage within a single chapter. Instead, we hope to provide a reasonably high-level view of what OODBs are, why they exist, and how they can be brought into existence.

In order to understand the increase of interest in OODBs we must differentiate between two quite distinct areas of database application. The first is straightforward data processing; this involves the processing of large amounts of static data of which the classic example is that of pay-roll programs. Once the initial data analysis has been completed and the large files of records set up, the structure of the database tends to be fairly static. If they do change, they will change very slightly and may entail system unavailability for a finite and acceptable time (for the application). Conventional database models continue to provide adequate support for such applications and have countless satisfied customers. The second area involves data and process intensive applications; these are situations where the data and the programs which manipulate them are heavily intertwined and both the structure of the data and programs will be subject to frequent alteration. An example of such an application would be an engineering design environment.

The ability to evolve and to maintain complex objects has resulted in OODBs attracting the very clientele that has been dissatisfied with conventional database models. Needless to say, OODBs have to perform the functions expected of conventional databases: they must provide persistence of data, sharing of data, and protection of data, and they must have acceptable levels of performance.

Who are the clients of OODBs? They come from application areas which require complex and evolutionary sets of data office information systems, knowledge based systems, CAD/CAM design systems, program support environments, and the like. If we consider design systems as a particular example [Zdonik,88], conventional DBMSs are simply not satisfactory for supporting them. Zdonik et. al.'s work has targeted the problems of supporting design systems, and features of the systems they produce specifically address these problems. Design environments have the following characteristics

- objects are built from other objects e.g. modules, sub-modules, books, chapters, sections, paragraphs etc.
- the process is inherently iterative as the design evolves; conventional DBs are "brittle" and do not cope with evolution easily
- they need multiple levels of abstraction consisting of multiple components and need to be able to look into these components
- the design task is shared amongst several designers. Designers will be modifying a certain part of the design and referring to the surrounding parts; there is a need to share component designs, and also to note that this sharing follows a certain pattern.

The rest of this chapter is structured as follows: in the next section, we concentrate on the area of semantics and semantic support for data. We hope to show the pressures that have brought a move away from conventional DB models and towards the development of semantic-rich OODBs. In section three, we give definitions and examples of OODB terminology that will be used in the remainder of the chapter. In section four, we detail some of the features we would expect of an OODB. Section five gives some detail on the underlying architecture required to support OODBs. A brief introduction to the idea of persistent programming is given in section six, and a summary is made in section seven. Section eight acts as an appendix and describes some of the OODB languages that end-users might expect to see.

7.2 DATA SEMANTICS

In the 1970's, Codd [Codd,70] revolutionized the database field with the introduction of the Relational Model. The model is based on set algebra, and gave the field a strong mathematical footing. Whereas the previous "big two" models, the hierarchic and the network model, seemed to follow slavishly the underlying physical model of the stored data, the relational model offered logical data independence.

In the years between the introduction of the model and its successful implementation, the model was used to assist in the analysis of data that would eventually be stored in hierarchic or network databases (today, the major commercial relational systems are Ingres, Oracle and IBM's DB2). The continuing commercial success of such systems is testimony to the acceptability of the model by a large number of satisfied customers. However, the relational model has failed to exploit any semantics inherent in the data.

Consider the following simple example which defines a relation

EMPLOYEE (name, age, gender, street, town)

From this relation, we can extract smaller relations (using the relational *project* operator) that can then imply that streets have genders and towns have ages (quite young ages!). What is needed, therefore, is some mechanism which allows us to define the permitted and sensible relationships. We also need to specify the *cardinality* of a relationship (one-to-one, one-to-many, many-to-many). The process of normalization, which produces minimal sets of relations by removing redundancy, requires this kind of support.

7.2.1 General Properties of Semantic Data Models

In an attempt to represent semantic structure in the data, a number of models have evolved. Increasing the semantic properties of the relational model is an area addressed by Codd himself as early as 1979 [Codd,79] and is the subject of on-going research (an excellent review of which can be found in [Gardarin,89]). Other DB models were introduced in an attempt to increase the semantics of data; various attempts include a classic paper by [Abriel,74], the Entity-Relationship (ER) model [Chen,76], and the Semantic Database Model [Hammer,81]. Before exploring the latter two, it is beneficial to cover some general properties of these models.

Semantic data models support the following four abstractions: generalization, aggregation, classification and association [Peckham,88].

Generalization/specialization In this, we have one of the most powerful tools for conceptual modelling -- after all, it underlies the process of abstraction. Consider the following

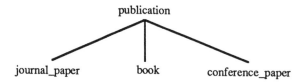

Figure 7.1: Generalization/specialization

In this example, a publication is a generalization of a journal paper, book and conference paper; conversely, a book is a specialization of a publication. You can form a generalization by considering a set of objects and, ignoring their differences, bring together their similarities, i.e. a publication will have a title and an author, whether it is a book or a paper.

Aggregation is the grouping of attributes into a relation (or fields into a record). For example, an aggregation of a TITLE and an AUTHOR forms a PUBLICATION

Publication (Title, Author).

Classification A collection of entities forms a higher-level object class. For example, we could introduce a new class BEST_SELLING_BOOKS, which consists of all BOOKS with sales greater than 10,000. An entity would be given this type if it has sales greater than 10,000. Thus, the object GONE_WITH_THE_WIND is an instance of the class BEST_SELLING_BOOKS.

Association The "is member of" relationship. The set DATABASE_BOOKS is an association of BOOK entities, as is the set AI_BOOKS. This is based on some predicate, for example if BOOKS has a topic attribute, then the DATABASE_BOOKS set consists of books that have topic = DATABASE. Consider the set of GOOD_BOOKS; this is a set whose membership is decided by the end-user, rather than the schema designer.

Classification and association appear similar given these two examples, because the results of these operations are both groups of BOOKS. To differentiate, consider the formation of a group of things which can go faster than 30 m.p.h. on land. This group would contain all sorts of land vehicles i.e. cars, trucks, motor bikes etc. but also animals such as cheetahs. This is another example of association. Thus, the result of a classification is a group of entities of the same type, while the result of an association is a group of entities with the same or different types.

Classification allows us to classify an entity when it is connected with the relevant type i.e. when the entity is created; association allows us to form sets of related objects.

Database schema should be based on abstract entities; we must be able to describe entities, their attributes, relationships among entities, collections of entities and structural interconnections among the collections.

As a lead up to O-O models for databases, in the next two sections, we examine two models -- the Entity-Relationship model, and the Semantic Database Model.

7.2.2. The Entity-Relationship Data Model
[Chen,76]'s Entity-Relationship data model, as its name suggests, offers two primary

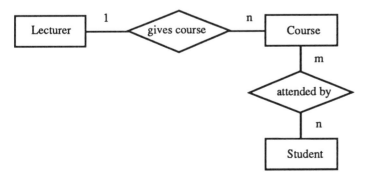

Figure 7.2: ER diagram

169

constructs, the entity and the relationship. Data is viewed as a collection of entity and relationship types, represented graphically. Entities are represented as rectangles, and diamonds represent relationships. Lines between entities and relationships are annotated by a number, indicating how many entities are involved with a single instance of a relationship (the relationship's cardinality).

For example, Figure 7.2 tells us one lecturer can teach many courses, and that many students can attend many courses. The ER model can be annotated by ovals giving the attributes of an entity.

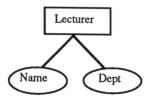

Figure 7.3: Entities and attributes

Figure 7.3 shows that a LECTURER entity has two attributes, a Name and a Dept.

Not only entities can be given attributes; relationships themselves may possess attributes. Consider the following.

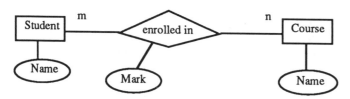

Figure 7.4: Relationships and attributes

Here, it is the relationship "enrolled in" which has the mark achieved by the student in the particular course. In this case, the attributes held by "enrolled in" represent intersection data. Of the four main semantic abstractions, the original ER model supports only aggregation (although there are more recent extensions to the model). The ER model is covered here to show the potential of treating relationships as entities in allowing them to have attributes; this is an area we will return to later.

7.2.3. The Semantic Database Model (SDM)
SDM came about as a realization that conventional models have limited semantic expressiveness; as they are unable to capture knowledge of the application area, they will inevitably lose information. The structures conventional models support are essentially record-oriented, and the record construct is significantly limited for expressing semantics. To this end, SDM views a database as a collection of entities. Entities are organized into meaningful collections called **classes**. Classes can be logically related by interclass connections. Entities and classes have **attributes** which describe their characteristics and

relate them to other entities. Attributes can be derived from other values in the database.

Each class has a set of attributes. An attribute has a name which is unique within the class's environment; it can have multiple synonymous names. Every attribute has a value which can be an entity or a set of entities. The value is extracted from a value class, which contains the permissible values of the attribute. This is analogous to an enumerated type in Pascal or to the domain of a field in the relational model. Attributes, as stated earlier, can belong to individual members or to the class as a whole. Attributes can be specified as single valued (at most one), multi-valued or mandatory (at least one); they can also be specified as not changeable. It is possible to derive the value of an attribute.

For example, take the following portion of a SDM definition for a university; in particular, a class called STUDENT. Like all classes, it has at least one name (STUDENT) although synonyms are allowed. Each class in SDM is a homogeneous collection of one type of entity. Each class has an optional textual class description; in this case, the class STUDENT should consist of all the students registered at the university. A class has a collection of attributes; there are two types of attribute -- member attributes and class attributes. A member attribute is an attribute that every entity belonging to the class must possess, i.e. every student has a name and a college. A class attribute is one that belongs to the class taken as a whole.

```
STUDENT
    Description:  all students registered with the University
    Member attributes:
        Name
                Value class:  NAME
                Not changeable
                May not be null
        College
                Value class:  COLLEGE
        Courses
                Value class:  COURSE
                Multivalued


COURSE
    Description:  all courses offered by the University
    Member attributes:
        Title
                Value class:  COURSE_TITLE
                May not be null
        Lecturer
                Value class:  LECTURER


LECTURER
    Description:  all lecturers working at the university
    Member attributes:
        Name
                Value class:  NAME
                Not changeable
                May not be null
```

```
Age
        Value class:   INTEGER
        May not be null
    Subject
        Value class:   SUBJECT
Class attributes:
    Average Age
        Value class:   INTEGER
        Derivation   average of all ages across all lecturers

SCIENCE_LECTURER
    Description:  all lecturers working at the University involved in
science.
    Interclass connection:   subclass of LECTURER
        where (Subject = Physics) or (Subject = Chemistry)
```

Note that the class attribute Average_Age of LECTURER is derived from the age attribute of all LECTURERS. Figure 7.5 represents the definitions above in a simple diagrammatical format. In (a) we can see the inter-object references which link individual students and lecturers via courses, while (b) represents the class of LECTURER and the sub-class of SCIENCE LECTURER.

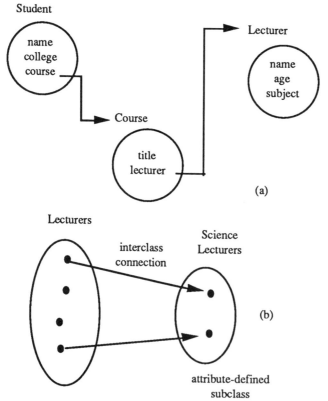

Figure 7.5: SDM definitions as a diagram

As stated earlier, the ER model supports only the abstraction of aggregation. SDM uses the four basic abstractions plus derivation, and is therefore a much more powerful model.

A class can be considered as a base or a nonbase class; a base class is independent of all other classes, and can be thought of as modelling a primitive entity. A nonbase class is defined in terms of one or more other classes, and is constructed using interclass connections. One type of connection is the subclass connection, and there are two ways of specifying such a connection. One is to associate a predicate on the member attributes of the superclass to specify which elements of the superclass are members of the subclass. Consider the subclass SCIENCE_LECTURER. This consists of all LECTURERS who teach physics or chemistry. Another technique is to allow the user to "manually" add/delete members to the subclass, i.e. the class BOOKS and the (user-selected) subclass GOOD_BOOKS. It should thus be seen that SDM's subclassing operation is used to support **generalization**. SDM also allows the use of set operations to define subclasses; we can apply intersection, union and difference to existing classes to form new classes.

SDM offers a grouping connection, whereby we can form groups based on an underlying class. For example, we can form a class LECTURER_SUBJECTS based on LECTURER where they are grouped on common values of "subject". The members of LECTURER_SUBJECTS are not lecturers, but groups of lecturers. We could use this technique to build classes of CHEMISTRY_LECTURERS, PHYSICS_LECTURERS etc. and then use set operators to union CHEMISTRY_LECTURERS and PHYSICS_LECTURERS into SCIENCE_LECTURERS. This ability to construct new types, the value of which is a set of objects of a particular type, is an example of **association**.

SDM is seen by many as the underpinning for OODBs. For example, the generalization mechanism is implemented through inheritance, and aggregation can be seen as the collection of attributes into an object.

7.3 SOME TERMINOLOGY AND DEFINITIONS

7.3.1 Sets, Types and Classes
We must now address the issue of terminology. Below, some informal definitions are given of the terms to be used in the remainder of this chapter. While this is a very brief section, the on-going discussion and controversy continues in the literature (and can be found in other chapters of this book) and cuts across all aspects of object-orientation.

Types Types allow us to define the structure and behaviour of an object. If object X is of type Pen, we know what to expect of X; we know what it looks like, we know how to inspect and set its values, we know what it can do. In this respect, we view types in this sense as the same as types in programming languages.

Sets A set is a collection of objects. If a set consists of objects of only one type (i.e. Pencils is the set of all pencils in the system) then they can be thought of as analogous to a relation (from the relational model referred to earlier). On the other hand, it is to be encouraged to have sets consisting of non-homogeneous objects. To borrow Cox's favourite example of a PencilCup [pp 60, Cox, 86], this is a container sitting on a desk, and can contain pens, pencils, scissors, etc.The description of such an object is made simple through the use of sets.

Beech points out most strongly that types are not sets. As he states [Beech,88] , "All objects "know" what types they are, i.e. this is regarded as intrinsic to them, but they do not necessarily "know" of which combinations they are members".

Classes This is the single most confusing term. Smalltalk 80 uses classes in the same way as our earlier description of types, as in programming languages. Classes in SDM are collections of objects of homogeneous type, i.e. LECTURERS and SCIENCE_LECTURERS, which we might term as sets. In an attempt to avoid further confusion, we will avoid the term class wherever possible.

7.3.2 The Definition of an Object

An object consists of a set of attributes and methods. Methods are groups of instructions which reference the attributes. Objects can be interrelated through relationships. The attributes, methods and relationships belonging to an object define that object type. At this level, a type can be viewed as a template for objects; objects are instances of a given type (or of given types). Objects have a unique unchanging identity, often referred to as the ID. The attributes and relationships (the state) of an object may change with time, but its identity will not. Moreover, an object is never identified by its state, but only by its identity. Below, we give the definition of a type PERSON.

```
type PERSON
      name:  STRING;
      birthdate:  DATE;
      gender:  BOOLEAN;
instance_method:
      age (): INTEGER; /* uses birthdate and today's date
                          to calculate age */
type_method:
      average_age(): INTEGER; /* uses all instances of
                                 type PERSON's age to
                                 calculate average age */
```

7.4 OBJECT-ORIENTED DATABASES

An OODB allows us to store, retrieve and manipulate objects. The schema of an OODB is represented by a collection of type definitions.

7.4.1 Inheritance

One of the main semantic abstractions is generalization/specialization, which we have already defined. In OODBs, inheritance is the mechanism used to pass on the properties (attributes and methods) of a general type to a more specific type. The inheriting type is referred to as the **subtype**.

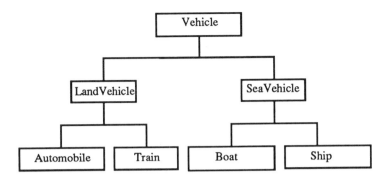

Figure 7.6: Inheritance hierarchy

In figure 7.6, we can see that LAND VEHICLE and SEA VEHICLE are subtypes of vehicle. Any attributes which belong to a vehicle also belongs to land and sea vehicles. The root of the hierarchy represents the most general type, with the leaves more specific types. The structure formed by inheritance is called the inheritance hierarchy. Returning to our earlier example, to specify the type EMPLOYEE, all we have to do is define the difference between employees and people (i.e., what do employees have that people do not?).

```
type EMPLOYEE
inherits PERSON
     employer:   FIRM;
     manager:   PERSON;
     national_insurance_number:   NI_NUMBER;
     salary:   INTEGER;
```

Any object of type EMPLOYEE also has the properties of PERSON; we can therefore legally refer to EMPLOYEE's name, age, gender, etc.

What about the type IBM_EMPLOYEE? Or OLD_AGE_PENSIONERS? Here again, the type vs set confusion rears its ugly head. Is IBM_EMPLOYEE a set or a type? IBM_EMPLOYEE is a subset of EMPLOYEE where employer = IBM; similarly, OAP is a subset of PEOPLE where ((age >= 60) and (gender = female)) or (age >= 65). One argument runs as follows; if OAPs are those elements of type PERSON who meet the boolean qualifier shown above, then they should be considered as a subset. If they have an attribute pension_amount, then OAPs must be a subtype because it has an extra attribute.

7.4.2. Multiple Inheritance

Increasingly more systems support multiple inheritance; a type can inherit the properties of more than one supertype. An example from [Banerjee,87] is presented in figure 7.7.

Instead of an inheritance hierarchy, we now have a network (or type lattice). This example raises a number of problems. If someone refers to a submarine's size, which size do we use? In the absence of more sophisticated semantics, we can view this as a graph-traversal problem, and choose the one that we meet first in the traversal algorithm, i.e. the one on the left-hand side (following the path motorizedVehicle and

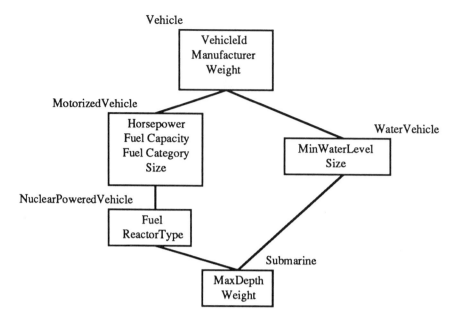

Vehicle

MotorizedVehicle

WaterVehicle

NuclearPoweredVehicle

Submarine

Figure 7.7: Multiple inheritance

`NuclearPoweredVehicle` (NPV)). The diagram assumes that NPV is listed as the first of Submarine's superclasses. This implies that the order of inheritance takes on a meaning; we can change the ordering of the graph by changing the ordering of the branches. The ORION system described in [Banerjee,87] offers the user two ways of by-passing the above convention and organizing multiple inheritance as they see fit

      a) the user can override the graph-traversal rule and specify inheritance of `WaterVehicle.size` as opposed to `MotorizedVehicle.size`.

      b) the user can inherit one or more instance variable/methods which have the same name and rename them within the new class i.e.

`WaterVehicle.size => CrewSize`
`NuclearPoweredVehicle.size => size`

7.4.3. Schema Evolution and Version Control

Schema information is meta-data; data about the data. We can think of it as a road map, and the data itself as the road. Traditionally, meta-data has been stored separately and treated specially. As [Oxborrow, 88] indicates, such a separation is unnatural; the integration of meta-data and data with uniform access is desirable to ease the problems of schema evolution. This orthogonality of treatment is carried very far in the ENCORE [Zdonik,85a,85b] system (parts of which will be considered in a later section). Two binary relational systems, ASDAS [Frost,81] and the Fact machine [McGregor and Malone,81], store schema information (referred to as rules in the Fact machine) along with the data. Any mechanisms applicable to the data can also be used on the meta-data. Logic-based systems such as Prolog support this concept, as a Prolog program is a collection of facts and rules.

      Version control is a necessary aspect of data processing systems, and OODBs are no different. Version control in ENCORE is handled by using a type called History-Bearing-Entity (HBE), which defines all the operations and attributes needed. Any type T which requires version control is defined to be a subtype of HBE and instances of T inherit the attributes previous-version, succeeding-version, and member-of-version-set. However, the fact that schema alterations are supported (and perhaps even encouraged in some circumstances) results in version control problems. Not only do we need to maintain versions of the data, but also of the schema. Old versions of the data will almost certainly be inconsistent with the current version of the schema; we cannot hope to find our way around the old roads (the old data) with a map showing the new roads (the current schema).

OODBs find application within areas that require complex data and evolutionary schemas. [Banerjee et al,87] give a taxonomy of schema changes (and the semantics of those alterations) supported by their ORION system. The multiple inheritance structure is a directed acyclic graph (DAG); similarly in the ENCORE system, the nodes in an inheritance structure represent types and the DAG is viewed as a type lattice [Skarra,86]. The main evolutions allowed can be briefly described as

* changes to the contents of a node, i.e. adding, deleting or modifying instance variables/methods; could arise when we discover a type requires an additional attribute, i.e. an Employee requires a telephone number. Conventional systems like dBaseII require us to recompile the whole database to achieve this. The dynamic applications OODBs cater for would find this an unacceptable option.

* changes to an edge, i.e. add or delete a type, or move a type to a new position in the type lattice; could occur if we change the inheritances. For example, we might introduce a further supertype, or delete an existing one, or change the order of supertypes. This last is important where the system has made a default selection of clashing attributes according to some rule based on ordering (as in ORION itself).

*changes to a node; occurs if we add, delete or change the name of a type.

In ENCORE, a class object represents a set of objects. Each class object has an associated predicate which defines the members of the class. These predicates form constraints on a type's class for containment by its superclasses and subclasses. (Earlier we described a subtype; if we return to figure 7.6, a Land Vehicle is a subtype or subclass of Vehicle; similarly, a Land Vehicle is a supertype or superclass of Automobile). The constraints essentially define a domain of values for an attribute to store. ENCORE thus faces the additional problem of evolution of these constraints.

The effects of evolution of the instances of type are readily seen; if the type changes, and the type acts as the definition of the instances, then the instances may be affected. Subtypes will be affected, as instances of subtypes are also instances of the type through inheritance or type/subtype matrix. There are type changes which can render instances of the type illegal, i.e., information stored in an instance will become missing, garbled or undefined according to the new type definition. If the new type has its properties rearranged, instances of the old type are garbled. These kinds of restructuring operations (addition, deletion and modification of properties) can also result due to type movement within the type lattice. If the ENCORE constraints have been altered, then illegal values may be stored.

Changes in type definition may also affect users of the instances; a program may attempt to access non-existent properties or to use values no longer within the domain of the property, as defined by the constraints. A program written according to the new interface may attempt to access a property which does not belong to the old instance. Conversely, a program written according to the old interface may attempt to access a property which has been deleted from the new instance.

As a crude example of the above, consider the following Person object

```
name:   array [ 1 .. 10 ] of character;
age:  0..99
gender:  character
```

Considered as a stream of bytes, this Person can be laid out in store as follows

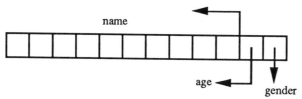

Figure 7.8: An object laid out as a byte stream

and now take an instance as an example

```
name:=  "Moira      "
age:=  21
gender:= "F"
```

If the order of attributes is altered to, say, age, gender and name, then a new program reading an old instance will consider the first two characters of a name to be age and gender (i.e. age is "M" and gender is "o"), and the remainder as the name (the last eight letters of the real name with age and gender appended i.e. "ira   \21F"). This means an old instance is garbled. If we remove an attribute (say age) then the age of an old instance will be interpreted as the gender.

The domain problem can be broken down into the reader's problem and the writer's problem. Consider the domain of Colours. If we have Red, Green and Blue, but now widen the domain to include Octaroon[1], an old program may read an unknown value from a new instance. Conversely, if we began with Octaroon included, but now decide we no longer believe in Magic and remove it thus narrowing the domain, a program using the new type definition may read a value from an old instance which is now outside the legal domain (and perhaps considered to be unknown).

If a constraint is relaxed (resulting in a wider domain), a program using the new type definition may attempt to write an illegal value to an old instance. Conversely, if a constraint is strengthened (resulting in a narrower domain), an old program may fail in trying to write a value to a new instance.

[Skarra and Zdonik,86] recognize the existence of two groups of database objects

---

[1] the colour of Magic,[Pratchett,83]

affected by a type definition change. Objects of the type (and its subtypes) are dependent on the type definition for their implementation and interpretation. Objects such as application programs that use objects of the type (and its supertypes) are dependent on the interface defined by the type. The problems thus face instances and users of instances.

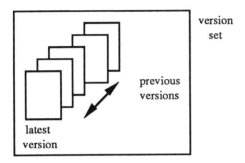

Figure 7.9: A version set

Instances are handled by providing a version set, which is an ordered collection of all incarnations of a particular object. It is possible to randomly or sequentially access members of a version set; one member of each set is designated as the current version. When a new type is created, a new version set is also created and initialized with the type's original definition; as the type is modified, a new version is added for each modification; when the type is deleted, so too is the version set. New versions of subtypes are automatically created and added to the corresponding version sets. All versions of a type remain instantiable and modifiable until deleted.

An instance of an object is bound to a single version of a type; its properties are defined by that one particular version of that type.

Users of instances face interobject errors which can be detected by either the object itself or the program using the object. When a program references a property undefined by the object or supplies a value outside a constrained domain, the object can detect the error. If an object returns a value outside the domain expected by the program, the program detects the error. These errors occur because an object is strictly bound to a single version of its type.

Different versions of the same type may provide different interfaces. However, if an abstraction of the interface defined by a type over time were available an object could be used as if it were bound to the type rather than to a single version of the type. As long as

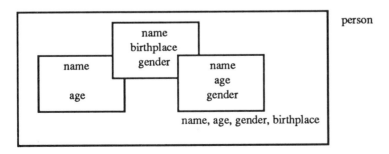

Figure 7.10: A version set of attributes and the interface

names of properties were unique and constant across all versions of the type, objects of different versions could be used interchangeably by programs. This concept is supported by a version set interface (see Figure 7.10).

The version set interface of a type is an inclusive summary of all the type's versions. Every property defined by a version of the type and every value declared as valid for a property is represented in the version set interface. Such an interface establishes a standard interface for all instances of a type, regardless of their version. The interface is the union of all version definitions for properties, and the constraints are the widest allowable (i.e. the least constrained domain). Nevertheless, to cope with the problems of reading/writing values outside the particular domain of a version, the system proposes error handlers that can be added to versions of a type for properties and domain values defined in the version set interface but not in the version's particular interface.

The success of the mechanisms outlined depend on an incremental evolutionary development of the type lattice rather than wholesale revolutionary changes, i.e. to use an example from [Skarra and Zdonik,86], from a frog to a prince.

7.4.4. Storing Relationships

There are four ways of storing a relationship between two objects.

(a) The first object may contain a reference to the second object within itself as an attribute. This is the approach taken in the example of a type PERSON shown below. Instances of type PERSON will store a reference to another instance of type PERSON as the value of their "married_to" attribute.
(b) The second object may contain a reference to the first.
(a) + (b) Both objects contain a reference to each other.
(c) The relationship itself can be modeled as an object. This is exactly the situation in our earlier ER example of the grade relationship between a student and a course.

Below, we augment our PERSON to use the (a)+(b) approach to represent "married_to" and to use the (a) approach to representing children.

```
type PERSON
    name:  STRING;
    birthdate:  DATE;
    gender:  BOOLEAN;
    married_to:  PERSON;
    children:  PERSON; /* can be multivalued
                        i.e. zero or more */
instance_method:
    age () integer; /* uses birthdate and today's date
                        to calculate age */
type_method:
    average_age(): integer;
```

We may choose to represent the spouse relationship as an object (option (c) above); this allows us to store some additional attributes referring to the relationship.

```
type MARRIED_TO
    spouse_one, spouse_two:   PERSON;
    wedding_day:   DATE;
    divorced_day:   DATE;
instance_method:
    years_wed():  INTEGER;
    husband(), wife():   PERSON;
        /* by accessing the gender attribute of spouse_one
              and spouse_two, we can implement these methods */
```

In Meyer's [Meyer,88] terminology, we are not inheriting the type PERSON when we use it as above; rather, the type PERSON is a client object of the type MARRIED_TO.

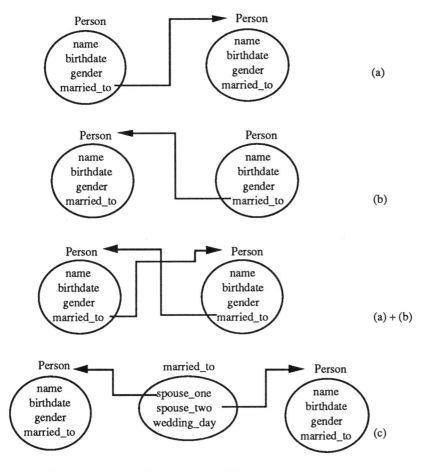

Figure 7.11: Representation of relationships

We can represent this as an (incomplete) ER diagram, as illustrated in Figure 7.12 below.

181

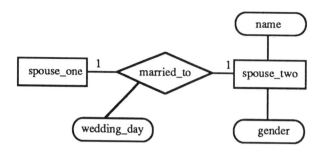

Figure 7.12: ER diagram of married_to relationship

7.4.5. Complex Objects

There are certain application areas -- such as those listed earlier, e.g. office information systems, CAD/CAM systems -- which require the representation of complex objects. Among the classic examples is parts explosion, where we must represent some object (an aeroplane wing, a car engine) as being composed of parts and composite parts, which in turn are composed of parts and composite parts, etc.

Consider the representation of a structured object -- specifically, a book -- in the relational model

```
BOOK (BOK#, PROPERTIES, ...)
CHAPTER (CHA#, BOK#, PROPERTIES, ...)
PARAGRAPH (PAR#, CHA#, PROPERTIES, ...)
SENTENCE (SEN#, PAR#, PROPERTIES, ...)
```

This can be shown diagrammatically as follows

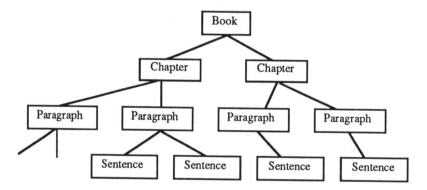

Figure 7.13: The hierarchic composition of objects

This illustrates how a single real world object (a book) becomes fragmented across a number of relations. The main problem with this approach is the retrieval of entire complex objects. At this point, it is worth introducing the relational integrity rule known as *referential integrity*, which can be defined as follows

If a base relation R2 includes a foreign key FK matching the primary key PK of

182

some base relation R1, then every value of FK in R2 must either (a) be equal to the value of PK in some tuple of R1 or (b) be wholly null (i.e., if FK is a multi-attribute key, each attribute must be null).

With respect to the above example of Figure 7.13, if a PARAGRAPH is held in a CHAPTER identified by CHA_4 (say), then the CHAPTER relation MUST hold a tuple with CHA# = CHA_4, as in Figure 7.14. If such a CHAPTER tuple does not exist, then we will be unable to find the PARAGRAPH. Without appropriate checking, we could register a PARAGRAPH as residing within a non-existent CHAPTER.

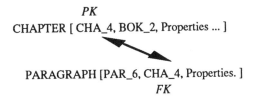

PK
CHAPTER [CHA_4, BOK_2, Properties ...]

PARAGRAPH [PAR_6, CHA_4, Properties.]
                    FK

Figure 7.14: Primary and foreign keys

This problem cannot arise within OODBs, due to the concept of object identity. For example, if a person tuple consists of the following fields

                PERSON(first_name, last_name, PROPERTIES)

and the primary key is (first_name, last_name), then if the person marries and changes last name, we have a different tuple, and in the name of referential integrity, we must update every appearance of this primary key as a foreign key.

Contrast this with the object situation as illustrated in Figure 7.15, where we only have to change the state of the object concerned (i.e. last_name); all other references to that object are made by its OID and do not require alteration.

Notice how the provision of the underlying concept of object identity allows us to

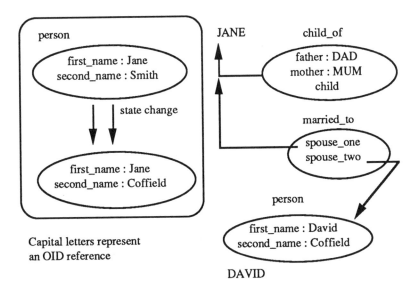

Figure 7.15: Object identity and state changes

handle the complexity of object structures intuitively; we can model the structure directly as follows

```
type BOOK
    name:   STRING;
    chapters:   type CHAPTER
        name:   STRING;
        paragraphs:   type PARAGRAPH
                            sentences:   type SENTENCE
                                            text:   STRING
                            end SENTENCE;
        end PARAGRAPH;
    end CHAPTER;
end BOOK;
```

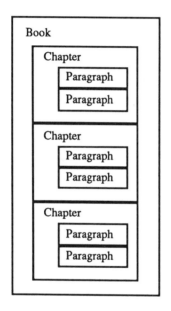

Figure 7.16: A thin tome

7.4.6 Type and Set Based Retrieval

The hierarchic diagram presented in figure 7.7 is enough to cause palpitations of the heart for those of us who remember the navigation-based query languages of the hierarchic and network models. The relational model freed us from those terrors with the powerful associative retrieval abilities of the relational calculus and algebra.

It is possible to use navigational techniques with the object model, and in many cases, this is highly desirable, as such abilities match quite readily with modern presentation techniques such as hypertext. However, this author would hate to see a return to navigational QLs. As we have tried to show, type methods allow us to compute values based on all instances of a given type, e.g. what is the average weight of all pencils known to the system? We can also have QLs (such as OSQL, supported by Iris) which allow relation-like queries. Equally important, however, is the ability to compute values based on membership of a set, e.g. what is the total weight of this PencilCup? Both forms of query should be supported, and preferably with the same syntax.

7.4.7. Remarks

Integrity constraints The example of married people leads us to a consideration of integrity constraints. When we add a new "married_to" object, how can we ensure that the spouses are of different gender, as required by law? The TAXIS semantic data model (as described in [Peckham,88]) supports preconditions (called prerequisites) which must evaluate to **true** in order for the operation to proceed. The action of recording a marriage would have the precondition that the spouses involved are of different genders

```
prerequisite
    different_genders?:
        (spouse_one.gender != spouse_two.gender)
```

Intensional and extensional facts Just as in conventional programming languages, we can implement a result-returning operation as a function or a table look-up (array access) i.e.

```
x := times2(5);      /* function call */
x := times2[5];      /* table look-up*/
```

Methods and attributes can be thought of in the same way:

```
sex := david.gender; /* table look-up */
age := david.age();  /* function call */
```

It can be argued that programming languages need the syntactic difference to remind the user of the cost of the operation chosen, but perhaps in an OODB we could use similar syntax. In fact, we are aiming at a PROLOG situation where a rule or a stored fact is written in exactly the same manner [Beech,87].

Schemas for OODBs are defined by introducing a group of types; generalization is supported by single and/or multiple inheritance. Manipulation of the types and the inheritance structure provides schema evolution; this presents us with a set of problems in the area of version control, which we have outlined and addressed in this section. OODBs are being used in applications where complex objects are used; if there is an additional need for distributed access to (portions of) these complex structures, we have some further issues of underlying support, and these are addressed in the next section.

7.5 UNDERLYING SUPPORT ARCHITECTURE

Section 7.4 explored the object-oriented database (OODB) model, its expected behaviour and the ramifications thereof; in this section, we examine the underlying support required for OODBMS (OODB Management Systems). The issues considered include distribution, transactions and the storage of complex objects.

Three systems are considered: ObServer [Skarra,87], the Object eXchange Service [Pathak,88] and, very briefly, Iris [Fishman,87], [Fishman,88]. In [Skarra,87], emphasis is placed on the management of transactions; in [Pathak,88], the emphasis is on the management of objects. We address both these considerations here, citing the approaches reported in the above papers in order to present a fuller coverage of the situation.

7.5.1. The Iris System Architecture

Chapter 13 of this book examines this system in depth. It is sufficient to consider the high-level architecture here with the aid of a diagram.

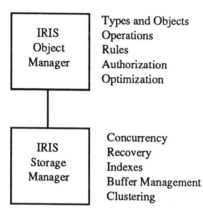

Types and Objects
Operations
Rules
Authorization
Optimization

Concurrency
Recovery
Indexes
Buffer Management
Clustering

Figure 7.17: Object manager layered on storage manager

It is interesting to note that (currently) the storage manager is a conventional relational storage subsystem. We leave detailed discussion of the Iris Kernel architecture to chapter 13.

7.5.2 Storage and Distribution of Objects: OXS and EXTOR

[Pathak et al.,88] describe an Object eXchange Service (OXS) and an EXTernal Object Representation (EXTOR) aimed at supporting the Zeitgeist distributed object-oriented database. EXTOR is the common representation which allows information to be stored on disk and shared among a network of machines, while OXS is a service which, using the concepts of object boundary, global objects and object closure, provides the exchange of information using EXTOR.

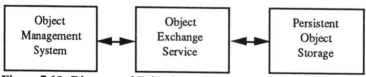

Figure 7.18: Diagram of Zeitgeist architecture

Zeitgeist, like the work described in [Skarra,87], provides transactions involving persistent objects to support cooperative design applications. We shall see later, in our discussion of transactions, how this particular domain can effect our handling of transactions.

Diskable and Transportable Representation of Objects EXTOR and OXS Any
system addressing the problems faced by Zeitgeist must resort to the translation of an in-
store object to a representation (for example, a byte stream) which can be easily stored
onto and retrieved from disk, and transmitted across networks. The EXTOR of any object
is an array of 16-bit elements, a linearized representation of the object in virtual memory
with type information encoded. Complex objects can be built up by allowing objects to
contain references to other objects within them, often with the use of an OID. In the
linearization process, EXTOR handles such object references using a **long pointer**,
which is an OID.

The conversion of an in-store object to a diskable representation is potentially a
costly operation in terms of efficiency; however, EXTOR is designed to preserve the
structure of an object's memory image form. As a result, the recreation of an object from
its disk representation does not incur high performance penalties.

The EXTOR of an object consists of a set of data types and values; some are
primitive types (numbers, characters and character strings), and some are composite
types (lists, symbols, arrays, records, functions and abstract data types). EXTORs also
contain relative and named references, which allow intra- and inter-object sharing.

As an example, consider the following declaration of an EXTOR array object

```
type StarFleetPersonnel
    age:   INTEGER;
    name:  (surname:  STRING, initials:  STRING);
    ship:  SHIP;
```

and an instantiation

```
(34,  ("Kirk",  "J.T."),  ENTERPRISE);
```

We can show this diagrammatically as follows

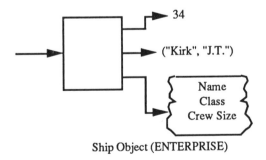

Ship Object (ENTERPRISE)

Figure 7.19 An EXTOR array object

The external representation of this array object is shown in figure 7.20 and can be
interpreted as follows. At word 0 (zero), we have the header. Word one contains header

187

information about the object; words two to four contain objects (or values) themselves (i.e. Kirk's age held at word two) or relative references to objects (i.e. the list object and ship object referred to at words three and four respectively). The two elements of the list are referenced at words five and six, with the actual values held at words seven and nine. Lastly, word eleven contains an external reference (an OID) to the ship object.

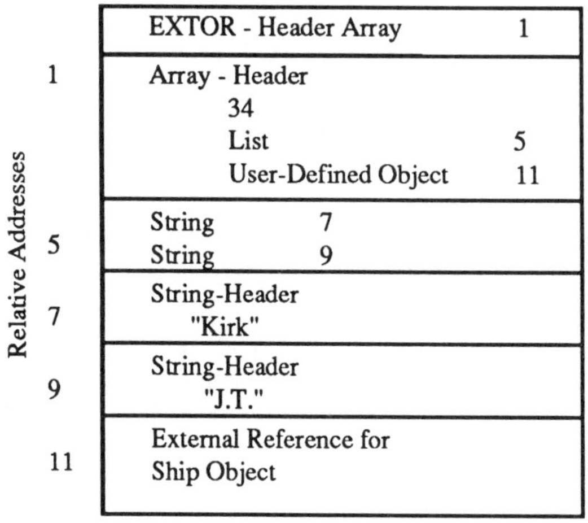

EXTOR - Header Array	1
Array - Header	
34	
List	5
User-Defined Object	11
String	7
String	9
String-Header	
"Kirk"	
String-Header	
"J.T."	
External Reference for	
Ship Object	

(Relative Addresses marked at 1, 5, 7, 9, 11)

Figure 7.20: The external representation of figure 7.19

When we consider the distribution of EXTOR objects, however, we find a number of other problems. Complex objects will contain many references to other objects. In order to linearize such an object, we may have to perform a transitive closure, causing us to access every object in memory. This problem is addressed by **object boundary and closure**. It is the responsibility of the OXS to provide the mechanisms for object boundary and object closure.

The object boundary gives the granularity of an object which can be handled by transport, locking, clustering, etc. Transporting an aircraft object in a CAD environment conceptually involves a closure of the aircraft object, bringing in wings, landing gear, etc. However, the object boundary (defined by the application) may indicate that components such as wings are separate objects to be referenced within the EXTOR as a long pointer. Object boundary is determined by three rules: sharing, potential sharing and size. Potentially shared objects are identified by heuristics; shared and potentially shared objects are automatically separate objects; and large objects are treated as separate objects, for network performance reasons.

Object closure is used to decide how much of an object should be restored (from its EXTOR) when requested by a user. Do we restore just the object itself, its first level closure, or its complete closure? A system-wide integer is used as the object closure level; by default, it indicates a firstlevel closure policy, although this can be tuned.

When a user accesses a reference to an object which is not in-store, this causes **object faulting**, and the required object is then fetched from disk and restored.

7.5.3. Transaction Support: ObServer

We turn now to the ObServer [Skarra,87] system for its treatment of distributed transactions. ObServer is a server which manages persistent objects in an object-oriented database system. A client interacts with the server during a session, and within a session by transactions. A transaction is a series of messages between client and server and is atomic and non-nested.

As with the Zeitgeist work, ObServer is aimed at supporting design applications. This has an effect on the requirements for transaction support. In addition to the traditional shorter transaction, long, interactive transactions must be supported. Efficiency of file access and interprocess transfer of objects had to be optimized. ObServer is used to underlie two distinct object-oriented systems: ENCORE, a database system, and GARDEN, an interactive programming environment. As both these systems have their own type systems, ObServer had to be able to cope with objects of arbitrary type.

ObServer provides two concurrency models one, serializable, is achieved using standard two-phase locking with read and write locks. The other, cached, also uses two-phase locking but read locks are not required for a read. Two novel lock types, notify and writekeep, are used to increase the availability of shared objects and decrease the IPC cost of committing a transaction. However, the cached scheme shifts some responsibility for maintaining atomicity to the client.

The cached model results in objects being transferred between processes only when they have been modified by one client and are needed by another. Rather than a read lock by a reading process, the process requests a notify lock. The server then sends a notify message every time a notify locked object is modified by a committed transaction. The reading process can then request an updated version of the object from the server.

A writekeep lock is used by a client in order to keep a written object beyond the point of transaction commit rather than return it to the server when it is not in demand. A client wishing to modify an object initially obtains a write lock; at transaction commit, it may ask the server to convert the lock to a writekeep lock; the system then keeps the object rather than return it to the server. The client may continue to modify the object in subsequent transactions. However, should another client request a copy or to lock the object, the server sends a message to the writekeeping client to return the object.

The cached model is especially appropriate for collaborative designers who are working on separate but related components. Each designer is only working on a small part of the design, and can obtain write/writekeep locks on those components they are modifying, and notify locks on any related components. Components need only be returned to the server when they are finished with or another designer needs them, therefore writekeep locks enhance performance. However, associated with the model is the risk that serializability and atomicity are not guaranteed. This is partially because we can notify lock an object, use the values within it to modify a further object, and commit the transaction before receiving a notify message from the server telling us the values of the first object have changed.

Storage of Objects: ObServer Every object stored has a 32-bit OID. Objects are stored using three files: the entity, index and log files. The log file is used to maintain consistency during transaction commit. The entity file contains the objects; the index file contains an entry for each object in the entity file that was written by a committed transaction. Index entries are organized sequentially by OID, and consist of the entity file

189

location and size of the object. Thus, only one file access is required to find the location of the object and one more to retrieve the object itself.

All objects sent to the server by clients are entered to the entity file; objects are written to the file according to a best-fit algorithm operating on a free-space list, and not to their old locations. This means that objects returned to the server by a client are organized into a block and stored as a block, the idea being that those objects have been grouped together for a logical reason (components of a complex object) and are likely to be used together at some later date. As a result of this, when objects are read they are sorted by location to take advantage of this blocking of written objects.

7.6 PERSISTENT PROGRAMMING

We have considered how to support OODBs in the traditional sense of a DB using transactions and distribution. An alternative is persistent programming, which uses objects but whose rules are different. If we can make a bold distinction, OODBs are the results of traditional DB workers moving towards more semantic expressiveness and dynamic schemas, whereas PPLs (Persistent Programming Languages) are the result of traditional PL researchers removing the "artificial" distinction between internal and external data structuring and manipulation.

This is an area worthy of lengthier treatment. This short section can only hope to provide a brief introduction and an indication of its relevance to databases in general and OODBs specifically.

In their excellent paper, [Atkinson and Buneman,87b] survey the support for types and persistence in database languages. The three principles they discuss are **persistence**, **type completeness** and **expressive power**. Persistency concerns the lifetime of a data structure; its persistence is the period of time for which it remains accessible. In most programming languages, the persistency of the data is a single activation of the code it resides within. If we require to access the data over a number of program runs, we must store it in a file at the end of one run and read it back in at the start of the next. If we are storing a complex data structure (which uses in-store pointers), the saving and restoring procedures may be awkward.

Atkinson and Buneman give three principles of persistence: persistence should be a property of all values and not limited to certain types, all values have the same rights to persistence, and while a value persists, so should its type.

Principles 1 and 2 refer to type completeness; all data types have equal status within the language. With regard to expressive power -- is it possible to write the whole application in a query language, or are there (say) numerical computations and complicated database manipulations that cannot be written in the database programming language? The traditional solution is to embed the query language in a "lower-level" language, i.e. SQL as ESQL in RTI's Ingres.

In [Atkinson,87a], a description is given of the treatment of objects in a conventional language. Firstly, we have objects (local variables) which are created when a procedure is invoked and destroyed when the procedure exits. Secondly, we have objects (global variables) which are passed in and out of procedures as parameters. Using structures and pointers in the normal way, we can build and navigate arbitrary complex object collections. Lastly, we have files or databases held in the file system; objects here are accessed through a set of interface procedures. A user wishing to access a large structured collection of objects would expect to use the second or third methods above. In conventional languages, the second method can only be used for accessing objects as they exist while the program is running. If the intention is to build a long-lived (and evolutionary?) collection, we must turn to the third method.

Persistent languages allow the second method to be used for accessing long lived or permanent data, as opposed to the traditional third method involving files or databases. Underlying any persistent language must be a suitable storage mechanism, and PISA (Persistent Information Space Architecture) [Atkinson,87a] is just such a mechanism. Objects under PISA are stored within the storage system; if we consider a distributed PISA, we must consider the problem of maintaining pointers between distributed objects. This is dealt with by considering the PISA store as being split up into localities, where a locality is normally the storage system of one machine. If an object has a pointer to another object in the same locality, then this is held as a local address. If an object has a pointer to another in a remote locality, it could use a network address to identify the remote locality plus the address of the object within that locality. Any general "pisa" implementation will have to face and address many of the issues raised in section five.

The PISA project has developed two persistent languages; PS-Algol and the more recent Napier [Atkinson,88].

To conclude this section, we examine some of the facilities of the type system of the persistent programming language Galileo [Albana,88]. All the examples used are taken from the above paper. Galileo is described as a programming language for database applications which supports the abstraction mechanisms of both modern programming languages and semantic data models (classification, aggregation and generalization). For example, it allows us to declare a tuple type, consisting of an unordered set of <identifier, denotable value> pairs. We can define

```
type Person := (  Name:    string
                 and Surname:  string
                 and BirthDate:   Date  )

and Student := (  Name:    string
                 and Surname:   string
                 and BirthDate:   Date
                 and School:   string  )
```

This demonstrates aggregation. We can use a more direct form of inheritance

```
type Person <=> ( Name:   string
                 and Surname:   string
                 and BirthDate:   Date  )

and Student <=> ( is Person
                 and School:   string  )
```

Galileo also supports multiple inheritance, i.e. we can introduce a further type Employed Student which is a subtype of both Student and Employee. We can, as usual, use our type network for generalization.

It is possible to build sequences of type variables, i.e.
```
1::[2; 3; 4]
```
produces a sequence
```
[1; 2; 3; 4]
```
where :: is the sequence operator, and the single value on the LHS has the same type as the values in the sequence on the RHS.

Subtyping makes this interesting; if we have a variable PaulBrown of type Person and MarySmith of type Student, then the typing and evaluation of

```
MarySmith :: [ PaulBrown ]
```

requires the use of the type hierarchy. MarySmith is a student, but as a student is a person, then we can obtain a least upper bound i.e. { student, person } is the set of possible instance types, and person is the most general (higher up in the type hierarchy). MarySmith is thus treated as a person, and the result of the concatenation is a sequence of values of type person, where MarySmith's contribution is solely drawn from those attributes she possesses by dint of being a person.

Classes are supported in Galileo by characterizing them with a name and a type which gives the structure of their elements. For example,

```
Persons class
   Person <->
      (
      Name:  string
      and Surname:  string
      and Birthdate:  Date )
```

The class identifier Persons is now bound to a modifiable sequence of Person values. Whenever a new Person is created, it can be automatically appended to the sequence of Persons. This is similar to the behaviour of ENCORE, as shown in the appendix.

In the appendix, comparisons may be drawn between the PPL approach and the DBL approaches.

7.7 SUMMARY

In this chapter, we have tried to show how the object model applies to a new generation of database systems, combining the features of the relational model and logic programming and trying to better them. We began by presenting the advantages of semantic-rich data handling, leading to a description of a model for objects within an OODB, and the expected behaviour of such a system. We outlined the architecture required to support OODBs, with particular consideration given to a small number of aspects. We concluded with a brief exploration of persistent programming. In the appendix which follows, we give an overview of some of the currently available OODB languages, with the aim of presenting the underlying features of OODBs.

The production of OODBMS is still a research area, even though several systems are now commercially available (Gemstone, Vbase etc.). We view the situation as similar to the early days of the relational model; the model was accepted and used long before viable largescale systems were available. Today, OODBMS systems are already available but it may be some time yet before systems yielding the true power and potential of objects are commonly available.

ACKNOWLEDGEMENT

To Thomas Rodden for his helpful comments on earlier drafts of this chapter.

REFERENCES

[Abrial,74] Abrial, J.R., "Data Semantics", in Data Base Management, J.W. Klimbie and K.L. Koffeman (eds), North Holland, 1974, pp 1-59

[Atkinson,87a] Atkinson, M.P., R. Morrison and G. Pratten, "PISA -- A Persistent Information Space Architecture", ICL Technical Journal, May 1987, pp 477 - 491

[Atkinson,87b] Atkinson, M.P., and O.P. Buneman, "Types and Persistence in Database Programming Languages", ACM Computing Surveys, Vol. 19, No. 2, June 1987, pp 105-190

[Atkinson,88] Atkinson, M.P. and R. Morrison, "Types, Bindings and Parameters in an Persistent Environment", pp 3-20, "Data Types and Persistence, Atkinson, Buneman and Morrison (Eds), Springer-Verlag, ISBN 3-540-18785-5, 0-387-18785-5, 1988

[Albana,88] Albana, A. et al., "The Type System of Galileo", pp 101-119, "Data Types and Persistence, Atkinson, Buneman and Morrison (Eds), Springer-Verlag, ISBN 3-540-18785-5, 0-387-18785-5, 1988

[Banerjee,87] Banerjee, J., et al., "Data Model Issues for Object-Oriented Applications", ACM Trans. on Office Information Systems, Vol. 5, No. 1, Jan. 1987, pp 3-26

[Beech,87] Beech, D, "Groundwork for an Object Database Model", in "Research Directionds in Object-Oriented Programming", B. Shriver, and P. Wegner, editors, pp317-554, MIT Press, 1987.

[Beech,88] Beech, D., "Intensional Concepts in an Object Database Model", OOPSLA '88 Proceedings, pp 164 -175

[Chen,76] Chen, P., "The Entity-Relationship model towards a unified view of data", ACM Trans. on Database Systems, Vol. 1, No. 1, March 1976, pp 9-36

[Codd,70] Codd, E.F., "A relational model of data for large shared data banks", Comm. of the ACM, Vol. 13, No. 6, June 1970, pp 377-387

[Codd,79] Codd, E.F., "Extending the database relational model to capture more meaning", ACM Trans. on Database Systems, Vol. 4, No. 4, Dec. 1979, pp 397-434

[Cox,86] Cox, B.J., "Object-oriented Programming An Evolutionary Approach", Addison Wesley 1986

[Shipman,81] Shipman, D.W., "The Functional data Model and the Data Language Daplex", ACM Trans. on Database Systems, Vol. 6, No. 1, March 1981, pp 140-173

[Fishman,87] Fishman, D.H., et al., "Iris An Object-Oriented Database Management System", ACM Trans. on Office Information Systems, Vol. 5, No. 1, Jan. 1987, pp 48-69

[Fishman,88] Fishman, D. et al, "Overview of the Iris DBMS", Internal Report, Database Technology Department, HP Labs, Palo Alto, California, June, 1988

[Frost,81] Frost, R.A., "Asdas -- A Simple Database System aimed at the naive user", Proceedings of 6th ACM European Regional Conference on Systems Architecture, IPC Business Press Ltd., London, pp. 234 - 240, Feb. 1981

[Gardarin,89] Gardarin, G., and P. Valduriez, "Relational Databases and Knowledge Bases", Addison-Wesley, 1989

[Hammer,81] Hammer, M. and D. McLeod, "Database Description with SDM a Semantic Database Model", ACM Trans. on Database Systems, Vol. 6, No. 3, Sept. 1981, pp 351-386

[Maier,86] Maier, D., Stein, J., Otis, A., and Purdy, A., "Development of an Object-Oriented DBMS", OOPSLA '86, pp 472-482

[McGregor and Malone,81] McGregor, D.R. and J.R. Malone, "The Fact Database System", in Research and Development in Information Retrieval, C.J. VonRijsbergen and P.W. Williams, Editors, Butterworth, pp 203-217, 1981

[Meyer,88] Meyer, B., "Object-oriented Software Construction", Prentice Hall 1988

[Oxborrow,88] Oxborrow, E.A., "Object-oriented Database Systems What are they and what is their future?", Database Technology, Vol. 2, No. 1, pp 31-39, 1988

[Pathak,88] Pathak, G., J. Joseph and S. Ford, "Object eXchange Service for an Object-Oriented Database System", draft version, Database Systems Branch Memo 88-06-01, Information Technologies Laboratory, Texas Instruments Incorporated, June 1988 (Accepted to the 5th International Conference on Data Engineering 1989).

[Peckham,88] Peckham, J., and F. Maryanski, "Semantic Data Models", ACM Computing Surveys, Vol. 20, No. 3, Sept. 1988, pp 153-189

[Pratchett,83] Pratchett, T., "The Colour of Magic", Corgi Books, ISBN 0-552-12475-3, 1983.

[Skarra and Zdonik,86] A.H. Skarra and S.B. Zdonik, "The Management of Changing Types in an Object-Oriented Database", OOPSLA 86 Proceedings, pp 483 - 495, Sept.

1986

[Skarra,87] Skarra, A.H., S.B. Zdonik, and S.P. Reiss, "ObServer An Object Server for an Object-Oriented Database System", Technical Report No. CS-88-08, Brown University, Dept. of Computer Science, July 1987

[Zdonik,85a] Zdonik, S.B., and Wegner, P., "A Database Approach to Languages, Libraries and Environments", Brown University, Department of Computer Science, Technical Report No. CS-85-10, May, 1985

[Zdonik,85b] Zdonik, S.B., and Wegner, P., "Language and Methodology for Object-Oriented Database Environments", Brown University, Department of Computer Science, Technical Report No. CS-85-19, November, 1985 this may have been published in Proc. of 19th Annual Hawaii Int. Conf. on System Sciences, Honolulu, Jan. 1986, pp 378-387

[Zdonik,88] Zdonik, S.B., Verbal Communication, St. Andrews Open Lecture Series,, 1988

7.8 APPENDIX: OBJECT-ORIENTED DATABASE LANGUAGES

In this section, we examine languages for manipulating OODBs, and through these languages reveal the underlying models and power. As our example data for some of this section, we take this set of relations.

```
Ship (         S_ID,   Name,        Class )
               S_1     Enterprise   Cruiser
               S_2     Reliant      Scout
               S_3     C-37D        Scout


Personnel (    P_ID,   Name,        Rank,           Birthplace )
               P_1     Kirk         Commander       Earth
               P_2     Spock        Lt. Commander   Vulcan
               P_3     Uhura        Lt. Commander   Earth
               P_4     Adams        Commander       Earth
               P_5     Ostrow       Lt. Commander   Earth
               P_6     McCoy        Lt. Commander   Earth


Assignment (   P_ID,   S_ID,        Post )
               P_1     S_1          Captain
               P_2     S_1          Science Officer
               P_2     S_1          First Officer
               P_3     S_1          Communications Officer
               P_4     S_3          Captain
               P_5     S_3          Chief Medical Officer
               P_6     S_1          Chief Medical Officer
```

To provide a base line, we examine Beech's [Beech,87] Object Database Model language (henceforth referred to as ODML).

7.8.1. Beech's ODML

In ODML, objects can be created and deleted

```
Create Object instances x,y,z;
Delete x;
```

Objects are instances of one or more type; types can be deleted and created

```
Create type  Navigator;
Create type Person
    (name String,
     birthplace Planet);
Create type Ship
    ( name String,
      class String);
```

196

```
Create type Assignment
   ( p_id Personnel,
      s_id Ship,
      post String);
Delete type Navigator;
```

The second create example shows how we define the state for instances of that type. The list of types of which an object is an instance can be modified as the object evolves over a long lifetime

```
Add type T1, T2 to y;
Remove type T2 from y;
```

Inheritance is supported in ODML with the use of supertypes, and the supertype relation forms a directed acyclic graph. A type can be inserted into the DAG at creation

```
Create type Personnel subtype of Person
   ( rank String );
```

The ODML allows the creation of an object and its association with a type in a more convenient form as follows

```
Create Personnel instance Kirk;
```

At a later time, we can associate the object Kirk with other types as

```
Add type Navigator to Kirk;
```

The state of an object can be set as follows

```
Set name(Kirk) = "J.T. Kirk",
   birthplace(Kirk) = Earth;
```

As we have seen, it is useful to be able to collect groups of objects together. ODML provides combinations and lists to support such collections. A combination is a finite collection without ordering or duplication. The example below illustrates the functions of a combination

```
Create Combination C1, C2;
Insert Hecht, Mendoza into C1;
Remove Hecht from C1;
if IsEmpty(C1) or Smith in C2
   Create List L1;
L1:= for each c in { Hecht, Mendoza }
SomeAction(c);
```

Ordered finite collections that may contain duplicates are lists.

```
Create List L2, L3, L4;
L2 := < Smith, Hecht, Mendoza >;
L3 := tail (L2);
L4 := < head(L2), L3 >;
```

The ODML includes the use of actions which are defined as formulae. An example of a formulae

```
Create action OnBoard ( Personnel e) -> Ship
as Select s_id (a)
    for each Assignment a
    where e = p_id(a)
```

In a later paper, [Beech,88], he develops a treatment for intensional concepts. Concepts are similar to Prolog rules, and allow us to derive intensional relationships such as "grandFather.of" from extensional relationships "parentOf" and "fatherOf".

```
Create Concept Father (Person p) as
    Select
    exists Person c
    where FatherOf (p,c);
Create Concept GrandfatherOf (Person gf, Person gc) as
    Select
    exists Person p
    where FatherOf (gf,p) and
        ParentOf (p,gc);
```

In short, we can access the elements of intensional and extensional sets in exactly the same way.

7.8.2. The IRIS Query Language: Object SQL
The IRIS DBMS takes many of the features of Beech's ODML and incorporates them in Object SQL. IRIS offers a functional viewpoint (derived from Shipman's model [Shipman,81]) which it includes within an extension to SQL. The three main extensions intended to adapt SQL to the object and function model are

> Users manipulate types and functions rather than tables
> Objects can be referenced by identity rather than state (i.e. keys)
> User-defined functions and Iris system functions may appear in **where** and
>   **select** clauses to give powerful retrieval.

We give some examples of Object SQL as a concrete implementation of the concepts of ODML. Taking our Starfleet example, we alter our view of the data as follows To create a type Person with property functions name, address and phone

```
Create Type Person
    ( name Charstring required,
    birthplace Planet);

Create Type Personnel subtype of Person
    ( rank String);
```

Note that properties may be multi-valued, and therefore types do not correspond directly with relational tables. Rather than use a further object (or relation) to store assignments, we relate Personnel to Ship by introducing a stored function, assignment, that, given a Personnel and a Ship, returns the post held by the Personnel on board that Ship (note we are altering the data by assuming that one Personnel can only hold one post on board one Ship).

```
Create function assignment (Personnel, Ship) -> String
```

We now create instances of Personnel

```
Create Personnel (name, birthplace, rank) instances
    Kirk ("J.T. Kirk", Earth, "Commander"),
    Spock ("Spock", Vulcan, "Lt. Commander"),
    McCoy ("L.H. McCoy", Earth, "Lt. Commander");

Set assignment (Kirk, Enterprise) = "Captain";
```

If we maintain a distinction between Personnel (those at Starfleet HQ or StarBases) and ShipBoardPersonnel (those on board ships), we can do so as follows

```
Create type ShipBoardPersonnel subtype of Personnel;
Add type ShipBoardPersonnel to Kirk, Spock, McCoy;

/* some queries */

Select name(Kirk); /* get name of Kirk */

Select name(sbp)
    for each ShipBoardPersonnel sbp; /* get names of all
                                        ship board personnel */

Select name(p)
    for each Person p
    where Vulcan = birthplace(p);    /* get names of all
                        people born on Vulcan */
```

Versions in Iris are supported by the Iris Object Manager (chapter 13). Briefly, versions are considered as snapshots of an object in certain states, and each version is modeled by a distinct object.

7.8.3. The Gemstone QL: OPAL

Gemstone [Maier,86] is a system based on Smalltalk. The corresponding QL, OPAL, thereby shares many of Smalltalk's features. The following examples are taken from the GemStone Product Overview, March 1988. For example, to create a new class Document as a subclass of the base Object class, we can say

```
Object subclass: 'Document'
   instVarNames: #('title' 'text' 'author')
```

This has defined the class to have three instance variables. We can also define behaviour for documents by adding inspection and access methods as follows

```
method: Document
title: aString
"A method that establishes the value of a Document's
'title' instance variable"
title := aString
%
method: Document
title
"A method that returns a Document's title"
^title
%
```

We can create a collection for holding documents by a special subclass of the Set class

```
Set subclass: 'SetOfDocuments'
   instVarNames: #()
```

We can add to the basic collection-handling methods inherited

```
method: SetOfDocuments'
findDocsEntitled: aString
"Use the method select: inherited from class Set to return
a SetOfDocuments entitled aString"
^self select:{:i|:i.title = aString}
%
```

Figure 7.21 shows a diagram of a more complex document object in GemStone. This diagram highlights the fact that attributes within an object can be other objects, and even sets of other objects. For example, the Bibliography attribute of a document consists of a set of other documents.

GemStone appears to handle versions by user-managed sets; in the above diagram, the set of documents Versions is used to store a list of object IDs representing the set of versions. To clarify further, it is the object IDs which are stored, not complete copies of the object. If an author is the author of several documents, it is the ID of the author which is stored in the separate documents. This use of object identify saves storage space, as well as meeting the referential integrity requirement stated earlier. Moreover, update

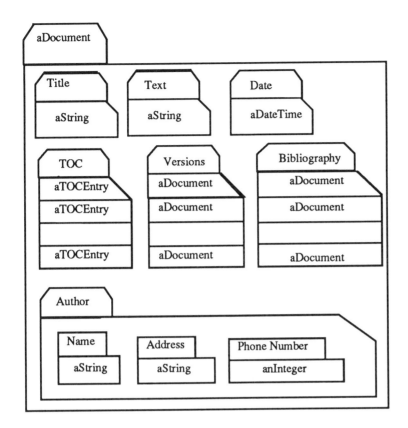

Figure 7.21 A complex document object in GemStone

problems are eased; if an author's phone number changes, this state information appears only once in the data, and only has to be updated once.

Naturally enough, we can use Smalltalk-like inheritance to further enhance and specialize classes i.e. we can create a class of NumberedDocument which are the same as Document with the addition of an instance variable for the DocumentNumber, and appropriate methods which use document numbers.

7.8.4 The ENCORE DBL
The ENCORE DBL [Zdonik,85a,85b] allows the declaration of types, consisting of a set of explicitly defined operations and properties, a possible list of supertypes, and an associated class (there's that word again!) to which objects of the type automatically belong. If no class name is given, a class with the same name as the type is automatically generated. A type T is defined as follows

```
Define Type T
Supertypes: < list of supertypes >
Associated Class: < class-name >
Operations:
```

```
< list of operations >
Properties:
< list of properties >
```

A class in ENCORE is a set which contains all declared instances of the type; we have assumed elsewhere that the set of all instances would be accessible by some arrangement, i.e. a relation with the name of the type, but here we see a concrete implementation approach to the problem. As soon as an instance is declared, it is added to the class.

As an example, ENCORE is used to specify the UNIX file system; a portion of the definition is given below

```
Define Type File
Operations:
    create-file() returns (F: file)
    open (F: File)
    close (F: File)
Properties:
    file-name:  String
    size:  Integer
    date-last-modified:  Date
```

In ENCORE, operations, properties and types are objects. For example, properties are objects and have types; therefore, they can have properties and attributes of their own. Thus the orthogonal treatment of operations, properties and types as objects results in powerful facilities.

ENCORE classes support associative retrieval of objects. The type Class supports the operation Select which has the form

```
Select ( C: Class, P: Predicate) returns (S:  Set)
```

The function call Select(C,P) returns a set containing all members of C that satisfy P. The predicate P is constructed using standard query language capabilities. As an example, to retrieve all files that have been modified today we can specify the following predicate that would be applied to all members of the class Files

```
P = Lambda (p)
    Get-property-value("date-last-modified",p) =
        todays-date())
```

This predicate can be used as follows in a Select instruction

```
Select(Files,P)
```

Chapter 8

Object-Oriented Design Methods

Andrew Ormsby
University College of Wales, Aberystwyth

ABSTRACT *Object-oriented design methods have recently begun to gain attention as an alternative to the more traditional ways of structuring large software systems. Much has been claimed of designing software on object-oriented principles, in particular, that it aids maintainability and increases reuse. This chapter views the current state of the art in object-oriented design methods, looking at Booch's OOD, the HOOD method and OOSD as examples of the object-oriented approach.*

8.1 BACKGROUND

8.1.1 Introduction

There has been much interest in object-oriented design in recent years. One reason for this interest is through the impetus provided by object-oriented programming languages. As has been described in earlier chapters of the book, these languages provide new means of structuring programs through the mechanisms of polymorphism and inheritance. Users of these new languages have come to realize that the current design methods which are available do not take advantage of the new and powerful facilities of these languages. Just as important as the development of these new languages has been the influence of the Ada programming language and the search for development methods suitable for use with it (e.g. [Freeman,82]). While Ada does not have the inheritance mechanism common to many object-oriented languages, nor the delegation mechanism available in some, there are many similarities between Ada and the object-oriented languages. Both encourage the design of systems built around building blocks which incorporate data and the routines that operate on those data. It is therefore not surprising that both the Ada and non-Ada camps have been moving towards design methods which can be called 'object-oriented', where an important part of the method is the intent to decompose designs into objects which encapsulate both data and code operating on that data. Some research in software reuse has also led to interest in object-oriented design. There is some dissatisfaction with current design methods which seem to place too much emphasis on designing for the task in hand and not enough on designing reusable software, or designing *with* reusable components.

8.1.2 What is a Design Method?

There is some controversy on what constitutes a software design method[1], and therefore what can be expected of a design method. In particular there is a line of argument with more than a grain of truth, that many current design methods are little more than notations for the expression of designs. True prescriptive software design methods do comprise more than just a notation, however. Such a method should provide guidelines on the steps that should be followed at each stage during the development and should cover the whole software development lifecycle [McDermid,84]. While an important aspect of design is related to how to decompose a complex system into smaller subsystems which can be easily understood, guidelines are not restricted to only this aspect of the design process. A comprehensive method should list and describe the deliverables that are to be produced at each stage. Some methods go so far as to provide some criteria by which quality assurance personnel can judge the deliverables and have some measure of certainty that the method has been applied correctly. Despite all of this, it is still the case that a design method usually incorporates one or more notations, often graphical, which can be used to express designs and to allow for their communication between designers.

Perhaps paradoxically, design methods cannot design for us. While a method can emphasize principles and provide guidelines for designers to follow, the act of designing a piece of software is ultimately a creative process which requires skill, experience and good taste to be performed well. It seems no more possible to design software automatically than it is to design any other complex artifact. One important guideline that design methods provide is to hint at the way in which large and complex systems can be decomposed into smaller units which can be dealt with more easily. The way in which object-oriented design differs from conventional design methods is the particular way in which the system is decomposed into these smaller units and the nature of the relationship between them.

With the construction of large and complex systems, and the availability to software engineers of advanced and powerful workstations, the provision of computer-based tools to support the use of design methods is increasingly important. These tools can take a wide variety of forms, ranging from diagram editors that help in the preparation of graphical notations relating to the design, type checkers for particular notations, transformation tools for assisting in the conversion of elements of a design from one notation to another, and eventually, distributed environments for the development of software in which the steps of the development process and the underlying method are animated by some executable model of the development process. While full support for all steps of the design process will probably not be available for some time, it is clear that immature methods without a recognized standard are going to be at a disadvantage when it comes to tool support.

Design methods are not always appropriate. They are intended to provide guidance for the development of large systems. It is perfectly possible to develop programs of a

---

[1]The word "method" is used throughout this chapter rather than the overused word "methodology" which is here taken to refer to the study of methods.

small number of thousands of lines without the use of any systematic development method. It is only when larger systems are attempted that design methods become useful and necessary.

8.1.3 History and Principles

Design is traditionally thought of as a top-down process. In methods such as Yourdon's Structured Design [Yourdon,79], the designer starts with a highlevel abstract description of the function of the overall system and progressively breaks this down and refines it to produce successively less abstract descriptions of the functions of smaller and smaller parts of the system. The designer decomposes the system into smaller units according to functional criteria.

Object-oriented design is based on the concept of the *object*. Rather than decomposition based on the various functions that elements of the system perform, *objects* from which a system is built model both the data and related operations corresponding to parts of the overall system. Unlike many other approaches to design, it is not possible to categorize object-oriented design as fundamentally top-down or bottom-up. It includes both approaches. When a designer is reusing an existing object or class, it could be said that a bottom-up approach is being used. However, when decomposing a large design into the smaller elements which will be mapped onto objects and classes, the approach is more a top-down one.

In [Freeman,83], Peter Freeman writes that "good designers understand intuitively that a successful design is one that matches the structure of the problem". In terms of software, this means that our designs should in some sense reflect the structure of our problem domain. Object-oriented approaches to design seek to do this by mapping objects in the real world onto objects in the software system.

Parnas. Parnas' paper on modularization [Parnas,72] describes a strategy for decomposing systems which has much in common with what has become known as object-oriented design. In this paper, Parnas describes two different decompositions of a simple software system. One follows a "conventional" method of decomposition in which the modules represent sub-functions in the overall system. The first module, for example, is concerned with input – it reads the data and places it into shared storage ready for use by the modules which follow. This decomposition is obvious enough – the designer has chosen to keep all the initialization processing in one module. This is superficially attractive: the decomposition has both functional cohesion (functionally related parts of the program are close together) and temporal cohesion (meaning that things which happen in juxtaposition are also close together in the program). The trouble with it is that it requires data to be shared between a number of modules, making all of the modules which access the shared data dependent on the representation chosen for the data. Each time the representation is changed, all the modules which know about the representation of the data will have to be modified. Parnas' second decomposition is based on the principle of information hiding. The overall system is split into modules which try to hide details of the internal representation of data from the other modules in the system. In the second decomposition, one module is responsible for the storage of data. It provides a subroutine which allows other modules to access that data in a controlled manner, but avoids the necessity of the other modules needing to know about the actual representation of that data. Parnas' contention is that while both of the decompositions will work, when it comes to modifying the design, the second decomposition is much easier to change.

Information hiding is closely related with the ideas of "high cohesion" and "low coupling". Designs in which the modules (in the case of object-oriented design, objects or classes) exhibit high cohesion are those in which the modules group together parts of the system which are closely related. Low coupling is the level to which one module in the system is dependent on other modules. Obviously the greater the amount of coupling between modules, the more complex the design and therefore the harder it will be to understand and maintain. Low coupling happens when the number of links between modules is small and the interfaces which modules present to other modules in the system are kept as simple as possible.

Parnas' work is also interesting as it shows that it is not strictly necessary to have the modularization features of a modern programming language in order to realize designs which exhibit information hiding.

Note that the emphasis here is on ease of modification and not necessarily on ease of building the software in the first place. It is well known that for large software systems, more is spent on maintaining them during their lifetime than is spent on constructing them in the first place. Information hiding makes change easier to cope with because it localizes knowledge of the low level details of the system. Parnas addresses the importance of making systems amenable to change in another paper [Parnas,79] in which he points out the extent to which other engineering disciplines design with future change in mind from the outset, whereas this is rarely the case in software engineering. In the longer term, making it easier to change or maintain systems also makes it cheaper to build new ones. This is because software reuse, the development of new software by reusing old pieces of software, is very similar to maintaining old software. In both cases, the software developer or maintainer is taking some existing software and changing it or adapting it to meet new requirements or to fix problems. An argument for object-oriented design in the context of software reuse is presented in much more detail in [Meyer,87].

Booch. "Object-Oriented Development" [Booch,86] was one of the first papers to discuss an object-oriented approach to design and to distinguish between OOD and object-oriented programming. Booch introduces 'object-oriented development' as an approach to software design "in which the decomposition of a system is based upon the concept of an object". This contrasts with the conventional methods, where the decomposition is guided by the idea that each module represents a step, or function, in the overall process. In Booch's paper, this new approach to the decomposition of designs is motivated by the need to use the structuring facilities of the Ada language. Booch's ideas on object-oriented development first appeared in a chapter on object-oriented design in [Booch,83]. The method is further expanded in Booch's later book [Booch,87].

Booch considers the shortcomings of traditional development methods to be:
- They don't address data abstraction and information hiding
- They are inadequate for problems with concurrency
- They are often not responsive to changes in the problem.

Booch concentrates on Ada, where the most significant structuring mechanisms from the point of view of object-oriented design are the package and the task. The ability to parameterize packages by the use of the Ada generic mechanism gives a further means for allowing generality to be expressed. Note, however, that Ada does not provide inheritance (or an equivalent mechanism), something that other authors, such as Meyer

206

[Meyer,88] and Cox [Cox,86], consider a significant drawback. In [Seidewitz,87], however, it is argued that although Ada does not provide direct support for object-oriented concepts such as inheritance, an object-oriented development method is still useful in providing an approach to the use of packages.

8.2 EXAMPLES OF OBJECT-ORIENTED DESIGN METHODS

In this section, some existing object-oriented design methods are described. The section begins with a description of Object-oriented Development, the method described by Booch in a number of publications and mentioned in the previous section of this chapter. Object-oriented development is significant because it was one of the earliest of the object-oriented approaches to design to be described in the literature. Booch's work has been taken considerably further in a handbook on object-oriented design produced by the US software company EVB. The extensions and clarifications in this handbook are described in 8.2.2. The new European method, HOOD, is described in 8.2.3 and following on from this, the rather different approach of OOSD is explained in 8.2.4.

8.2.1 Object-Oriented Development

Booch's method is a prescriptive one in which the steps of the method are described in some detail, though there are some variations in the approach described in the various publications which describe it. The general approach, however, is as follows:

- Identify the objects and their attributes;
- Identify the operations suffered by and required of each object;
- Establish the visibility of each object in relation to other objects;
- Establish the interface of each object; and
- Implement each object.

These steps are now described in slightly more detail:

Identify the objects and their attributes. According to Booch, this step "...involves the recognition of the major actors, agents, and servers in the problem space plus their role in our model of reality". Booch suggests that these are often identifiable as nouns used in the description of the problem space. Booch also suggests that where there are a number of objects that share characteristics, the objects can be collected together into a class. Other than these instructions, Booch gives very little advice on how to identify the fundamental objects in the system.

Identify the operations suffered by and required of each object. This step is an attempt to determine the behaviour of each of the objects. Booch distinguishes between the "static semantics" of the object and the "dynamic semantics". The former is given by the list of operations that can be performed on the object or by the object. The latter is the time and space constraints that the object must meet.

Establish the visibility of each object in relation to other objects. This step identifies the "static dependencies" between the objects.

Establish the interface of each object. At this stage, the module specification is produced. Booch uses Ada as the language at this point. Booch talks of this specification as "forming a contract between the clients of an object and the object itself".

Implement each object. This means deciding on a representation for the object or class and implementing the interfaces described in the previous step. In some cases, Booch admits, it may be necessary to go back to the method once more to further decompose objects or classes which have been "found to consist of several subordinate objects". In other cases, and Booch claims this is more common, composition rather than decomposition will be what is required, as the object is implemented by building on top of existing lower level objects or classes.

What the method does not say is quite how the designer should decide whether further decomposition at any stage is possible or desirable. Nor are guidelines provided for judging the quality of a particular decomposition versus another one (though this is very difficult).

The place of OOD in the lifecycle. Booch says that object-oriented development is not a complete lifecycle method. It concentrates on the design and implementation stages. Booch quotes Abbott [Abbott,80]: "although the steps we follow in formalizing the strategy may appear mechanical, it is not an automatic procedure [...] it requires a great deal of real world knowledge and intuitive understanding of the problem". As a result of this, Booch suggests that OOD should be combined with suitable other methods. Booch refers to JSD and SREM as possibilities for the requirements analysis stage of the lifecycle. Booch does not attempt to use these methods with OOD in the example in the paper nor in the examples in the books [Booch,83], [Booch,87].

In [Booch,86], Booch goes on to contrast the design for a cruise control system using both object-oriented and functional approaches. It is perhaps interesting to note that in both the functional and object-oriented approaches, Booch suggests a data flow diagram as a means to "capture our model of the problem space". The next stage in the functional approach would be to draw a structure chart (Yourdon), identifying the major functions in the overall process. In the object-oriented approach, the decomposition of the system is based on the objects that exist "in our model of reality". There is no requirement in Booch's method that the objects in the system represent physical objects that exist in the real world; this contrasts somewhat with the requirements for entity identification in JSD [Jackson,83].

8.2.2 EVB

EVB Software Engineering produce a handbook [EVB,85] for object-oriented design. The handbook describes a method which is based largely on Booch. Indeed, the EVB handbook makes no claims to be an OOD tutorial and recommends that the first seven chapters of [Booch,83] are read before attempting the handbook. Chapter 4 of the EVB handbook re-works the five examples from [Booch,83] in more detail, going right from the problem definition to Ada source code for one example, a simple electronic mail system. Like Booch, EVB state that OOD is only applicable to part of the software lifecycle. However, while OOD is thought to be most useful during the design phase, EVB's handbook also highlights its usefulness for design and re-design during maintenance. More importantly, EVB list some potential limitations to OOD:

There are few mechanisms for determining requirements. "OOD assumes that there has been some prior analysis, and that the software engineer has a basic understanding of the problem". EVB suggest Structured Analysis (and related tools) as a means of determining requirements, but admit that SA does not lend itself particularly to real-time systems. There has been more work on requirements and systems analysis and OOD and some of this work is mentioned later in this chapter.

The method does not provide mechanisms for defining algorithms and representations of data structures. In OOD, the software engineer has to develop the specification parts of the Ada program units, but nothing is said about the implementation of the bodies of these units, except in the case where these are decomposed further using OOD. This is only to be expected seeing where OOD fits into the development process. Nobody claims that OOD will assist in designing mathematical algorithms, for example.

While EVB admit that there has not been much experience with OOD, it must be remembered that their handbook was published in 1985 and there have been a number of substantially-sized developments using the object-oriented approach since then. EVB claim that software developed in Ada using OOD will frequently require less source code than more conventional languages. A similar argument, this time in favour of object-oriented programming languages and Objective-C in particular, appears in [Cox,86]. EVB claim that applications re-written in Ada have reduced the amount of source code required by a factor of ten.

EVB's OOD in detail. The EVB handbook devotes a chapter to a detailed description of the steps that must be carried out. For each step, the rationale for that step, instructions on how to perform it, and some suggestions for checks that might be made by quality assurance personnel are listed. It can be seen from the following that the steps of the EVB version of OOD are much the same as those given by Booch. EVB list:

Definition of the problem
    Statement of the problem
    Analysis and clarification of the givens
Development of an informal strategy
Formalization of the strategy
    Identification of the objects of interest
        Identification of objects and types
        Association of attributes with the objects and types of interest
    Identification of the operations of interest
        Identification of operations
        Association of attributes with the objects and types of interest
        Grouping operations, objects and types
    Definition of the interfaces
        Formal description of the visible interfaces
        Analysis and clarification of high-level design decisions
        Graphical annotation of the visible interfaces
    Implementation of the solution
        Implementation of the operation interfaces
        Stepwise refinement of the highest-level program unit
        Stepwise refinement of other program units
    Recursive application of OOD

The first stage of the problem definition is the statement of the problem in a single sentence. Of course, stating the problem in a single sentence is something that can only be done reasonably once the developer has some appreciation of the nature of the problem. The handbook suggests that for complex systems, some prior analysis of the problem will have taken place. If the system is a complex one, it may be hard to express the nature of the problem in a single sentence. However, at a sufficiently abstract level, it is possible to describe an arbitrarily complex system in a single sentence.

The second step, the "analysis and clarification of the givens", will depend on what has gone before. If some sort of analysis method has been used in the earliest stages of the design, then this step consists mainly of the organizing of the output of that work into a suitable form. However, where another method has not provided the input for this method, the handbook lists four processes that will have to be performed during this substep. These are (quoted from the handbook): gathering of information pertinent to solving the problem; analyzing the gathered information; organizing the analyzed information; and clarifying any problems (ambiguities, contradictions, omissions, etc). These four steps are repeated until the designer is happy with the statement of the problem.

The deliverables that will be produced by these substeps consist of "all [the] information necessary to solve the problem". The information may be of a wide variety of types. For a real-time system, this information will include the timing constraints that have to be met. The problem statement will list the objects in the problem space (as opposed to those which will exist in the solution) and any information regarding them which has come to light during the analysis phase. What is clear is that the deliverables produced during this phase will vary widely depending upon the method that has been used to assist in requirements analysis. JSD Entity Structure diagrams and Structured Analysis "Structured Specifications" are mentioned as possible examples. Where an analysis technique has been used which yields an "object-oriented" view of the problem, there will obviously be less work to do than those which produce a description in some other form.

The distinction between objects in the problem space and those in the solution is an interesting one as it shows that object-oriented design is not simply a matter of spotting the real world objects and modelling them in software. In some cases, there will be objects in the problem which, after due study, appear to have no place in the solution. Equally, the designer may choose to invent objects considered appropriate to a solution.

Developing an informal strategy. The informal strategy takes the form of a single paragraph describing the system to be built. EVB suggest that the informal strategy should all be at one level of abstraction. If the informal strategy is at the level of the entire system, the paragraph should not describe the system in terms of low level details. The informal strategy is a description of an informal solution to the problem.

Formalization of the strategy. The substeps which make up this step of the method involve identifying the objects of interest (i.e. those which are of use in the solution) and associating attributes with them. This is done by looking for nouns and pronouns in the informal strategy and making a list of the objects which are so identified. Attributes relating to objects are identified by looking for adjectives which are used to describe the object in the informal strategy. The designer draws up a table listing the objects, their attributes and an identifier which will be used in the final implementation.

Once the objects have been identified, the next stage is to look for the operations. Again, this step takes the informal strategy as its basis. This time, the developer looks for verbs, verb phrases and predicates. Each operation should act on only one object. This provides "functional cohesion". In a similar manner to the stage in which the objects and types are identified, it is suggested that the developer produce a table with the columns "operation", "space", "object" and "identifier", then read the informal strategy underlining the verbs, verb phrases and predicates.

As with the objects, a separate step is identified in which it is the task of the designer to list the attributes of the operations which have been identified. The handbook suggests that the developer looks for adverbs and related phrases.

Finally, the designer explicitly states which operations act on which objects and may define a hierarchy for the objects if this is appropriate.

Defining the interfaces. From this stage onwards, the development method becomes increasingly concerned with the implementation of the final system in Ada.

The "Formal description of the visible interfaces" is intended to produce an outline description of the highest level of the Ada code of the solution. The highest level program unit is identified, and the units which will interface directly with the highest level unit are also identified. Objects, types and operations which are are nested within the program units which have been identified will be listed. The nesting and dependency information can be shown in a graphical form if required, though this is optional according to the method.

Analysis and clarifications of high-level design decisions. Additional operations, objects and types are added to the basic solution arrived at in the previous solution. The objective is not to change the functionality or interfaces of the objects in the solution space objects, but to create additional objects, types and operations which will be helpful in arriving at the final Ada implementation. If changes are made to the objects etc. identified in previous steps, the developer should be prepared to step back as necessary to make the change and propagate the changes through the entire process. This step may produce a modified version of the output from the previous step and a discussion and rationale for any of the changes in the solution.

Graphic annotation of the visible interfaces. This step generates the Booch diagrams, familiar to readers of [Booch,83].

Implementing the solution. This major step produces the Ada source code. Modules which are too large to write directly are produced by a form of stepwise refinement. The OOD method can be applied recursively where necessary to achieve a suitable breakdown.

The EVB handbook comes much closer than any of the Booch texts to providing something that is recognizable as a prescriptive design method. It builds on the basis of Booch's method and provides some useful guidelines for software engineers and gives some pointers to quality assurance. Even so, EVB's OOD is not a fully fledged method. It does not cover the full software lifecycle. The incompleteness of the method is most noticeable at the requirements analysis phase where, like Booch, EVB suggest that the developer examines some other method for guidance. JSD is suggested as an example of a method that can be used with OOD.

Both EVB's method and Booch's method rely on the simple English language textual description of the problem as a starting point.

8.2.3 HOOD

HOOD is a design method developed under contract to the European Space Agency (ESA) by CISI Ingéniérie and Matra, for use on the ESA's Columbus and Hermes projects. The method is also being used on the development of the software for the European Fighter Aircraft. Both of these projects will produce software which will be in use for many years, which will be large and complex and incorporating real-time constraints, distributed across a number of computers and will need to be maintained during a long lifetime. HOOD designs are intended to be mapped easily into Ada, like the approaches of Booch and EVB.

HOOD itself is still under development. ESA fund a HOOD Working Group which is currently organizing the development of a standard. HOOD stands for Hierarchical Object-Oriented Design, and the method is aimed at the development of Ada software. The primary reference for HOOD is the HOOD Manual [HOOD,88], though a description of the method also appears in [Heitz,88].

Like the Booch and EVB approaches already described, the HOOD method is not a complete method in terms of covering the whole of the software lifecycle. The HOOD manual states that HOOD "is an architectural design method which can be continued into the Detailed Design Phase". The authors suggest the use of an Ada-PDL for detailed design. Again, like Booch and EVB, HOOD says little about establishing requirements. The manual admits that the "transition from requirements to design is a critical activity" (p.33), but as far as requirements analysis itself is concerned, the manual only notes that there may be several representations of the requirements – entity relationship diagrams, functional views and SADT diagrams.

According to the HOOD manual, HOOD is based on work done at Matra on Abstract Machines and CISI's work on OOD. The manual claims that the combination of the two in HOOD results in a hierarchical structure which is not present in ordinary OOD. HOOD has not one, but two types of hierarchies, a seniority hierarchy and a parent-child hierarchy. The seniority hierarchy gives a means of providing a layered structure to the system. The "senior" objects at the top of the hierarchy use the "junior" objects which are below them in the hierarchy. The second type of hierarchy is called the parent-child hierarchy and allows objects to be composed of other objects. HOOD also distinguishes between active and passive objects. Active objects are objects in which control flows are interacting, or where the object responds to some external stimulus, whereas passive objects are those where control is passed to the object. Active objects can *use* any other kind of object, whereas passive objects can only use other *passive* objects. There is a further restriction that passive objects cannot use each other in a cyclical manner. Active objects correspond to Ada tasks.

The parent-child hierarchy is defined through the include relationships in the system. The child objects that are included in a parent object "collectively provide the functionality of the parent".

There is a difference in the nature of decompositions that can be produced with active and passive objects. If a passive object is decomposed into a number of child objects, the parent object must retain control over the operations that are provided by the child objects. In contrast, the decomposition of an active object may include a child object which controls the operation of the other child objects in the system, or may split the control within an object between a number of child objects.

The HOOD method has a graphical notation for the description of objects, with the distinction between active and passive objects clearly made and the control, data and exception flows shown.

The HOOD design process is considered by its authors to be "globally top-down". A number of "basic design steps" are executed, in which objects are broken down into their constituent objects and each documented in what HOOD calls a chapter .

The HOOD basic design step
The HOOD basic design step identifies the child objects and the relationships of a parent object to the existing objects. The basic design step is made up of four sub-steps: definition and analysis of the problem; elaboration of an informal strategy of solution; formalization of the strategy and formalization of the solution. As with the other OOD methods, the HOOD manual suggests that the method can be applied recursively.

HOOD Details
Problem definition. The problem definition phase is the first step of the HOOD method. The problem definition phase itself is split into two substeps:

(i) Statement of the problem. The HOOD manual suggests that the developer should try to state the problem in one sentence, giving a precise definition of the problem and defining the overall context and environment. The HOOD manual explains that by restricting the outline description of the problem to a single sentence, the developer is forced to adopt higher-level abstractions for larger and more complex problems, whereas simple problems can be described more directly.

(ii) Analysis and structuring of the requirement data. This step is to allow the designer to develop a complete understanding of the problem. The output of this stage includes a description of the environment of the system, a user's manual for the final system and technical notes that provide more information about any problems that have arisen from more detailed examination of the requirements analysis. Note that the HOOD method starts with the assumption that the requirements analysis has already been done. SADT, data-flow diagrams and entity-relationship methods are suggested as requirements analysis techniques which are applicable.

Elaboration of an informal solution strategy. The elaboration of the solution consists of expanding the single sentence describing the problem into a paragraph. The solution need not be precise or complete, but HOOD suggests that "dynamic descriptions" (describing the actions between objects) are to be preferred over "static descriptions" in order to avoid the danger of merely rephrasing the description of the problem which has come before. The description should only concern itself with one level of abstraction, should be simple and describe the solution in terms which are close to the real world. One of the reasons for the last point is that the HOOD manual recommends that the text produced by this phase of the process should be reviewed by the customer and by an expert in the application domain.

Formalization of the strategy. This stage consists of a number of substeps. Like the

EVB handbook, the HOOD manual warns that difficulties in formalizing the solution often arise when something has been missed out or a concept described inadequately. The substeps of the formalization phase are:

(i) Identification of objects. The goal of this step is to identify the objects in the solution. These may be represented by active objects, passive objects, classes, types or "simple data". The exact structure that evolves will depend upon the behaviour of the system and on the hierarchies which are established.

As with the other object-oriented methods, the HOOD manual's main suggestion for the identification of objects is to underline the nouns (and noun phrases) in the strategy document. Each of the objects identified in the solution space is given an identifier. The HOOD manual warns that some objects may be mentioned more than once in the strategy, though they may be described using slightly different terms. Some objects may only exist in the strategy to aid understanding of the document and may have no place in the solution. HOOD suggests that these are listed in the object list, but are not given an identifier.

(ii) Identification of operations. In a similar manner to the other object-oriented methods, HOOD suggests that the verbs and verb phrases in the strategy are underlined, given a suitable identifier, and associated with a corresponding object.

(iii) Objects and operations. This step analyses the relationship between the objects and the operations. The objective is to produce a HOOD "object skeleton", a description of the interfaces of the objects in the system.

(iv) Graphical description. In this step, the developer produces a HOOD diagram showing the objects and their operations. Figure 8.1 shows a simple stack defined using the HOOD graphical notation. The stack provides two operations, shown in the box on the left of the main object, called "push" and "pop". The stack object can also raise two exceptions, "empty" or "overflow", both of which are indicated by the crossed arrows. In a complete design, these arrows would be connected to the objects which handle the exceptions.

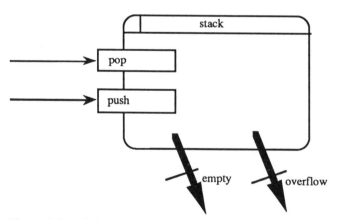

Figure 8.1: HOOD graphical notation example

Formalization of the solution. The formalization builds on the identification of the objects and operations in the previous phases to produce a formal description (in HOOD terms) of the objects, their attributes and the relationships between the objects.

Formal description of the interfaces. For each "child" object, the description of the interface is produced. This is the description of the required and provided operations of the object and is used to fill out the object definition skeleton (ODS). The HOOD manual states that an Ada-PDL is to describe the control structure of the objects, though this would seem a little premature.

Definition of the parent object. In this sub-stage, according to HOOD, the "parent" object is described completely and formally. Again, the description is in the form of an ODS. The method is somewhat confused at this point. Although the previous step has the title "formal definition of interfaces", it seems to be assumed that the control structure of the child object is done here. On the other hand, nothing is said in the guidelines about the control structure of the parent object.

A parent object will usually contain several child objects. Figure 8.2 shows how a more complex HOOD parent object might contain three child objects. Children 1 and 2 collectively provide the interface of the parent object through their exported operations. The thick arrow connecting child 2 to child 3 indicates that 3 provides an interface which is used by 2, (the HOOD "use" relationship), but no more detail than this is shown in the figure.

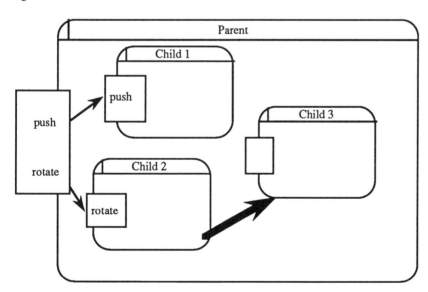

Figure 8.2: Parent and child objects in HOOD

Implementation of the parent object. According to the manual, this step should "describe the implementation strategy for specific target environments and produce a formal description of the parent object". This step is essentially the transformation of the ODS into Ada. HOOD suggests that with suitable tools, this step could be performed automatically.

215

Validation. The HOOD manual has a page suggesting the kind of validation and QA procedures that might be applied to ensure that the method has been applied properly. These are in the form of general suggestions and do not contain the level of detail to be found in the EVB handbook.

General Guidelines

As well as the more detailed information on how to perform the various steps of the HOOD method, the HOOD manual also provides some more general guidelines for the developer in describing how to set about designing objects. These include principles for designing "good" objects (defined as an object which represents a problem domain entity hiding closely related information which is likely to change), and describing four kinds of abstraction which are employed:

- Entity abstraction in which a problem domain entity is modelled, such as a real piece of hardware, or something more abstract such as a compiler symbol table

- Action abstraction, modelling actions rather than entities

- Virtual machine abstraction, grouping operations which are used together by some superior level in the system, and

- Logistic abstractions, which are not abstractions at all, but merely convenient collections of operations.

HOOD Tools

As was pointed out in the introduction to this section, HOOD is still under development. However, ESA have funded the development of two toolsets which support HOOD. One is produced by Software Sciences Ltd., the other is available from Systematica Ltd. Both provide a means of producing and manipulating HOOD object diagrams.

Problems with HOOD

One of the major difficulties is the inadequacy of the HOOD Manual [HOOD,88] as it exists at the moment. The manual lacks explicit guidance on how to perform many steps of the method. It is not really very clear how a HOOD development should start, or indeed at what point it should end.

While the two types of hierarchy which are present in HOOD may seem like a useful idea at first, there are certain problems with the idea. The seniority hierarchy makes it necessary for interfaces provided by lowerlevel objects to be propagated up through the more senior objects in the system if they are to be used by objects in other branches of the hierarchy. There is also a problem in that the emphasis on the seniority hierarchy could work against reuse by imposing a structure on the system which is too static and too closely related to the project in hand.

Since HOOD is oriented towards implementations in the Ada language, it is perhaps not surprising that the role of classes is not addressed. This limits the use of HOOD for use with other programming languages, but also may be a limitation even with Ada. Although Ada has no explicit class construct, a package exporting a type can be used to achieve some of the same effect and provides for the same basic need, that is to be able to express the commonality of a number of objects.

Like the other OOD methods described so far in this chapter, the HOOD method does not mention inheritance. Again, given the use of Ada as the implementation language for HOOD designs, this is understandable. However, it does limit the usefulness of the method with other programming languages. There is an argument that even when the final implementation language does not have a mechanism for inheritance, it may still be useful at higher levels in the design process, where, like the class construct, there is a requirement to exploit the commonality of a number of objects.

These criticisms may seem a little harsh. As has already been mentioned, the method is still under development and was originally conceived as a method for use on one specific project within ESA. The method is bound to develop further in the future and it it likely that shortcomings mentioned here will be addressed in later versions of the method.

8.2.4 OOSD

OOSD (Object-Oriented Structured Design) is described in a recent paper by Anthony Wasserman and his colleagues from Interactive Development Environments [Wasserman,89]. Like the HOOD method just described, OOSD is seen as an architectural design method, the phase in the design "at which the *what* becomes the *how*". The developers of OOSD are ambitious: the "goal of OOSD is to provide a single architectural design notation that can support every software design". OOSD aims to be useful to software designers working in a wide range of different application areas, including concurrent systems. The method emphasizes the interfaces that modules present to the rest of the system and the visibility of these interfaces throughout the system as a whole. It is perhaps somewhat strange that the developers of the method have chosen to base OOSD on Structured Design rather than on object-orientation because of "the desire to keep modularity as the most critical component of an architectural design method".

One of the requirements mentioned for OOSD mentioned in [Wasserman,89] is that

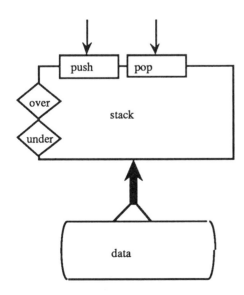

Figure 8.3: Stack object in OOSD

217

it is "methodology independent". The reason given for this is that OOSD can therefore be used as the architectural design method for a wider range of systems. This author would argue that the real reason for this method independence is that OOSD is not a design method at all by the criteria mentioned at the start of the chapter. Rather, it attempts to be a comprehensive diagrammatic notation which can encompass a very wide range of software designs. IDE, for whom the authors of OOSD work, market a CASE tool called Software Through Pictures. Clearly, the intention of the authors is that OOSD can be used with Software Through Pictures in a large number of cases where there would be no chance of the organization concerned completely changing their approach to software development.

One of the ideas of OOSD is to provide a diagrammatic notation sufficiently complete to allow code to be generated from it. OOSD diagrams are therefore considerably more complex than HOOD diagrams, where much detail can be relegated to the text documents associated with the method. This leads to a diagram syntax which is very complex. However, as a simple example of the OOSD notation of Figure 8.3 shows a stack object, again exporting two operations and two exceptions. The data store used by the stack object is shown, made visible to the stack object itself by the thick arrow connecting it to it.

8.2.5 Eiffel

Bertrand Meyer is the president of Interactive Software Engineering Inc., and his book, "Object-Oriented Software Construction" [Meyer,88] describes another approach to software development.

Meyer defines object-oriented design as "the method which leads to software architectures based on the objects every system or subsystem manipulates rather than 'the' function it is meant to ensure". He goes on to provide what might be considered the overriding guideline to designers employing the object-oriented approach, namely: "Ask not first what the system does: Ask what it does it to!". By using an object-oriented approach, Meyer argues, the designers avoid for as long as possible the need to describe and implement the top level function of the system. Meyer points out that software systems can frequently be regarded as operational models of the real world. Once this is recognized, the object-oriented approach seems much more natural.

Meyer illustrates his ideas on object-oriented design with examples written in the Eiffel programming language. Eiffel has multiple inheritance, so unlike HOOD and the methods of Booch and EVB, Meyer advocates an approach to software design based around *classes*. Meyer emphasizes the importance of making the classes from which the design is composed as autonomous as possible. This is mainly for reasons of reuse. If a class is nested within another class, in the way in which one procedure might be nested within another in a block-structured language, it is difficult or impossible for the inner class to be reused. This is not the same as saying that one object cannot contain another in the final system. This is referring to the textual definition of the classes in the design. For instance, an object in a software system might contain a *stack*, but the class definition for the object concerned would not *contain* the definition of the stack; instead it would refer to one defined elsewhere.

Meyer's book also illustrates many important principles of object-oriented design. For instance, the need for the units of design to map easily into the implementation language (in this case, classes and Eiffel); the need for the number of interfaces to be kept small so as to reduce complexity; the need for the interfaces themselves to be small, (really a restatement of the information hiding principle in slightly different terms); and the need for interfaces to be explicit, avoiding hidden communication between the various units in the program which may seem obvious to the original programmer, but are rarely so to those who follow and try to maintain the system.

Although Meyer's explanations are clear and his examples excellent, his book does not describe a design method in the sense intended here. It does, however, present a number of useful ideas which could be adopted in a design method.

8.2.6 JSD

JSD [Jackson,83] is mentioned as a method which may be suitable for use with OOD in both Booch's paper on object-oriented development [Booch,86] and the EVB handbook on object-oriented development [EVB,85], not as a method for requirements analysis, but as a way of helping to give structure to the requirements. Several authors have examined the similarities between JSD and OOD, e.g. [Masiero,88] and [Birchenough,88]. In particular, the "entity action step" has some similarities with the early stages of OOD. From [Jackson,83] we see that "...the ideas of entity and action are very closely related: an action is always performed or suffered by one or more entities, and an entity is characterized by the actions which it performs or suffers, and their ordering in time. [...] A JSD entity must perform or suffer actions, in a significant time ordering.". It is the emphasis on the time ordering of events which is one of the major differences between JSD and OOD. Nonetheless, the suggestions that JSD makes for identifying the entities and actions bear a striking resemblance to the OOD suggestions for identifying objects and operations: "...make a comprehensive list of nouns and verbs we encounter in our study of reality: each noun is a possible entity; each verb is a possible action".

8.3 CONCLUSION

OOD is not yet a mature system development method. It does not, for example, meet the requirements for a design method listed in [Freeman,82] or [McDermid,84], where an important requirement is that a method should "cover the entire development process, simplifying transitions between project phases". While there is much interest in the object-oriented approach, the growing multiplicity of methods and tools labelled "object-oriented" inevitably means that a certain amount of scepticism is in order when looking at the new approach. Object-oriented methods are being increasingly used in industry, however, and the use of HOOD by the European Space Agency is one example of the way ahead.

OOD is not a complete design method. None of the descriptions of OOD addresses the requirements analysis phase of the software lifecycle. Most authors in the area suggest that some other appropriate method be used as a "front-end" to OOD at this stage. This author believes that this is an area where much more research needs to be done. Any structuring of requirements is a form of highlevel design. A designer needs to be careful that this is done in a way which is compatible with the object-oriented approach. For example, it is unlikely that a functional breakdown of a system will lead in a natural way to a good object-oriented design.

None of the object-oriented design methods gives much assistance in identifying objects. Booch, EVB and HOOD all concentrate on the highlighting of nouns and verbs in the informal strategy as a means of identifying candidate objects and operations. Meyer in [Sowizral,88] states that it is a myth that there are simple methods for finding objects; others claim that it is simple once an object-oriented "mindset" has been achieved. What is clear is that the developer should be prepared to make more than one attempt at identifying the objects for a complex system. There is a tendency for the textbooks on OOD to describe systems in which identifying the objects is very easy, or at least to present the description of a design in such a way that it is made to look easy. It would be useful to see examples of decompositions which have gone wrong as well as those which seem to have worked. In the design of a large, complex system, identification of objects and the establishment of the relationships between them is likely to take some time. It is also important to remember that identifying classes is not the same as identifying objects. The objects have a life in the running system, whereas the classes are a means of expressing commonality of objects when building the system.

As well as new methods coming into existence, the influence of OOD is being felt in other areas. Existing design methods are changing to adapt to a new object-oriented view of the world. This is particularly evident with SA, the analysis technique which is the companion to the almost archetypical function-oriented decomposition technique, SD. In [Shlaer,88], SA is described as an object-oriented analysis technique.

Many people writing about object-oriented design say that there will be significant changes to the software lifecycle as a result of the new ways of working which OOD brings in its wake. While this is probably true, it is also the case that the simple views of the software lifecycle are being questioned. More sophisticated views such as Boehm's spiral model [Boehm,88] attempt to address issues such as the need for prototyping and risk assessment during the development process. Many writers in the object-oriented world have identified the need for methods and lifecycles which permit the kind of iterative development and gradual change which occurs in the development of large systems. Object-oriented design assists in this because of the way in which the objects or classes which are being built are independent of each other.

In summary, true object-oriented development methods which are well defined and cover the entire lifecycle, supported by appropriate tools for which the criteria which were identified at the beginning of this chapter, do not yet seem to exist. The situation is changing, however, and as experience with the object-oriented approach grows, we can expect more mature methods and their associated tools to appear. Work on object-oriented design methods continues, particularly in extending the approach to cover more of the lifecycle. Work describing object-oriented requirements analysis (OORA) and object-oriented domain analysis (OODA) (for example, [Schlaer,89]) is now beginning to appear.

8.4 ACKNOWLEDGEMENTS

The author is currently working on the DRAGON project of the ESPRIT programme and gratefully acknowledges the financial support of the Commission of the European Communities.

The participants in the DRAGON project are: TXT SpA, GSI-Tecsi, Dornier System GmbH, the University College of Wales Aberystwyth, Lancaster University, Imperial College, Politecnico di Milano, and the Universities of Genoa and Passau.

REFERENCES

[Abbott,80] Abbott, R., "Report on Teaching Ada," *Science Applications Inc., report SAI-81-312WA,* December 1980.

[Birchenough,88] Birchenough, A., and Cameron, J.R., "JSD and Object-oriented Design," *Proc. 7th Ada UK Conference* , York, UK., pp. 66-71, 1989. (Published in *Ada User* Vol.9 Supplement).

[Boehm,88] Boehm, B. W., "A Spiral Model of Software Development and Enhancement," *IEEE Computer,* pp. 61–72, May 1988.

[Booch,83] Booch, G., *Software Engineering with Ada,* Benjamin Cummings, Menlo Park, California, 1983.

[Booch,86] Booch, G., "Object-Oriented Development," *IEEE Transactions on Software Engineering,* pp. 211-221, February 1986.

[Booch,87] Booch, G., *Software Components with Ada* Benjamin Cummings, Menlo Park, California, 1987.

[Cox,86] Cox, B.J,, *Object-oriented Programming – An Evolutionary Approach,* Addison-Wesley, 1986.

[EVB,85] EVB, *An Object-oriented Design Handbook for Ada Software,* EVB Software Engineering Inc., Frederick, Maryland, 1985.

[Freeman,82] Freeman, P. and Wasserman A. I., "Ada Methodologies: Concepts and Requirements," US Department of Defense, November 1982.

[Freeman,83] Freeman, P., "Fundamentals of Design," *IEEE Tutorial on Software Design Techniques,* pp. 2–22, 1983.

[Halbert,87] Halbert, D.C. and O'Brien P.D., "Using Types and Inheritance in Object-Oriented Languages," *Proc. European Conference on Object-oriented Programming (ECOOP '87),* Paris, France, pp. 20-31, June 1987.

[Heitz,88] Heitz, M. and Labreville B., "Design and Development of Distributed Software using Hierarchical Object-oriented Design and Ada," *Proc. Ada-Europe International Conference,* Munich, FRG., pp. 143-156, June 1988.

[HOOD,88] CISI Ingéniérie, CRI A/S, Matra Espace, *HOOD Manual Issue 2.2* European Space Agency, Noordwijk, Netherlands, 1988.

[Jackson,83] Jackson, M., *System Development,* Prentice-Hall, Englewood Cliffs, New Jersey, 1983.

[Johnson,88] Johnson, R.E. and Foote, B., "Designing Reusable Classes," *Journal of*

Object-oriented Programming, pp. 22-35, June/July 1988.

[**Masiero,88**] Masiero P.C. and Germano F.S.R., "JSD as an Object-Oriented Design Method," *ACM Software Engineering Notes,* Vol.13 No.3, pp. 22-23, July 1988.

[**McDermid,84**] McDermid J. and Ripken K., *Life Cycle Support in the Ada Environment*, Cambridge University Press, Cambridge, UK, 1984.

[**Meyer,87**] Meyer, B., "Reusability: The Case for Object-Oriented Design," *IEEE Software*, pp. 50-64, March 1987.

[**Meyer,88**] Meyer, B., *Object-oriented Software Construction*, Prentice-Hall, Hemel-Hempstead, England, 1988.

[**Parnas,72**] Parnas, D.L., "On the Criteria to be Used in Decomposing Systems into Modules," *Communications of the ACM*, pp. 1053-1058, December 1972.

[**Parnas,79**] Parnas, D.L., "Designing Software for Ease of Extension and Contraction," *IEEE Transactions on Software Engineering*, pp. 310–319, March 1979.

[**Seidewitz,87**] Seidewitz, E., "Object-oriented Programming in Smalltalk and Ada," *Proc OOPSLA '87*, Orlando, Florida, pp. 202-213, October 1987.

[**Shlaer,88**] Shlaer, S. and Mellor S.J., *Object-Oriented Systems Analysis: Modelling the World in Data*, Yourdon Press, Englewood Cliffs, New Jersey, 1988.

[**Shlaer,89**] Shlaer S. and Mellor S.J., "An Object-Oriented Approach to Domain Analysis," *ACM Software Engineering Notes,* pp. 65–77, July 1989.

[**Sowizral,88**] Sowizral H.A., "7-8 Panel Session," *Special Issue of SIGPLAN Notices,* vol.23 no.5, Orlando, Florida, pp. 7-8, May 1988.

[**Wasserman,89**] Wasserman, A.I., Pircher P.A. and Muller R.J., "An Object-Oriented Structured Design Method for Code Generation," *ACM Software Engineering Notes,* pp. 32–55, January 1989.

[**Wegner,87**] Wegner, P., "Dimensions of Object-Based Language Design," *Proc. OOPSLA '87*, Orlando, Florida, pp. 168-182, October 1987.

[**Yourdon,79**] Yourdon, E.N. and Constantine, L.L., *Structured Design: Fundamentals of a Discipline of Computer Program and Systems Design*, Prentice-Hall, Englewood Cliffs, New Jersey, 1979.

Chapter 9

Distributed Systems and Objects

David Hutchison and Jonathan Walpole
Lancaster University

ABSTRACT *This chapter discusses the application of the object-oriented paradigm to distributed systems. First, we present an overview of the specific problems encountered in programming distributed systems as opposed to centralized systems. Then, in order to alleviate some of the confusion in this particular area, we outline the evolution of object-oriented distributed systems through a discussion of the various distributed systems models which led to its development. This is followed by a discussion of the current application of the object-oriented paradigm to distributed systems and a brief survey of recent distributed object-oriented languages and systems. Finally, the use of objects in distributed systems architectures, and in particular in the international standards work on Open Distributed Processing, is introduced and some of the important aspects of the work emphasized.*

9.1 DISTRIBUTED SYSTEMS

There is almost as much contention over the meaning of the term 'distributed system' as there is over the meaning of the term 'object-oriented'. The different interpretations cover a spectrum which includes vector processors at one extreme and world-wide networks of autonomous computers at the other. In this book, the term distributed system is defined as follows:

Definition: A distributed system consists of multiple processors which do not share primary memory, and which communicate by sending messages over a communications network.

(The communications network could be a local area network, a metropolitan area network, or a wide area network.)

A large number of research projects which address distributed *systems* work also address the *language* issues associated with programming distributed systems and applications. In many cases it is difficult to identify where the systems work ends and where the language work begins. With the arrival of object-oriented distributed systems, this division of responsibility has been almost completely removed and many projects could be classified equally accurately as distributed systems projects or as distributed language projects. Throughout this chapter, the term 'distributed system' will also be used to encompass distributed application and language projects.

9.1.1 Programming Distributed Systems

In addition to the array of different types of distributed systems, there is a wide variety of distributed applications, many of which have different design goals. However, the reasons for programming a distributed system rather than a centralized system usually fall into one or more of the following categories:-

* Performance can be improved through the introduction of parallelism, i.e. processing can take place on more than one node at the same time.
* The application is inherently distributed. This can be due to either the geographical separation of communicating entities (as in mail systems), or the functional specialization of distributed resources (as in automated factory floor systems and automated chemical plants).
* Reliability can be increased through the replication of data and processing entities on a number of nodes.

In order to achieve the above goals, distributed programming systems must address a number of important issues which do not arise in centralised systems. These issues are listed below and will be used in section 9.3 as a framework for discussing the application of the object-oriented paradigm to distributed systems:

* location of distributed entities (e.g. are they fixed at a location or can they migrate)
* distribution transparency (in terms of object location, partial failure, etc.)
* support for parallelism
* communication between distributed entities
* synchronization: if parallelism is supported, how do cooperating entities synchronize?
* behaviour sharing and distribution.

Prior to this, however, we examine briefly the trends which have led to the development of object-oriented distributed systems.

9.2 THE EVOLUTION OF OBJECT-ORIENTED DISTRIBUTED SYSTEMS

There is considerable confusion in the distributed systems world over what constitutes an object-oriented distributed system. The term "object-oriented" has been attached, inappropriately in our view, to the different categories of system discussed below. The discussion will attempt to show why such confusion arose and to what extent the respective categories of distributed system contributed to the development and acceptance of object-oriented distributed systems.

9.2.1 Clients and Servers

From the early days of distributed computing, distributed systems have been programmed using conventional high-level languages with extensions to handle inter-process communications. These languages are used to write programs which implement processes running on separate nodes. The processes communicate via message passing and are typically organized as either clients or servers. The client/server model allows the communicating entities in a distributed system to be identified and it provides a rudimentary technique for modelling their behaviour. In this way, services in a distributed system can be viewed as being encapsulated within a server which implements a well defined interface through which the other entities in the system (clients) can access the service.

Communication in the client/server model is provided by the underlying operating system and is accessed by programmers through the use of special operating system routines. Consequently, communication between clients and servers is explicit and programmers are faced with a considerable degree of distribution complexity. In the client/server model there is a clear distinction between the responsibilities of the system and those of the language; only the system is concerned with distribution. There are several examples of this approach in the literature [Wilkes80,Mullender87].

9.2.2 Remote Procedure Calls

The introduction of the remote procedure call paradigm [Birrell84] was a significant step towards well structured distributed systems (and towards object-oriented distributed systems). Remote procedure calls allow programmers to represent the entities in a distributed system and their communications interfaces using facilities which are supported at the language level.

Communication between distributed entities is no longer explicit at the programming interface. Communication is made transparent by hiding it within the procedure calling mechanism of the programming language (in practice, this is not entirely possible because in the event of a partial failure during a remote call, transparency is broken and an unexpected error condition arises). Therefore, programmers are shielded from the complexities of distribution through the use of a higher-level programming abstraction, namely the remote procedure call.

The remote procedure call (RPC) is frequently used in conjunction with the client/server model. This approach expedites the construction of distributed systems through the use of powerful high level abstractions. However, procedure calling (with the usual synchronous wait semantics) is a serial language paradigm and therefore it can be used to make distribution transparent only at the additional expense of parallelism.

The significance of the contribution made by the remote procedure call paradigm is that it provides a convenient and familiar model to the programmer while hiding the underlying mechanisms for supporting distribution. Examples of this approach are covered in [Xerox81, Wilbur87].

9.2.3 The Object Model

The object model as introduced by Jones in [Jones78] is probably the most commonly used abstraction for building recent distributed systems. Jones borrowed the language concepts of object and type and showed how they could be applied to the design of operating systems.

As a system structuring construct the object model is more powerful and flexible than the client/server model. Distributed entities can be modelled as user-defined typed objects. The type of an object specifies the operations which can be performed on it. Therefore, if the type of an object is known it is possible to determine its interface. In addition, the object model uses a message passing paradigm and does not require that communication semantics match those of a procedure call. Asynchronous communications may be adopted, giving scope for the increased use of concurrency. Therefore, as a communication model, it is more flexible than the remote procedure call model.

Significantly, the object model introduces the use of more powerful language concepts for distributed systems design. The concepts of object and type are not specific to conventional programming languages and therefore they can be used to present a powerful high-level abstraction for programming distributed systems without restricting parallelism.

9.3 ISSUES IN OBJECT-ORIENTED DISTRIBUTED SYSTEMS

In this section we examine the application of the object-oriented paradigm to distributed systems. In particular, we study the various approaches taken by object-oriented systems in tackling the issues outlined in section 9.1.1.

9.3.1 Object Location

In object-oriented distributed systems the unit of distribution is the object. Distributed systems are composed of a number of cooperating objects which can be located on separate nodes. Several different strategies exist for the mapping of objects to processors. Firstly, this mapping can be either determined automatically by the compiler and operating system, or it can be explicitly under the control of the programmer. The former requires the system to use information about the object and processor concerned in order to perform a sensible mapping. However, the correct mapping of objects to processors is often dependent on the application being supported. Application specific information is not usually available to the system and therefore some control over object location is often given to the programmer through special language primitives.

Depending on whether object location is under the control of the programmer or the system, there are also a number of choices concerning the time at which objects are mapped to processors. The location of an object can be fixed at compile time or objects can be allowed to migrate dynamically during execution. There are a number of advantages and disadvantages associated with each of these approaches. Fixing an object's location at compile time allows the programmer to take advantage of the fact that an object's location is known For example, communication between objects which are located at the same node can be made more efficient. However, the static location of objects is too inflexible for some applications. Object migration may be required for a number of reasons: to match the semantics of the application; to achieve better performance through load balancing; to implement more efficient parameter passing (see section 9.3.4).

If the application being supported requires high reliability, objects can also be replicated. In this case, it is clearly important that the replicas of an object are kept on different nodes.

9.3.2 Distribution Transparency

In object-oriented distributed systems the location of an object may or may not be transparent at the programming language level. In either case, communication between objects is achieved by explicitly sending messages. Furthermore, the object model does not distinguish between local or remote message passing. Hence (physically) distributed systems can be programmed using the same abstractions as non-distributed systems.

One difficulty in maintaining total distribution transparency arises when the treatment of partial failures is considered. The failure of a single node in a distributed system causes all the objects held on that node to become unavailable for a period of time. This event can be viewed by the other objects on other nodes in the system in several possible ways: one object could send a message to a remote object which was already unavailable; or the remote object could become unavailable during the processing of a message. In both cases the remaining object would not receive a reply (whether or not a reply is expected also depends on the semantics of the message passing protocol - see section 9.3.4). Alternatively, the underlying system could inform the surviving object that a crash had been deduced, by returning a specific error condition. In either case however, the semantics of remote object invocation are different from those for local object invocation and hence distribution is not completely transparent.

9.3.3 Parallelism

A variety of different approaches to parallelism occurs in the object model. Some object-oriented languages/systems allow parallelism to occur within objects. In such systems, objects either support multiple parallel processes, in which case the unit of parallelism is a process, or the language itself supports parallel instructions for programming objects, in which case the unit of parallelism is the instruction.

A more common model however is to support parallelism only between objects. There are several different sets of semantics which can be associated with computation between objects. These significantly affect the level of parallelism that can be supported. In order to discuss these different approaches, it is first necessary to distinguish between passive and active objects.

We define passive objects to be those which are used in the following way: objects are only activated when they receive a message; while the receiver of a message is active the sender waits for a reply and is passive. Therefore, only one object is active at any time and there is no parallelism.

There are several ways in which this situation can be improved to increase parallelism:-

* allow an object to be active without having received a message.
* allow receiving objects to continue execution after they have returned a result.

227

* allow senders to send messages to several objects at the same time;
* allow senders to proceed in parallel with receivers
    (i.e. through the use of asynchronous message passing).

Various combinations of the above approaches are used in current distributed object-oriented systems (see sections 9.4 and 9.5).

9.3.4 Communication

Communication between objects is usually based one one of the following models: remote procedure call in which the sending object blocks until it receives a result; synchronous message passing in which the sender blocks until it receives an acknowledgment; or asynchronous message passing in which the sender continues execution immediately after sending a message.

In addition to the various strategies for inter-object communication already covered above, it is also necessary to consider the methods used for invoking operations on remote objects. Of particular interest are the various possible parameter passing semantics. In object-oriented systems, parameters often refer to other objects. Therefore, the natural way to pass parameters is by reference. However, in distributed systems this approach causes several problems. Firstly, references (addresses) are context dependent and therefore have no meaning on a remote machine. Secondly, call-by-reference can be expensive because passing a reference to an object which is remote (to the invoked object) requires that object to perform a further remote operation. In remote procedure call systems, and in the Argus system [Liskov82], these problems result in parameters being passed by value for remote invocations. However, this changes the semantics of the object model for remote operations and destroys distribution transparency.

Several techniques are used to maintain call-by-reference semantics for invocations on remote objects. One solution is to send a copy of the parameter object(s) with the message which invokes the remote operation. However, this solution introduces consistency problems since there are now multiple copies of the parameter object(s). To alleviate such problems this approach is typically used for small objects which are immutable and hence do not introduce a consistency problem.

A more general solution is to use proxy objects. A proxy object is a representative of a remote object on a local machine. The call-by-proxy parameter passing technique causes a proxy of the parameter object to be passed to the remote node. Messages to the proxy object are forwarded to its remote object. The remote object executes the associated operations and sends the reply to the proxy. The proxy then forwards the reply to the original sender. This approach also maintains the semantics of call-by-reference and is more flexible than the call-by-copy technique described above.

Although call-by-proxy is a general solution to implementing remote invocations, it still incurs the overhead of remote execution which can, in many cases, be avoided. In some cases a more efficient solution to this problem is to move the parameter object to the required node when the operation is invoked. This maintains the semantics of call-by-reference since all parameters can be referenced locally. However, whether this is worthwhile depends on a number of factors. These include: the size of the parameter object; other current or future operations on the parameter object; the number of invocations which will be issued by the remote object to the parameter object; and the relative cost of moving the object, local invocation and remote invocation. It is important to note that this approach requires the support of object migration whereas call-by-proxy does not (as discussed in 9.3.1).

9.3.5 Synchronization and Recovery

The synchronization mechanisms required in object-oriented distributed systems depend largely on the level of parallelism supported. If parallelism is supported within an object the object must contain mechanisms to control concurrent access to its shared data. These mechanisms usually consist of locks, semaphores or monitors [Hoare74].

Recent research [Detlefs88, Shrivastava87] is also exploring the use of user defined object types which exhibit particular synchronization and recovery characteristics. These object types can then be placed in an inheritance hierarchy to allow particular synchronization and recovery characteristics to be inherited by sub-types.

In some systems it is also necessary to provide mechanisms which allow operations to be performed atomically on groups of objects. This is usually achieved by channeling messages to the members of the group through a special object which is designated as the manager or guardian of the group. This technique is used in the Argus language [Liskov82] and is discussed in more detail in section 9.4.

9.3.6 Behaviour Sharing and Distribution in Class Based Systems

A new problem which is introduced by the use of the object-oriented paradigm in distributed systems is the distribution of class hierarchies. The interaction between objects in an object-oriented system takes two forms: interaction between instances; and interaction between an instance and its corresponding class or 'concrete' data type. This latter form of interaction can also involve interaction between classes and their super-classes (recursively).

Several object-oriented models (e.g. Smalltalk) take the view that classes are also objects, and that the interaction between instances, classes and super-classes can be treated uniformly (using the techniques described above). However, this approach has several drawbacks in distributed systems. The invocation of an operation on an object typically involves a number of interactions. First, the class of the instance must be contacted in order to access the code for the required operation. This code may be defined within the class of the instance, or it may have been inherited from a super-class. If it has been inherited, each super-class above the current position in the hierarchy must be contacted until the relevant piece of code has been located. If the instance, class and various super-classes are located on different nodes of the distributed system this chain of interaction will be extremely expensive.

There are several solutions which make the invocation of operations in distributed inheritance systems more efficient. These include the following:

* allow instances to reside only on nodes which hold their associated classes.
* maintain a master copy of the hierarchy and cache slave copies on the required machines.
* replicate the class hierarchy on a number of nodes.
* associate pointers with instances which store the location of the appropriate class object.

However, each of these approaches has serious drawbacks. Forcing objects to reside only on the same nodes as their classes severely restricts object mobility. The master slave approach suffers from problems of maintaining consistency of cached copies. Replication also suffers from the same consistency problems, since updates must be correctly propagated to every node. One solution to this problem is to make classes immutable, i.e. allow class evolution only through the creation of sub-classes and not through the modification of existing classes. However, this approach may present an intolerable restriction on class evolution. Finally, the association of pointers with objects, in order to locate their classes, can limit the mobility of classes since it is often necessary for classes to migrate in the same way as other objects. Several variations of this approach have been suggested in order to support class migration [Bennett87].

The above problems have led a number of distributed object-oriented system designers to consider other approaches to behaviour sharing which are not based on inheritance. Alternatives include models based on prototypes [Lieberman86] and abstract data types [Black87].

9.4 DISTRIBUTED OBJECT-ORIENTED LANGUAGES

This section discusses various object-oriented developments which originated in the language area, while the following section discusses relevant projects whose origins are in the systems area. As discussed earlier, the object-oriented paradigm has caused some convergence of the two areas. Consequently, there is considerable overlap between some of the systems/languages discussed.

Since the object-oriented paradigm is inherently distributed, it could be claimed that all object-oriented languages should be categorized as distributed programming languages. However, there are a number of projects which have explicitly addressed the problems of distribution in object-oriented languages. In this section we outline a representative selection of those projects and present a more detailed discussion of one such project, Emerald, to show how some of the problems outlined in the previous section have been tackled.

9.4.1 Argus

Argus [Liskov82,Liskov87] is an early distributed object-oriented language which was developed at MIT during the mid 1970s by Liskov et. al. Argus is based on CLU [Liskov81] and was designed specifically for supporting fault tolerance. The main features of Argus are guardians and actions. Guardians are Argus modules which contain data objects and procedures for manipulating those objects. Guardians are active entities and they control the synchronization and recovery characteristics of objects.

Communication in Argus is through handler calls which are a form of remote procedure call. Parallelism is supported by allowing guardians to execute in parallel and by allowing processes to execute in parallel within guardians. Instances of guardians are created by sending messages to creator procedures. Argus also provides a number of built in atomic data types which determine the amount of parallelism that is allowed between actions.

9.4.2 Distributed Smalltalk

Several projects have addressed the problem of distributing Smalltalk [Schelvis88, Bennett87, McCullough87]. These projects can generally be characterized according to the level at which they introduce distribution.

Most approaches to distributing Smalltalk introduce distribution at the Smalltalk image level and leave the underlying Smalltalk virtual machine untouched. This is usually achieved by introducing proxy objects into the address spaces of the sender and receiver which handle remote invocations. Two examples of this general approach are [Bennett87, McCullough87]. However, the motivation behind distributing Smalltalk is different in each case.

The first project [Bennett87] is concerned with providing support for programming distributed applications in a Smalltalk system which is not necessarily multi-user. Therefore, in this case there is a logically distinct address space for each user, and some additional primitives for distribution are provided within the language. Classes are replicated on several nodes, and object mobility is limited to only those nodes which contain an object's class. This requires a check when an object moves to ensure that the class on the destination node is the same as the one on the object's original node.

The second project [McCullough87] is concerned with providing support for sharing a Smalltalk system between multiple programmers on a local area network of workstations. Therefore, at the programming level, distribution is transparent and multiple programmers share a common Smalltalk image.

An alternative approach to distributing Smalltalk is to modify the virtual machine in order to present distribution transparency at the image level. This approach is taken in [Schelvis88] and has the advantage that it maintains the semantics of centralized Smalltalk programs. Heavily used objects, especially classes, are replicated within the virtual machine. Objects can migrate from one node to another (as long as their class is present on the destination node) and forwarding objects are left behind when an object leaves a node. The virtual machine uses these forwarding objects to locate an object which has migrated. Again, proxy objects are used for remote invocation, and distribution can become visible through the return of distribution specific error conditions.

9.4.3 Guide

Guide [Decouchant88] is a language for programming applications in the Guide distributed operating system which is currently under development at the University of Grenoble. As such, this discussion could also have been placed in the following section on object-oriented distributed systems.

An important aim of Guide is to make distribution transparent at the language level. This is achieved by providing facilities for supporting distribution within the underlying operating system. The operating system normally requires that objects are not to be split across nodes. However, there are special facilities for supporting composite objects which can be distributed across several nodes. In addition, Guide also supports object migration.

The computation model supported by Guide is synchronous in that senders must wait for the result of invocations on other objects. However, Guide also provides primitives for expressing parallelism. Parallelism is supported by allowing messages to be sent to a number of other objects in parallel. A number of different rules are presented for resuming activity following the sending of a message. The default synchronization policy for objects is implemented using a simple mutual exclusion algorithm. However, specialized synchronization constraints can also be specified within object classes. In this case the specialised synchronization mechanism will then apply to all the instances of the class.

Guide uses a distributed inheritance mechanism which generates a 'stub' class on the same node as the calling object (instance). Interaction between the instance and its class then takes place using a remote procedure call.

9.4.4 Emerald

Emerald [Black86, Black87, Black88] is an object-oriented language and system for constructing distributed applications. A key feature of Emerald is the tight coupling between the compiler and the run-time kernel. The Emerald compiler can determine the requirements of objects and can use context to generate different implementations from the same piece of source code.

Objects have unique network-wide names, data, operations and an optional process. Emerald objects may be either active or passive. Objects which contain processes are said to be active, objects without processes are passive. Parallelism is supported by allowing objects to contain several threads of control concurrently. Synchronization is provided by monitors.

Significantly, Emerald is not based on inheritance which the designers claim does not seem to be entirely appropriate in a distributed context. Instead, Emerald is based on a model of abstract data types. See chapter 4 for detailed discussion of this point.

Another key feature of Emerald is its support for object mobility. Both coarse and fine grained objects can migrate and the Emerald language provides primitives for supporting mobility. These primitives include the following:

LOCATE: to determine the node at which an object resides.
MOVE: to relocate an object.
FIX: to fix an object at a node.
UNFIX: to make an object mobile again.
REFIX: to relocate an object by automatically performing
an UNFIX followed by a MOVE and a FIX at the new location.

A special type of object, called a node object, is used to provide an abstraction of a physical machine. The MOVE primitive can be used to relocate an object either at a specified node or at the same node as another named object. This latter facility helps to provide an extra degree of flexibility, since programmers often require objects to be on the same node, but do not care which specific node they are on.

Emerald also provides facilities which allow programmers to attach objects to other objects. This is particularly useful when deciding which objects should be moved together. Attached objects are usually those which are required for the execution of one of the object's operations. Hence moving an object together with its attached objects can reduce the number of remote operations and therefore increase performance (attachment is transitive but not symmetric).

Emerald's comprehensive support for object mobility allows a variety of different parameter passing mechanisms to be considered. In all cases Emerald's parameter passing semantics are call-by-reference, or more correctly call-by-"capability" where a capability is a ticket of permission that details the nature of access that may be made as well as the

232

reference itself. However, to achieve reasonable performance for remote operations Emerald provides a number of variations of the call-by-move technique discussed in section 9.3.4.

As shown in section 9.3.4 there are several factors which affect whether it is worthwhile moving an object. In the case of small (parameter) objects, Emerald supports the notion of immutable objects which are copied to the remote site. Since the objects are immutable, no consistency problems are introduced by making copies. Emerald also supports two variations of call-by-move. In the first case an object which is moved to the remote site for invocation is left there. In the second case, the object is also moved, but after the remote invocation it is returned to its original site. These parameter passing modes are called call-by-move and call-by-visit respectively. The Emerald compiler is capable of determining the appropriate parameter passing mode for a given context.

9.5 DISTRIBUTED OBJECT-ORIENTED OPERATING SYSTEMS

In contrast to the language area, full object-oriented models are not common in distributed operating systems. The models used for building distributed operating systems have not progressed past the object model introduced by Jones [Jones78]. This is partially due to the different levels of abstraction at which languages and operating systems work, and partially due to the recent trend in operating systems towards providing only minimal facilities within an operating system kernel, i.e. process creation, memory management and inter-process communication. This latter aspect has effectively lowered the level of abstraction at which distributed operating systems are treated, to such an extent that some object-oriented features such as polymorphism are no longer applicable.

However, there are several distributed operating system projects whose design is based on the concept of objects and message passing, and which present a good base on which to build distributed object-oriented systems. Three of these are discussed below.

9.5.1 Eden
The Eden project [Almes85] began in 1980 at the University of Washington. Eden was influenced by Hydra [Wulf75], an earlier project at Carnegie Mellon University, which used the concept of objects in the design of a multi-processor operating system. Eden is not typical of the systems discussed in this section because it is an integrated language and distributed operating system. As such, it addresses a wider range of issues than the other systems in this section and is an early example of a project which blurs the distinction between language and system responsibilities for distribution.

The Eden kernel is implemented as a user process on top of a conventional kernel that provides processes, virtual address space and to provide access to disk and network. Eden's associated programming language (EPL) is an extension of concurrent Euclid. EPL provides a remote procedure call mechanism and supports multiple lightweight processes which makes it possible to manage many synchronous remote invocations concurrently. Facilities are also provided to allow objects to checkpoint. That is, they can atomically write values to stable storage.

Eden objects may be either active or passive (in Eden terminology). Active objects have an associated process, whereas passive objects are stored on disk as core images. All Eden objects are persistent (i.e. once created, they exist independently from the program that created them) and encapsulated at the system level. That is, an object's data part is protected such that the object exists until it is explicitly deleted and it can only be accessed via the object's invocation interface. Objects are named using capabilities which exist in a single uniform system-wide name space. Capabilities do not specify the location of an object; however, the underlying system can locate an object given its capability. Furthermore, objects can migrate and the invocation of operations on objects is location independent.

Several important lessons were learned from the Eden project [Black85]. The following relate specifically to distribution. Firstly, objects should be typed according to their behaviour rather than their implementation. This provides extra degrees of flexibility and extensibility which are important in distributed systems.

Secondly, synchronous communication was found to be very successful when combined with support for multiple concurrent processes within objects. This allows objects to handle multiple remote invocations simultaneously and to separate the concerns of managing concurrency from those of managing remote objects (concurrency within objects tends to be handled using monitors).

Thirdly, the system programming language and the system itself should be integrated. Two central features of Eden which allow this are the language support for capabilities (location independent naming) and invocations (either local or remote operation requests).

Finally, it is important to provide distribution transparency where required, but also to provide primitives within the language which allow distribution to be controlled.

9.5.2 Chorus

Chorus [Armand86] is a message passing distributed operating system, developed by Chorus Systemes in Paris. Several versions of Chorus have already been implemented; the following discussion relates to Chorus version 2.

Chorus is based on the actor model of computation in which processing is carried out by sequential processes called actors. Actors do not share memory, but communicate with other actors by sending messages, which are arbitrary-length byte strings. Each message received by an actor triggers the execution of a processing step which ends with the transmission of one or more messages. An important characteristic of processing steps is that they are indivisible.

Each actor defines a number of ports on which to receive messages. Ports also have associated priorities which are used to determine which message to process next. The processing carried out by an actor depends on the messages it has received at its ports and the relative priorities of those ports. Each actor defines one special port on which to receive signals. This port has the highest priority of all the actor's ports and enables signals to preempt the sequential processing of an actor by jumping to the front of its message queue.

In order to create an actor, it is necessary to specify the node on which the actor is to reside. This node can either be named explicitly, or it can be described by its characteristics, which are then used by system actors to determine its location (the local node is the default). Once created, actors are bound together by exchanging port descriptors. There are several ways in which these can be obtained: by inheritance from a parent actor; by communication from another actor; or by resolving a symbolic port name within the name directory of the chorus file system. Reconfiguration of actors is also supported by allowing actors to change ports. Furthermore, multiple ports can be grouped together, and hence, multi-cast communication can be supported by allowing messages to be addressed to these groups.

The building blocks of actors, ports, messages and processing steps are well suited to supporting object-oriented environments. Actors can be used to model objects, programming steps can be used to implement object operations and ports can be used to represent the entry points for an object. However, the fact that processing steps are indivisible means that only one thread of control can be within an actor (object) at any time. This restriction is removed in Chorus version 3 which will support multi-threaded actors.

Finally, a layer has been built on top of the Chorus kernel to present an object-oriented programmer's interface to the kernel facilities. This is currently the subject of experimentation and is reported in [Deshayes89].

9.5.3 Clouds

The Clouds distributed operating system [Bernabeu88] is currently under development at Georgia Institute of Technology. All instances of programs, services and data in Clouds are encapsulated in objects. Objects are persistent and an object system replaces the conventional notion of a file system. Fault tolerance and transaction processing are important aspects of the Clouds project.

An early version of Clouds, Clouds-v1, has already been implemented on a network of minicomputers. The current version of Clouds has redesigned Clouds-v1 and adopts a minimal kernel approach, i.e. that a kernel should be as small and efficient as possible by containing only essential facilities. The new kernel, called Ra, runs on bare hardware and provides support for location-independent invocation of operations on objects.

Clouds is being built on top of Ra using system level objects to provide system services such as user object management, synchronization, naming and atomicity. The building blocks presented by Ra include partitions (for persistent storage), segments (for memory) and processes. These building blocks are used to construct a large virtual address space which contains objects. Therefore, at the lowest level of abstraction, Clouds objects are disjoint virtual address spaces.

Objects are structured, and contain a data segment, a code segment and a mechanism for extending their storage allocation. The data segment of an object can only be accessed from the code segment of the same object. Furthermore, the only way data can be moved in and out of an object is as parameters of the object's entry points. Object naming is supported through the use of capabilities which are globally unique, and objects can migrate transparently between nodes. Significantly, Clouds objects do not contain any processes and are therefore passive.

The active entities in Clouds are called threads. Threads are implemented as lightweight Ra processes consisting of a process control block and a stack, but no virtual address space. Computation is supported by allowing a thread to execute within an object. A thread enters an object through one of several entry points and on completion of the execution it leaves the object. Threads can pass from one object to another (under the control of Ra) via the invocation operation (similar to a procedure calling mechanism).

Threads which cross machine boundaries (i.e. those which pass from an object to a remote object) are implemented by several processes, one per machine. Whenever a thread moves to another object, addressing is then limited to that object's address space.

In this way, objects present a firewall (i.e. the address spaces of different objects are disjoint and addresses are only meaningful within the context of the enclosing object). Furthermore, several threads can execute concurrently within an object. This is supported by a variety of customized concurrency control (and recovery) mechanisms within Clouds.

9.6 RESEARCH ISSUES

Object-oriented distributed systems are still largely in the research domain. This section outlines a number of research issues associated with distributed object-oriented systems which have not been discussed in the previous sections.

9.6.1 Nested Objects

A classical approach to solving large problems is to split them recursively into smaller problems until all that remains is a (possibly large) number of small solvable units. If the interaction between these smaller units can be controlled, then the overall problem can be solved.

This approach to problem solving can be supported using object-oriented models by dividing problems into a number of parts and representing each of those parts by an object. The same technique can then be used for each of the resulting objects, until objects of a manageable size and complexity are produced. However, this approach requires some support for nested or composite objects, the management of which is a non-trivial task in distributed systems.

Firstly, nested objects complicate issues such as call-by-move. If a nested object, or a part of a nested object, is passed as a parameter, it is difficult to determine whether the object should be moved. This problem arises because nested objects usually dictate a pattern of interaction between their sub-objects. Therefore, when considering whether to do a call-by-move on a nested object or sub-object, it is not clear which other objects should also be moved.

Secondly, it is unclear how sub-objects should view their parent: should they have free access to the internal variables of their parent object or should they be forced to use their parent's external interface? It is also necessary to consider how parent objects access their sub-objects and whether sub-objects can be accessed independently of their parents. These issues compound the problem of deciding whether or not nested objects should be kept intact, i.e. together on the same node. The following section shows how the use of nested objects can also affect the synchronization mechanism used in an object-oriented distributed system.

9.6.2 Concurrency and Synchronization

One of the great values of the object-oriented paradigm is that it can be used in such a way that synchronization is implicitly supported. Message passing is a well established synchronization model in which concurrent computations send messages to a synchronization entity which then processes the messages serially. In this way the operations of the concurrent computations are synchronized. Since message passing is an integral part of the object model, objects can, if they choose, process messages serially and hence implement their own synchronization. In this case concurrent activity is supported between objects but not within objects (since processing messages serially removes all opportunity for concurrent activity within an object).

There are a number of problems associated with using an object's message passing interface as its synchronization mechanism. Firstly, there is the issue of object granularity. For all but atomic objects (i.e. those with only one internal variable) there is usually scope for supporting some degree of concurrent execution within the object without losing the consistency of its variables. This argument is especially true for nested objects which can potentially support concurrent execution between their constituent sub-objects [Martin87].

Secondly, if concurrent activity within objects is not supported, the problem of controlling the concurrent activity which is allowed between objects becomes more difficult. The reason for this is that objects which initiate concurrent activity amongst other objects are forced to combine, and hence confuse the issues of communication and synchronization.

However, if synchronization is not implemented within the message passing interface, another separate mechanism must be introduced. Unfortunately, this compromises the conceptual simplicity of the original model.

The arguments above are concerned with controlling concurrent activity within objects. In some circumstances, it is also necessary to control concurrent activity across a number of objects. The latter problem is the domain of object-oriented transaction mechanisms. When nested objects are considered the concepts of inter-object and intra-object concurrency control are combined and require nested transactions. The support of nested transactions in object-oriented distributed systems is currently a difficult research problem.

9.6.3 Heterogeneity

Heterogeneity is an issue which arises at a number of different levels in distributed systems, all of which cause problems for supporting distributed object-oriented systems. Firstly, there is the issue of heterogeneous hardware. The hardware architecture of a system significantly influences the models which can be layered above it. Even the representation of data types such as integers may differ from one machine to another and this alone can cause serious problems for distributed systems builders. The support of object migration and remote invocation of operations on objects is considerably more complex and compounds this problem considerably.

Secondly, distributed systems may support heterogeneous systems software, i.e. a number of different operating systems may be supported within the same distributed system. Again, this can cause problems for inter-object communication and object mobility, because the interface presented by the operating system influences the models which can be layered above it.

Finally, the issue of heterogeneity also arises at the object model level. If a number of different object models are simultaneously supported in a distributed system it may be a requirement that objects within one model should be able to communicate with objects of another model. In this case the system would need to provide some generic support for object interaction.

One approach to these problems is to abstract out the common or generic properties of various object models and to provide support for these on an intelligent network access board [Lea89]. This approach also allows the translation of hardware and system software specific characteristics to be performed separately from the heterogeneous host systems themselves. In this way the construction and integration of heterogeneous systems can be simplified. A major benefit of devolving object support to a network access board may be in significantly improving system throughput, particularly if in time the functionality of such a board is implemented on silicon.

There is, however, a much larger initiative aimed at solving the problem of building heterogeneous distributed systems. Called Open Distributed Processing, this is an International Standards Organisation (ISO) work item that began in 1988, and we describe it in the next section.

9.7 OPEN DISTRIBUTED PROCESSING

In this section, we present a body of work aimed at establishing an architecture for modelling and building open distributed systems. This comes out of the Advanced Networked Systems Architecture (ANSA) project which was supported under the UK Alvey research project between 1984 and 1988 [ANSA89]. ANSA has subsequently gone forward into Europe as ESPRIT project ISA (Integrated Systems Architecture). The work done under ANSA has been the primary technical input to a new area of international standardization called Open Distributed Processing (ODP) which aims to establish a reference model for the subject, that is a framework in which specific distributed processing standards can be developed.

The goal of the ANSA/ISA projects is to develop a generic architecture that enables the interworking and integration of distributed applications using equipment from different vendors. The applications could be from different domains, particularly in the areas of office, factory and telecommunications.

9.7.1 The ANSA Architecture
The essence of an architecture is that it forms a framework for performing all the tasks necessary to specify, design and implement a system, in this case a distributed system. Much of the work of ANSA has been to draw up a set of concepts for reasoning about all aspects of distributed systems, and in doing this the project has drawn heavily on previous research worldwide, including the work on remote procedure calls and on distributed systems projects such as Emerald.

An ultimate goal is to produce a set of languages suitable for tackling the different aspects of distributed systems building, and to this extent the definition of an architecture can be stated as:

1. a set of concepts for expressing all the necessary structures and activities associated with systems building;
2. a set of languages for describing systems in all their aspects.

The ANSA project, after considerable investigation, has proposed that there are five different aspects or projections from which distributed systems are viewed by the different people concerned with them, namely:

* enterprise
* information
* computing
* engineering
* technology

These may be described briefly as follows.

The enterprise model is concerned with the relationships between the system owners, operators and users, in other words with the role of the distributed system in the enterprise or business that it is intended to serve. The major concerns of this model are the interface between the distributed system and the external world, and the human and organizational issues involved. Although this is not an area that the ANSA project has investigated in detail, it is becoming recognized as an increasingly important subject, and one that demands the joint attention of computer scientists and business specialists.

The information model, as its name suggests, has as its main concern the information that exists about and within a distributed system. The issues divide into two: information engineering, which deals with the abstract 'information' about a system; and data engineering, dealing with the representation of information within the system. Much has been done, of course, in computer science on the latter, but relatively little coherent work has been done on information engineering.

A key area of investigation in information engineering is in requirements capture, the first (and absolutely crucial) phase in building a system. No implemented system is likely to function correctly if its requirements have not been accurately established. It is necessary to develop a language that will enable the formal capture of user requirements - - a difficult problem because, most often, users express their needs in a very imprecise and ambiguous way. But first an information-based model needs to be developed, and speech act theory is a possible basis for this, since it models information systems as acts of communication (for example factual statements, or promises) that can be captured and analysed [Auramaki88].

In the computing projection the main concerns are with the specification, structure and logical operation of distributed applications. This has been, along with the engineering projection, the main thrust of the ANSA work so far. The model developed is based on objects, where encapsulation and access to operations and data through strictly defined interfaces are key features in representing a distributed computation environment.

In general, a program consists of several computational objects that are connected together and to the 'environment', i.e. the external world which would typically be people (users, managers) and/or sources/sinks of data. The objects could be physically distributed in a number of different possible ways.

Inherent in the computing model is the notion of *trading* (and subsequent *binding*). When a client or user wishes a service, it presents a template of characteristics that it requires (for example read, write, open, close in the case of basic file access). The trader uses these to find a match within the possible available services and returns a suitable binding if it can satisfy the request. It may be possible to provide an approximate match so long as the service located has at least the characteristics that the user seeks, i.e. by matching subtypes (as discussed in chapter 4). In general, the trader will operate on behalf of the user only in the permissible domain of that user (i.e. a subset of the possible trading space of the whole distributed system). This ANSA model is more general and more powerful than the client-server system outlined in section 9.2.1. Much influence on the model has come from distributed systems projects worldwide, for example from the Emerald project [Black86, Black87].

The engineering model deals with the provision of operating systems and networks on which the distributed application programs will run. The ANSA work adopts the notion of a platform, above which are the applications and below which are the (distributed and possibly heterogeneous) computer systems and networks. Again, ANSA has been influenced by research work elsewhere, for example Carnegie Mellon University's Mach distributed operating system [Accetta86] and the Emerald project outlined in section 9.4.4. Between the platform and the applications are possible transparency mechanisms, that is mechanisms for hiding aspects of service provision that the user need not or should not be concerned with.

The ANSA work highlights the importance of distribution transparency. In general, the object model provides for logical distribution, leaving the engineering projection (and the technology projection for implementation aspects) responsible for the realization of distribution and the difficult problems this brings. Six types of transparency that have been identified are as follows:

* access transparency: local and remote services are accessed in the same way

* location transparency: the user need not know the whereabouts of a service

* migration transparency: if a service moves location, this is not apparent to the user

* replication transparency: if there are several (replicated) services, the user is not aware of this

* concurrency transparency: if there are several users accessing a service concurrently, each user is unaware of the others

* fault transparency: the presence of a fault is hidden from the user.

However, transparencies may be used *selectively*: the engineering model allows the choice of any of the transparency mechanisms depending on circumstances. For example, if communication overheads are high it may be sensible to maintain control over which objects are distributed, grouping strongly interacting objects together. On the other hand, performance gains may be made by distributing processor intensive objects and arranging for them to execute concurrently. In general, trade-offs will be necessary to meet the user or application requirements.

Finally, the technology projection deals with the implementation of distributed systems in terms of real components including computer hardware, run-time operating systems and (reusable) software packages. This view of the distributed system is essentially a blueprint ready for implementation.

Much of the above has been taken over into ISO's Open Distributed Processing work, and forms an initial basis for establishing a reference model or architecture of ODP. A key element of ODP is its emphasis on precise concepts in the descriptive model of the architecture. There are four parts to this model: the overview that explains the motivation for ODP and gives the key definitions; the descriptive model itself, containing concept definitions and notation; the prescriptive model that specifies the necessary characteristics for open distributed processing; and the user model, that describes the ODP from a system engineer's point of view. Where possible, formal description techniques are being adopted, for example an object-oriented form of LOTOS [Cusack89] is being explored for use in ODP standards, but at present it is unclear which formal tools and techniques will be most suitable to apply within each of the viewpoints.

In parallel with the ISO activity, the European Computer Manufacturers Association (ECMA) is investigating the provision of a support environment for ODP (SE-ODP). Also, the CCITT DAF (Distributed Application Framework) standards project has a goal similar to that of ISO ODP, to establish a reference model for Open Distributed Processing. The ISO, CCITT and ECMA activities are maintaining close contact to ensure the most rapid progression of ODP standards.

ODP is now the subject of significant international effort and seems likely to have the same impact on distributed systems work that Open Systems Interconnection (OSI) has had on computer networking. In chapter 14, we will discuss the prospective future developments in ODP and in particular we will examine the role of object-oriented computing in assisting these developments.

REFERENCES

[Accetta86] Accetta M., Baron R., Bolosky W., Golub D., Rashid R., Tevanian A. and Young M., 'Mach: a New Kernel Foundation for Unix Development', Proceedings of USENIX Summer Conference 1986, pp. 93-112, June 1986.

[Almes85] Almes, G. T., Black, A. P., Lazowska, E. D. and Noe, J. D., 'The Eden System: A Technical Review', IEEE Transactions on Software Engineering, vol. SE-11, no. 1, pp. 43-59, January 1985.

[ANSA89] 'The ANSA Reference Manual', version 01.00, Architecture Projects Management Ltd., Poseidon House, Castle Park, Cambridge, UK, 1989.

[Armand86] Armand, F., Gien, M., Guillemont, M. and Leonard, P., 'Towards a Distributed Unix System - The CHORUS Approach', Proceedings of the EUUG Autumn'86 Conference, Manchester, England, September 1986.

[Auramaki88] Auramaki, E., Lehtinen, E. and Lyytinen, K., 'A Speech-Act-Based Office Modelling Approach', ACM Transactions on Office Information Systems, Vol. 6, No. 2, pp. 126-152, April 1988.

[Bennett87] Bennett, J. K., 'The Design and Implementation of Distributed Smalltalk', OOPSLA'87 Proceedings, pp. 318-30, October 1987.

[Bernabeu88] Bernabeu, J., Khalidi, Y. A., Ahamad, M., Appelbe, W. F., Dasgupta, P., LeBlanc, R. J. and Ramachandran, U., 'Clouds - A Distributed Object-oriented Operating System: Architecture and Kernel Implementation', Proceedings of the 88'EUUG Conference, Cascais, Portugal, October 1988.

[Birrell84] Birrell, A. D. and Nelson, B. J., 'Implementing remote procedure calls', ACM Transactions on Computer Systems, vol. 2, pp. 39-59, February 1984.

[Black85] Black, A. P., 'Supporting Distributed Applications: Experience with Eden', Proceedings of the 10th ACM Symposium on Operating System Principles, Orcas Island, Washington, pp. 181-93, December 1985.

[Black86] Black, A., Hutchinson, N., Jul, E. and Levy, H., 'Object Structure in the Emerald System', OOPSLA'86 Conference Proceedings, special edition of SIGPLAN Notices, vol. 21, no. 11, September 1986.

[Black87] Black, A., Hutchinson, N., Jul, E., Levy, H. and Carter, L., 'Distribution and Abstract Types in Emerald', IEEE Transactions on Software Engineering, vol. SE-13, no. 1, January 1987.

[Black88] Black, A., Hutchinson, N., 'Types and Polymorphism in the Emerald Programming Language', private communication, December 1988.

[Cusack89] Cusack, E., Rudkin, S. and Smith, C., 'An Object-Oriented Interpretation of LOTOS', Proceedings of the 2nd International Conference on Formal Description Techniques (FORTE89), 1989.

[Decouchant88] Decouchant, D., Duda, A., Freyssinet, A., Riveill, M., Rousset de Pina, X., Vandome, G. and Scioville, R., 'Guide: An implementation of the COMANDOS object-oriented distributed system architecture on Unix', Proceedings of the 88'EUUG Conference, Cascais, Portugal, October 1988.

[Deshayes89] Deshayes, J., Abrossimov, V. and Lea R., 'The CIDRE Distributed Object System Based on Chorus', Proceedings of the TOOLS'89 Conference, Paris, 1989.

[Detlefs88] Detlefs, D. L., Herlihy, M. P. and Wing, J. M., 'Inheritance of Synchronization and Recovery Properties in Avalon/C++', IEEE Computer, vol. 21, no. 12, pp. 57-69, December 1988.

[Hoare74] Hoare, C. A. R., 'Monitors: an operating system structuring concept', Communications of the ACM, vol. 17, no. 10, pp. 549-57, 1974.

[Jones78] Jones, A. K., 'The object model: a conceptual tool for structuring software', Operating Systems - An Advanced Course, pp7-16, Springer-Verlag, 1978.

[Lea89] Lea, R., 'Network Support for Distributed Objects: Coping with Heterogeneity in Models and Architectures', PhD thesis, University of Lancaster, UK, March 1989.

[Lieberman86] Lieberman, H., 'Delegation and Inheritance: Two Mechanisms for Sharing Knowledge in Object-oriented Systems', Journees Langages Orientes Object. 1986.

[**Liskov81**] Liskov, B., Atkinson, R., Bloom, T., Moss, E., Schaffert, C. J., Scheifler, R. and Snyder, A., 'CLU Reference Manual', Springer Verlag, vol. 114, 1981.

[**Liskov82**] Liskov, B. and Scheifler, R. W., 'Guardians and actions: linguistic support for robust, distributed programs', ACM Transactions on Programming Languages and Systems, vol. 5, no. 3. pp. 381-404. 1982.

[**Liskov87**] Liskov, B., Curtis, D., Johnson, P. and Scheifler, R., 'Implementation of Argus', Proceedings 11th Symposium on Operating System Principles, Austin, Texas, pp. 111-22, ACM-SIGOPS, November 1987.

[**Martin87**] Martin, B. E., 'Modeling Concurrent Activities with Nested Objects', Proceedings of the Seventh International Conference on Distributed Computing Systems, West Berlin, West Germany, September 1987.

[**McCullough87**] McCullough, P., 'Transparent Forwarding: First Steps', OOPSLA'87 Proceedings, pp. 331-341, October 1987.

[**Mullender87**] Mullender, S. J. (ed), 'The Amoeba distributed operating system: Selected papers 1984 - 1987', CWI Tract 41, Amsterdam, 1987.

[**Schelvis88**] Schelvis, M. and Bledoeg, E., 'An Implementation of Distributed Smalltalk', Proceedings of the European Conference on Object-Oriented Programming, Oslo, Norway, June 1988.

[**Shrivastava87**] Shrivastava, S. K., Dixon, G. N. and Parrington, G. D., 'Objects and actions in reliable distributed systems', IEE Software Engineering Journal, vol. 2, no. 5, pp. 160-8, September 1987.

[**Wilbur87**] Wilbur, S. and Bacarisse, B., 'Building distributed systems with remote procedure call', IEE Software Engineering Journal, vol. 2, no. 5, pp. 148-59, 1987.

[**Wilkes80**] Wilkes, M. V. and Needham, R. M., 'The Cambridge Model Distributed System', Operating Systems Review, vol. 14, no. 1, January 1980.

[**Wulf75**] Wulf, W., Levin, R. and Pierson, C., 'Overview of the Hydra Operating System Development', Proceedings of the 5th ACM Symposium on Operating System Principles, Austin, Texas, 1975.

[**Xerox81**] Xerox Corporation, 'Courier: the remote procedure call protocol', Xerox Systems Integration Standards, Stamford, Connecticut: Xerox Corporation, 1981.

Chapter 10

Interactive User Interfaces

Stephen Cook, George Coulouris, Jean Dollimore, Kieron Drake and John Francis
Queen Mary College, University of London.

ABSTRACT *In this chapter, the application of object-oriented ideas and languages to the construction of interactive user-interfaces is described. A discussion of general principles is followed by a description of the Smalltalk-80 Model-View-Controller framework, leading to an overview of more modern window systems and their associated toolboxes. The final section on MacApp shows how object-oriented techniques can be used to build an application framework, capturing the Apple Macintosh user interface guidelines in software.*

10.1 INTRODUCTION

Object-oriented ideas and techniques have achieved considerable use at the interface between computers and their users, particularly for programming their interactive visual aspects. Recent years have seen massive increases in computer power and display capability, and at the same time, techniques for implementing interactive interfaces have been developed which take advantage of the increased power and bandwidth to make the control of the machine much more accessible and apparent to the human user. Three main basic design principles characterize many of the most recent and popular interactive systems; these are *WYSIWYG* ("What You See Is What You Get"), the elimination of *modes* in the interface, and *direct manipulation*. The techniques which have developed to support these principles are a combination of windows, icons, mouse and pop-up menus, pioneered at the Xerox Palo Alto Research Center and subsequently adopted first by the Apple Macintosh and then in many other personal computers and workstations. These interactive user-interface ideas have developed hand-in-hand with object-oriented programming technologies.

10.1.1 WYSIWYG
The principle of WYSIWYG has by now become almost second nature in the design of

interactive interfaces. WYSIWYG first appeared in the development of screen-based text editors. Earlier text editors were based on a precept of editing one line at a time, by issuing instructions to change the current line, and to display parts of the current contents of the text file. Such editors could be used with teletypes, and even in a batch mode by creating a deck of punched cards containing all the desired changes to the file. In a WYSIWYG editor, the current contents of a file are displayed on a screen, with the same appearance as they would have when output on a printer. A cursor or a selection point indicates visually the current focus of interaction within the display of the text. The cursor is moved around by means of cursor direction keys or a special device such as a mouse or joystick. The results of any action are immediately displayed. The end result of a good WYSIWYG design can be a highly intuitive program which can be used immediately by people with little or no previous experience with computers.

10.1.2 Modes

The principle of eliminating modes from the interface developed alongside the ability to display large amounts of information on a screen. An interface with modes is one in which the interpretation of a command or input is dependent on the mode the system is in. With such interfaces novice users will frequently not know what mode they are in, or how to get out of a mode, while expert users tend to develop safe strategies for finding out what the current mode is. The development which had the most impact on reducing interface modes was the idea of dividing the display space into multiple overlapping areas, called windows, each representing a separate context for interaction. The idea of overlapping windows is credited to Alan Kay, the inventor of Smalltalk, by Larry Tesler in [Tesler81]. Overlapping windows can avoid the kind of mode normally associated with "being in a program"; in a multiple-window interface different programs can be run within different windows and control can be transferred from one to another merely by moving the screen cursor into the new window.

Even with windows, modes can still exist within a single interaction context, particularly for various kinds of command; for example, many screen-based text editors have an "insert mode" for inserting new characters into the text, and a frequent error with such an editor is to forget which mode it is in. These modes can be eliminated by careful design of the command syntax. Much work on eliminating modes from the interface was carried out by the designers of the Smalltalk system at Xerox PARC between 1972 and 1980, and is embodied in the user interface to the Smalltalk-80 system.

10.1.3 Direct Manipulation

Direct Manipulation is a general term used to describe ways of interacting with a computer where the user has the experience of being directly in control of what is going on on the computer screen, with no apparent intermediary. Objects of interest appear on the screen and are operated on by direct reference and rapid, reversible, incremental actions whose impact on the object is immediately visible. This kind of interface often provides elaborate graphics, multiple ways for giving the same command, multiple asynchronous input devices, and rapid *semantic* feedback, where the response to user actions is determined by specialized information about the functions of the objects involved in the action. Descriptions and characterizations of direct manipulation interfaces can be found in [Schneiderman87], and in [Hutchins86]. Common examples of direct manipulation interfaces include the Finder and many other programs for the Apple Macintosh, video games and computer-aided design (CAD) systems.

An important distinction, made by [Hutchins86] and by [Laurel86], sets out two primary metaphors for interacting with computers: the *conversation* or *second person* metaphor and the *model world* or *first person* metaphor. In a system built according to the conversation metaphor, users experience themselves as having a dialogue with an anonymous agent inside the machine which is carrying out instructions on their behalf. In contrast a direct manipulation interface exemplifies the model world metaphor; in such an interface a user perceives himself or herself as the direct agent in the interface instead of conversing with an agent in the machine.

Hutchins, Hollan and Norman [Hutchins86] give a detailed characterization of direct manipulation in terms of cognitive concepts which they call *engagement* and *directness*. *Engagement* is the feeling of dealing "not with programs, not with the computer, but with the semantic objects of our goals and intentions .... when an interface presents a world of action rather than a language of description, manipulating a representation can have the same effects and the same feel as manipulating the thing being represented". *Directness* measures "the distance between one's thoughts and the physical requirements of the system under use."

Direct manipulation interfaces and object-oriented programming have developed together. Descriptions of direct manipulation interfaces are naturally formulated in terms of the objects that appear on the screen. A suitable technology for building direct manipulation user interfaces is based on the idea of re-usable visual elements, such as words, windows and their parts, icons, pictures, controls, buttons and sliders. Using object-oriented programming terminology, the basic behaviour of each element can be represented by a class. Specialized elements for particular purposes can be created by specialization from the class using inheritance. General attributes of all elements, to do with displaying, positioning and control, can be represented in a common superclass which captures their abstract interface. The interface of the common superclass represents a protocol for glueing elements together into complex interfaces. The relationships between interface elements can be represented in a framework consisting of a set of related classes which provide a starting-point for the development of interactive applications through the mechanisms of inheritance and instantiation. Such a framework can effectively capture a set of user-interface design styles, while providing hooks for the development of a wide variety of applications which follow those styles.

10.1.4 User Interface Architecture and Construction

Figure 10.1 shows a very simplified picture of the architecture of a modern interactive user-interface. The dotted lines indicate that the divisions between applications, higher level interface construction environments and toolkits are often hard to define. For instance a bit-map editor might be at various stages an application, part of an icon design package provided for user interface constructors or a toolkit component for inclusion in an interactive application — when it might form the picture editor part of a multi-media document processing system.

In many cases the activities required to implement behaviour at each level are broadly similar:

1. create an entity with some sort of interactive significance (windows, menus, buttons, etc.), with some pre-defined (default) behaviour and representation;

2. modify its normal (default) attributes in some way (size, position, labels, behaviour); and
3. "plug it in" to some conceptual framework that is presented to the constructor by the environment.

These operations are analogous to the
- class and instance division,
- inheritance and specialization
- and late-binding facilities,

respectively, offered by object-oriented systems and environments. In a general way this explains the widespread success of the object-oriented paradigm in user interface construction.

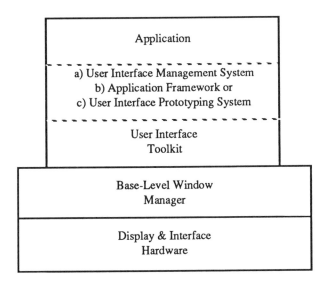

Figure 10.1: Architecture of an interactive user interface.

10.2 USER INTERFACE MANAGEMENT SYSTEMS

Building complex visual interactive interfaces is complicated. The user interface portion of an application is a significant fraction of the code, often as much as 50% and sometimes up to 88% according to studies quoted by Myers [Myers88]. As well as programmers and software designers, different people with specialist skills such as graphic artists, human factors specialists, cognitive psychologists, and the ultimate users of the application, may be involved in the design of a complex interactive system. The only reliable method for ensuring the quality of these interfaces, again according to reports quoted by Myers, is to evaluate prototypes with actual end users and modify the prototypes based on this evaluation.

The development of User Interface Management Systems (UIMS) is motivated by the need for a framework which separates out the various aspects and elements of interactive interface design and construction, thereby making it easier to create and modify prototypes. A UIMS can be seen as somewhat analogous to a 4th generation language (4GL) in the sphere of database processing. A UIMS provides an interface designer with a vocabulary of elements together with a model in which the elements can be readily combined to produce a wide variety of interfaces. The elements include primitive and composite visual elements, elements to handle user input and other events, elements to provide control and management both locally and generally, and elements encapsulating specific application behaviour.

The fundamental idea behind any UIMS is to give an interface designer some kind of high-level language or notation in which a wide variety of interfaces can be efficiently expressed. This language, which might be visual or gestural rather than textual, will compile into a run-time system which implements the interface. Myers [Myers88] classifies UIMS by the kind of language they use to specify the interface, and identifies the following language types: menu trees, state transition diagrams, grammars, event languages, declarative languages, object-oriented languages, direct graphical specification, and automatic creation. Green [Green86] investigates models for UIMS specification languages, and compares transition networks (including augmented and recursive networks), context-free grammars and event languages. His main conclusion is that event languages can be used to implement the other formalisms, and therefore at the lowest level the event model is the most appropriate, although there may be a need for the other models at higher levels to give more expressive power for certain applications.

Hudson in [Hudson87] considers the implications of *direct manipulation* interfaces for the design of UIMS. He points out that more traditional approaches, which divide an interface into lexical, syntactic and semantic components, are not good candidates for supporting direct manipulation interfaces. Engagement will be reduced by having a syntax for the entire system; instead syntax "should be in terms of individual objects, should be as simple as possible, and should involve physical actions such as pointing or dragging instead of more linguistic concepts". Hence systems based on transition networks or grammars which describe the overall syntax for the system are unsuitable for direct manipulation interfaces. Hudson also emphasizes the importance of semantic feedback and flexibility in the design of interaction techniques. He concludes that the architecture of a UIMS for direct manipulation should represent an application as *shared active objects*, with a separate presentation component to handle input and output.

10.3 MODEL-VIEW-CONTROLLER

The Smalltalk-80 programming environment [Goldberg84] introduced a number of important architectural ideas for constructing interactive user interfaces. The Smalltalk-80 user interface itself is built around an architectural framework called Model-View-Controller (MVC), which although problematical in some respects has been an inspiration and starting-point for most subsequent designs. MVC was one of the earliest abstract functional decompositions of interactive interface behaviour, and was also one of the first examples of a window manager.

10.3.1 The Basic Framework
The purpose of the MVC framework is to represent how to build up a window from

components, and to manage the interaction within windows. As its name indicates, it consists of three fundamental parts.

The *model* is the part that implements the interface to the application, e.g.

- a counter can be represented by an integer, with the model providing methods to increment and decrement it;
- an account can be represented by a list of credits and debits and a balance, with the model providing methods to add new entries and to report the balance;
- a drawing can be represented by a set of shapes and positions, with the model providing methods to add, remove and alter shapes;
- a simple text editor can be represented by a string of characters and a current insertion point, with the model providing methods to insert and delete characters.

The purpose of a *view* is to display some aspect of a particular application. The display may be textual or graphical or mixed. A view sends a message to the associated model requesting information about its current state before attempting to display it. There may be several views of the same model. The model and the views work together, the role of the model being to provide the interface which enables the application to be viewed and to co-ordinate the views which share it.

The purpose of a *controller* is to interpret user input actions (via mouse or keyboard) and thereby cause changes to the application via the model. Interpretation of the primitive input actions depends on the current visual context, in particular the position of the cursor on the screen and the objects displayed near the cursor point. For example:

- when selecting an operation from a menu, cursor movements cause selection feedback to indicate which menu entry would be selected if the mouse button were released;
- the cursor may be positioned over a set of buttons that may be set on or off;
- the cursor may be in a text entry box in which case keyboard events will cause text characters to be displayed;
- the mouse may be used to manipulate the displayed object directly, for example by dragging or stretching it.

A controller, which is associated with a specific view, contains the information needed to apply the appropriate interpretation, if necessary referring to the view and model to determine their current state. As a result of the interpretation it may send messages resulting in changes to the model and view.

10.3.2 The Structure of a Window

A Smalltalk-80 window is a composite object constructed from nested components. There is normally a single model, and a number of view-controller pairs. The views are arranged in a hierarchy corresponding to their visual relationship. There is always a *top view* which is normally an instance of the class StandardSystemView, together with a corresponding instance of the class StandardSystemController.This view and controller together implement the behaviour which is common to all Smalltalk-80 windows: expanding, collapsing, framing, moving and closing.

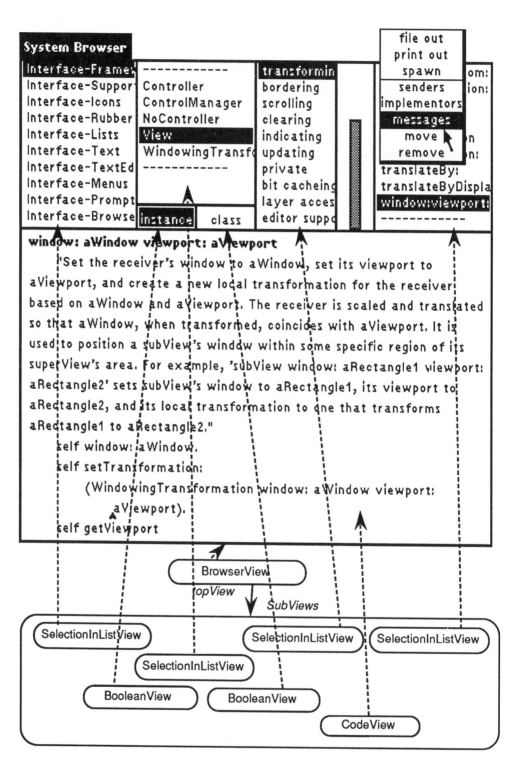

Figure 10.2: The Smalltalk-80 browser

Subviews of this view, together with their controllers, implement behaviour specific to particular *panes* within the window. Figure 10.2 shows the Smalltalk-80 browser, and illustrates the relationship between the views and subviews which make up its structure. In the figure, the top right-hand pane of the browser is selected, and the pop-up menu associated with this pane is displayed at the cursor point.

All views belong to a subclass of the abstract class View. This class represents an abstraction of display behaviour and takes care of displaying an image, clipping it to the available display space, giving it a border where necessary, and organizing transformations between the co-ordinate systems in which it is represented and displayed. Similarly, all controllers belong to a subclass of the abstract class Controller, which represents an abstraction of control behaviour, in particular the way control is passed between controllers and dispatched within them when input events are detected.

Each controller is associated with a single view. The hierarchy of views and subviews within a window establishes a corresponding hierarchy of the associated controllers, and this hierarchy is used to determine how control is passed between them as the cursor is moved around within the window. The controller associated with the top view is called the *top controller*.

Object	Object
View	Controller
BinaryChoiceView	BinaryChoiceController
DisplayTextView	MouseMenuController
FormView	BitEditor
ListView	FormEditor
SelectionInListView	ScrollController
ChangeListView	ListController
StandardSystemView	ParagraphEditor
BrowserView	TextEditor
InspectorView	StringHolderController
NotifierView	FillInTheBlankController
StringHolderView	TextCollectorController
FillInTheBlankView	TextController
TextCollectorView	CodeController
SwitchView	StandardSystemController
BooleanView	NotifierController
TextView	NoController
CodeView	ScreenController
OnlyWhenSelectedCodeView	SwitchController

Figure 10.3: View and controller classes

The overall control flow in the Smalltalk-80 interface is coordinated by a *control manager*, which regains control whenever this is relinquished by the top controller of a window. The control manager keeps a list of all the top controllers of all the windows on the screen, and gives control to one that wants it. This becomes the *active* controller, and the control manager forks a new process which sends the active controller the message startUp. The active controller retains control until it no longer requires it, at which point the control manager looks for a new controller to schedule. If none of the controllers associated with windows want control, this is given to the screen controller which manages a menu of system operations available on the area of the screen where there are no windows.

The controllers operate in a mutually co-operative manner. They only request control when they actually require it, and they explicitly relinquish it when it is no longer needed. Any new controller class must be written according to this co-operative principle.

Figure 10.3 shows some of the Smalltalk-80 class hierarchy, with the main classes of views and controllers.

10.3.3 Co-ordinating Updating with Dependents

Display updating is co-ordinated with changes to the model by a dependency mechanism. Every model has associated with it a collection of *dependents*, which normally comprises the set of views which refer to it, i.e. all of the views and subviews within the window (or windows) which the model is co-ordinating. Each subview is associated with a particular aspect of the model, and the dependency mechanism allows for a view to update only when its associated aspect of the model has changed.

Whenever a controller action results in a change which needs displaying, the message changed is sent to the model, which automatically results in the message update being sent to all its dependents, i.e. to all its views. The changed method and dependency mechanism is implemented in the class Object and inherited by all objects[1].

Each view on receiving the update message takes whatever action is necessary to create the appropriate visual appearance. Co-ordination between the aspects of a model and the associated views is achieved by parameterizing the messages changed: and update: with an object, normally of class Symbol, to distinguish which aspect of the model has been changed. The update: methods in each view tests this parameter to determine if it is necessary for a particular view to update for this change.

As a simple example, consider the thermometer pictured in Figure 10.4. This thermometer has two subviews, a MercuryView and a ScaleView. The height of the mercury depends on the temperature, and the appearance of the scale depends on the particular temperature scale in use. The model responds to the message temperature, replying with an integer value, and to the message scale with an instance of class Symbol, either #Fahrenheit or #Celsius. Whenever the magnitude of the temperature changes, the model is sent the message changed: #Temperature, which (because of the inherited dependency mechanism) causes the message update: #Temperature to be sent to each of the views. Each view tests the parameter to the update: message to determine whether it should take action; only the MercuryView needs to do so, and sends the model a message to discover the new temperature so that it can display it on the screen. The method for update: within class MercuryView is this:

```
update: aspect
    aspect == #Temperature ifTrue:
        [self displayMercuryWithHeight: model temperature].
```

---

[1]In later versions of Smalltalk-80 the dependency mechanism is implemented in a separate class Model from which all models inherit.

The method for `update:` within class `ScaleView` is this:

```
update: aspect
    aspect == #Scale ifTrue:
        [model scale == #Fahrenheit
            ifTrue: [self displayFahrenheitScale]
            ifFalse: [self displayCelsiusScale]].
```

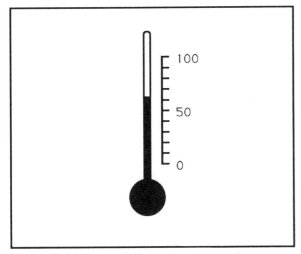

Figure 10.4: Thermometer with two subviews

10.3.4 Co-ordinate Systems

Each view maintains the relationship between two co-ordinate systems, called the *window* and the *viewport*. The window is a rectangular portion of some conceptual coordinate system associated with the particular aspect of the model being displayed in this view. The viewport is the corresponding rectangle expressed in the co-ordinate system of the superview, or the screen in the case of the top view. The relationship between the co-ordinate systems for any view is represented by an instance of the class `WindowingTransformation` called the *local transformation*, which provides the ability to translate either way between the two co-ordinate systems. Each view also maintains an additional instance of the class `WindowingTransformation`, called the *display transformation*, which represents the relationship between the window co-ordinate system of the view and the co-ordinate system of the screen. This transformation is re-calculated whenever the view is moved or resized by composing the local transformations of the view and all its superviews. The calculation is carried out by methods inherited from the abstract class view. The local and display transformations can be used in methods of the view and controller to translate between points in the co-ordinate systems.

10.3.5 Pluggable Views

In the Smalltalk-80 environment, there are a number of cases where very similar views are used in different contexts. To avoid the proliferation of classes which would occur if a different class were defined for each context, Smalltalk-80 introduces the concept of a *pluggable view*. A pluggable view is parameterized with the various messages it sends to the model to access and update its state. The view retains the symbols for these messages as instance variables, and sends the messages using the Smalltalk-80 message `perform: aMessage` (this is defined in class `Object` in such a way that evaluating an expression of the form `obj perform: aMessage` has exactly the same effect as evaluating `obj aMessage`).

An example of a pluggable view which is used throughout the Smalltalk-80 system comprises the classes `SelectionInListView` and `SelectionInListController` which together provide a way of displaying a list of items and making a selection from the list. These classes can be used with the same model in a variety of different ways, for example in the various panes of the standard browser which display lists representing different aspects of the Smalltalk-80 environment.

10.3.6 Menus and Dialogues

The Smalltalk-80 interface also provides a number of menu and dialogue box classes to enable the programmer to get the user to answer simple structured questions or make simple selections. In most cases these facilities are started up by a controller of a window. They normally pre-empt control, so that the user is unable to do anything else until the interaction is completed.

`Menus` return a selection which the controller deals with. `BinaryChoices` require the user to answer *yes* or *no* to some textual enquiry. `FillInTheBlanks` require the user to enter some text to answer some enquiry. `Notifiers` are different in that they are full Smalltalk windows and not preemptive. These provide the ability to start up a debugging window with a title explaining the problem, and a body that shows the most recent entries in the method activation stack. Further interaction with them requires the user to decide to open up the full debugger.

10.3.7 Critique of MVC

A number of criticisms may be levelled at the Smalltalk-80 MVC framework in the light of experience. This is not to detract from its accomplishment as probably the first coherent interactive user-interface architecture, but instead to point out some deficiencies highlighted by developments since MVC was created.

No Concurrency The major drawback of MVC is that the entire framework is built with the overriding assumption that there will be essentially no concurrency, i.e. that only one window can be active at one time and that no part of the active window will be obscured. This assumption holds throughout the structure of views and controllers, and building an interface which violates this assumption would require major modifications to MVC to add two concepts: independent drawing surfaces, and events.

Independent drawing surfaces would provide the ability for independent concurrent controllers to cause view updates without being concerned about the view being on top.

Controllers in MVC poll the input devices to discover the current input state. This only works under the assumption that a maximum of one controller is concurrently active. A system of events created on user input and subsequently dispatched to appropriate controllers would allow several controllers to operate concurrently with the same multiplexed input stream.

Co-ordinate Systems and Transformations The system of co-ordinate transformations in MVC does not do much, and in many cases does not do what is required. They must be used explicitly by any methods in the view and controller which need to translate between points in the different co-ordinate systems: there is no concept of a graphics state or graphics pipeline taking automatic care of co-ordinate systems. In addition they provide defaults which in some cases are inappropriate; for example views containing text (rendered by transferring bitmaps from fonts directly onto the screen) completely ignore their transformations, which are thus an unnecessary overhead.

Graphics Primitives All of the display operations in Smalltalk-80 use bitmaps, the fundamental display primitive being the `BitBlt` (Bit Block Transfer) operation, which combines a source and destination bitmap with rules designed for the rapid display and update of rectangular portions of images. The graphics classes provided in Smalltalk don't provide the ability to describe pictures in terms of high-level device-independent abstractions, only in terms of primitive paths and bitmaps. A higher-level graphics model based on device-independent primitives, such as the ones used in the PostScript page description language and exploited in the NeWS window system (see 10.4.6), would provide a more expressive language for describing and composing pictures, and would localize the device-dependent aspects of the graphics. A further limitation of the standard Smalltalk-80 graphics architecture is that it does not include any representation of colour. An extension of Smalltalk-80 to incorporate colour is described in [Wirfs-Brock88].

Dependencies The MVC dependency mechanism is based on sending the message `changed:` to the model and using the parameter to this message to distinguish what kind of change is occurring. This mechanism is too coarse-grained. Many models have appreciable internal structure, with complex logical relationships between their parts, and this internal structure should be describable independently of the other dependencies e.g. the structure of windows used to view the model. A finer-grained architecture would provide an abstract framework for representing the internal structure of models, and would keep this framework separate from the mechanism for co-ordinating control and maintaining view updates. Mechanisms based on constraints, as described later in this chapter, provide a potentially sound basis for implementing such a finer-grained architecture.

Classes vs. Prototypes The MVC framework is essentially static, the structure of any particular kind of window being represented by the relationships between a number of Smalltalk-80 classes. In a class-based system like Smalltalk-80, the process of constructing an object like a window is equated to the process of constructing the classes which represent it and its parts. However, user-interface building is more fundamentally a prototyping activity, and it would be highly advantageous to be able to assemble windows and other visual objects in the user interface by direct manipulation, by taking existing components and composing them visually. An approach based on prototypes would permit new windows to be constructed by taking copies of old ones and altering them. Systems based on prototypes are inherently more dynamic than systems based on classes. In such systems the distinction between making and using an object becomes blurred, and objects can alter their behaviour dynamically. The feasibility of this approach has been demonstrated by a number of systems, notably Thinglab [Borning81], HyperCard [Goodman87], ExperInterfaceBuilder [Hullot87], the Alternate Reality Kit [Smith86] and languages like Self [Ungar87] which eschew classes in favour of prototypes (see also [Lieberman86]).

10.4 WINDOW SYSTEMS

Window systems provide the lowest level, above the hardware, of a typical interactive system. They generally provide facilities for creating, managing, drawing on and destroying various independent, and possibly overlapping, drawing surfaces as well as facilities for managing the various input devices and making their outputs available to window system clients. This latter process often involves multiplexing the various device outputs into a single event stream which can be selectively demultiplexed and filtered, generally on the basis of drawing surfaces or screen regions. Thus window systems provide a virtual display and input model above the actual hardware devices. This may or may not be device independent to some extent — the virtual devices may, or may not, hide the details of definition limits, available colours, co-ordinate systems orientations and ranges, etc.

The preceding paragraph describes the facilities provided by a typical *base-level* window manager, like X11 [Scheifler86] or Sun's NeWS (Network-extensible Window System) [Densmore87]. Most other window systems also provide *window managers* as an integral part of the windowing system. Here *window manager* normally refers to the interactive facilities available to the user by which the window hierarchy can be manipulated and windows can be created, destroyed, resized, iconized, etc. In the context of systems like X11 these functions are provided by a separate program which is a client of the window system — it makes use of its facilities — just like any other interactive program. In this case users can choose which window manager, and associated user interface, to use or can even write their own.

10.4.1 Drawables as Objects
When designing an object-oriented window manager the most obvious class to provide is a class which represents the general concept of a drawable or displayable object. Each "drawable" would be an instance of this class with instance variables specifying position, size, shape, etc., and all behaviour inherited from the class. This would include basic graphics drawing operations, input event filtering, movement,visibility, resizing, stowing as icons, etc.

10.4.2 Window Relationships
In most window systems each window is part of a hierarchy with the framebuffer being the root of the tree (see Figure 10.5). Indeed it is generally referred to as the root window and is the one window that does not need to be created by a client program. In these systems each window has a parent and there are generally restrictions to these children; they may not be able to extend outside of their parent, they may lie in front of their

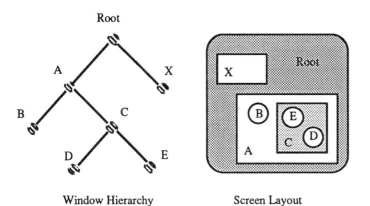

Window Hierarchy   Screen Layout

Figure 10.5: Window hierarchy and corresponding screen layout

parent, they may be made visible or invisible when a common parent is, etc. The
positions of child windows are often defined with respect to their parent so that as an
interior node of the window tree (e.g. **A** in Figure 10.5) is moved then all of its
descendants (i.e. **B, C, D & E** in Figure 10.5) will move as well.

10.4.3 Windows as Collections of Drawables
Although the term "window" has been loosely used as essentially interchangeable with
"drawable" the two may need to be distinguished when dealing with window managers
(i.e. programs that offer user manipulation of the drawables). In this case what a user
perceives as a window may well consist of a group of drawables all sharing a common
parent. The client programs may well refer to the group as a single entity by means of the
common parent. Typical components of such a window would be an interior and a frame
with the latter containing various buttons and scroll bars for stowing windows, scrolling
the contents, etc. In an object-oriented system referring to a group as a whole in this way
can be handled by appropriate message relaying in a manner opaque to the client
program. The LiteWindow class provided as part of NeWS is structured in this way - a
window object actually has a number of child drawables (canvases in NeWS
terminology) for the interior, frame buttons and labels, etc.

10.4.4 Operations on Windows
In an object-oriented system each operation on a window would be provided by sending
an appropriate message to the window object. In general window operations can be
thought of as belonging to two sets:

Graphics Operations These include drawing lines and curves, filling and moving
regions (to and from the screen as well as within it, including text), clipping to regions,
etc. Many window systems restrict their idea of regions to rectangles but this need not
always be the case. Some systems support the notion of one (or more) graphics contexts -
specifying attributes like line width, dash/dot patterns, fill textures, etc. - as one (or more)
instances of a `GraphicsContext` class. Various graphics operations, e.g. an `update`
operation to display the current state of a graphics object on the screen, can be applied
both to individual objects of different kinds and to groups of objects. In the case of a

257

group of objects, the collection implementing the group will forward the operation to the individuals within the collection, which might be groups in their own right. Object-oriented message polymorphism is a natural mechanism for implementing such operations.

Interaction Operations Operations in this category include receiving input events, notification of display changes, etc. Event distribution to clients of a window system can be managed by creating an instance of an EventQueue class for each client. Each client will have particular selection criteria for the events that interest it: events in a certain area of the screen, associated with a certain window or device, and so on. The EventQueue instance associated with the client can encapsulate the selection criteria so that the client simply needs to request the next relevant event, which it can then process appropriately.

10.4.5 The Programming Interface

As window systems provide the most basic and widely used layer of a typical interactive system, they provide an opportunity for standardization which has become almost irresistible given the availability of base-level window systems like X11 with their user selectable window managers and the ability to connect to client programs on the same or different machines. The very ubiquity of these window systems has meant that they have been designed so as to be implementable on the lowest levels of hardware and software functionality. Object-oriented programming languages and environments are not yet that widely available or standardized, so they have not been generally adopted for these low-level systems. With the wider use and availability of languages like C++ and Objective-C, providing a more or less object-oriented environment without requiring sophisticated hardware or software resources and with some degree of compatibility with existing languages, this situation is likely to change.

It is at the level of the programming interface that some window systems assume an object-oriented disguise. It is possible to provide an interface library, written in C++ say, to provide clients with an object-oriented view of such a window system. This involves the library objects and classes keeping track of information, state and "objects" that are internal to the window system. This is a technique known as *shadowing*, often called *client-side shadowing* in the context of NeWS and X11. Of course, in the case of a truly object-oriented window system the programming interface would be the set of classes that comprise the window system itself, or some suitable subset of them, rather than shadow objects on the client side of the interface.

10.4.6 NeWS LiteWindow

LiteWindow is the "window manager" layer on top of Sun NeWS. The NeWS interpreter is not object-oriented but it interprets an extended PostScript which can be used as an object-oriented environment providing classes, instances, inheritance and prototyping.

LiteWindows are instances of a window class which is itself made from a collection of drawables (canvases). Each such instance has a parent drawable which is quoted as the argument to the *new* message sent to the class when creating an instance. Thus one would create a new instance of the LiteWindow class and keep a reference to it named win as follows:

```
/win
```

```
framebuffer /new LiteWindow send
def
```

Here the `send` operator (itself defined in PostScript) is being used to pass the message `new` to the class `LiteWindow` with a single parameter `framebuffer`. The result is a new instance of the `LiteWindow` class which is assigned into the variable named `win` by the `def` operator.

Subsequently further messages can be sent to this instance to, say, interactively position and size it, make it visible, etc.

```
/reshapefromuser win send
/map win send
```

Apart from the details of instances, classes and messages, this is not that different from the standard procedural interface provided by many existing window systems and their interface libraries. The advantages of an object-oriented system become apparent when one considers how the desired text and graphics are to be painted onto a window or how extra features, like scrollbars, are to be added to windows.

Consider first the way that a single line, say, would be painted onto the window created above:

```
win /paintClient {
        10 10 moveto
        50 50 lineto
        stroke
} put

/paintclient win send
```

Here a procedure, `paintClient`, is being defined within the `LiteWindow` instance. The `LiteWindow` class defines a `paintclient` method, which calls the `paintClient` procedure for the particular instance, if one exists. The `paintclient` method is called every time the window is damaged in any way and is expected to recreate the display of the window's contents. In the last line of the example above, the `paintclient` method will cause the new `paintClient` procedure for the individual instance of `LiteWindow` to be called. This will draw a line from (10,10) to (50,50) in the co-ordinate space of the window.

The important point is that all instances of `LiteWindow` will respond to being sent the `paintclient` message and they will respond appropriately. Thus once the required drawing instructions have been "loaded" into a window by defining its particular `paintClient`, the window can be treated as a self-contained object with its own behaviour. The facility to define methods on a per-instance basis as illustrated here is a particularly useful feature of the NeWS implementation of object-oriented programming.

10.5 TOOLKITS

Once a set of windows are available then part of a simple interactive application could be constructed, but if anything more advanced than a simple text entry and editing system, say, is required then other components need to be supplied. These typically include

- Menus — pop-up, pull-down, scrolling, pull-right & pie menus.
- Buttons
- Radio Buttons
- Sliders and Scroll Bars
- Collections of Windows, Buttons, etc often provided as Paned Windows — laid out like the Smalltalk browser, for example.
- Text Entry Windows for form filling and dialog boxes, possibly scrollable.
- Dialog Boxes
- Alert Boxes

Note that most of the items in the list describe classes of item in fairly general terms while in actual use each menu, for instance, has to be supplied with details of size, position, contents, etc. even if the general behaviour of all of them is the same. This is exactly the sort of facility directly provided by a class mechanism.

Additionally many of these items are refinements of others in the list, e.g. alert boxes and dialog boxes, while many others are composite items which contain others, e.g alert and dialog boxes contain buttons, text windows, etc. and radio buttons come as groups with the "radioness" provided by the container. These facilities are directly provided by inheritance and message polymorphism, respectively.

These object-oriented features can be provided in a number of ways. One solution is to have a real object-oriented programming language and environment available, e.g. Smalltalk-80, but for many reasons (performance, cost, licensing, memory limitations, portability, etc.) this may not be an option. In this case some simulation of the required features must be provided with more or less limitation in the ease of use and flexibility of the resulting toolkit depending on the accuracy and completeness of the simulation.

10.5.1 The X11 Toolkit

One of the most widespread user-interface toolkits currently available is that provided for use with the X window system, version 11. This toolkit, or more accurately this set of facilities upon which a toolkit can be based, is called the *X Toolkit*, or *Xtk* or *Xt* for short [McCormack].

The X Toolkit is written in C so that it can be used by the widest range of users. As C does not provide object-oriented programming constructs, a simulation of those required is provided. The Xtk solution is to define a toolkit core, called the *Intrinsics*, which provide mechanisms for constructing classes and instances, various generic operations and a limited degree of late binding. In Xtk terminology objects are called *Widgets* and classes are called *Widget Classes*.

Widget Classes are essentially statically defined and initialized C structures. These contain further structures both for the class and for any superclasses. Thus a Widget Class*W* which is a subclass of *Simple* which is in turn a subclass of *Core*, say, would be represented as follows:

```
typedef struct {
        int             just_one_class_variable;
} WClassPart;
```

```
typedef struct {
        CoreClassPart core_class;
        SimpleClassPart      simple_class;
        WClassPart     w_class;
} WClassRec;
```

While the actual widget structure is defined (but not declared yet, it will use dynamically allocated storage) as follows:

```
typedef struct {
        int             just_one_instance_variable;
} WPart;

typedef struct {
        CorePart        core;
        SimplePart      simple;
        WPart           w;
} WRec;
```

Note that all of the classes on the same path through the inheritance tree have been concatenated in the data structures. Thus in order to create a new subclass it is necessary to know all of the classes on this path rather than just the immediate superclass.

When this class comes to be declared and initialized, which it must be exactly once, then further knowledge of the parent classes is required. In particular the layout and the type of the fields of the parent class structures must be understood. This makes the process of constructing new widget classes very much harder. Most Xtk users either use the provided widget classes unaltered or they exploit the limited facilities for dynamically changing the binding between events and actions. These will be discussed further below.

The major part of the Intrinsics facilities are accessed via the fields in the *CoreClassPart* component of the widget class structure given above. These include, among many others, the following:

- pointer to superclass structure
- class name
- size of widget (instance) structure
- pointer to an initialization procedure for the class
- pointers to functions for various generic operations:
  — initializing instances
  — destroying instances
  — setting and getting instance variables by string names
  — accepting the input focus
- an action table
- the default widget translation table

Creation of new instances (widgets) is provided by other Intrinsic routines which use information from the core part, like the size of the widget structure (i.e. the size of a *WRec* in the example above) to allocate suitable amounts of heap storage and then apply whatever instance initialization procedures are defined, in the class record, for instances of the given class.

A notable feature of the X Toolkit is the ability to access certain instance variables by string name, although macro definitions of the string are normally used. Thus programmers can use widgets and widget classes without needing to know the details of the actual data structures. A small amount of public knowledge is all that is required to use a widget class effectively. This is in contrast to the widget constructor who has to know much more, both about the Intrinsics and the superclasses, in order to produce a new widget class.

Finally, the X Toolkit provides a limited form of late binding, i.e. it is possible to have widgets respond differently to the same event, where these are largely limited to the X11 Event repertoire. Thus it is possible to change the event that causes a button to invoke its user-supplied action procedure from being the up-transition of the mouse button (the default) to being the down-transition. This mechanism also allows for a degree of polymorphism but is limited because although the translation from events to actions is dynamic and is held on a per-widget basis the action table which contains all of the possible actions is static and defined when the widget class is constructed. Thus only the actions considered by the widget constructor are possible.

Overall the X Toolkit can be seen to have provided classes and instances and a form of inheritance although this latter feature requires a lot of specialist knowledge on the part of the widget constructor if it is to be exploited. Users of the widget classes need to know very little about them, on the other hand. Xtk also provides a degree of "message" polymorphism, where "messages" corresponds to the small set of generic operations as well as the interactively significant X11 Events. There is also some opportunity for prototyping, or instance specialization, via the translation tables although the range of actions to choose from is static and predefined. The X Toolkit is, however, portable to almost any C environment.

10.6 MACAPP: AN APPLICATION FRAMEWORK

The Apple Macintosh is a personal computer which has been extremely influential in bringing direct manipulation interfaces into widespread use. Several of the team who worked on the development of the Macintosh software had previously worked on the development of Smalltalk-80, and many ideas which first emerged in Smalltalk-80 have been refined and re-applied in the Macintosh context.

Macintosh users and the Macintosh user interface guidelines [Apple87] insist on a direct manipulation style of user interface, so all applications require access to windows, mouse and graphics. Direct manipulation requires user-driven sequencing of actions, which implies event-driven programs (i.e. programs must be prepared to respond to mouse, keyboard and window events).

MacApp is a library of object classes designed to:
a) avoid the need to re-program the main event loop and the standard user interface components in every application, for example menu and dialogue handling, scrolling, zooming, re-sizing, moving and closing windows;
b) support the Macintosh User Interface standards and guidelines, e.g. the menu bar, the standard menus (, *File and Edit*) and the clipboard by implementing them in a reusable form as definitions for the object classes common to most applications;

c) enable the programmer to provide behaviour appropriate for a particular application by overriding the methods of these classes.

MacApp is based on Object Pascal and includes a library of pre-defined object classes that support most of the standard look and feel and much of the standard behaviour found in Macintosh applications. Applications are developed by taking a framework that consists of a working but "empty" interactive program, adding new object classes that inherit some of their methods from the pre-defined classes while other parts of their behaviour are specified by *overriding* the pre-defined methods.

Object Pascal is an extended version of Pascal developed by Apple. The extensions are designed as a minimal set to provide the support required for object-oriented programming. It provides modules (called *UNITS*) that support data abstraction with separate *interface* and *implementation* files as in Modula-2, a notation for defining object classes and operations for creating and disposing objects and for accessing their instance variables and their methods [Schmucker,86 Chapter 3].

10.6.1 The MacApp Classes
The most important generic classes of objects in MacApp are shown in Figure 10.6 in which arrows show a "has a" relationship. These classes named in Figure 10.6 are defined at the level of abstractions such as views and commands rather than windows and menus. With these classes MacApp provides a generic application framework containing a substantial part of the user interface, with a standard "look and feel" based on the user interface components of the Mac toolbox (windows, scrollbars, pull-down menus), enabling applications to be built using more powerful abstractions.

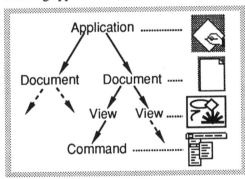

Figure 10.6: MacApp's idea of the structure of a Macintosh application

The MacApp object classes can be described in relation to the components of the MVC paradigm:

Application: There is no direct MVC analogue for the MacApp application class. It represents a running program and invokes the event loop to await keyboard, mouse and other events.

Document: MacApp *document* objects provide the *model* part of the MVC paradigm. A *document* is an object used to represent the changing state of an ongoing task (e.g. making a diagram, editing a chapter of a book), together with methods for altering the state as required by the task.

263

View: As in MVC, a MacApp *view* contains the methods for 2-D presentation of a document. Multiple concurrent views are useful: e.g. outlining and editing in MSWord, magnified views in drawing programs. Presentation of a view may be in a window or printed on paper.

Command: MacApp *command* objects provide the *controller* part of the MVC paradigm. Each command object is an "actor" created for a specific interactive dialogue, e.g. menu selection, object dragging, and it initiates the implied changes in the document.

Windows do not appear explicitly in Figure 10.6. In MacApp, windows are created and associated with views when the views are created. All of the subsequent actions required to maintain each window and its contents are handled by the view with which it is associated. So we have the following definition:

Window: A screen area through which all or part of a view is made visible. Scrolling, resizing and uncovering windows merely require a part of the view to be re-drawn and can be handled by standard code.

The application framework defines classes of objects by defining the methods (procedures in Object Pascal) that can be applied to the objects and the data values (instance variables) that are associated with each object. The main classes correspond to the components of Macintosh applications, but abstracted to include only their common characteristics. An application consists of instances of the object classes provided in the framework and instances of sub-classes defined by the application developer.

If the objects had always to be instantiated from those defined in the framework there could be only one application type, so application developers must define *sub-classes* with some of their behaviour defined by methods inherited from the generic classes (*default behaviour*) and other behaviour defined by methods that override or extend the default behaviour.

10.6.2 The Propagation of Changes

As in Smalltalk-80 MVC, a MacApp controller interprets user input and notifies its model accordingly. When there is a change in the model, the views may need to be updated. To achieve this, the model notifies each of its views whenever it changes. A view can then send a message (procedure call in Object Pascal) requesting information about the state of the model and change the display accordingly. In MacApp the model (document) must have instance variables holding references to each view of the model. When the model changes, it sends a change message to each view. It needs no specific knowledge about the views.

The views do not directly update the screen. They merely post a record of the rectangle that needs updating in a list of invalid areas. The list is processed by the Event Handler at the next update event; it invokes the *Draw* method of each view that has updates pending, requesting them it to re-draw the invalid area.

10.6.3 Example: the "Counter" Application

As an example consider an application that simulates a mechanical counter (Figure 10.7), with both a digital and a graphical display of the counter's current value.

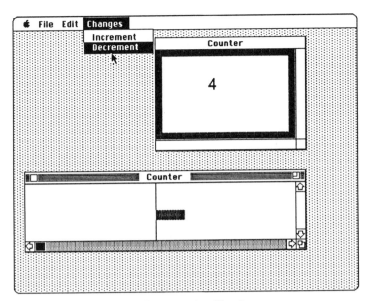

Figure 10.7: Screen for the Counter Application

The Counter application can be described in terms of the MVC paradigm:

- The **model** is the part of the program that implements the application semantics. A counter can be modelled by an integer, together with methods to initialize and to increment and decrement its value. A subclass `CounterDocument` of the MacApp class `Document` implements a data abstraction representing a single integer value with methods for initializing, incrementing and decrementing the value.
- The purpose of a **view** is to display some aspects of a particular model. The counter is displayed in two views – as a number and as a bar of length proportional to its value. Subclasses `NumericView` and `BarView` of the MacApp class `View` implement windows displaying a number giving the current value of counter, and a bar with its length proportional to the value of the counter.
- The purpose of a **controller** is to manage dialogues for making changes to the model. The Counter application provides two types of controller:

  — a dialogue for the selection of menu options to increment or decrement the counter;
  — a dialogue for the use of the mouse to set the counter value by "stretching" its graphical representation.

Subclasses `MenuCmd` and `BarDragger` of the MacApp class `Command` implement a menu giving a choice of increment or decrement operations, and a mouse dialogue handler for dragging the end of the bar.

Figure 10.8 shows the communication required between objects when the state of the counter changes. It shows user input to the *controllers* `MenuCommand` and `BarDragger`. These two controllers send `DoIncrement` and `DoDecrement` messages to `CounterDocument` which is the *model*. The model sends `change`

265

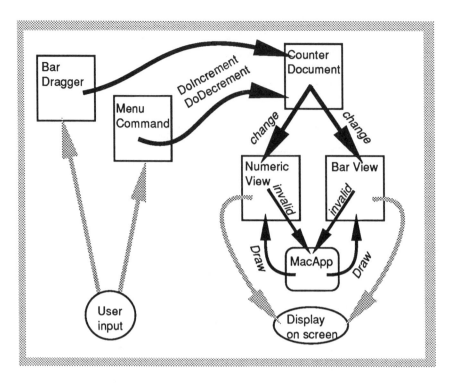

Figure 10.8: Communication between objects needed to update views

messages to the two views, NumericView and BarView. The views send invalid
messages to their super class which posts an *invalid area* event in the application's queue
of pending events. When an *invalid area* event is processed by the EventHandler
object that is associated with each MacApp program, the Draw method specific to the
relevant view is invoked to re-draw the invalid area.

The counter application is implemented by the following sub-classes of the MacApp
classes:

> *CounterDocument* – an object class representing a single integer value with methods
> for initializing, incrementing and decrementing the value;
> *NumericView* – a view showing the current value of counter in numerals;
> *BarView* – a view showing the current value of the counter as a bar whose length is
> proportional to its value;
> *MenuCmd* – menu giving choice of increment and decrement operations;
> *BarDragger* – a mouse dialogue handler for dragging the end of the bar.

Figure 10.9 lists the main methods and instance variables of some of the classes defined
for the counter application. Each class is shown in a separate box with the names of the
instance variables in the top part and the methods in the bottom part. Names of inherited
instance variables are underlined.

10.6.4 Summarizing MacApp
MacApp is the first object-oriented framework that has become widely available for the
development of production software. Its success demonstrates the effectiveness of the

object-oriented approach and the MVC paradigm. It is highly productive. The support that it provides for the Macintosh user interface guidelines and system interface (including, sound, colour and the LocalTalk network), means that programmers need not be familiar with the details of these. The performance penalties incurred in using MacApp are minimal. Schmucker quotes a worst-case speed penalty of 10%.

Our experience in using it in teaching at the MSc level is encouraging: students with no previous knowledge of object-oriented programming or user interface implementation have assimilated the necessary skills to build real applications in a few weeks.

CounterDocument	(parent class: Document)
fValue	an integer holding the value of the the counter
fNumericView	set by DoMakeViews
fBarView	set by DoMakeViews
fWindowList	set indirectly by DoMakeWindows
DoMakeViews:	creates and initializes the two view objects
DoMakeWindows:	create and initialize an object of class Window
DoDecrement:	Decrements the counter
DoIncrement:	Increments the counter
DoSetValue:	Sets a value in the counter
DoInitialize:	Initializes the counter
DoInvalidateCounter:	Informs the views that the counter has changed

NumericView	(parent class: View)
fDocument	A reference to the CounterDocument object
Draw:	Displays the counter value in textual form
InvalidateCounter:	Informs MacApp that an area of the view needs to be re-drawn
DoSetupMenus:	Sets up the menu containing increment and decrement
DoMenuCommand:	Called when the user selects a menu item; creates a controller of class MenuCmd

MenuCmd	(parent class: Command)
fNumericView	the View that created the command, set by DoMenuCommand
fCounterDocument	the document, set by DoMenuCommand
IMenuCmd:	Initialize a command
DoIt:	Perform the command
UnDoit:	Undo the last menu command
ReDoit:	Redo the last menu command

Figure 10.9: Subclasses in the counter application

Object Pascal is not Smalltalk – there is no interactive programming environment and no automatic "dependents list" mechanism for notifying Views about model changes. Good encapsulation is possible but not mandatory in Object Pascal.

The Macintosh software architecture is restricted to non-communicating application programs, hence the class *Application* is the top of the MacApp hierarchy, whereas if there could be a class *Process* and a class *Network*, modularity and re-usability might extend to the level of whole programs (*cf* Unix pipelines).

10.7 CONCLUSION

This chapter has described several of the different ways that object-oriented programming techniques can support the construction of interactive user interfaces, and illustrated the discussion with a brief description of several real systems. The discussion of UIMS, window systems, toolkits and application frameworks shows that object-based mechanisms can be applied at many architectural levels. One of the most fundamental properties of object-oriented technology which makes it appropriate for building user interfaces is the ability to build contexts into which elements may flexibly be plugged. In interactive software there are many elements, such as windows and their components, which have strong similarities as well as strong differences, and the classification mechanisms of object-oriented programming are ideal for expressing these elements.

REFERENCES

[**Apple87**] Apple, *Macintosh User Interface Guidelines*, Addison-Wesley, 1987.

[**Borning81**] A.Borning, "The Programming Aspects of Thinglab, a Constraint-Oriented Simulation Laboratory", *ACM Transactions On Programming Languages and Systems*, Vol. 3 No. 4, pp. 353-387, October 1981.

[**Densmore87**] O.M.Densmore and D.S.H.Rosenthal, "A User Interface Toolkit in Object-Oriented Postscript", Computer Graphics Forum, Vol. 6 No. 3, pp. 171-181, 1987.

[**Goldberg84**] A.Goldberg, *Smalltalk-80: the Interactive Programming Environment*, Addison-Wesley 1984.

[**Goodman87**] D.Goodman, *The Complete Hypercard Handbook*, Bantam Books, 1987.

[**Green86**] M.Green, "A Survey of Three Dialogue Models", *ACM Transactions on Graphics*, Vol. 5 No. 3, pp. 244-275, July 1986.

[**Hudson87**] S.E.Hudson, "UIMS Support for Direct Manipulation Interfaces", *Computer Graphics*, Vol. 21 No. 2, pp. 120-124, April 1987.

[**Hullot87**] J-M.Hullot, *Exper-Interface Builder*, ExperTelligence Inc., 1987.

[**Hutchins86**] E.L.Hutchins, J.D.Hollan and D.A.Norman, "Direct Manipulation Interfaces", in *User Centered System Design*, ed. D.A.Norman and S.W.Draper, pp. 87-124, Lawrence Erlbaum Associates, 1986.

[**Laurel86**] B.K.Laurel, "Interface as Mimesis", in *User Centered System Design*, ed. D.A.Norman and S.W.Draper, pp. 67-86, Lawrence Erlbaum Associates, 1986.

[**Lieberman86**] H.Lieberman, "Using Prototypical Objects to Implement Shared Behaviour in Object Oriented Systems", OOPSLA'86, *ACM SIGPLAN Notices*, Vol. 21 No. 11, pp. 214-223, Nov. 1986.

[**McCormack**] J.McCormack, P.Asente and R.R.Swick, "X Toolkit Intrinsics - C Language X interface", X Version 11 Release 2 Documentation.

[Myers88] B.A.Myers, "Tools for Creating User Interfaces: An Introduction and Survey", *Carnegie Mellon University Computer Science Technical Report* CMU-CS-88-107.

[Scheifler86] R.W.Scheifler and J.Gettys, "The X Window System", ACM Transactions on Graphics Vol. 5 No. 2, pp. 79-109, April 1986.

[Schmucker86] K.J.Schmucker, *Object-Oriented Programming for the Macintosh*, Hayden Book Company, 1986.

[Schneiderman87] B.Schneiderman, *Designing the User Interface: Strategies for Effective Human-Computer Interaction*, Addison-Wesley, 1987.

[Smith86] R.B.Smith, "The Alternate Reality Kit: An Animated Environment for Creating Interactive Simulations", *Proceedings of 1986 IEEE Computer Society Workshop on Visual Languages*, pp. 99-106, Dallas, June 1986.

[Tesler81] L.Tesler, "The Smalltalk Environment", *BYTE Magazine*, Vol. 6 No. 8, pp. 90-147, August 1981.

[Ungar87] D.Ungar and R.B.Smith, "Self: The Power of Simplicity", OOPSLA'87, *ACM SIGPLAN Notices*, Vol. 22 No. 12, pp. 227-242, Dec. 1987.

[Wirfs-Brock88] R.Wirfs-Brock, "An Integrated Color Smalltalk-80 System", OOPSLA'88, *ACM SIGPLAN Notices*, Vol. 23 No. 11, pp. 71-82, Nov. 1988.

Chapter 11

REKURSIV - Object Oriented Hardware

David M Harland and Brian Drummond
Linn Smart Computing Ltd, Glasgow, Scotland, UK

ABSTRACT *The REKURSIV computer architecture is the first processor dedicated uncompromisingly for the object-oriented paradigm to be released in VLSI technology. This chapter describes its general features and introduces the general design philosophy of Lingo, the systems programming language which exploits its capability to support high level instructions.*

11.1 INTRODUCTION

HADES is the first product incorporating Linn's *REKURSIV* processor. It plugs into a standard Sun 3/100 series (or larger) workstation, to provide all disk and I/O facilities in a standard environment. The *REKURSIV* architecture provides unprecedented hardware support for the operations required by the most advanced of programming languages, those which are object-oriented. The *REKURSIV* is a microcodable processor, capable of supporting instructions of any complexity, with memory management based on arbitrary-sized objects and capable of performing all necessary checking in parallel with other processing to manipulate objects in a secure persistent environment.

The *REKURSIV* architecture represents objects directly, maps them into a persistent store, automatically swaps them in and out of memory, performs range checking and by supporting very high level instruction sets it can guarantee their semantic integrity.

The *REKURSIV* is a tightly coupled cluster of processors, but unlike the typical network which is composed of many general purpose elements, each processor in the *REKURSIV* is optimised for a specific kind of operation traditionally considered to be an 'overhead' (one checks types, one checks index ranges, one maintains the one-level store etc.). The major disadvantage of employing a tightly coupled cluster - the overhead of the communications protocol which would be the case in a network - is overcome in the *REKURSIV* by using a single control word to synchronize all the elements. To allow operations for various processors to be specified in parallel, for a given clock cycle, it is necessary to widen the machine's control word; there will be a given number of processing elements and a field must be provided for each, with as wide a range of operations as possible.

But it is pointless having a wide control word to permit many separate activities to be specified in parallel, if there is contention for some vital component in the system which can only be allocated to one activity on a given cycle. For example, if a variety of registers could be loaded at the same time except for the fact that all would have to use the same data path to acquire their information, then that data path is a bottleneck which must be remedied if the potential parallelism is to be realized.

In addition to such architectural bottlenecks, there is another, less obvious and quite different form of technological bottleneck, one which places tremendous constraints on architectural parallelism. Thus, although the modern tendency towards on-chip RAM makes large amounts of fast memory available, because the memory chip can be addressed only once per clock cycle, only one memory location can be accessed on a given microinstruction. This is irrespective of how the RAM may be logically segmented and the number of special data paths that have been provided. Similarly, the incorporation of banks of RAM into ALUs makes available a number of fast registers to hold the most vital system information, but even if multi-ported it restricts any algorithmic parallelism associated with access to such data.

If a program's data space, code area, stacks etc. are 'memory mapped' onto a single massive memory chip, electrically at most one of these supposedly distinct areas can be accessed on any given cycle.

The *REKURSIV* processor is heavily fragmented into many distinct banks of memory, for stacks, code and data. Each memory should be directly accessible and manipulable by the associated processing elements, independently of the main system bus. In addition, each memory should have an appropriate system of control registers and sufficient local arithmetic logic to support the necessary address calculation, thereby obviating the processing of addresses in the main ALU, further reducing the need for bus traffic.

Each stack memory, therefore, is controlled by a separate addressing system. Each control register can be controlled individually, and offset addresses can be computed independently of the ALU. Addresses for each stack can be carried directly to the memory which implements that stack. Similarly, because memories for code and data are distinct and are controlled by different parts of the control word, not only can the next instruction be fetched and decoded in parallel with data operations, it can be carried out independently of the bus, without inhibiting computation.

In most general purpose machines, the processor cannot take direct responsibility for the paging strategy and memory allocation; this is left to the operating system. The consequences for the microcoder are tremendous: when an instruction detects a 'page fault' during address translation it must back up the instruction to a point at which it can be re-entered, saving the 'microstate', and then invoke a system call in the host operating system to handle the fault. Then, when the fault is fixed, that instruction must be restarted, from the middle. Some microcoders, faced with only a few instructions which need to be backed up, or are too complex to back up, adopt the simple expedient of arranging for the re-run to invoke one of a number of special 'recovery instructions', each of which is dedicated to recovering from a specific point in a given main instruction. But this is not a general solution, and it consumes valuable opcodes. Clearly, for an instruction which implements a high level algorithm during which memory is frequently accessed, the microstate may become very complex and the recovery process quite costly, not to say difficult to write and test (faults are fairly non-deterministic). The LOGIK sequencer overcomes this limitation.

Microcode for the *REKURSIV* can manipulate arbitrarily structured data and paging is automatic; there is no need to back up an instruction because page faults are handled 'below' the processor by the interface to the object-oriented store (the disk processor, DP). When a page fault (a 'DPFLT') occurs, the *REKURSIV* is halted while the storage system fixes the fault by loading in the desired item from disk, updating the page tables and then restarting the *REKURSIV*, which then continues oblivious to the fact that it had been frozen. This would not be possible if the *REKURSIV* had to call 'upwards' to an operating system utility to place the new item into memory. The storage system must be autonomous if there is to be a clean division between the processes of computational and storage management. The OBJEKT memory management unit achieves this.

Since so few programmers microcode their own instruction sets, most do not realize that because so many microcycles are spent packaging up data at the end of one instruction only to have it opened up again at the start of the next, a microcoded algorithm can run an order of magnitude faster than machine code. With special hardware assistance for critical operations the increase in performance will be even greater.

If large segments of microcode can be written, then to a large extent this kind of data transfer can be obviated and the remaining segments of activity can be merged to form a single larger instruction. Performance can be improved further still by overlapping the various independent operations of an algorithm.

There is actually an 'algorithmic threshold point', beyond which performance increases dramatically. This is triggered by the microcodability of nested and even recursive higher-order and data-driven algorithms in instructions. To achieve this it is necessary to design a different kind of architecture, a recursive architecture. Conventional microcodable machines do not really achieve this threshold, so only low-to-medium level instruction sets can be implemented. They can be microcoded with specific loops, so long as the loop's body can recover from the page faults, but loops within arbitrary algorithms cannot. This is why machines have such low level instruction sets; or, more correctly, it is why they have so far been unable to provide high level instruction sets. The *REKURSIV* has changed all that. By addressing for the first time not some but all of the consequences arising from the existence of the semantic gap, by providing an object-based persistent storage system and a processor capable of executing truly high level instructions, the *REKURSIV* represents a leap forward in computer architecture to a generation of flexible, secure and efficient information processors.

Unlike Lisp machines, which tag pointers, the *REKURSIV* attaches a fixed size header to each object's storage image, thereby giving direct support to a very large number of types. This format is ideal for Smalltalk's objects, having an object's size and type (or, as Smalltalk would call it, its class) attached to the object.

Backing store and main memory form a single object store, the storage format is the same in each case; the memory could be regarded as a large cache into the main object store on disk. Accordingly, objects are referred to in a memory independent manner; specifically the *REKURSIV* maps position-independent object references, called 'object numbers', into the current physical addresses of objects, and will page them in from the backing store if necessary.

At the heart of the *REKURSIV*'s memory management system is a 64K element 'memory map'. This contains the physical addresses for the objects which have been loaded into memory. Similar tables hold corresponding type (class) and range information and another holds the first word of each object (that is, the most frequently accessed element). Thus, there are tables to hold an object's size, an object's type or class, an object's current address in memory, and the first word of the object. Each table element is indexed by the object number, modulo the table size. The object number to be paged can be brought off the main system bus or provided by various sources internal to the paging system. In each case the object number is folded over to form a sixteen bit index in order to address the pager tables. Each table is accessed at the same time, to fill individual output registers at the end of the paging cycle. These can then be fed into range checking logic so that checks can rapidly be carried out when the components of an object are accessed. In order to achieve this, whilst catering for a very large number of datatypes (that is, despite the fact that it cannot simply employ a few tag bits at the top of a pointer), the *REKURSIV* has been designed to eliminate auxiliary access to an object's image in memory to extract type and range information. And, obviously, the *REKURSIV* undertakes as many such checks as possible at the same time, in parallel with address translation and, should any check fail, inhibits memory access to maintain the semantic integrity of the store.

11.2 THE OBJECTIVE CHIPSET

The basic processor architecture, as outlined in Figure 1, is built around the OBJECTIVE chipset comprising three gate arrays :

(1) OBJEKT: object-oriented memory management unit
(2) LOGIK: microsequencer and stack addressing unit
(3) NUMERIK: data manipulator

The memory management unit and microsequencer are mounted in 299-pin ceramic pin grid array (CPGA) packages. The data manipulator is mounted in a 223-pin package. Each of these devices is implemented in complementary metal oxide semiconductor (CMOS) 1.5 micron technology using a 'sea-of-gates' array.

In addition to these VLSI components, the processor employs a number of high-speed static RAM (SRAMs) each of which has some specific dedicated purpose and some dynamic RAM (DRAM) for the main memory.

11.3 THE CONTROL WORD

In each clock cycle, a word of microcode is read from the Control Store, and latched into the Control Store Output Register (CSOR) at the end of the cycle. During that cycle, the previous contents of CSOR form the Control Word (microcode word) for that cycle.

The control word is composed of 41 fields, typically 1 to 5 bits wide. Each field is fed to a different part of the processor, to control the function of that part during the current cycle. Thus the *REKURSIV* processor can be seen as a tightly-coupled set of parallel processors, each dedicated to a few simple operations, controlled by a single (very wide) stream of instructions. Some fields are common to more than one ASIC (Application-Specific Integrated Circuit).

11.3.1 The D-Bus
The D-Bus is common to the three ASICs, the VME interface and various board-level devices, and it is the primary means of communication between them. It should obviously only be driven by one source at a time, and this is achieved by decoding the DX (D-Bus Control) field of the Control Word to determine the active source.

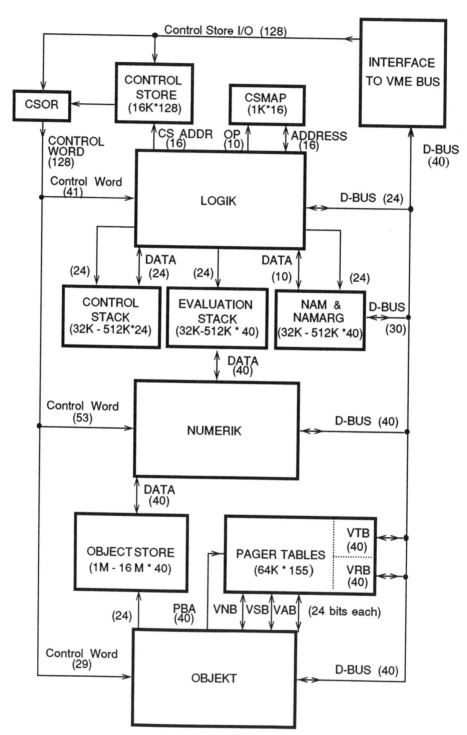

Figure 1. *The REKURSIV processor*

11.3.2 Condition Codes

Condition codes are fed from the ASICs and board-level logic onto the Condition Code (CC) line. This is "read" by the sequencers and the pager tag logic when executing conditional opcodes. The CCX field controls which CC source is multiplexed onto the CC line, as the DX field does for the D-Bus.

Several of the SEQX sequencer opcodes are conditional; i.e., their effect depends on the CC line in the current cycle. The CC signal may be inverted before being sensed by these opcodes using the 1-bit CCMODEX field.

11.3.3 SYSCLK and the Machine Cycle

The *REKURSIV* executes one microinstruction every SYSCLK cycle. The start of a cycle is denoted by the rising edge of SYSCLK. As this clocks CSOR, the control word will be valid a short while later.

By the falling edge of SYSCLK, the D-bus and all address buses should be valid, and memory accesses take place in the second half of the SYSCLK cycle. A consequence of this is that all memory reads are registered, and can only source the D-Bus on a following cycle. Condition codes and DPFLTN are valid by the end of the cycle.

Because different operations take different times, the speed of SYSCLK is programmable by the SPEEDX control word field. The microcode assembly software generates the correct value for the slowest operation in a cycle. There are eight possible cycle lengths, from 100 to 300 nS.

Main memory accesses are an exception to this, as their duration may not be known. (The external memory card may run at a different speed and, if error correction is employed, it may slow up certain cycles). There is a DTACK line (Data Transfer Acknowledge) into the SYSCLK generator on LOGIK to allow this.

11.4 CONTROL STORE LOGIC

Control Store is 128 bits wide, organized as sixteen fast SRAM devices. The address bus is 16 bits wide. It may be supplied from LOGIK during normal operation, or from the VME address bus for control store writes or DP fault handling.

A 128 bit word is written to control store as 4 words of 32 bits each, at successive addresses in the VME bus address space. There are 4 banks of 32 bit buffers, each between the VME data bus and a 32 bit block of control store.

Control Store Output Register (CSOR) is fed from the 128 bit wide data bus, latched on every rising SYSCLK edge (the start of a cycle) and enabled on CSOREN.

To stop the machine, CSOREN is held high, tri-stating CSOR, and the entire control word is held high by pullup resistors. For each field in the control word, the opcode consisting entirely of "1"s has been arranged to be a "NO-OP", thus the *REKURSIV* idles until CSOREN is dropped.

Linn Smart Computing reserves the top 1k of control store for diagnostic and interfacing microcode.

11.5 OBJEKT - THE OBJECT PAGER

OBJEKT encapsulates an unique approach to the problems of memory addressing, virtual memory management and data security. Main memory addresses simply do not exist - even at the microcode level.

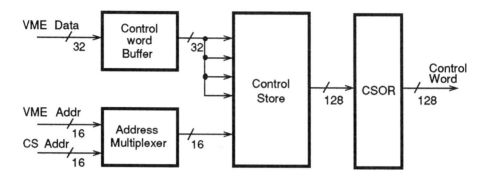

Figure 2. *Control Store logic.*

A data object, of any size or any type, is not mapped onto a specific range of addresses in memory (as would happen in a conventional processor). Instead, to create an object, the user specifies its size and type, and is given an unique identifier (called the Object Number) in return. Underlying hardware allocates a block of memory and notes the start address in the pager table. To access a specific word within an object, (to "index into it"), the object is paged (with the object number on the D-Bus or in a local register) in one cycle, indexed in the second cycle and read/written in the third cycle. Successive accesses may be pipelined at one cycle per access, because indices may be manipulated in parallel with memory accesses.

When the object is paged, it may not be in memory. In this event, a DPFLT (Disk Processor Fault) is raised and the CPU stops until the Disk Processor has placed the object in memory. Then execution continues as though nothing had happened. (In a conventional processor, the entire instruction would typically be re-started after a page fault - so high-level instructions such as recursive algorithms, which cannot be re-started, cannot be implemented on such machines).

When the object is indexed, the index (from the D-bus or a local register) is added to the object's base address in memory (invisible to the programmer) to address the relevant component. At the same time, the index is checked against the object's size, (0 < Index <= size), to test for unauthorised accesses. When the object is accessed, the access will be inhibited if it was unauthorised, providing data security. There is no peek/poke capability which could compromise security!

11.5.1 Objects and Object Numbers
Integers, arrays, structures etc. are all represented on the *REKURSIV* as objects. An object can be identified by its object number, and its size, type and value are all found by "paging" the object number (asking for the object).

Data paths in the *REKURSIV* are normally 40 bits wide, and object numbers are distinguished from other items by having Bit 39 (the MSB) set to "1". Bit 38 is also set in the case of a special entity, known as the Compact Object. The remaining 38 bits provide for 2^{38} unique objects, excluding compact objects.

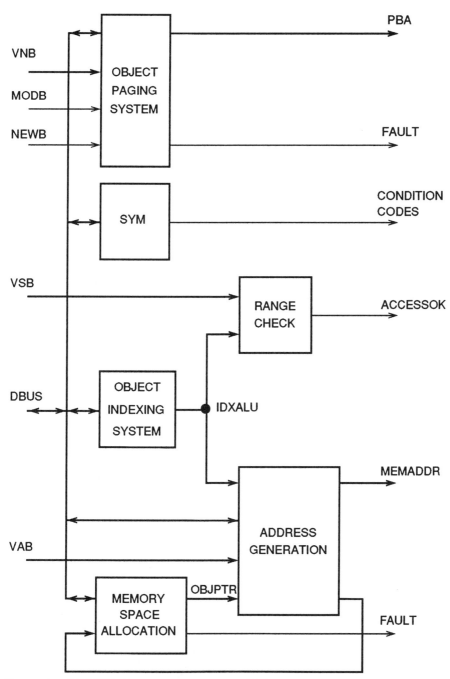

Figure 3. *OBJEKT Memory Management Unit*

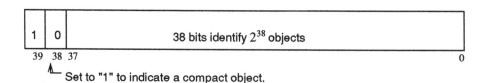

39 38 37   0

↑— Set to "1" to indicate a compact object.

Figure 4. *Object Identifier.*

The size of each object may be up to 2^{24} words, and is used for memory/disk space allocation, and for range checking to eliminate illegal accesses. The type of an object will be checked when performing an operation on that object, to ensure that the operation is permitted for that object

11.5.2 Pager Tables
All of the functionality above relies on the object pager tables, which hold paging information for up to 65536 objects at once. Each object currently held in memory has an entry in the pager table, holding :-
>   VNB - its object identifier or object number (top 24 bits)
>   VSB - its size (24 bits)
>   VAB - its base address in memory (24 bits)
>   VTB - its type (40 bits)
>   VRB - REP 1, the first word of the object itself (40 bits)
>   NEWB,MODB,TAGB - three flags indicating its status. (1 bit each)

Representation of an example 3-word object on disk.

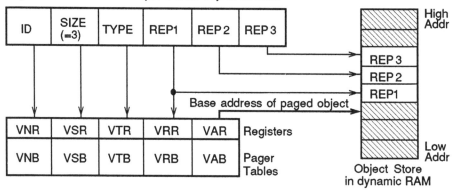

Figure 5. *The persistent image of an object on disk and its form in memory.*

Each pager table has an associated register, (denoted by VNR etc.) into which a pager table entry is loaded when that object is paged. Figure 5 illustrates an object's representation on disk, and how this relates to the pager tables. On disk, each object comprises a "header" and a "representation", concatenated as shown.

When an object is paged, the object number is placed on PBA, the Pager Buffer Address bus. The lower 16 bits of PBA are used as an address in the pager tables.

The upper 24 bits are compared with VNB to determine whether or not the object is in memory. If not, the Disk Processor (DP) must fetch it, allocate space for it in memory and update the pager tables. How it does this is described in the HADES VME Card Data Book.

The size and base address are loaded into OBJEKT, the flags are cleared and the type and range registers VTR and VRR are loaded from VTB and VRB respectively. Figure 6 illustrates the pager table lookup process.

On the HADES card, the pager tables total 155 bits in width, 64k words deep. This is formed of 19 hybrid SRAM modules, each 64K*8, and 3 surface mounted 64K*1 devices. The TAGB flag, used in garbage collection, is handled by a PAL (Programmable Array Logic).

11.5.3 VTR and VRR

These are board-level logic, basically connecting the D-Bus to the type table VTB and representation table VRB respectively. They provide buffers from D-Bus to memory and registers from memory to D-Bus. These registers are gated onto the D-Bus by the board-level DX decoder.

11.5.4 Compact Objects

Compact objects enable the single word quantities such as literal integers, found on conventional machines, to be handled as objects, without occupying pager table slots or memory locations. The overhead of paging them in or out, or of reading memory is also avoided.

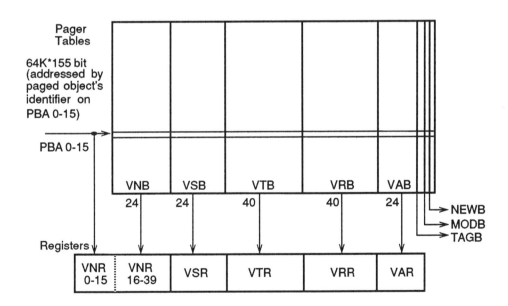

Figure 6. *Pager table addressing.*

A compact object is simply an object number (so bit 39 is set), flagged as a compact object by setting bit 38. Bits 33 to 37 indicate the type of the object, bit 32 is 0, and bits 0 to 31 represent its value.

When a compact object is paged, the pager tables are not involved at all. Its size, address, and the flags are meaningless anyway. Instead, if Bit 38 of the object number on PBA is set, the type bits are fed into VTR (and VTR bit 39 is set) and the lower 32 bits are fed into VRR to give the compact's type and value directly. The Size and Address registers are set to 0.

Note that :

Types are themselves objects, as VTR bit 39 is set
Object number zero is the nil object
Object numbers 0 to 31 are reserved for the types of compact objects.

The meaning of an object's type is purely determined by software. VTR contains the object number of an object containing the description of the current object's type, together with a dictionary of valid operations which may be performed on the current object.

11.5.5 The Object Store
5 MBytes of DRAM provide 1 million 40-bit words of object store on the HADES card. 1MByte hybrid memory modules are used. Two 50-way IDC connectors at the front of the card provide all necessary connections to an external memory card which could contain up to 16 million words.

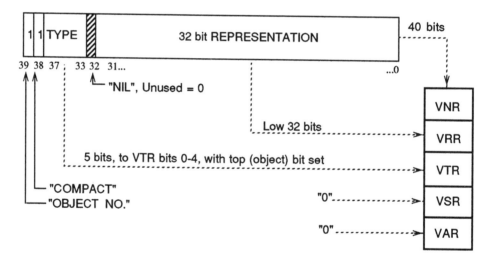

Figure 7. *A Compact Object.*

Data is protected by parity logic. In the event of a parity error, a DPFLT is raised, and the disk processor attempts to repair the damage. The byte in error may be determined by reading the MPC (Main Processor Card) Diagnostic register via the D-Bus. The MOD and NEW flags for the damaged object (from MODB and NEWB in the pager tables) should be inspected, and if it is not modified and not new, it may safely be paged back in from disk, without the knowledge of the executing instruction. Otherwise, the DPFLT handler should warn the user or abort the program, depending upon the application.

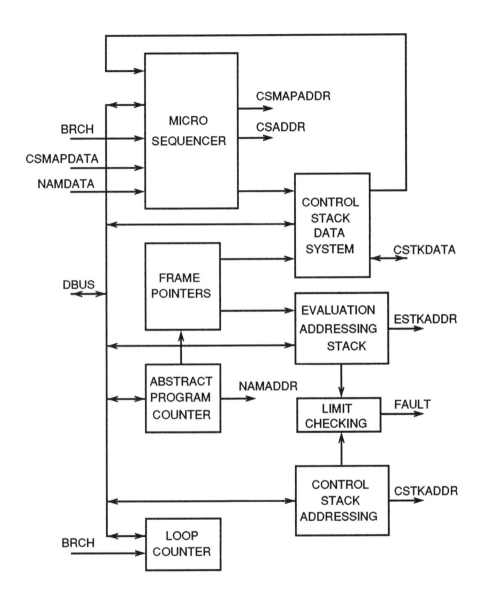

Figure 8 *Logik Sequencer and Stack Controller*

11.6 LOGIK - THE SEQUENCER

LOGIK integrates the microcode sequencer and the method sequencer with the addressing logic for both evaluation and control stacks. The microcode sequencer generates Control Store addresses, and the sequencer generates addresses in NAM, which is the method cache. LOGIK also generates the variable-speed SYSCLK by dividing down the 50 MHz input frequency. Additional supporting logic handles the arguments (NAMARG) to the method cache (NAM). Memory is provided on the HADES card for NAM and NAMARG (addressed in parallel), Control Store Map and the Control Stack. The relationship between LOGIK and its support is shown in Figure 9.

11.6.1 Methods

Method instructions have 10 bit opcodes with 30 bit arguments. They may be fetched from either NAM directly or by caching them from the object store via the D-Bus. Each instruction causes a routine in microcode to be executed, and the "next" instruction to be fetched.

In principle, any algorithm may be microcoded and represented as a single instruction. This includes recursive algorithms, and further instructions may be fetched and executed within such an instruction. It is possible to microcode the interpreter for any token stream, or build a "virtual machine", and eliminate the performance disadvantage associated with an interpreted language.

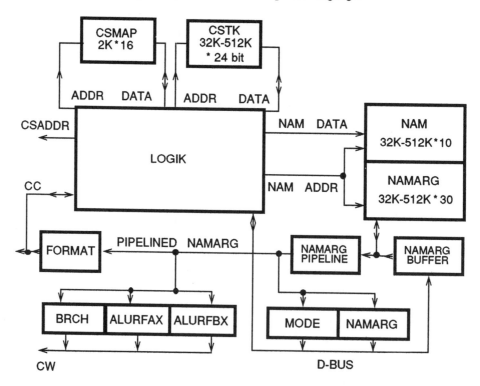

Figure 9. *LOGIK etc.*

11.6.2 NAM and NAMARG

Method code is held in NAM as 10-bit opcodes, each associated with a 30 bit argument (NAMARG). NAM memory, therefore, has a 40 bit data bus, addressed by a 24 bit address bus. The opcodes are translated into microcode start addresses in CSMAP. This sequencer may be thought of as an interpreter implemented in hardware.

NAMARG, which allows the arguments to be used in several ways, is implemented as board level logic. There are two basic argument formats, distinguishable by a bit which may be read as a condition code by the "FORMAT" CCX opcode.

Format 0.	Opcode:	bit 0 - 9	(10 bit opcode)
	Constant:	bit 10 - 25	(16 bits, may substitute BRCH field)
	Mode:	bit 26 - 29	(4 bits, may specify addressing mode etc.)
	Src:	bit 30 - 33	(4 bits, may specify source register in ALU)
	Dst:	bit 34 - 37	(4 bits, may specify destination register in ALU)
	Format:	bit 38	(Set to 0 to indicate this format)
		bit 39	(unused - zero to avoid confusion with object number)

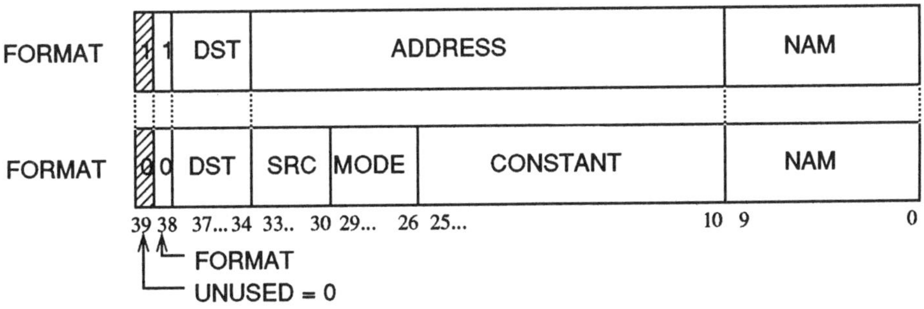

Figure 10. *NAM & NAMARG Formats.*

Format 1.	Opcode:	bit 0 - 9	(10 bit opcode in NAM)
	Address:	bit 10 - 33	(24 bits, used for short constant or address)
	Dst:	bit 34 - 37	(4 bits, may specify destination register in ALU)
	Format:	bit 38	(Set to 1 to indicate this format)
		bit 39	(unused - zero to avoid confusion with object number)

Address may source the D-Bus, driving bits 0 to 23. Format is available as a condition code on the board-level CC multiplexer, to allow a microcoded instruction to do different things according to the format of its argument. MODE is

283

read via the D-bus, to allow an instruction to determine what to do with its argument.

Constant, Src and Dst may substitute fields BRCH, ALURFAX and ALURFBX in the control word, according to the SUBX field. This allows one instruction such as ADD to operate on any combination of registers, or add immediate-mode data from BRCH etc. This facility adds greatly to the flexibility of register-based instructions. Note that all of the above fields are pipelined to match the NAM pipeline.

11.6.3 Control Store Map

Control Store Map (CSMAP) performs the translation of opcodes (10 bits wide) from NAM into the start address of the microcode routine in control store (16 bits wide). It may be loaded by microcode, using special purpose opcodes. Although it need only be 1K*16, it has been implemented as 2K*16 on the HADES card to use commonly available devices.

Linn Smart Computing reserves map slot 0 - 255 for system software, slots 256 -1023 are available for user defined instructions.

11.6.4 Control Stack

Both the microcode and method sequencers may store information on the control stack. Stack addresses and method code (NAM) addresses are 24 bits in width, while control store addresses are only 16 bits wide. The control stack has its own address and data buses (both 24 bits in width) and its own address arithmetic unit optimised for stack addressing. The control stack is 24 bits in width.

It is the ability to store microcode states on the stack, allowing arbitrary recursive algorithms to be microcoded within an instruction, which gives the sequencer its power, and the *REKURSIV* its name.

11.7 NUMERIK - THE DATA MANIPULATOR

NUMERIK is the main data processor in the *REKURSIV*. It incorporates a powerful set of tools, and it is not heavily burdened with address calculations or range checks, which have been off-loaded onto special-purpose hardware. Data I/O bandwidth can be maximised because the D-Bus and the ESTK may be accessed in parallel, in addition to the dual-port register file in the ALU. Unlike a load/store architecture, I/O and processing may take place in the same cycle. In addition, because NUMERIK and OBJEKT are independent, operations in NUMERIK can take place in parallel with object access.

The processing tools include a 32-bit ALU and 64 bit shifter, a true 32 bit multiplier producing a 64 bit result, and a 32 bit barrel shifter allowing single-cycle normalisation. In addition, NUMERIK provides facilities for building compact objects and the data path to main memory (the object store), which also runs in parallel with the D-Bus.

11.7.1 Evaluation Stack

The Evaluation Stack (ESTK) is closely associated with NUMERIK, but it is addressed from LOGIK by an addressing unit similar to that for the control stack. The address bus is still 24 bits wide, but the data in this case is 40 bits wide, to

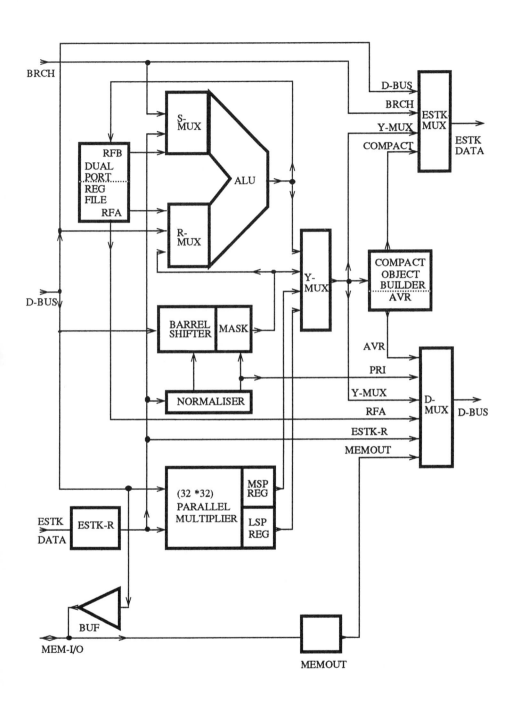

Figure 11. *NUMERIK Arithmetic and Logic Unit.*

285

accept object numbers and compact objects. It uses fast SRAM to allow stack accessand processing in the same cycle.

11.7.2 DP Faults

Various conditions occurring inside the processor require outside intervention. These are typically errors, memory overflows and page requests for an object not currently in memory, akin to page faults on a conventional virtual memory system.

Conventionally, these would abort the current instruction and escape to the operating system. The problem would be fixed, and the instruction would restart. This prohibits the use of sophisticated microcode, which cannot be undone and, therefore, limits the usefulness of the resulting instructions.

On the *REKURSIV*, a fault asserts the DPFLTN line (active low), which halts the *REKURSIV* (by tri-stating CSOR) and interrupts the Disk Processor. The DP may execute microcode cycles on the *REKURSIV* to diagnose and rectify the problem. After this, the failed activity is patched by the Disk Processor and the instruction continues from where it left off, unaware that a fault occurred.

Of course, it is essential that the microstate (register contents etc.) are not corrupted by the DP. Most of these may be read via the D-Bus. The rest may be saved in shadow registers, and restored at the end of the DPFLT service routine, using special SAVE and RESTORE opcodes. This implies that DPFLTs may not be arbitrarily nested.

In addition to DPFLTs, there are 15 I/O faults, explicitly generated by the CSEQBRK sequencer opcode, which also stop the *REKURSIV* and interrupt the DP (or a separate processor) to request I/O. Their treatment is similar to DPFLTs.

11.8 THE VME INTERFACE

The interface allows the *REKURSIV* to communicate with the user via I/O devices on the Sun, and it allows the Sun to act as an intelligent disk interface for the *REKURSIV*.

The *REKURSIV* occupies a 2 Mbyte page in the VME system's memory space, and up to 4 may be installed in one SUN. The card is configured as a VME bus slave and interrupter. That is, it cannot initiate VME bus operations, but it can interrupt the bus master and wait to be serviced. The master, when servicing the interrupt, is responsible for interrogating the *REKURSIV* to determine the cause of the interrupt and transferring data accordingly.

11.9 HADES CONFIGURATION

The HADES card requires a host system such as a VME-based SUN 3 or SUN 4 workstation. All communications are routed through the host, which is required to provide both I/O to the outside world, and the backing store required for a persistent system.

Several applications are possible :

(1) The host may be a diskless node on a network, providing user I/O and *REKURSIV* power for an AI workstation. Paging to backing store through the network may not be fast, but the host should cache disk blocks internally, to reduce traffic.

(2) If the host is a disk-based workstation, the combination forms a powerful AI workstation. Sharing objects around a network of such machines - a "distributed object space" has enormous potential.

(3) The host may have a large disk, and communicate with users exclusively through the network to form an object server. This has obvious attractions in multiple-access database applications, for example.

The CPU has been integrated with 5 MBytes of main memory (object store) and an interface to the VME bus, on a single PCB. It is a triple-height (9U) quadruple-extended Eurocard, 367mm*400 mm, to match the SUN-3 form factor. Power consumption of HADES is approximately 9 Amps at 5 Volts.

Within a host machine, various configurations allow increasingly powerful machines to be built.

(1) Figure 12 illustrates a typical VME system incorporating a single HADES. It illustrates that the SUN provides user, disk and network I/O, while the VME bus is used for communications to the *REKURSIV* and other special function cards. Note that the J2 Bus (VSB) and any proprietary bus on J3 are not affected by the HADES card.

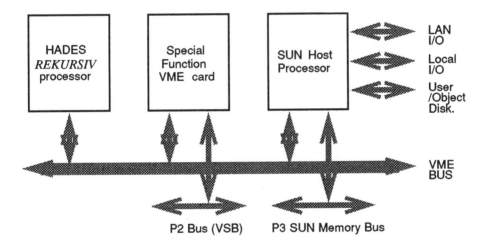

Figure 12. *REKURSIV System 1.*

(2) Figure 13 shows how this may be expanded by the addition of an external memory card. This should provide 8 to 16 MWords of memory, and error correction is considered essential on a memory card of this size. The memory card would also have a VME interface, capable of performing DMA operations. This would make the paging of large objects considerably faster.

11.10 ISSUES OF SYSTEM DESIGN

For any given application, a systems analyst will be able to suggest an optimal solution, and a language implementor will be able to make a language with just sufficient capability to perfectly match these requirements, and the result will be a

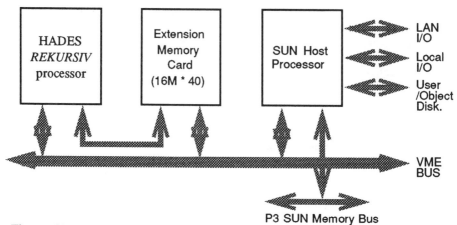

Figure 13. *REKURSIV System 2.*

system that doesn't suffer any major inefficiencies arising from the implementation tools employed.

The problem is, though, that for each such application a different set of requirements, and hence a different set of constraints on the power of the implementation tools, will result. If each application was in itself an immense undertaking, or the absolute peak of performance had to be achieved, whatever the cost, then a variety of implementation toolkits may be justifiable. But, in such an environment, the potential for subsequent integration of the resulting applications will be severely limited, or made impracticable. In addition, of course, the effort of duplication that would go into making all these slightly different systems could well be prohibitive.

The alternative, is a single, very general system in which all these applications could be built, and later integrated, but at the cost of each application having directly exploited only a subset of the potential power of the underlying system (or to put it another way, each individual application being subject to some inefficiencies as a result of running on top of generalisations which it did not actually need or exploit).

Object-oriented systems tend to support this latter paradigm of a single very powerful system, with all applications being implemented on top of a small number of very general mechanisms. True, for almost every individual case this mechanism (namely message passing) will impose a considerable overhead over a dedicated but less flexible system, but it is to be hoped that if the overall performance level is acceptable the fact that the very last ounce of efficiency has not been squeezed out of the system will not be crucial. If this is the case, and the OOPS techniques are employed on a wide scale, then for the first time truly flexible, reliable and well integrated systems of applications (note the plural) can be achieved.

Any builder of computer systems, therefore, must weigh up the trade-offs of whether the system is to be a one-off, or whether it will later be extended and integrated with other (perhaps bought in) applications, and whether, even if it is a single application, if it is to undergo considerable modification during its working life. All these things are factors in the decision of which kind of computational system to use.

For the providers of OOPS there are two decisions: is the system they provide sufficiently general, and does it perform adequately when in use.

Clearly, unless it is overwhelmingly powerful, a very general system will impose real overheads. Whether a system with a given level of generality, implemented in a particular way, or on particular hardware, will give adequate performance, depends largely on the applications to be tackled using it. Or, to put it another way: for any practicable system (balancing generality and power) there will always be some applications which hit pathological deficiencies in the underlying system. The key, therefore, is to achieve as wide a range of potential applications as possible, allow them to be integrated (whilst recognising that not everything will be possible) and implement this as well as possible.

11.11 LINGO

Lingo has been designed to make full use of the *REKURSIV*'s unique capabilities, particularly those implementing the persistent object store. Lingo is designed to be efficient too.

The *REKURSIV* is a processor for manipulating objects. It sees only objects, there is no concept of a linear store of words composed of bits, so there is no notion of an address. There are only objects, and each object is given a unique identifier at the time that it is created which serves to identify that object until it is discarded and garbage collected. This is a non-positional identifier, so it remains the same no matter where the object sits in memory, or on disk. Unlike other processors, therefore, the paging system translates object identifiers into physical addresses for low level access, rather than from virtual to physical addresses.

One major consequence of this scheme is that objects can be passed freely between different processes, and between any two languages; they are not in the "address space" of either, they are objects.

In any design, a specific balance is reached between many potentially conflicting requirements. In the case of the *REKURSIV*, it has been assumed that there will be a great many (millions) objects in all, but that relatively few (hundreds of thousands) of them will be required at any one time. It is also assumed that objects will generally be long-lived data structures, so provision has been made for their persistence over prolonged periods. Furthermore, it is assumed that these objects will be real data, not parts of the computational process; that is, that when an object is created it is to form part of the data set of the application. Or, to put it another way, that objects are not wasted implementing control structures, whose lifetimes are transient, often in the extreme, that objects will represent real data.

Unlike Smalltalk, which relies upon the message passing metaphor for absolutely everything, including control flow, Lingo, although message-based, incorporates a range of algol-like control constructs which do not incur the overhead of message passing. Of course, Lingo permits message-oriented control flow abstractions to be constructed, but the core of the language can be extremely efficiently implemented if it does not depend upon this technique.

Lingo has been designed to minimise the rate of consumption of resources - namely of object identifiers and of space in the object store - as well as being fast to execute.

Lingo minimises the use of both identifiers and space by employing "compact" objects wherever possible. These implement the word-sized quantities of traditional computers by incorporating the 32-bit representation directly in the 40-bit object identifier which identifies them. In this way, no space in the object store is consumed. And, since the structure of these quantities is known to the machine, the *REKURSIV* is able to implement this optimisation particularly efficiently - no time is wasted examining objects to see if they are "compact" or "real". Compacts provide a particularly effective way of saving space; observations of Lingo in action have indicated that compacts can outnumber real objects by a factor of 1000 or more.

One way in which Lingo exploits the *REKURSIV*, which such a language cannot do on conventional processors, is the almost perfect one-to-one mapping between syntactic clauses and instructions. Each clause in the language generally produces a single machine instruction in the code stream. This means that the code is very compact, does not take up much space in the object store, can rapidly be cached into the method store, and lots of code modules can be cached at any given moment, as well as meaning that the code runs quickly. Particularly, it eliminates the need for the complex prefetch hardware that is so characteristic of today's processors (RISC especially).

Message sending is, therefore, a single instruction on the *REKURSIV*, whereas on a conventional processor it would have to be a whole sequence of instructions, each of which would have to be loaded into the instruction cache, and in which each sub-branch will disrupt the prefetch pipeline. On the *REKURSIV*, with a single opcode invoking the whole operation, branches take place in the microcode where there is no such pipeline break, and in a control store which is, by its very nature, always "cached in" and in any case runs faster than the main memory in which the program would otherwise have to be stored. The Lingo code structure is, therefore, very simple, and only a few very generalised instructions are necessary to implement its high level constructs. In effect, therefore, the machine sits just below the level of the language, and the process of compilation and code generation is comparatively trivial because it exploits this virtual elimination of the "semantic gap".

Lingo is designed to compile into an extremely compact high-level instruction set. The basic unit of code is the "module". Methods are compiled into modules. These contain linearised instruction sequences. The individual instructions can be very high level. Control flow occurs at two levels. There is the low-level control flow implemented by jump instructions, and there is the high-level control flow of message passing, implemented by the Send instruction. Jumps are all relative to the jumping instruction. They can be either forward or backward, but are limited to destinations within the module in which the jump appears. Larger-scale flow is via messaging.

Since jumps are relative, and methods are identified by symbolic "selectors" (the messages of Smalltalk parlance), there are no addresses as such. Consequently, all code modules are completely relocatable. Much of benefit flows from this simple fact.

Although modules are objects, and reside in the object store, as they are needed they are cached in the "nam". The fact that they are position-independent means that they can be loaded anywhere. Also, given that modules will cause other modules to be executed (by sending them messages) a specific module may get deleted from the cache before the lifo execution sequence runs back down into it, so when it is needed again it may in fact find itself at some other point in the cache. The Lingo instruction set is very high level, so modules are very compact, and so consume little space in the cache (and, indeed, in the object store). In practice, therefore, it often happens that most of the modules required by a given program can be cached, with little swapping taking place.

It is desirable to have an object store transparently distributed over a number of *REKURSIV*s, possibly even over a network of geographically remote machines. Lingo is designed to exploit this *REKURSIV* capability. It never deals with addresses, only object identifiers, and it is the nature of these identifiers which permit it to reach across a network, as if it were a single level object store.

For example, an expert system may operate on a large number of objects scattered across a network, most of which once created are retained, all of which represent information to be processed by the expert system, and, specifically, that the act of running the system does not flood the object store with a great many transient control-flow objects. In such an application, therefore, although the number of objects potentially accessible may be very large (there may be information on a great variety of subjects), relatively few will be required at any one time (queries will be on a particular subject area), and although these may be heavily used, the act of processing the information will not cause active objects to be swapped out.

It is for this kind of system that the *REKURSIV* has been designed, as a down-loaded expert system delivery vehicle for computationally intense object-manipulation.

Its paging system has been designed to hold vital information on up to 64,000 objects at any one time, providing rapid access to the type, size, base address of any in a single cycle, and to provide validated component access to any object in three cycles (two if updating).

The overall design assumes relatively low paging rates. If, therefore, you load it up with a system designed to run with a quite different object allocation strategy, the paging rate may quickly become excessive, indeed prohibitive. A language like Lisp, therefore, or to a lesser extent Smalltalk, is rather antagonistic. Such a system uses objects very heavily for the act of computation. Lisp makes cons elements at a prodigious rate, and Smalltalk tends to do the same for its execution contexts, both of which will consume objects "needlessly" and accelerate the paging rate.

A language like C++ may well run on a stack, making control flow inexpensive, and employ the object store only for real data. However, the language C makes it very difficult to embed semantics into objects, as methods on classes, because C code tends to assume that it is able to work in a linear code stream, and relies too much on the address model as a result. It is very hard to split C code modules up into independently relocatable segments, and have them stored out in the object store, and even harder to arrange to have these modules then shared between various applications using that set of objects, let alone to have the whole system dynamically extensible. A conventional language like C, therefore, as a "hybrid" object system, is very attractive on a single processor, for a single application, but it is not easy to scale it up for a distributed object store shared amongst a number of different applications. Objects in such systems, therefore, tend to be data structures, pure and simple, not "objects" in the true sense of the word, where data and semantics are inseparably joined together and passed around as a whole.

Lingo is a balance between these two and, not surprisingly, it suits the *REKURSIV*. It maps control flow onto a stack for efficiency, and so does not waste objects or accelerate the paging rate. It uses the object store for data. However, unlike a hybrid approach, Lingo code forms completely relocatable modules which can be passed around the network. It is a good balance and can be scaled up to form a distributed object store.

11.12 THE LINGO INSTRUCTION SET

There are fourteen instructions in the Lingo instruction set. These are set at a level just below the Lingo language's constructs, to eliminate the semantic gap.

The Lingo system manipulates the stack primarily through its higher level instructions, accessing objects and sending messages without resorting to the basic push/pop level; however, this is sometimes necessary.

STACK		mode	count

This instruction pushes a variety of frequently used objects (nil, true, filedescriptors, etc.), duplicates and pops the stack.

The Lingo system manipulates the object store primarily through its higher-level instructions, each executing in their own right many object-accesses; however, it is often necessary to directly manipulate objects.

GET	index

The object on top of the stack is replaced with the component whose offset is specified by the operand. If the index is invalid, nil is pushed.

PUT	index

The stack holds the replacement value above the container object, and this value is written into the container object at the index specified by the operand. The result is the object, or is nil if the index is invalid.

Making objects in the object store is done by one of a variety of instructions.

ALLOC	size

This instruction takes a type from the stack and replaces it with an object of that type, whose **size** is specified by the operand. The components are initialized to nil. If the **size** is zero, a valid empty object is created. No provision is made to ensure that all empty objects of a given type are, in fact, unique instances of that type of object.

CREATE		mode	count

This instruction makes an object of a type specified by the stack, and initializes it with the adjacent count stack elements, replacing them all with the new object's identifier.

COMPACT		type

The following word's low 32 bit are formed into an object of the desired compact type and push it onto the stack.

STRING	count

This instruction will cause a String object to be loaded onto the stack. The string is built up from the characters packed into the words that follow, the number of words being given by **count**.

MODULE	count

This 24-bit operand specifies the number of codewords following the instruction. A Module of size **count** is created. This is then initialized from the codestream and the instruction pointer advanced to the next instruction. The module is pushed on the stack.

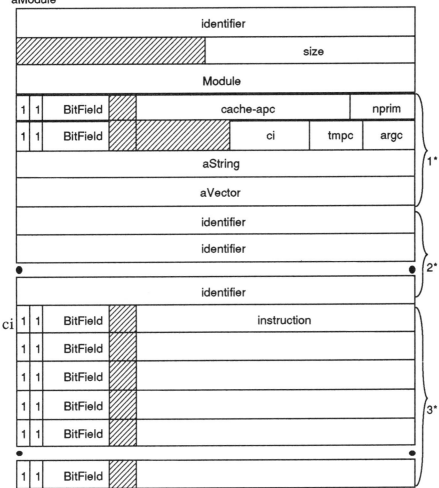

1* denotes - standard header
2* denotes - optional literals
3* denotes - instructions

KERNEL CLASS		objid

The object identifier of the kernel class to be initialized is specified by objid. This is the low 5 bits of the 40 bit identifier. The stack has a count above that number of components, and a type at the bottom, with which to initialize the specified kernel class. Make the class of that type, filling in its components and type from the stack.

The Lingo system's flow of control is driven primarily through its higher level instructions, sending messages which invoke methods. Within each method's module, however, local control flow is controlled by a variety of low level jump instructions. These are all relative jumps; there is no global addressing scheme -

modules are cached dynamically and are position-independent code segments.

The Instruction Pipeline is largely unobtrusive at this level, addresses are not directly available; just plant the offset in terms of distance from the instruction following the current instruction in the codestream, the jumps (apc is one ahead of the current instruction) and the destination instruction.

JUMP	////	mode	offset

There are jumps forwards and backwards, with options to pop the stack, on stack-top being true or not.

SEND	C	S	nargs	selector#

This instruction takes arguments on the stack, and looks up the method with the **selector** specified by the operand on the class of the receiver. The receiver is the first argument, so Send always has at least one argument. If necessary, Send will follow the single-inheritance superchain off the receiver's class in order to find the method. If no method is found the method for *unknownSelector* is invoked in Object.

The method will be either primitive, or abstract. In the case of a primitive, the appropriate microcode will be executed immediately, and the number of arguments and their types checked as appropriate to each operation. For an abstract method, it will be verified that there is the correct number of arguments, and that method will then be invoked.

If a primitive method fails, the stack will be reset, with the method for that selector on the stack above the arguments, and then the corresponding abstract method will be invoked. Usually such a 'failure' will merely report an error, but this mechanism can also be employed to cater for unusual cases for which the microcoded primitive form has no option.

When an abstract method is invoked all temporary variables are initialized to nil.

Notes :
(1)   Argument one is the receiver
(2)   There are up to 63 arguments allowed
(3)   Selectors are sixteen-bit binary codes (these are converted into compact objects of type Selector within the machine).
(4)   If s is set, the "receiver" on the stack will actually be a class, this will cause Send to invoke a superclass-Send, starting with that class rather than the class of the receiver. The class on the stack is replaced by the proper receiver before the method so found is invoked (this is available to the instruction in the receiver register).
(5)   If c is set, the instruction takes a module on the top of the stack above an argument group and "calls" that module with those arguments.
      This stack pattern corresponds to :

      how the stack would look at the point in a "perform" method by which the module (the receiver to the perform selector) has been rotated up onto the top of the stack, or

      how the stack would look at the point in a message send by which the

294

selector (on top of the stack) has been replaced by the module
implementing the method with that selector for a given receiver.

Typically, therefore, this option will be used in code which has been optimised
for a particular class configuration by having had all the methods frozen into the
codestream during computation.

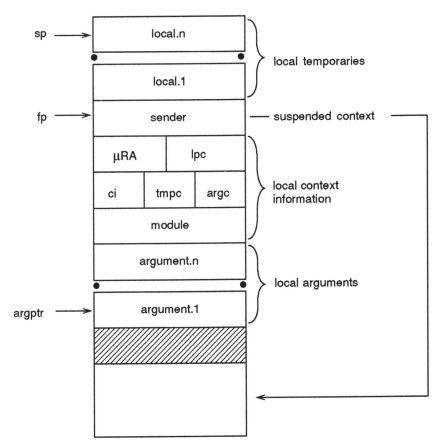

Figure 14. *A Stack Frame*

This exits from a module returning to the suspended 'sender' context. If
necessary the resumed context's code will be re-cached.

IV		mode	offset

This instruction operates on instance variables, loading onto the stack or storing
from the stack as appropriate.

LV		mode	offset

This instruction operates on module variables (argument or temporary), loading onto the stack as storing from the stack as appropriate.

Measurements running Lingo show instructions by dynamic frequency of :

%	
29	Send a message, invoke the appropriate module
29	Load a local variable
11	Jump within a module
15	Load a special value (nil, true, etc.), and pop
6	Exit a module
4	Load an instance variable
1	Get a component of an object

~95%

showing that every *third* instruction is a message sending instruction, and by elapsed time

%	
72	Send a message
8	Exit a module
5	Load a local variable
5	Jump within a module

~90%

where the time counted as Send includes the time in microcoded primitive methods and some 80% of messages sent were to primitives. Examining the primitives used, dynamic frequency counts showed that some 75% were to fairly trivial operations, viz :

%	
16	=
13	at:
12	+
10	size
9	>
7	stringCompare:
5	class
4	not

~76%

Clearly, therefore, message sending at the instruction set level is dominant just as it is at the conceptual level of object-oriented programming. It is also obvious that the presence of local control flow instructions (jumps) contributes significantly to performance by obviating what would otherwise have to be further message sending instructions if Lingo were to be like Smalltalk and employ "blocks" for control flow rather than the built-in constructs.

11.13 CONCLUSION

REKURSIV is a novel approach in implementing object oriented systems. It has been designed for distributed object systems, rather than personal object systems. Lingo (see Appendix 1) is a language explicitly designed for the *REKURSIV*. It exploits well the capability of the *REKURSIV* to support high-level instructions. Measurements indicate that this combination is very powerful.

ACKNOWLEDGEMENTS

We would like to thank Kirstine Lambie and Anne Marie Hunter for preparing this manuscript.

REFERENCES

REKURSIV Object-oriented Computer Architecture, by D.M.Harland, published by Ellis Horwood, 1988

APPENDIX 1 - SYNTAX

```
expression =           binary-expression { keyword-selector binary-expression }
                           [("and"|"or") expression]

binary-expression =    unary-expression { binary-selector unary-expression }

unary-expression =     . primary { unary-selector }

primary =              name
                     | literal
                     | classname ["[" { primary } "]"]
                     | "module" { name } ["of" name {name}]"["
                           { name } "]" expression
                     | "if" expression "then" expression "else" expression
                     | "(" expression ")"
                     | "{" sequence "}"
                     | "case" [ expression ] "of"
                           {expression "=>" expression ";" }
                                       "default" ["=>" expression]

statement =            "raise" identifier
                     | "when" identifier
                           ("do" statement | "then" statement "else" statement)
                     | variable ":=" expression
                     | ( "if" | "unless" ) expression "do" statement
                     | "if" expression "then" statement "else" statement
                     | ( "while" | "until" ) expression "do" statement
                     | "repeat" statement ( "while" | "until" ) expression
                           [ "do" statement ]
                     | "repeat" statement "forever"
```

```
                        |   "{" [ statement { ";" statement } [ ";" ] ] "}"
                        |   [ "^" ] expression
                        |   "case" [ expression ] "of"
                                    {statement "=>" statement ";" }
                                            "default" ["=>" statement]

class =                 classname "is"classname
                            [ namelist ] [ "{" [ namelist ]{ method } "}" ]{ method }

method =                message-pattern "[" { [":"] name } "]"
                            ["primitive" ["("selector")"]] [expression ] "."

sequence =              [ statement { ";" statement } [ ";" ] ] [ "->" expression ]

namelist =              "[" { name } "]"

message-pattern =       unary-selector
                        |   name unary-selector
                        |   name binary-selector name
                        |   name keyword-selector name { keyword-selector name }
```

Literals of the grammar are quoted (in "..." quotes). A vertical bar, |, interspersed in a sequence delineates alternatives. Brackets [and] delineate an option, which may be present zero or one times. Brackets { and } delineate an option which may appear zero or many times. A hyphen in a name is not significant. A piece of text between brackets < and > provide an informal specification of a clause.

Chapter 12

Basic Principles of the BETA Programming Language

Ole Lehrmann Madsen
Aarhus University

Birger Møller-Pedersen
Norwegian Computing Center

ABSTRACT *A conceptual framework for object-oriented programming is presented. The framework is independent of specific programming language constructs. It is illustrated how this framework is reflected in the BETA programming language. In addition the language mechanisms are compared with the corresponding elements of other object-oriented languages. Main issues of object-oriented programming are considered on the basis of the framework presented here.*

12.1 INTRODUCTION

The origins of object-oriented programming may be traced back to Simula [Simula,67]. The important contributions of Simula were the introduction of the class and subclass concepts and the notion of virtual procedure. These constructs have become the core of most languages supporting object-orientation. In Simula it is also possible to model concurrency by means of coroutines. An instance of a class behaves like a coroutine. The history of the Simula development has been described in [Nygaard,81].

Simula has been used by a relatively small community for many years. The real breakthrough for object-oriented programming came with the development of Smalltalk [Goldberg,83]. The Smalltalk style of programming has especially caught on in Lisp communities. This has resulted in a number of substantial contributions like Flavors [Cannon,83] and Loops [Bobrow,83]. The notion of object-orientation has also started to impact traditional software construction. The most influential contribution seems to be C++ [Stroustrup,86]. Another contribution is Eiffel [Meyer,88].

Even though object-oriented programming has a long history, the field is still characterized by experiments, and there is no generally accepted definition of object-oriented programming.There are as many definitions of object-oriented programming as there are papers and books on the topic. This paper is no exception. It contributes with yet another definition. According to this definition there is more to object-oriented programming than message passing and inheritance, just as there is more to structured programming than avoiding gotos.

While other programming perspectives are based on some mathematical theory or model, object-oriented programming is often defined by specific programming language constructs. Object-oriented programming is lacking a profound theoretical understanding. The purpose of this chapter is to go beyond language mechanisms and contribute with a conceptual framework for object-oriented programming. Other important contributions to such a framework may be found in [Stefik,86], [Booch,84], [Knudsen,85], [Shriver,87], [ECOOP] and [OOPSLA].

The following definition of object-oriented programming is a result of the BETA Project and has formed the basis for the design of the object-oriented programming language BETA, [BETA,87a].

Many object-oriented languages originate from SIMULA, either directly or indirectly via Smalltalk. Most of these languages represent a line of development characterized by everything being objects, and all activities being expressed by message passing. The definition and language presented here are built directly on the philosophy behind SIMULA, but represent another line of development.

SIMULA was developed in order to describe complex systems consisting of objects, which in addition to being characterized by local operations also had their own individual sequences of actions. In SIMULA, this led to objects that may execute their actions as coroutines. This has disappeared in the Smalltalk line of development, while the line of development described here, has maintained this aspect of objects. While SIMULA simulates concurrency by coroutines, the model presented here incorporates real concurrency and a generalization of coroutines.

BETA represents the so-called Scandinavian school of object-oriented programming, whereas the line of development from Smalltalk is often referred to as the American school [Cook,88].

12.2 THE CONCEPTUAL FRAMEWORK

The following description of a conceptual framework for object-oriented programming is an introduction to the basic principles underlying the design of BETA. In section 3 the framework is illustrated by means of the BETA language. It is not attempted to give a complete and detailed description of the basic principles nor to give a tutorial on BETA. Readers are referred to [DELTA,75], [Nygaard,86] and [BETA] for further reading. This chapter addresses the fundamental issues behind BETA. There is, however, also a practical side. The Mjølner [Mjølner] and Scala projects have produced an industrial prototype implementation of a BETA system, including compiler and support tools on SUN, Apollo, Vax and Macintosh.

12.2.1 Short Definition of Object-Oriented Programming
In order to contrast the definition of object-oriented programming, we will briefly characterize some of the well-known perspectives on programming.

Procedural programming *A program execution is regarded as a (partially ordered) sequence of procedure calls manipulating data structures.*

This is the most common perspective on programming, and is supported by languages like Algol, Pascal, C and Ada. This view of programming may be traced back to the origins of computers. A computer was then mainly conceived as a programmable calculator with registers and operations. This was reflected in the programming languages where variables (data structures) correspond to registers and procedures to operations. However, this perspective may be working well when performing small calculations; but for large computations it is not possible to keep track of the values in the registers (variables). The problems with global variables and side effects have led to the development of perspectives and languages based on mathematical modelling.

Functional programming *A program is regarded as a mathematical function, describing a relation between input and output.*
 The most prominent property of this perspective is that there are no variables and no notion of state. Lisp is an example of a language with excellent support for functional programming.

Constraint-oriented (logic) programming *A program is regarded as a set of equations describing relations between input and output.*
 This perspective may be seen as a generalization of functional programming. Instead of just using functions to describe relations between data, more general types of relations can be used. In general a set of equations describe the relations between data. In order to implement such a language, it is necessary to put some restrictions on the kind of equations being allowed. This perspective is supported by e.g. Prolog.

The definitions above have the property that they can be understood by other than computer scientists. A definition of object-oriented programming should have the same property. We have arrived at the following definition:

Object-oriented programming *A program execution is regarded as a physical model, simulating the behaviour of either a real or imaginary part of the world.*
 The notion of physical model shall be taken literally. Most people can imagine the construction of physical models by means of e.g. LEGO bricks. In the same way a program execution may be viewed as a physical model. While functional programming and constraint-oriented programming are attempting to eliminate the notion of a variable changing state over time, the notion of objects (variables) changing state over time is central in object-oriented programming.
 Functional programming and constraint-oriented programming are based on well understood mathematical concepts like equations, relations, predicates, etc. For object-oriented programming a similar well understood conceptual framework does not exist. In this chapter the notion of physical model will be elaborated in order to contribute to a conceptual framework for object-oriented programming.

12.2.2 Introduction to Physical Models

Physical models are based upon a conception of the reality in terms of *phenomena* and *concepts*, and as it will appear below, physical models will have elements which directly reflect phenomena and concepts.

Consider accounting systems and flight reservation systems as examples of parts of reality. The first step in making a physical model is to identify the relevant and interesting phenomena and concepts. In accounting systems there will be phenomena like invoices, while in flight reservation systems there will be phenomena like flights and reservations. In a model of an accounting system there will be elements that model specific invoices, and in a model of a flight reservation system there will be elements modelling specific flights and specific reservations.

The flight SK451 may belong to the general concept of flight. A specific reservation may belong to the general concept of reservation. These concepts will also be reflected in the physical models.

In order to make models based on the conception of the reality in terms of phenomena and concepts, we have to identify which aspects of these are relevant and which aspects are necessary and sufficient. This depends upon which class of physical models we want to make. The physical models, we are interested in, are models of those parts of reality we want to regard as *information processes* [Nygaard,86].

Aspects of phenomena For information processes three aspects of phenomena have been identified: *substance, measurable properties* of substance and *transformations* on substance. These are general terms, and they may seem strange at a glance.

Substance is physical matter, characterized by a volume and a position in time and space. Examples of substances are specific persons, specific flights and specific computers. From the field of (programming) languages, variables, records and instances of various kinds are examples of substance.

Substance may have *measurable properties*. Measurements may be compared and they may be described by types and values. Examples of measurable properties are a person's weight, and the actual flying-time of a flight. The value of a variable is also an example of the result of the measurement of a measurable property.

A *transformation on substance* is a partially ordered sequence of events that changes its measurable properties. Examples are eating (that will change the weight of a person) and pushing a button (changing the state of a vending machine). Reserving a seat on a flight is a transformation on (the property reserved of) a seat from being free to being reserved. Assignment is an example of a transformation of a variable.

Aspects of concepts Substance, measurable properties and transformations have been identified as the relevant aspects of phenomena in information processes. In order to capture the essential properties of phenomena being modelled it is necessary to develop abstractions or concepts.

The classical notion of a concept has the following elements: *name*: denoting the concept, *intension*: the properties characterizing the phenomena covered by the concept, and *extension*: the phenomena covered by the concept.

Concepts are created by *abstraction*, focussing on similar properties of phenomena and discarding differences. Three well-known sub-functions of abstraction have been identified. The most basic of these is *classification*. Classification is used to define which phenomena are covered by the concept. The reverse sub-function of classification is called *exemplification*.

Concepts are often defined by means of other concepts. The concept of a flight may be formed by using concepts like seat, flight identification, etc. This sub-function is called *aggregation*. The reverse sub-function is called *decomposition*.

Concepts may be organized in a *classification hierarchy*. A concept can be regarded as a *generalization* of a set of concepts. A well-known example from zoology is the taxonomy of animals: mammal is a generalization of predator and rodent, and predator is a generalization of lion and tiger. In addition, concepts may be regarded as *specializations* of other concepts. For example, predator is a specialization of mammal.

12.2.3 Elements of Physical Models

Up till now we have only identified in which way the reality is viewed when a physical model is constructed, and which aspects of phenomena and concepts are essential. The next step is to define what a physical model itself consists of.

Objects with properties and actions, and patterns of objects A physical model consists of *objects,* each object characterized by *attributes,* and a sequence of *actions.* Objects organize the substance aspect of phenomena, and transformations on substance are reflected by objects executing actions. Objects may have part-objects An attribute may be a reference to a part object or to a separate object. Some attributes represent measurable properties of the object. The *state* of an object at a given moment is expressed by its substance, its measurable properties and the action going on then. The state of the whole model is the states of the objects in the model.

In a physical model the elements reflecting concepts are called *patterns*. A pattern defines the common properties of a category of objects. Patterns may be organized in a classification hierarchy. Patterns may be attributes of objects.

Notice that a pattern is not a set, but an abstraction over objects. An implication of this is that patterns do not contribute to the state of the physical model. Patterns may be abstractions of substance, measurable properties and action sequences.

Consider the construction of a flight reservation system as a physical model. It will a.o. have objects representing flights, agents and reservations. A flight object will have a part object for each of the seats, while e.g. actual flying time will be a measurable property. When agents reserve seats they will get a display of the flight. The seat objects will be displayed, so that a seat may be selected and reserved. An action will thus change the state of a seat object from being free to becoming reserved.

Reservations will be represented by objects with properties that identify the customer, the date of reservation and the flight/seat identification. The customer may simply be represented by name and address or as a reference to a customer object in a customer data base. The flight/seat identification will be a reference to the separate flight object/seat object.

As there will be several specific flights, a pattern Flight defining the properties of flight objects will be constructed. Each flight will be represented by an object generated according to the pattern Flight.

A travel agency normally handles reservations of several kinds. A train trip reservation will also identify the customer and the date of reservation, but the seat reservation will differ from a flight reservation, as it will consist of (wagon, seat). A natural classification hierarchy will identify Reservation as a general reservation, with customer identification and date, and Flight Reservation and Train Reservation as two specializations of it.

Actions in a physical model Many real world systems are characterized by consisting of objects that perform their sequences of actions *concurrently*. The flight reservation system will consist of several concurrent objects, e.g. flights and agents. Each agent performs its task concurrently with other agents. Flights will register the reservation of seats and ensure that no seats are reserved by two agents at the same time. Note that this kind of concurrency is an inherent property of the reality being modelled; it is not concurrency used in order to speed up computations.

Complex tasks, as those of the agents, are often considered to consist of several more or less independent activities. This is so even though they constitute only one sequence of actions and do not include concurrency. As an example consider the activities "tour planning", "customer service" and "invoicing". Each of these activities will consist of a sequence of actions.

A single agent will not have concurrent activities, but *alternate* between the different activities. The shifts will not only be determined by the agents themselves, but will be triggered by e.g. communication with other objects. An agent will e.g. shift from tour planning to customer service (by the telephone ringing), and resume the tour planning when the customer service is performed.

The action sequence of an agent may often be decomposed into *partial action sequences* that correspond to certain routines carried out several times as part of an activity. As an example, the invoicing activity may contain partial action sequences, each for writing a single invoice.

Actions in a physical model are performed by objects. The action sequence of an object may be executed *concurrently* with action sequences of other objects, *alternating* (that is at most one at a time) with action sequences of other objects, or as *part* of the action sequence of another object.

The definition of physical model given here is valid in general and not only for programming. A physical model of a railroad station may consist of objects like model train wagons, model locomotives, tracks, points and control posts. Some of the objects will perform actions: the locomotives will have an engine and the control posts may perform actions that imply e.g. shunting. Patterns will be reflected by the fact that these objects are made so that they have the same form and the same set of attributes and actions. In the process of designing large buildings, physical models are often used.

12.2.4 Object-Oriented Programming and Language Mechanisms

The notion of physical models may be applied to many fields of science and engineering. When applied to programming the implication is that the *program executions* are regarded as physical models. The ideal language supporting object-orientation should thus be able to prescribe physical models. Most elements of the framework presented above are represented in existing languages claimed to support object-orientation, but few cover them all. Most of them have a construct for describing objects. Constructs for describing patterns are in many languages represented in the form of classes, types, procedures/methods, and functions.

Classification is supported by most existing programming languages, by concepts like type, procedure, and class. Aggregation/decomposition is also supported by most programming languages; a procedure may be defined by means of other procedures, and a type may be defined in terms of other types.

Language constructs supporting generalization/specialization (often called subclassing or inheritance) are often mentioned as the main characteristic of a programming language supporting object-orientation. It is true that inheritance was introduced in SIMULA and until recently inheritance was mainly associated with object-oriented programming. However, inheritance has started to appear in languages based on other perspectives as well.

Individual action sequences should be associated with objects, and concurrency should be supported. For many large applications support for persistent objects is needed.

12.2.5 Benefits of Object-Oriented Programming
One of the generally accepted benefits of object-oriented programming is that the class/subclass mechanism (inheritance) has new possibilities for **re-usability** of existing code. This has turned out to be of major practical importance. This is however not the only benefit of object-orientation.

Physical models reflect reality in a natural way One of the reasons that object-oriented programming has become so widely accepted and found to be convenient is that object-orientation is close to the natural perception of the real world: viewed as consisting of objects with properties and actions. Stein Krogdahl and Kai A. Olsen put it this way (translated citation from [Krogdahl,86]):

> "The basic philosophy underlying object-oriented programming is to make the programs as far as possible reflect that part of the reality, they are going to treat. It is then often easier to understand and get an overview of what is described in programs. The reason is that human beings from the outset are used to and trained in perception of what is going on in the real world. The closer it is possible to use this way of thinking in programming, the easier it is to write and understand programs."

Physical model more stable than the functionality of a system The principle behind the Jackson System Development method (JSD, [JSD]) also reflects the object-oriented perspective described above. Instead of focussing on the functionality of a system, the first step in the development of the system according to JSD is to make a physical model of the real world with which the system is concerned. This model then forms the basis for the different functions that the system may have. Functions may later be changed, and new functions may be added without changing the underlying model.

12.3 THE BETA PROGRAMMING LANGUAGE

The conceptual framework presented above is directly reflected in the programming language BETA. The following gives a description of part of the transition from framework to language mechanisms. Emphasis is put on conveying an understanding of major language mechanisms, and of differences from other languages. The BETA language will not be described in all details.

305

12.3.1 Objects and Patterns

The BETA language is intended to describe program executions regarded as physical models. From the previous it follows that by physical model is meant a *system* consisting of a collection of interacting objects. A BETA program is consequently a description of such a system. An object in BETA is characterized by a set of attributes and a sequence of actions. Attributes portray properties of objects. The syntactic element for describing an object is called an *object descriptor* and has the following form:

```
Super
(#
        Decl1; Decl2; ...; Decln
enter In
do
        Imp
exit Out
#)
```

where `Super` is a the superpattern, `Decl1; Decl2; ...` `Decln` are declarations of the attributes, `In` is the input parameters, `Imp` describes the actions of the objects in terms of imperatives, and `Out` is the output parameters. Attributes make references to objects or patterns. The various parts of an object descriptor will be explained in the following.

Pattern declaration In BETA a concept is modelled by a *pattern*. A pattern is defined by associating a name with an object descriptor:

```
P: Super
   (# Decl1; Decl2; ...; Decln
   enter In
   do
      Imp
   exit Out
   #)
```

The intension of the concept is given by the object descriptor, while the objects that are generated according to this descriptor, constitute the extension. So, while patterns model concepts, the objects model phenomena. A pattern is a generalization of abstraction mechanisms such as class, type, procedure, function and method. In BETA there are no special constructs corresponding to these abstraction mechanisms. A pattern may be used as class, type, procedure, function, etc. The fact that there is only one abstraction mechanism does not mean that it is not useful to distinguish between different kinds of patterns. In the following we shall refer to concepts like *class pattern* and *procedure pattern* for patterns that are used as classes and procedures respectively. Note, however, that technically there is no distinction in the language.

During the design of BETA it has been useful to have only one abstraction mechanism. This has resulted in a uniform treatment of class, type, procedure, function, etc. One example of this is that the notion of subclassing is also available for procedures. In the current implementation of BETA the pattern mechanism is being used in practice. It is currently being investigated to add facilities to restrict the usage of a given pattern. It might e.g. be desirable to express that a given pattern may only be used as a procedure. The reasons for doing this could be a matter of documentation and for efficiency purposes.

Object Generation The fact that pattern and object are two very different things is reflected in their specification. An object according to the pattern P may be declared in the following way:

```
aP: @ P
```

where aP is the name of the object, and P identifies the pattern. aP is an example of a reference attribute., which will be further explained below.

Singular Objects The fact that some objects model singular phenomena is reflected in BETA: it is possible to describe objects that are not generated according to any pattern, but are singular. The object specification

```
S: @ Super
     (#  Decl1; Decl2; ...; Decln
   do
        Imp
   #)
```

describes a singular object S. The object S is not described as belonging to the extension of a concept, i.e. as an instance of a pattern. Singular objects are not just a convenient shorthand to avoid the invention of a pattern name. Often an application has only one phenomenon with a given descriptor, and it seems intuitively wrong to form a concept covering this single phenomenon. A search for a missing person in the radio includes a description of the person. This description is singular, since it is only intended to cover one specific phenomenon. From a description of a singular phenomenon it is, however, easy to form a concept covering all phenomena that match the description.

The framework presented here makes a distinction between phenomena and concepts, and this is reflected in the corresponding language: objects model phenomena and patterns model concepts. A pattern is not an object. In contrast to this distinction between objects and patterns, Smalltalk-like languages treat classes as objects. Concepts are thus both phenomena and used to classify phenomena. In the framework presented here, patterns may be treated as objects, but that is in the *programming process*. The objects manipulated in a programming environment will be fragments (e.g. patterns) of the program being developed.

Delegation based languages do not have a notion corresponding to patterns. They use objects as prototypes for other objects with the same properties as the prototype object.

12.3.2 Class Patterns
A pattern may be used as a class as shown in the following example

```
        Seat:
(#   Reserved: ↑ Reservation;
      Class: @ ClassType;
      Smoking: @ Boolean;

      Reserve: (# ... #);
      Cancel: (# ... #);
      isReserved: (# ... #)
#)
```

This pattern only contains declaration of attributes. The enter-, do- and exit-clauses are empty just as no superpattern has been specified. When no explicit superpattern is specified, the superpattern is assumed to be the most general pattern *object*.

The class pattern Seat is intended to be used in a description of a flight reservation system. Each flight is characterized by a number of Seat objects. Each seat object will have a reference Reserved to an object representing the reservation, a reference Class representing the class of the seat and a reference Smoking representing if smoking is allowed on that seat. In addition it has operations Reserve, Cancel, isReserved. These operations are patterns and will explained below.

12.3.3 Reference Attributes
The attributes Reserved, Class, and Smoking are examples of reference attributes. A reference denotes an object. A reference may be either static or dynamic.
The reference Reserved is an example of a dynamic (or variable) reference. A dynamic reference may denote different objects during the program execution. In this sense a dynamic reference corresponds to a qualified reference in Simula and an instance variable in Smalltalk.

The references Class and Smoking are examples of static (or constant) references. A static reference denotes the same object during the whole program execution. The object being denoted is generated as part of the generation of the enclosing object. When a Seat object is generated, an instance of ClassType and an instance of Boolean is generated and these objects are denoted by the references Class and Smoking respectively.

The substance of a phenomenon may consist of the substances of part-phenomena. In BETA this is reflected by the possibility for objects to have part objects. Static references support the modelling of part objects. Part objects are integral parts of the composite object, and they are generated as part of the generation of the composite object.

12.3.4 Procedure Pattern Attributes
The attributes Reserve and Cancel defined in the pattern Seat are examples of pattern attributes used as procedures (methods). If S denotes an instance of the class pattern Seat, then the imperative

```
S.Reserve
```

implies that an instance of the procedure pattern Reserve is executed. Most object-oriented languages has a construction like this. From Smalltalk it has become known as "message passing", even though concurrent processes are not involved. It has the same semantics as a normal procedure call, the only difference is that the procedure is defined in a remote object and not globally. SIMULA introduced the notion of "remote procedure call" for this construction.

The details of `Reserve` and the other pattern attributes will be shown later. This includes specification of parameters.

12.3.5 Indexed References

It is possible to describe an indexed collection of references as shown in the following example:

```
Flight:
    (#  Seats:  [560] @ Seat;
        ...
    #)
```

The pattern `Flight` contains a declaration of an indexed set of `560` static references to `Seat` objects. A single `Seat` object may be denoted by an expression of the form `Seats[inx]`. Instead of static references, the indexed collection might contain dynamic references. Also the indexed collection contains a fixed number of references. In general the range of the collection may be computed at run-time.

12.3.6 Generation of Objects and Assignment of References

A `Flight` object may be instantiated either as a part object or by means of a dynamic generation. Consider the following two attributes:

```
F1: @ Flight;
F2: ↑ Flight;
```

`F1` is a static reference denoting a part object being generated as part of the enclosing object. `F2` on the other hand is a dynamic reference which may denote different objects during the program execution. `F2` may be given a value by means of a reference assignment:

```
F1[]  →  F2[]
```

This assignment implies that the object referenced by `F1` will also be referenced by `F2`. The box `[]` means that it is the reference that is manipulated and not the object itself. BETA does also have a notion of value assignment. This will however not be discussed here.

It is also possible to create objects dynamically at run-time. The following evaluation creates an instance of `Flight` and assigns the reference to `F2`

```
&Flight[]  →  F2[]
```
The operator `&` corresponds to `New` in Simula and Smalltalk.

12.3.7 Qualified References

References in BETA are *qualified* (typed) by means of a pattern name. The qualification of a reference restricts the set of objects that may be denoted by a reference. In the pattern `Seat` the references `Reserved`, `Class` and `Smoking` are qualified by `Reservation`, `ClassType` and `Boolean` respectively.

A static reference will constantly denote an instance of the qualifying pattern. A dynamic reference may denote an instance of the qualifying pattern or an instance of a subpattern of the qualifying pattern (subpatterns will be further described below). The dynamic reference `Reserved` may thus denote instances of the pattern `Reservation` or instances of subpatterns of `Reservation`, i.e. the reference `Reserved` may then not by accident be set to denote, e.g. an instance of the pattern `ClassType`.

The notion of qualified reference originates from Simula and is one of the major characteristics of strongly typed object-oriented languages.

12.3.8 Class Pattern Attributes

The attributes `Reserve` and `Cancel` of pattern `Seat` are examples of pattern attributes used as procedures. A pattern attribute may also be used as a class as shown in the next example:

```
FlightType:
   (#   source, destination: ↑ City;
        departureTime,
        arrivalTime: @ TimeOfDay;
        flyingTime: @ TimePeriod;

        Flight:
        (# Seats: [NoOfSeats] @ Seat
           actualDepartureTime,
           actualArrivalTime: @ TimeOfDay;
           actualFlyingTime: @ TimePeriod;

           DepartureDelay:
                (#
                exit actualDepartureTime
                        - departureTime
                #)
        #);

        DisplayTimeTableEntry: (# ... #);
        ...
   #)
```

The pattern `FlightType` is supposed to be used for modelling entries in a flight timetable. For each entry in the time-table there will be a an instance of the pattern `FlightType`. Examples of such instances are `SK451` and `SK273`, which describe two different flight types offered by SAS.

```
TimeTable:
   (# ...
      SK451: @ FlightType;
      SK273: @ FlightType;
      ...
      Initialize:
         (# ...
         do ...
            'Copenhagen' -> SK451.source;
            'Los Angeles' -> SK451.destination;
            ...
         #)
   #)
```

A FlightType object has information about source, destination, departure time, arrival time, flying time, etc. The flight SK451 between Copenhagen and Los Angeles will actually take place most days of a year. An attribute like departureTime is thus actually modelling the scheduled departure time. The actual departure time may vary from day to day.

A table for handling reservations must contain an entry for each day the flight takes place. Each such entry should have information about reservation of seats for that day. In addition it might include information about the actual departure time, etc. in order to compute various kinds of statistics .

Each FlightType object has a local class pattern Flight, which models the actual flights taking place. Instances of the pattern Flight will have attributes characterizing a given flight. These attributes include an indexed collection of Seat objects, the actual departure time, the actual arrival time, and the actual flight time.

The reservation table may thus be described by the following pattern:

```
ReservationTable:
   (#
      SK451Flights: [365] ↑ SK451.Flight
      SK273Flights: [365] ↑ SK273.Flight
      ...
   #)
```

Note that SK451Flights is an indexed collection of references to instances of the class pattern Flight of the object denoted by SK451, whereas SK273Flights denotes instances of the Flight pattern being an attribute of SK273.

Assume that the reference ResTable89 denotes an instance of the pattern ReservationTable. The actual flight SK459 taking place at day no. 111 of year 1989 is thus modelled by the object denoted by

```
ResTable89.SK451Flights[111]
```

Seat no. 48 for the flight of that day may then be reserved by executing

```
ResTable89.SK451Flights[111].Seats[48].Reserve
```

When the flight has taken place, the actual times for departure, arrival and flight time may be entered into the flight object. The difference between the estimated flight time and the actual flight time may then be computed by executing

```
ResTable89.SK451Flights[111].DepartureDelay
```

which returns the difference between `actualDepartureTime` and `departure-Time`. Note that `DepartureDelay` refers to the global reference `departureTime` in the enclosing `FlightType` object. (Execution of actions will be further explained below.)

In the example above `Flight` is a class pattern attribute of `FlightType`. In addition `FlightType` instances have the reference attribute `destination` and the procedure pattern attribute `DisplayTimeTableEntry`. For the different instances `SK451` and `SK273` of the pattern `FlightType`, the attributes `SK451.destination` and `SK273.destination` are different attributes. Also `SK451.DisplayTimeTableEntry` and `SK273.DisplayTimeTableEntry` are different procedure patterns, since they are attributes of different instances. In the same way the class patterns `SK451.Flight` and `SK273.Flight` are different since they are attributes of different `FlightType` objects. For further exploitation of "class attributes" see [Madsen,86].

12.3.9 Procedure Patterns

A consequence of the above definition of object-oriented programming is that every action performed during a program execution is performed by an object. A pattern may be used as a procedure. Execution of a procedure pattern consists of creating an instance of the pattern and then executing that instance. The following example is a detailed description of the procedure pattern attribute `Reserve` of pattern `Seat`:

```
Reserve:
  (# aReservation: ↑ Reservation;
     wasReserved: @ Boolean
  enter aReservation[]
  do
     (if isReserved
      // True then
         aReservation[] → Reserved[];
         True → wasReserved
      // False then
         False → wasReserved
     if)
  exit wasReserved
  #)
```

The enter-part of an object descriptor describes the possible input-parameters. The do-part describes the actions to be executed. The exit-part describes possible output-parameters. `Reserve` has one input parameter, `aReservation`, and one output parameter, `wasReserved`.

The do-part of `Reserved` consists of one single if-imperative. If the `Seat` object is not reserved, the input parameter `aReservation` is assigned to the reference variable `Reserved`. Finally the exit parameter returns the value `True` if the reservation was successful.

```
(if (Res[]  →  S.Reserve)
 // True then
    'Was successfully reserved!'  →  Screen.Display
 // False then
    'Could not be reserved!'  →  Screen.Display
if)
```

where `S` denotes the seat to be reserved and `Res` denotes the reservation made by the customer.

In BETA `Reserve` is a pattern attribute. While `Seat` is a pattern defining objects with attributes only, `Reserve` has an action-part, describing how `Seats` may be reserved. The objects in BETA will thus have different functions (or missions) in a program execution, depending on their descriptor . No objects are a priori only "data objects with methods" and no objects are a priori only "methods". Class patterns may also have an action-part. Examples of this will be given below.

12.3.10 Measurable Properties

As an example of a measurable property, consider the percentage of occupied seats of a flight. A flight has parts like seats, but is has no part representing the percentage of occupied seats. This is a property that has to be measured. The value "85 %" is not an object, but is rather a denotation of the *value* of some measuring object.

Actions producing measurements In BETA a measurable property is reflected by an object that produces a *measurement* as a result of executing the object. The representation of a measurement is described by the exit-part. This consists of a list of evaluations that represents the value of the object. In the following example the pattern `Occupied` is an example of a measurable property of `Flight` objects

```
Flight:
  (#  Seats: [NoOfSeats] @ Seat; ...

    Occupied:
      (# NoOfRes: @ Integer
      do
          (for inx: NoOfSeats repeat
              (if Seats[inx].isReserved
              // True then
                  NoOfRes+1  →  NoOfRes
```

```
              if) for)
           exit (NoOfRes/NoOfSeats)*100
           #)
    #)
```

If F is a Flight object, then an execution of F.Occupied will perform a measurement of the percentage of occupied seats in F. Technically an instance of F.Occupied will be created and executed. This instance will however only exist temporarily while the measurement is computed. It does not model a part of a Flight object in the same way as the Seat objects.

The pattern DepartureDelay is another example of an attribute modelling a measurable property of a Flight object. Notice that the result of the measurement does not only depend on the Flight object. It does also depend on the enclosing Flight-Type object.

In other languages the aspect of measurable properties is to some degree covered by function attributes.

Actions resulting in state changes Change of state is usually associated with assignment to variables. In physical models there is a duality between observation of state (measurement) and change of state. A measurement is reflected in BETA by the execution of an object and production of a list of values that represents the value of the measurement. Correspondingly a change of state is reflected by reception of a list of values followed by execution of the actions of an object.

The patterns Reserve and Cancel are examples of actions that result in state changes. The enter-part represents the values that are to be imposed upon the state.

Often a pattern attribute describes an action that results in both state changes and produces a measurement.

The association of reception of values with actions are also found in other languages (active, annotated values).

12.3.11 Classification Hierarchies
In this section the meaning of the super-part (Super) of an object descriptor will be explained. The super-part is intended for modelling classification hierarchies (generalization, specialization) as discussed in section 2 of this chapter. Due to the generality of the pattern mechanism, the superpart is available for both class patterns and procedure patterns.

Class patterns As mentioned above a travel agency will normally handle reservations of several kinds. Classification of reservations into a general Reservation and two specializations Flight Reservation and Train Reservation will be reflected by corresponding patterns.

```
    Reservation:
       (#
          Date: @ DateType;
          Customer: ↑ CustomerRecord;
```

```
    #)
FlightReservation: Reservation
    (#
        ReservedFlight: ↑ Flight;
        ReservedSeat: ↑ Seat;
    #)

TrainReservation: Reservation
    (#
        ReservedTrain: ↑ Train;
        ReservedWagon: ↑ Wagon;
        ReservedSeat: ↑ Seat;
    #)
```

The patterns FlightReservation and TrainReservation both have a super-part specifying the pattern Reservation. The effect of this is that all the attributes of Reservation are also attributes of FlightReservation and TrainReservation.

We will say that FlightReservation and TrainReservation are *subpatterns* of Reservation and that Reservation is the *superpattern* of FlightReservation and TrainReservation. The term *inheritance* is often used to express the fact that properties of the superpattern are inherited by the subpattern.

Besides supporting a natural way of classification, this mechanism contributes to making object-oriented programs compact. The general pattern only has to be described once. A revision of the pattern Reservation will have immediate effect on both subpatterns. It also supports re-usability. All object-oriented languages, except delegation based languages, have this notion of class/subclass.

Given this classification of reservations, the Reserved attribute (qualified by Reservation) of each Flight object may now denote Reservation, FlightReservation and TrainReservation objects. In order to express that it may only denote FlightReservation objects, it is qualified by FlightReservation:

```
    Reserved: ↑ FlightReservation
```

Procedure patterns One of the advantages of the single pattern mechanism is that inheritance is also available for procedure patterns. This makes it possible to describe a classification hierarchy of action-sequences. Consider the concept *HandleReservation:* An element in the extension of this concept is an action-sequence performed by an agent when making a reservation. This concept may then have specializations like *HandleFlightReservation* and *HandleTrainReservation*. Inheritance for procedures is in addition useful for re-usability of code. Consider the following example:

```
    ScanReservations:
        (#  F: ↑ Flight; CurrentSeat: ↑ Seat
        enter F[]
        do (for inx: F.Seats.Range repeat
```

315

```
(if F.Seats[inx].isReserved // True then
    F.Seats[inx][] → CurrentSeat[];
    INNER
if)
for)
#);


DisplayReservations: ScanReservations
(#
do CurrentSeat.Reserved.Display;
   INNER
#);
```

The pattern ScanReservations scans through all reservations made for a given flight denoted by F. The for-loop steps through all the Seats of the flight. If a given Seat is reserved then that Seat is assigned to the "index variable" CurrentSeat. The **INNER** imperative describes how the actions of ScanReservations are combined with the actions of a possible subpattern.

The pattern DisplayReservations is a subpattern of ScanReservations. An execution

```
SomeFlight[] → DisplayReservations
```

is carried out as follows: An instance of DisplayReservations is generated and the actual parameter SomeFlight is assigned to the enter-part F. The execution of the instance start by execution of the action-part of the superpattern ScanReservations. Whenever **INNER** is executed, the actions of DisplayReservations are executed. i.e. the actions of DisplayReservations includes the actions of ScanReservations. ScanReservations is an example of a pattern used as a control structure.

12.3.12 Virtual Patterns

When making a classification hierarchy, some of the pattern attributes of the superpattern are completely specified, and these specifications are valid for all possible specializations of the pattern. The printing of date and customer of a reservation will be the same for both kinds of reservations. Other attributes may only be partially specified, and first completely specified in specializations. The printing of reservations will depend upon whether a FlightReservation or a TrainReservation is to be printed. This means that it will not be possible to fully specify a display pattern attribute of Reservation. A display pattern may be given for FlightReservation and TrainReservation. However these display patterns will both have the code for displaying the date and customer of a Reservation. It would be more efficient to have that code as part of Reservation. This can be obtained by specifying a virtual pattern attribute Display of Reservation.

```
Reservation:
   (# Date:...; Customer:...;
      Display:<
         (#
         do {Display Date and Customer};
            INNER
         #);
   #);

FlightReservation: Reservation
   (# ReservedFlight:...;ReservedSeat:...;
      Display::<
         (#
         do {Display ReservedFlight and ReservedSeat}
            INNER
         #)
   #)
```

The pattern `Display` of `Reservation` has been specified virtual (the symbol <
means virtual). This implies that

- In every subpattern of `Reservation`, `Display` can be specialized (extended) to
  what is appropriate for the actual subpattern.
- Execution of `Display` of some `Reservation` object, by

    `SomeReservation.Display;`

where `SomeReservation` denotes some `Reservation` object, means
execution of the `Display`, which is defined for the `Reservation` object
currently denoted by `SomeReservation`.

In the pattern `FlightReservation` the description of `Display` has been extended
(the symbol `: <` means extend virtual). The effect of this is that the `Display` pattern of
`FlightReservation` is a subpattern of the `Display` pattern described in `Reservation`. A similar extension can be made of the pattern `Display` in `TrainReservation`.

Execution of a virtual pattern implies late binding of the `Display` pattern of the actual object denoted by `SomeReservation`. The qualification (`Reservation`) of
`SomeReservation` implies that it may only denote instances of pattern `Reservation` or of subpatterns of `Reservation` The qualification, however, ensures that
`SomeReservation.Display` will always be valid. `SomeReservation` will not be
able to denote objects that do not have a `Display` attribute.

In languages like Smalltalk and Flavors all methods are virtuals, while in BETA,
C++ [Stroustrup 86] and SIMULA it must be indicated explicitly. This means, that message-passing in Smalltalk and Flavors always implies late binding, while non-virtuals in
C++ , BETA and SIMULA may be bound earlier and thereby be executed faster. It also
has the implication that with non-virtual methods it is possible to state in a super-pattern

317

that some of the methods may *not* be specialized in sub-classes. This is useful when making packages of patterns. In order to ensure that these work as intended by the author, some of the methods should not be re-defined by users of the packages.

As methods in BETA are represented by pattern attributes, the ordinary pattern/sub-pattern mechanism is also valid for these. The virtual concept and specialization of methods are further exploited in [BETA,87b]. The above example of a virtual pattern demonstrates the virtual concept for procedure patterns. It is however also possible to specify *virtual class attributes*. For examples of this see [BETA,89].

It is well-known that object-oriented design greatly improves the re-use of code. The main reason for this is sub-classing combined with virtuals [Meyer,87]. For many people this is the main issue of object-orientation. However, as pointed out above, modelling which reflects the real world is an equally important issue.

12.3.13 Individual Action Sequences

As mentioned above all actions in a BETA program execution are executed by objects. Each object has an individual sequence of actions. The model identifies three ways of organizing these sequences: as concurrent, alternating or partial sequences. In BETA, these are reflected by three different *kinds* of objects: *system* objects, *component* objects and *item* objects.

Concurrent action sequences System objects are *concurrent* objects and they have means for synchronized communication: a system object may *request* another system object to execute one of its local objects and the requester will wait for the acceptor to do it. When the requested object *accepts* to execute this local object, possible parameters will be transferred and the local object executed. If parameters are to be returned, then the requesting object must wait until the object has been executed.

In the BETA model of the flight reservation system mentioned above, agents and flights may be represented by concurrent objects, reflecting that there will be several agents, each of which at some points in time tries to reserve seats on the same flight. Seat reservations will take place by synchronized communication (the `Flight` object will only perform one reservation at a time), so double reservation of the same seat is avoided.

The pattern `Flight` may be extended with an operation for reserving seats . In addition it will have an action-part for communication with agents.

```
Flight:
  (# ...
     ReserveSeats: @
        (#
        enter(noOfSeats, Smoking, someClass)
        do ...
        exit Result
        #)
  do
     Cycle(#do  <?ReserveSeats   #)
  #)
```

318

Assume that the reference F denotes the SK451.Flight instance handling reservations for a given day. An agent object may then reserve 5 non-smoking seats on business class by performing the following request

```
(5,False,Business) → F>?ReserveSeats → someResult
```

The operation F>?ReserveSeats requests the Flight system object denoted by F to execute the object ReserveSeats. The operations <?ReserveSeats describes that the Flight object is willing to execute ReserveSeats for some system object.

If several agents at the same time request the ReserveSeat operation, then only requests from one agent at a time will be accepted. The descriptor of ReserveSeat may be extended with a specification saying that only requests from agent objects will be accepted. It may even restrict this to one specific agent object.

As each object may have their individual action sequence it may at different stages in this sequence accept different requests. In the above example, a Flight object repeatedly executes a cycle where it only accepts requests for ReserveSeats. In a complete reservation system, a Flight object should also be able to accept requests for cancelling seats. Similarly, when the flight is fully booked, it should not accept further requests for ReserveSeats. The BETA mechanisms for describing this will not be explained here.

The underlying model of a language determines to a certain degree which kind of concurrency is supported. While languages supporting objects as the main building blocks will have objects executing actions concurrently (even if this may only be accomplished by concurrent execution of methods as in Concurrent Smalltalk), Lisp-based languages will have concurrency based on concurrent evaluation of expressions (futures).

Alternating action sequences Component objects in BETA are alternating objects, i.e. objects where at most one object is executing at a time and where the shift of control from object to object is non-deterministic.

In the BETA model of the tour reservation system, there may be objects supporting the agents with various activities such as tour planning, invoicing and customer service The action-sequence of such an object may be described as an alternation between action-sequences supporting each of these activities. The pattern AgentServer below has internal objects corresponding to these activities.

```
AgentServer:
(#  TourPlanning:...
    Invoicing: ...
    CustomerService: ...
do...;
    (| TourPlanning | Invoicing | CustomerService |)
        ...
#)
```

The construct (| ... |) describes that execution alternates between the objects.

The activity TourPlanning may consist of planning a series of tours that are bought earlier, and just wait to be planned. Correspondingly, the activity `Invoicing` may consist of writing invoices for a series of tours. The activity `CustomerService` consists of waiting for customer requests and fulfilling them. A shift from `TourPlanning` or `Invoicing` to `CustomerService` will thus only take place, when there is a request for it, so it will not be part of the descriptor of either `TourPlanning` or `Invoicing` when this shall happen.

Partial action sequences The example above with the execution of an object according to the `Display` attribute of some `Reservation` object is an example of a partial action sequence, represented by an item object. The action sequence of `Display` is executed as part of the "calling" object.

All languages have a notion of partial action sequences. The notion of procedure and function covers this aspect of actions. Method invocation as a result of message passing is a special case of a partial action sequence, where the procedure to perform is defined in an object different from the invoking object.

One of the characteristics of most other object-oriented languages is that everything is an object with methods and all activity is expressed by message passing and method invocation. Objects in these languages do not have any individual action sequence; they are only "executing methods" on request. Thus, objects in these languages may not support alternating or concurrent action sequences. One exception is the Actor model of execution [Agha,86], where the objects are concurrent, but sub-classes are not supported in the common sense of the word. Work has been initiated to make concurrent Smalltalk, but this work does not include giving the objects their own sequence of actions.

12.4 OTHER ASPECTS OF OBJECT-ORIENTATION

As mentioned in the introduction many properties are associated with object-oriented programming. In this section we will comment on some of these.

12.4.1 Methods and Message Passing
A property common to most object-oriented programming languages is that everything has to be regarded as an object with methods and that every action performed is message passing. The implication of this is that even a typical functional expression such as

```
6+7
```

gets the unnatural interpretation

```
6.plus(7)
```

However, 6 and 7 are objects (integer objects), and they are also in the definition of object-oriented programming presented here, so there is no reason that + may not be regarded as an object that adds two integer objects:

```
plus(6,7)
```

Thinking object-oriented does not have to exclude functional expressions when that is more natural. Functions, types and values are in fact needed in order to describe measurable properties of objects.

12.4.2 Automatic Storage Management

According to the definition of object-oriented programming given here it has not necessarily anything to do with dynamic generation of objects. and automatic storage management. This is one of the properties often associated with object-oriented programming. Many people have found Simula to be too inefficient because it requires a garbage collector. With modern technology people seem more willing to accept automatic storage management.

In many object-oriented languages it is only possible to generate objects dynamically. But whether objects are parts of other objects or generated independently and dynamically, is not crucial for whether program executions are organized in objects or not. It is demonstrated above that in BETA it is possible to specify part-objects. Program executions are still organized in objects with attributes and actions, but some of the objects are allocated as part of other objects. As shown above a Flight object consists of Seat objects, and these are constituent parts of a Flight object. When objects are generated dynamically, as e.g. Reservation objects will be in the example above, it is, however, important that the implementation includes an automatic storage management system.

12.4.3 Late Binding

Object-oriented programming does not necessarily imply *late and unsafe binding of names*. As mentioned above, pattern attributes of BETA objects and procedures in C++ objects may be specified as non-virtual, which means that late binding is not used when invoking them.

When Smalltalk or Flavors objects react on a message passed to it with "message not understood", it has nothing to do with Smalltalk or Flavors being object-oriented, but with the fact that they are untyped languages.

The combination of qualified (typed) references and virtuals in BETA implies that it may be checked at compile time that expressions like "aRef.aMethod" will be valid at run time, provided of course that aRef denotes an object and not **none**. And still a late binding determines which aMethod (of which sub-pattern) will be executed. Which aMethod to execute depends upon which object is currently denoted by aRef.

In the example above the reference SomeReservation will be qualified by Reservation. This means, that SomeReservation may denote objects generated according to the pattern Reservation or sub-patterns of Reservation. As Display is declared as a virtual in Reservation, it is assured that

        SomeReservation.Display

is always valid and that it will lead to the execution of the appropriate Display. However, the use of untyped references in Smalltalk-like languages has the benefit, that recompilation of a class does not have to take the rest of the program into consideration .

What makes late binding slow is not only the method look-up. If a method in Smalltalk has parameters, then the correspondence between actual and formal parameters must be checked at the time of execution. `Display` will e.g. have a parameter telling how many copies to print. This will be the same for all specializations of `Display`, and should therefore be specified as part of the declaration of `Display` in `Reservation`.

In BETA this is obtained by *qualifying virtuals*. The fact that `Display` will have a parameter is described by a pattern `DisplayParameter`:

```
DisplayParameter:
    (# NoOfCopies: @ Integer;
    enter(NoOfCopies)
    do ...
    #)
```

Qualifying the virtual `Display` with `DisplayParameter` implies that all specializations of `Display` in different sub-patterns of `Reservation` must be sub-patterns of `DisplayParameter`, and thus have the properties described in `DisplayParameter`. This implies that `Display` in all sub-patterns to `Reservation` will have an Integer `NoOfCopies` input-parameter.

If object-oriented programming is to be widely used in real application programming, then the provision of typed languages is a must. As Peter Wegner says in "Dimensions of Object-Based Language Design":

"..., the accepted wisdom is that strongly typed object-oriented languages should be the norm for application programming and especially for programming in the large."

As demonstrated above it does not have to exclude flexibility in specialization of methods or late binding.

12.4.4 Inheritance and Code Sharing

Since inheritance has been introduced by object-oriented languages, object-oriented programming is often defined to be programming in languages that support inheritance. Inheritance may, however, also be supported by functional languages, where functions, types and values may be organized in a classification hierarchy.

In most object-oriented languages classes are special objects, and inheritance is defined by a message forwarding mechanism. Objects of subclasses send (forward) messages to the super-class "object" in order to have inherited methods performed. This approach stresses *code sharing*: there shall be only one copy of the super-class, common to all sub-classes. With this definition of inheritance it is not strange that "distribution is inconsistent with inheritance" [Wegner,87] and that "This explains why there are no languages with distributed processes that support inheritance" [Wegner,87].

In the model of object-oriented programming presented here, the main reason for sub-classing (specialization) is the classification of concepts. The actual implementation of inheritance should not be part of the language definition.

According to the definition of patterns and objects in BETA given above, patterns are not objects, and in principle every object of pattern P will have its own descriptor. It is left to the implementation to optimize by having different objects of P share the descriptor. Following this definition of patterns and objects there is no problem in having two objects of the same sub-pattern act concurrently and even be distributed. The implementation will in this case simply make as many copies of the pattern as needed, including a possible super-pattern. This does not exclude that a modification of the super-pattern will have effect on all sub-patterns.

12.4.5 Multiple Inheritance

Multiple inheritance has come up as a generalization of single inheritance. With single inheritance a class may have at most one super-class, whereas multiple inheritance allows a class to have several super-classes. Inheritance is used for many purposes including code sharing and hierarchical classification of concepts. In the BETA language inheritance is mainly intended for hierarchical classification. BETA does not have multiple inheritance, due to the lack of a profound theoretical understanding, and also because the current proposals seem technically very complicated.

In existing languages with multiple inheritance, the code-sharing part of the class/sub-class construct dominates. Flavors has a name that directly reflects what is going on: mixing some classes, so the resulting class has the desired flavor, that is the desired attributes. For the experience of eating an ice cone it is significant whether the vanilla ice is at the bottom and the chocolate ice on top, or the other way around. Correspondingly, a class that inherits from the classes (A, B) is not the same as a class that inherits from the classes (B, A).

If, however, multiple inheritance is to be regarded as a generalization of single inheritance and thereby as a model of multiple concept classification (and it should, in the model presented here), then the order of the super-classes should be insignificant. When classifying a concept as a specialization of several concepts, no order of the general concepts is implied, and that should be supported by the language.

Single inheritance is well suited for modelling a strict hierarchical classification of concepts, i.e. a hierarchy where the extensions of the specializations of a given concept are disjoint. Such hierarchies appear in many applications, and it is often useful to know that the extensions of say class predator and class rodent are disjoint.

By classifying objects by means of different and independent properties, several orthogonal strict hierarchies may be constructed. A group of people may be classified according to their profession leading to one hierarchy, and according to their nationality leading to another hierarchy. Multiple inheritance is often used for modelling the combination of such hierarchies. It may, however, be difficult to recognize if such a non-strict hierarchy is actually a combination of several strict hierarchies.

12.4.6 Object-Oriented Design

The benefits of object-orientation do not apply only to programming, but also to system design in general, including requirement analysis and functional specification. The framework presented here may therefore also be applied to languages and methods used in these activities.

Functional specification of a system is intended to give the functionalities of the system, and this is often done in terms of the behaviour of a system seen as a black box, given certain input values, stimuli or more generally the behaviour of the environment of the system. In their role as contracts between customers and suppliers, it has emerged that the specification of behaviour is not the only interesting thing, especially for non-professional customers. Even more important is the specification of which phenomena and which concepts from the application area that are covered by the system. A first interesting question on a reservation system would be a question like "Are customers covered as phenomena (and thus integrated with our customer data base) or do they just turn up as name and address on reservations?" A more advanced question would be: "Is the notion of actual flights covered, in addition to the notion of scheduled flights"

It is also reported that the main difficulty in requirements capture [Borgida,85] is deciding which phenomena and concepts are relevant and should be covered.

The framework presented in this chapter has not only been used in the design of BETA. Part of it has also been used in the design of an object-oriented extension, OSDL [OSDL], of the CCITT recommended specification language SDL [SDL]. The language mechanisms of SDL support concurrency (processes, that is extended finite state machines), alternation (by service decomposition of processes) and partial action sequences by transitions (from one state to the next state) and procedures. OSDL adds to this specialization of process types, of block types (consisting of processes), and of procedures. It incorporates virtual procedures in almost the sense described here. Virtual transitions are for specializations of action sequences of processes and procedures, and they correspond to the INNER construct of BETA. While most concurrent object-oriented languages have started with simple objects and added on concurrency, OSDL has as a starting point a language supporting concurrency.

12.5 CONCLUSION

The programmer's perspective on programming is perhaps more important than programming language constructs. Object-oriented programming should not be defined only by specific language constructs. It is absolutely possible to think and program object-oriented even without a language that directly supports it.

It is, however, a great advantage to use an object-oriented language that directly supports object-orientation. Such a language should support:

- Modelling of concepts and phenomena, i.e. the language must include constructs like class, type, procedure.
- Modelling classification hierarchies, i.e. sub-classing (inheritance) and virtuals.
- Modelling active objects, i.e. concurrency or coroutine sequencing, combined with persistency.

The benefits of object-oriented programming may be summarized as follows:

- Programs reflect reality.
- Model is more stable than functionality.
- Sub-classing and virtuals improve re-usability of code.

The above statements are of course not objective, in the sense that it is arguable what is natural, easy and stable. For a mathematician it may be more natural to construct a model using equations.

Finally we would like to stress that a programming language should support other perspectives than object-orientation. There are many problems that may be easier to formulate using procedural, functional or constraint-oriented programming. BETA supports procedural programming and has good facilities for functional programming. Work is going on to improve the support for functional programming and to include support for constraint-oriented programming. The overall perspective will still be object-oriented, but transitions may be described as functions without intermediate states. Support for constraint-oriented programming will allow for expressing constraints and for a more high level description of transitions. Loops is an example of a language supporting several perspectives.

12.6 ACKNOWLEDGEMENTS

The framework presented here is mainly a result of the authors' participation in the BETA project. In addition to the authors, Bent Bruun Kristensen, Aalborg University Centre, Denmark and Kristen Nygaard, University of Oslo, Norway, have been members of the BETA team. Jørgen Lindskov Knudsen, Kristine Stougård Thomsen, Jon Skretting and Einar Hodne have contributed with useful discussions and by commenting on the paper. A previous version of this paper has been presented at ECOOP, the European Conference on Object-Oriented Programming, Oslo 1988. A very early version (in Danish) appeared in the special December 1987 issue of Nordisk Datanytt edited by Stein Gjessing.

REFERENCES

[Agha,86] Agha G., "An overview of Actor Languages," *Sigplan Notices*, Vol.21, No.10, Oct. 1986.

[BETA,87a] Kristensen, B.B., Madsen, O.L., Møller-Pedersen, B. and Nygaard K., "The BETA Programming Language,". In: [Shriver,87].

[BETA,87b] Kristensen, B.B., Madsen, O.L., Møller-Pedersen, B. and Nygaard K., "Classification of Actions or Inheritance also for Methods," In [ECOOP,87].

[BETA,89] Madsen, O.L and Møller-Pedersen, B., "Virtual Classes - A new Dimension in Object-Oriented Programming," Draft 1989.

[Bobrow,82] Bobrow, D.G. and Stefik, M., "Loops: An Object-Oriented Programming System for InterLisp," Xerox PARC 1984.

[Booch,86] Booch, G., "Object-Oriented Development," *IEEE Trans. on Software Engineering*, Vol. SE-12, No. 2, Feb. 1986.

[Borgida,85] Borgida, A., Greenspan, S. and Mylopoulos, J. "Knowledge Representation as the Basis for Requirements Specification," *IEEE Computer*, April 1985.

[Cook,88] Cook, S. "Impressions of ECOOP´88," *Journal of Object-Oriented Programming*, Vol. 1, No. 4, 1988.

[DELTA] Holbaek-Hanssen, E. Haandlykken, P. and Nygaard, K., "System Description and the DELTA Language," Publication no. 523, Norwegian Computing Center, 1975.

[ECOOP] Proceedings of European Conference on Object-Oriented Programming, Conference Proceedings 1987 and 1988, *Springer Lecture Notes in Computer Science*, Vol. 276, 1987, Vol. 322, 1988, Heidelberg.

[Flavors] Cannon, H. "Flavors, A Non-Hierarchical Approach to Object-oriented Programming," Draft 1982.

[Goldberg,83] Goldberg, A., Robson, D., *Smalltalk 80: The Language and its Implementation*, Addison Wesley 1983.

[JSD] Jackson, M., *System Development*, Prentice Hall 1983.

[Knudsen,85] Knudsen, J.L. and Thomsen, K.S., "A Conceptual Framework for Programming Languages," Computer Science Department, DAIMI PB-192, Aarhus University, April 1985.

[Krogdahl,86] Krogdahl, S. and Olsen, K.A., "Modulær- og Objekt Orientert Programmering", *DataTid* , Nr.9 , Sept. 1986.

[Madsen,86] Madsen O.L., "Block Structure and Object Oriented Languages," In [Shriver,87].

[Meyer,87] Meyer, B. "Reusability: The Case for Object-Oriented Design," *IEEE Software*, Vol.4, No.2, March 1987.

[Meyer,88] Meyer, B., *Object-Oriented Software Construction*, Prentice Hall, 1988.

[Mjølner] Dahle, H.P., Løfgren, M., Magnusson, B. and Madsen, O.L., "Mjølner, A Highly Efficient Programming Environment for Industrial use," *In Proceedings of Software Tools 87*, Online Publications, London 1987.

[Nygaard,81] Nygaard, K. and Dahl, O.-J., "Simula 67," In *History of Programming Languages*, ed. R.W. Wexelblatt, 1986.

[Nygaard,86] Nygaard, K.: "Basic Concepts in Object Oriented Programming," *Sigplan Notices*, Vol. 21 No. 10 October 1986.

[OOPSLA] OOPSLA, Object-Oriented Programming Systems, Languages and Applications, Conference Proceedings, 1986, 1987 and 1988, *ACM Sigplan Notices*, Vol. 21, No. 11, 1986, Vol. 22, No. 12, 1987 and Vol. 23, No. 11, 1988.

[OSDL] Møller-Pedersen, B., Belsnes, D. and Dahle, H.P., "Rationale and Tutorial on OSDL: An Object-Oriented Extension of SDL," *Computer Networks*, Vol. 13, No. 2, 1987.

[SDL] CCITT, "Functional Specification and Description Language (SDL)," CCITT Red Book Vol. VI-Fascicle VI.10, z.100 - CCITT Report com X-R15-E, Geneva, Jan. 1987

[Shriver,87] Shriver, B. and Wegner, P., *Research Directions in Object-Oriented Languages*, MIT Press, 1987.

[SIMULA 67] Dahl, O.J., Myhrhaug, B. and Nygaard, K. "SIMULA 67 Common Base Language," Norwegian Computing Center, February 1968, 1970, 1972, 1984.

[Stefik,86] Stefik, M. and Bobrow, D.G., "Object-Oriented Programming, Themes and Variations," *The AI Magazine*, Vol. 6, No. 4, pp. 40-62, Jan. 1986.

[Stroustrup,86] Stroustrup, B., *The C++ Programming Language*, Addison Wesley 1986

[Wegner,87] Wegner, P., "Dimensions of Object-Based Language Design," *Tech. Report No. CS-87-14*, Brown University, July 1987.

Chapter 13

An Overview of the Iris Kernel Architecture

Peter Lyngbaek and Kevin Wilkinson
Hewlett-Packard Laboratories

ABSTRACT *We describe an architecture for a database system based on an object/function model. The architecture efficiently supports the evaluation of functional expressions. The goal of the architecture is to provide a database system that is powerful enough to support the definition of procedural functions that implement the semantics of the data model. The architecture has been implemented to support the Iris Database System.*

13.1 INTRODUCTION

The Iris object-oriented database system being developed at Hewlett-Packard Laboratories [Fishman,87] is intended to meet the needs of new and emerging database applications such as office information and knowledge-based systems, engineering test and measurement, and hardware and software design. These applications require a rich set of capabilities that are not supported by the current generation of relational DBMSs. In addition to the usual requirement for permanence of data, associative access, controlled sharing, backup, and recovery, the new capabilities that are needed include: rich data modeling constructs, including constructs for modeling of behavior, direct database support for inference, novel and extensible data types, and multiple versions of data. Data sharing must be provided at the object level, allowing a given object to be accessed by applications that may be written in different object-oriented programming languages.

In order to meet the above needs, the Iris data model is based on object and function concepts that support high-level structural as well as behavioral abstractions. Queries are written as functional expressions and function values can be modified by database procedures. Extensibility is provided by allowing users to define new functions.

One of the long-term goals of the Iris implementation is to be able to describe and implement the Iris system in terms of its own functions and procedures [Lyngbaek,86].

To do this, it is necessary to identify an appropriate set of primitive operations for object creation and function updating that can be used to define higher level operations. That way, new data model operations can be easily prototyped as ordinary database functions. This approach allows us to experiment with different semantics of, for example, multiple inheritance, versioning, and complex objects with little re-implementation effort. The nature of the Iris database language and its impact on the system architecture is the subject of this chapter. An initial draft of the material has appeared in [Lyngbaek,89].

In an earlier Iris implementation [Lyngbaek,87b], all the operations of the Iris Data Model, e.g., operations for object and function creation, were implemented as C language subroutines and provided as separate Iris entry points. In that approach, it is not possible to support a database language in which complex database procedures are written from the primitive built-in system operations.

In addition, meta-data access was internally provided via a C subroutine library that maintained a cache of the Iris system functions, i.e., the system catalog. These subroutines were not accessible as ordinary Iris functions and their use and control-flow was rather ad-hoc. Furthermore, the cached system functions were updated in a different manner than ordinary functions. Adding new system functions was tedious since they were supported via two different access mechanisms: one for users and one for Iris internally.

Since the essence of the Iris Data Model is function application and updating, the Iris system is being rearchitected around the single operation of invoking a function. Thus, the reimplementation consisted of two tasks: we must define the capabilities of the Iris language to be supported and we must reimplement internal meta-data access and system operations as Iris functions.

The challenge is to find efficient solutions for both tasks. We must limit the features of the Iris database language to those that we know how to compile and optimize efficiently. We must also devise efficient execution strategies for system functions to limit the overhead and path length for those that are frequently invoked. We prefer the simplicity of a single function execution mechanism for all operations, both user-accessible and internal to the system, but it must perform efficiently.

The rest of this chapter is organized as follows. Section 13.2 gives a brief overview of the Iris Data Model, Section 13.3 discusses the new system architecture and its constituents, Section 13.4 gives examples, and Section 13.5 provides some concluding remarks.

13.2 OVERVIEW OF THE IRIS DATA MODEL

The Iris Database System is based on a semantic data model that supports abstract data types. Its roots can be found in previous work on Daplex [Shipman,81] and the Taxis language [Mylopoulos,80]. A number of recent data models, such as PDM [Manola,86] and Fugue [Heiler,88], also share many similarities with the Iris Data Model. The Iris data model contains three important constructs: *objects, types* and *functions*. These are briefly described below. A more complete description of the Iris Data Model and the Iris DBMS can be found in [Lyngbaek,86; Fishman,87]

13.2.1 Objects and Types

Objects in Iris represent entities and concepts from the application domain being modeled. Some objects such as integers, strings, and lists are identified by their content. Those are called *literal objects*. A *surrogate* object is represented by a system-generated *object identifier* or *oid*. Examples of surrogate objects include objects representing persons and departments.

Types have unique names and represent collections of objects that are capable of participating in a specific set of activities. These activities are modeled by functions. Objects serve as arguments to functions and may be returned as results of functions. Objects are constrained by their types to be operands for only those functions defined on the types.

Types are organized in an acyclic type structure that supports generalization and specialization. A type may be declared to be a subtype of other types (its supertypes). The graph of the system types is shown in Figure 13.1.

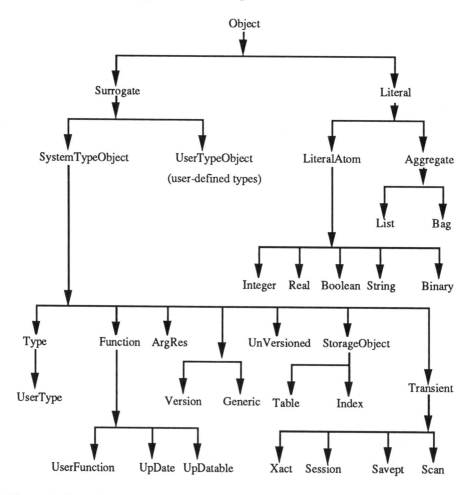

Figure 13.1: IRIS system types

The type graph models inheritance in Iris. A function defined on a given type is also defined on all the subtypes. In order to support stepwise refinement of functions, function names may be overloaded. That is, different functions defined on different types may be given identical names. When a function call is issued using an overloaded function name, a specific function is selected for invocation. Iris chooses the function that is defined on the most specific types of the actual arguments.

Surrogate objects may belong to multiple types even if the types are not related by a subtype/supertype relationship. In addition, objects may gain and lose types dynamically. For example, an object representing a given person may be created as an instance of the Employee type. Later it may lose the Employee type and acquire the type Retiree. When that happens, all the functions defined on Retiree become applicable to the object and the functions on Employee become inapplicable. This feature enable us to better support database evolution.

Objects in Iris may be versioned. Conceptually, versions of an object are snapshots of the object in certain states. An object being versioned is represented by a *generic* object and a set of distinct *version* objects corresponding to each version of the object. The generic object may have properties whose values are inherited by all its version objects. References to the generic object as well as references to specific version objects are supported. A reference to the generic object may be resolved automatically to a specific version object. By default objects are not versioned, i.e. they have the type UnVersioned. The Iris versioning mechanism is further described in [Beech,88].

13.2.2 Functions

Attributes of objects, relationships among objects, and computations on objects are expressed in terms of functions. Functions are defined over types and they may be multi-valued and have side-effects. In Iris, the declaration of a function is separated from its implementation. This provides a degree of data independence.

A type can be characterized by the collection of functions defined on it. The Employee type might have the following functions defined over it:

JobTitle: Employee → String

EmpDept: Employee → Department

Manager: Employee → Employee

SalHist: Employee → Integer * Date

ChangeJob: Employee * String * Department → Boolean

If Smith is working as a software engineer in the Toolkit Department reporting to Jones then the function values are as follows:

JobTitle(Smith) → "Software Engineer"

EmpDept(Smith) → ToolKit

Manager(Smith) → Jones

The SalHist function is multi-valued. It is also an example of a function with multiple result types. Each value consists of a pair of salary and date objects. The date indicates when the salary was changed. If Smith was hired on 3/1/87 with a monthly salary of $3000 and given a raise of $300 on 3/1/88 then the salary history function has the following value:

SalHist(Smith) → [<3000, 3/1/87>, <3300, 3/1/88>]

The function ChangeJob has side-effects. It assigns a given employee to a given department and changes the job title as specified. This is an example of a function with multiple argument types. The promotion of Smith to Project Manger in the Applications Department can be reflected in the database by the following function invocation:

ChangeJob(Smith, "Project Manager", Applications)

In this invocation, Smith and Applications denote oids.

A new function is declared by specifying its name together with its argument and result types:

create function Manager(Employee) = supervisor/Employee;

Before a function may be used, an implementation must be specified. This process is described in Section 13.2.4.

13.2.3 Database Updates and Queries
Properties of objects can be modified by changing the values of functions. For example, the following operations, expressed in the OSQL database language [Fishman,87], will cause the JobTitle function to return the value "MTS'" in a future invocation with the parameter Smith and add another salary and date pair to Smith's salary history:

set JobTitle(Smith) = "MTS";

add Salhist(Smith) = <3800, 1/1/89>;

In addition to setting and adding function values, one or more values may be removed from the value-set of a multi-valued function. Not all functions are updatable.

The database can be queried by specifying a list of results using variables and function applications, a list of existentially quantified variables, and a predicate expression on objects and function values. The predicate may use variables, constants, nested function applications, and comparison operators. The execution of a query causes the variables to be instantiated. The result of a query is all the instantiated values of the variables and the results of the function applications specified in the result list. The results are returned as a bag. Queries are side-effect free. The following query, expressed in the OSQL database language, retrieves all the dates on which Smith's salary was modified:

> select d
> for each Date d, Integer s
> where SalHist(Smith) = <s, d>;

and the query:

> select Manager(Smith);

returns Smith's manager.

13.2.4 Function Implementation

So far, we have discussed the declaration of functions and their use in queries and updates. An important additional characteristic of a function is the specification of its behavior. Function values may be explicitly stored in the database or they may be computed. The method used is user-specified and is called the function's *implementation*. In general, functions can be used in queries regardless of how they are implemented provided they are side-effect free. Iris supports three methods of function implementation: *Stored, Derived,* and *Foreign.*

In the process of implementing a function a compiled representation of the function is generated. The compiled representation is stored in the system catalog in an optimized form. When the function is later evaluated, the compiled representation is obtained and interpreted.

Stored functions The extension of a function may be explicitly stored in a persistent data structure. Currently, table-like structures, similar to the ones used by relational database systems, are provided to support stored functions. Corresponding argument and result values of a function (the mapping of the function) are maintained in a single table. Several functions may be clustered in the same table in order to improve performance. Stored functions may be updated, that is, the mappings from argument values to result values can be explicitly specified (Section 13.2.3). The actions of retrieval and updates are implicitly defined in terms of relational operations on the tables. A formal treatment of the mapping of Iris functions to relational tables can be found in [Lyngbaek,87a].

Derived functions A function may be computed from other functions that are either stored, derived or foreign. Derived functions are intensionally defined in terms of Iris database language expressions (Section 13.2.3). Derived functions support associative access to sets of objects and can be optimized by the Iris Query Translator. The goal of the Iris language is to provide a database language that is powerful enough to support the definition of procedural functions that implement most of the operations of the data model. Foreign functions, described below, achieve the full generality of a general-purpose programming language.

A derived function without side-effects can be thought of as a view of the stored data. The update semantics of such a function are not always well-defined. For example, if the derivation expression of a given function requires joining several tables, the function cannot be directly updated. However, the actions of updates are implicitly defined by Iris in those cases where it can solve the "view update" problem. Functions that are defined as inverses of stored functions are examples of updatable derived functions. In other cases, the update semantics may be explicitly specified as part of the function definition.

A function defined by a sequence of update statements can be thought of as a database procedure. Such a function has side-effects and cannot be updated.

Foreign functions A foreign function is defined in terms of a program written in some general-purpose programming language and compiled outside of Iris. The object code is stored in the Iris database. When the foreign function is invoked, the program is dynamically loaded and executed. The program defining a foreign function must adhere to certain interface conventions. Foreign functions provide flexibility and extensibility. Since the Iris database language is not computationally complete, there are certain functionalities that cannot be expressed as derived functions. Foreign functions provide a mechanism for incorporating such functionalities into the system. Furthermore, existing programs can be integrated with Iris through the foreign function mechanism by making them adhere to the interface conventions. Foreign functions cannot be optimized by the Iris system. However, their usage in queries can potentially be optimized.

Foreign functions and the mechanisms with which they are supported in Iris are described in [Connors,88].

13.2.5 Iris System Objects
In Iris types and functions are also objects. They are instances of the system types Type and Function, respectively. The Iris system types and their subtype/supertype relationships are illustrated in Figure 13.1. Like ordinary user-defined types, system types have functions defined on them. The system functions are implemented as stored, derived, or foreign functions and they may have side-effects. The collection of system types and functions model the Iris metadata and the Iris operations. This approach allows the metadata to be modeled in the Iris data model.

System functions without side-effects can retrieve data as well as metadata. Examples of functions retrieving meta-data include a function that returns the name of a type or function, a function that returns the number of arguments and results of a function, one that returns the subtypes of a type, one that returns the declared types of the arguments and results of a function, and one that retrieves the compiled representation of a function. The Select system function supporting the queries illustrated in Section 13.2.3 is an example of a system function capable of retrieving both metadata and user-data.

The Iris system functions that have side-effects are called *system procedures*. They implement updates to the stored data. For example, the OSQL update statements illustrated in Section 13.2.3 are supported by the Update system procedure.

Certain system functions are implemented as foreign functions. These *system foreign functions* cannot be expressed in the current extended relational algebra or they are more efficiently implemented as foreign functions. Typically, system foreign functions implement the system procedures that correspond to the operations of the data model. For example, functions for creating an object or a type, declaring a function, and implementing a function are system foreign functions. System foreign functions are also used to implement transaction support, e.g., Commit and Rollback, and facilities for source code tracing and timing.

13.3 IRIS KERNEL ARCHITECTURE

The Iris kernel is a program that implements the Iris data model. It is accessed via a single entry point, `iris_eval`, that serves as a function call evaluator, or more generally, an expression tree evaluator. Iris requests are formatted as expression trees. Each node in an Iris expression tree is self-identifying and consists of a header and some data fields. The header defines the node type[1]. The possible node types are: object identifier, variable, function call and one node type for each Iris literal type (i.e. *integer, real, boolean, string, binary, bag, list*).

The Iris kernel operates as a server in an infinite loop of: *accept request, execute request, send reply*. A kernel request is formatted as a functional expression tree. All user and system functions are invoked via function calls (including such basic functions as comparison or equality checking). The kernel is organized as a collection of software modules. They are layered as illustrated in Figure 13.2.

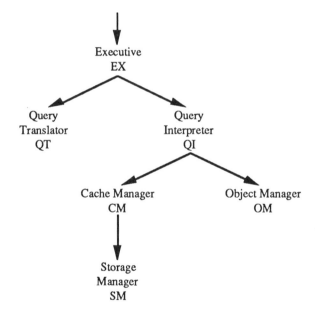

Figure 13.2: IRIS kernel architecture

The top-level module, EX (the Executive), implements the kernel entry points and the basic server loop. For each request, it calls the query translator, QT, to construct a relational algebra tree for the request [Derrett,89]. It then passes the relational algebra tree to the query interpreter, QI, to yield the results.

The Object Manager, OM, is a collection of system foreign functions. The Cache Manager, CM, is an intermediate layer between the Iris kernel and the Storage Manager,

---

[1]This is a distinct notion from an object type. Node types merely identify interface data structures.

SM. It provides prefetching and cache management for data retrieval and data updates between the kernel and SM. The SM module is the Iris storage manager. It provides data sharing, transaction management and access to stored tables.

The remainder of this section describes the Iris kernel modules in more detail.

13.3.1 Iris Executive

Client interface The Executive module, EX, manages interaction between the Iris kernel and its clients. It provides an external interface to clients, accepts requests and returns results to the client.

The EX module implements the server loop of: *accept request, execute request, send reply*. A request consists of a functional expression tree, a result buffer and an error buffer. The error buffer is used to return errors encountered during the processing of the request. The result buffer is filled with the result objects generated by evaluating the expression tree.

Request processing consists of two steps: compile and interpret. The compilation step, performed by the QT module, converts the functional expression tree into an extended relational algebra tree. The relational algebra tree is then passed to the query interpreter, QI, which traverses the tree and produces the result objects for the request.

Note that the current version of Iris differs from other expression tree evaluators (e.g. LISP) in that Iris does not contain a sophisticated *eval-apply* loop. The conventional eval-apply algorithm operates on expression trees by first *evaluating* the arguments of a function call, then *applying* the function to the results of the argument evaluation. In the current Iris, every request expression tree must be rooted by a function call and the function call arguments must be constants. Thus, the Iris *eval* operation is trivial since the function arguments need no evaluation.

Actually, Iris permits specific arguments to some system functions to be non-constant. Currently, these are treated as special-case exceptions. For example, the *select-expression* argument to the `Select` system function (see Section 13.4.2) may be an arbitrary expression tree containing variables and nested function calls.

We plan to extend Iris in the future by first allowing any function call argument to be a nested function call and later by allowing variables. However, the semantics of such expression trees remain to be defined. Conventional *eval-apply* algorithms may not be consistent with Iris semantics. For example, Iris expressions may be bag-valued or may be re-ordered by query optimization.

Iris result objects are also formatted as expression trees. However, a result expression tree consists entirely of constant nodes (i.e., literals or oids). The content and structure of the result tree depend on the function invoked by the request expression tree. For example, invocation of the `ObjCreate` system procedure (create an object) would return an expression tree consisting of a single node, an object identifier. However, invoking a multi-valued function or a function with more than one result type returns a bag or a list, respectively. For example, the `Select` system procedure (find a collection of objects) returns a bag of objects.

Entry points The primary entry point of the Iris kernel is `iris_eval`[2] which takes a

---

[2]This is somewhat of a misnomer since, when compared with other expression tree evaluators, iris_eval corresponds more closely to the apply operation.

request expression tree and a result buffer, then compiles and evaluates the request and places the results in the result buffer. If the result buffer is too small to contain the entire result object, as much of the result is returned as will fit in the buffer. It is the client's responsibility to ensure that enough space exists.

Often, the result size is unpredictable or it is impractical to preallocate a large buffer. In this case, the client must open a scan over the result objects to ensure that no results will be lost. The `ScanOpen` system function takes a request expression tree as an argument and returns a scan object that identifies the result bag. The `ScanNext` system function can then be used to extract a specified number of objects from the result bag.

It is expected that opening a scan will be a frequent operation for the client. Thus, as a convenience, the kernel provides the additional entry points: `iris_open`, `iris_next`, `iris_close`. These provide the same functionality as the Iris system procedures `ScanOpen`, `ScanNext`, `ScanClose`, respectively. However, they save the user the task of having to rewrite an existing request expression tree with a call to `ScanOpen`.

Actually, Iris supports two sets of EX entry points: one for clients, the other for internal kernel calls. This was done to decrease the internal path length and improve performance for recursive kernel calls. This is possible because the internal EX calls can be considered safe. Thus, the internal EX entry points can avoid some of the type checks and sanity checks that are necessary for ordinary client requests. The internal entry points also provide a form of security. Certain system functions may only be invoked through the internal entry points and, therefore, they can be hidden from the client.

Client/Server configurations The Iris kernel may be configured either as a server process or be tightly-coupled with the client application. The particular configuration is transparent to the source code of the client. In a tightly-coupled environment, the client and kernel execute in the same address space. In a serverized environment, the client and kernel run as separate processes and communicate via messages.

The client invokes the Iris kernel via one of the subroutine entry points described in the preceding subsection. In the non-serverized environment, the client is linked directly to those entry points. In the serverized environment, the client is linked with stub subroutines for the entry points. These stubs offer the same interface as the actual entry points. They make the inter-process communication transparent by packing the request expression tree as a message, sending the message to the server process and awaiting and unpacking the results. In either case, the client is unaware of the location of the Iris kernel code.

Note that each copy of the kernel (either serverized or non-serverized) runs as a separate process. The Storage Manager uses a shared memory buffer among the different processes for concurrency control and transaction logging.

The choice of running in a serverized or non-serverized environment is dictated by performance. The serverized configuration is safer since the Iris kernel and client are protected from each others' errors. However, there is a performance cost due to the inter-process communication overhead.

Recursive kernel calls In the course of processing a request, the Iris kernel may need to invoke itself, recursively. This is done for two reasons. First, the kernel accesses the Iris metadata through the same system functions provided to external clients. For example, to retrieve the object identifier for a named function, QT must construct an expression tree to call the appropriate system function and invoke an internal EX entry point.

The second reason for recursive kernel calls is that some system procedures and functions may be defined in terms of other system functions. For example, creating a function involves updates to several stored system functions. When such a system procedure is implemented as a system foreign function, it must recursively call the kernel in order to invoke the other system functions.

Iris metadata In order to compile and execute functions, the Iris system needs access to metadata (a system catalog) that describes the database schema. For example, given a type, Iris must be able to find all its subtypes. Given a function, Iris must find the name of the function, the argument and result parameters (which are, themselves, system objects with their own descriptions), the function implementation, and whether the function is single-valued. For an arbitrary object, Iris must be able to determine all its types.

The Iris system catalog is maintained as a collection of database tables (currently about 15). These tables contain the extensions of stored system functions. This notion of modeling system metadata as functions is similar to relational database managers in which the system metadata is modeled as relations. In other words, metadata is implemented using the primitives of the data model.

Since the system functions are frequently accessed together (i.e. get the name and arguments for a particular function), most of the functions for a particular type of object are clustered together into a single table. However, metadata for some objects may be represented in several different tables. For example, because of their size, the compiled representations of functions are stored in a separate table from the rest of the function metadata.

13.3.2 Query Translator

As mentioned above, requests to the Iris kernel are formatted as an Iris functional expression tree, or *F-tree*. The nodes of an F-tree tree include function calls, variables, and literal nodes. The query translation process consists of three main steps. First, the F-tree is converted to a canonical form. This involves a series of tree transformations that are done to simplify subsequent transformations. For example, nested function calls are unnested by introducing auxiliary variables. Type checking is also performed. The actual arguments in a function call must match or be subtypes of the corresponding formal argument types.

The second step converts the canonical F-tree to an extended relational algebra tree known as an *R-tree*. This is a mechanical process in which function calls are replaced by their implementations (which are, themselves, R-trees). For example, comparison function calls (e.g. equal, not-equal, less-than, etc.) are converted to relational algebra filter[3] operators. The logical function, *And*, is converted to a cross-product operator.

The resulting R-tree consists of nodes for the relational algebra operations of project, filter and cross-product. To increase the functionality of the Query Interpreter, there are some additional nodes. A *temp-table* node creates and, optionally, sorts a temporary table. An *update* node modifies an existing table. A *sequence* node executes each of its

---

[3]In order to distinguish the Iris system function, Select, from the select operator of the relational algebra, the term, filter operator, will be used to denote the latter.

subtrees in turn. A *foreign function* node invokes the executable code that is the implementation of a foreign function.

The leaves of an R-tree actually generate the data that is processed by the other nodes. A leaf may be either a table node or a foreign function node. A table node retrieves the contents of a Storage Manager table. A projection list and predicate can be associated with the table node to reduce the number of tuples retrieved. A foreign function node simply invokes a foreign function.

The semantics of the tree are that results of a child node are sent to the parent node for subsequent processing. For example, a project node above a table node would filter out columns returned by the project node. Joins are specified by placing a filter node above a cross-product node to compare the columns of the underlying cross-product[4].

The final, and most complex, step is to optimize the R-tree. The optimizer is rule-based. Each rule consists of a test predicate and a transformation routine. The test predicate takes an R-tree node as an argument and if the predicate evaluates to true, the transformation routine is invoked. The predicate might test the relative position of a node (e.g., filter node above a project node) or the state of a node (e.g., cross-product node has only one input). The possible transformations include deleting the node, moving it above or below another node, or replacing the node with a new R-tree fragment. As in [Dewitt,87], the system must be recompiled whenever the rules are modified.

Rules are organized into rule-sets which, together, accomplish a specific task. For example, one rule-set contains all rules concerned with simplifying constant expressions (e.g., constant propagation and folding). Optimization is accomplished by traversing the entire R-tree for each rule-set. During the traversal, at a given node, any rule in the current rule set may be fired if its test predicate is true.

The optimization steps (i.e., rule-sets) can be roughly described as follows. There is an initial rule set that converts the R-tree to a canonical form. The canonical form consists of a number of query blocks. A query block consists of a project node above a filter node above a cross-product node (any one of these nodes is optional). A leaf of a query block may be either a table node, a foreign function node or another query block. A query block may be rooted by a temp-table node, an update node or a sequence node.

A second rule-set eliminates redundant joins. This has the effect of reducing the number of tables in a cross-product. A third rule-set is concerned with simplifying expressions. A fourth rule-set reorders the underlying tables in a cross-product node to reduce the execution time. A fifth rule-set handles Storage Manager-specific optimizations, for example, finding project and filter operations that can be performed by the Storage Manager.

The final (optimized) R-tree is then sent to the Query Interpreter which processes the query and returns the result to the user. However, the R-tree may not represent a query but may, instead, be the newly defined body of a derived function. In this case, the R-tree is simply stored in the database system catalog for later retrieval when compiling queries that reference the derived function.

The Query Translator is flexible and can accommodate any optimization that can be expressed in terms of a predicate test on a node and a tree transformation. Of particular interest is the ability to optimize the usage of foreign functions. As a simple example, given a foreign function that computes simple arithmetic over two numbers, rules could

---

[4]Of course, joins are rarely executed this way because the filter predicate is typically pushed down below the cross-product to produce a nested-loops join.

be written to evaluate the result at compile time if the operands are constants.

13.3.3 Query Interpreter

The Query Interpreter module evaluates an extended relation algebra tree (R-tree) which yields a collection of tuples that become the result objects for the request expression tree. The Query Interpreter traverses the R-tree and pipes data between parent and child nodes. Conceptually, each node in the R-tree may be viewed as a filter with the filter inputs coming from the subtrees of the node. In the implementation, each node must implement three operations: *open*, *next*, and *close*.

An *open*, *next*, or *close* operation may call the Query Interpreter, recursively, to evaluate a sub-tree. For example, given a project node, the portion of the R-tree below the project node represents the source of the tuples for the project operation. Thus, an *open* operation on a project node must recursively open the sub-tree in order to get its input tuples. The leaf nodes of the tree are the data sources. An *open* operation on a table node creates a Storage Manager scan.

The *next* operation returns the next tuple in the pipeline. A *next* operation on a table node results in a call to the Storage Manager to fetch the next tuple in the previously opened scan. Similarly, a *next* operation on a foreign function node will invoke the foreign function to generate the next tuple value.

The only variation is with cross-product nodes. If a cross-product node is marked as having a nested-loops implementation (see Section 13.3.2), then the processing order for the subtrees is different. In a nested-loops algorithm, the subtrees are processed left-to-right where each subtree is completely scanned for each tuple in the subtrees to its left. In other words, the processing order is: *open* subtree$_i$, *next* subtree$_i$, *open* subtree$_{i+1}$, *next* subtree$_{i+1}$, ... *next* subtree$_{i+1}$, ... *close* subtree$_{i+1}$, *next* subtree$_i$, *open* subtree$_{i+1}$, *next* subtree$_{i+1}$, etc.

Note that a *next* operation on an update node has side-effects. For this reason, if the subtree of an update node references the stored table that is being updated, the update tuples are spooled into a temporary table. This prevents cycles in the data pipeline. Typically, the result tuple for an update operation is a single boolean value indicating success or failure.

The Query Interpreter is fully re-entrant. It can handle R-trees of arbitrary complexity, not just the simple project - filter - cross-product trees mentioned earlier. In particular, nested queries can easily be processed.

13.3.4 Object Manager

The semantics of some Iris system functions can be defined and implemented in terms of other Iris system functions. Essentially, this is the job of the Iris Object Manager. It is a collection of system foreign functions. These functions provide services that are essential to Iris but whose implementations either cannot be expressed as a stored or derived Iris function or are more efficient written in an external programming language. For example, type creation is a system foreign function. It involves creating a typing function and updating several stored system functions. Such a complex update is difficult to express as a relational algebra expression. Another example is a system function that returns the time of day.

In the current version of Iris, most of the system procedures (system functions that update the metadata) are implemented as foreign functions. These system procedures call the Storage Manager directly (bypassing the cache) to update the system functions stored as tables. As the number and complexity of the system procedures has increased, the direct SM calls have become a problem. First, because the Storage Manager is called from many places in the Object Manager, it will be difficult to modify Iris to use a different Storage Manager. Making Iris independent of any particular storage subsystem is a long-term goal. Indeed, it should be possible to view the Storage Manager as just another foreign function.

A second problem with direct Storage Manager calls is that the semantics of an operation are hidden inside the procedure. Thus, it is not possible to optimize the procedure. In addition, it means that Iris is not self-describing.

Thus, the next step is to reimplement the Iris system procedures as extended relational algebra expressions. An initial step along these lines has been taken. An *update* node and a *sequence* node have been added to the set of R-tree nodes. These nodes are currently used only to modify user functions. The next step is to use these nodes to update the system tables. Then, the complex system procedures could be implemented as derived function using a sequence of updates to individual stored system functions. This work is currently under investigation. It may require the addition of more relational algebra nodes, e.g. a branching node.

13.3.5 Cache Manager
The Iris Cache Manager, CM, implements a general-purpose caching facility between the Iris kernel and the Storage Manager. An important point is that, since the Query Interpreter operates on relational algebra trees, CM caches tables not functions. Retrieval performance could be significantly improved if Iris cached function values because a function call could be directly evaluated without compiling it into a relational algebra tree. However, updates to stored tables pose a challenge since a single tuple in a stored table may contain values for many functions (e.g. when functions are clustered together in one table; see [Lyngbaek,87a]). The individual function caches would need to be located and updated in an efficient manner. This problem is currently under investigation. The present implementation supports only table caches as provided by CM.

The Cache Manager maintains two types of caches: a *tuple cache* and a *predicate cache*. The tuple cache is used to cache tuples from individual tables. A table may have at most one tuple cache. A table cache is accessed via a column of the table and that column must be declared as either *uniquely-valued* or *multi-valued*. If a column is declared as multi-valued, the cache ensures that whenever a given value of that column occurs in the cache, all tuples of the table with the same column value will also occur in the cache. This guarantees that when a cache hit on a multi-valued column occurs, the scan can be entirely satisfied from the cache without having to invoke the Storage Manager.

When a scan is opened, the scan will be directed at a tuple cache if the table has a tuple cache and: (1) the scan has an equality predicate on a column with a unique index, or (2) the scan has an equality predicate on a multi-valued column. The Cache Manager can only support caching on one multi-valued column per table cache (although the underlying table may have several multi-valued columns).

A table may have many predicate caches. A predicate cache contains tuples from a table that satisfy a particular predicate. Thus, a predicate cache has an associated predicate and projection list. An open-scan operation will be directed at a predicate cache if the scan's predicate and projection list match the predicate and projection list of the cache.

The tuple cache is primarily intended to support caching of system tables. However, user tables may also be cached in this way. The predicate cache is useful in caching intermediate results during query processing.

Information in that cache is always kept consistent with the storage manager. If an update request is too complicated to preserve cache consistency, the table will be automatically uncached.

13.3.6 Storage Manager

The Iris Storage Manager is (currently) a conventional relational storage subsystem, namely that of HP-SQL [HP]. HP-SQL's Storage Manager is very similar to System R's RSS [Blasgen,77]. It provides associative access and update capabilities to a single relation at a time and includes transaction support.

Tables can be created and dropped at any time. The system supports transactions with savepoints and restores to savepoints, concurrency control, logging and recovery, archiving, indexing and buffer management. It provides tuple-at-a-time processing with commands to retrieve, update, insert and delete tuples. Indexes and threads (links between tuples in the same table) allow users to access the tuples of a table in a predefined order. Additionally, a predicate over column values can be defined to qualify tuples during retrieval.

One of the basic functions of the Storage Manager is the retrieval of tuples from tables. A retrieval request includes a table identifier and may include a filter predicate, a projection list and a preferred access method. The Storage Manager begins by opening a scan on the table. The scan specifies any projection list, filter predicate and whether the scan should be sequential or via an access method. The filter predicate is composed of conjunctions and disjunctions of operators applied to constants and column values.

13.4 EXAMPLES

To provide a better understanding of the Iris architecture, in this section we describe the kernel processing for two system functions.

13.4.1 Type Creation

The creation of a new type is the task of the system foreign function, TypeCreate. To invoke this function, the request expression tree contains a single function call node. The call node specifies the function to be invoked along with an argument list. The function identifier may be either a string or an Iris object identifier. In this case, the function identifier is "TypeCreate". The argument list contains two elements: the name of the new type and its super-types. The super-type argument is itself a list containing the object identifiers of the super-types of the new type.

The Iris kernel is then invoked via the iris_eval entry point. The Executive immediately passes the expression tree to QT for compilation. QT first checks to see that the function arguments are the correct type. If the argument types are correct, QT retrieves the R-tree implementation for the function and substitutes the actual arguments for the formal arguments.

Since this request was a simple function call, no further optimization of the R-tree is required (since R-trees are stored in a pre-optimized form). However, certain system functions, such as `Select`, require more complete optimization as discussed below.

QT returns the optimized R-tree for the request back to the Executive. The Executive then passes the R-tree to the Query Interpreter to extract the results. In this case, the R-tree is a single foreign function node, which calls the foreign function that implements the Iris `TypeCreate` system function. Since the function is known to be single-valued, there is no need to open a scan on the result. Thus, the query interpreter simply invokes the foreign function and returns the result which is the object identifier of the newly created type.

The foreign function that creates a new type performs the following actions. It first performs some sanity checks that the type name is unique and that the supertypes exist. This is done by calling the appropriate system functions for metadata checking using `iris_eval`. It then calls the Storage Manager directly to update the system table containing the type metadata. Finally, it creates a *typing function* for the new type. The typing function maintains the extension of the type. Typically, a typing function is used to determine if an object has a particular type, e.g. `UserFunction(x)` returns `True` if the object identified by x is a user function.

Function creation is performed by the Iris system procedure (`FunctionCreate`). Thus, Iris must call itself recursively to create the typing function. `TypeCreate` builds an expression tree to invoke `FunctionCreate` and calls `iris_eval` in order to create the typing function. If the function is successfully created, `TypeCreate` returns the object identifier of the new type object. Otherwise, the type object is deleted and an error is returned to the client.

As an aside, note that it would be possible to create a function by updating the stored system functions, directly. These updates could be included as part of the `TypeCreate` implementation, thus avoiding the recursive Iris call. But, because the number and sequence of the updates is dependent on the structure of the Iris metadata, which may change, it is better to encapsulate the updates in a single system procedure.

Also note that all system procedures establish a *savepoint* before any modifications to the stored system functions. Should errors occur during the procedure, the modifications are undone by restoring the database to the savepoint.

13.4.2 Select Function

In this section, we describe the sequence of events in executing the Iris `Select` function. This function better illustrates the role of the Query Translator and the Query Interpreter. As before, the client must build a request expression tree for the `Select` call. The arguments to `Select` are a list of result variables and their types, a list of existential variables and their types, a *distinct* flag and a *select-expression*. The select-expression is itself an expression tree containing function calls, variables and constants.

The semantics of `Select` may be roughly described as follows. The result and existential variables are bound to the cross-product of the extensions of their types. For each binding of the variables, the select-expression is evaluated to produce a bag of result objects that is then projected on the result variables. These partial results are accumulated and the entire collection is returned to the user as one large result bag. If the *distinct* flag is `True`, duplicates are eliminated from the final result bag.

The request expression tree for `Select` is received by EX and sent to QT for compiling. Type checking consists of ensuring that the result and existential lists are in the correct format and that the distinct flag is a Boolean value. Note that the *select-expression* can be any object, including another function call. This is one case where the arguments to a function call may be non-constant. The remainder of the compilation task is more complicated than the simple parameter substitution in the previous example.

QT considers `Select` an *intrinsic* system function. The intrinsic system functions are those that QT can compile directly into a relational algebra tree. In the previous example, the call to `TypeCreate` was simply compiled into a call to a foreign function. That foreign function actually interprets the function call and implements type creation since there is no relational algebra tree to express the various system function changes necessary to create a type.

However, the intrinsic system functions have corresponding relational algebra trees that QT can compile and optimize. Examples of other intrinsic system functions include `FunUpdate`[5], `Sequence`, `And`, and the six comparison operators (i.e. `Equal`, `NotEqual`, `LessThan`, etc.).

For `Select`, compilation proceeds as follows. First, the select-expression is converted to a simplified form in which function calls are unnested. This may result in the introduction of auxiliary variables for the results of the nested function call. The select-expression is then converted to an R-tree by replacing all function calls by their stored implementations and substituting the actual parameters. This is described in more detail in Section 13.3.2.

The R-tree is then checked to ensure that all declared variables are bound to a column value of their declared type. This ensures that the query is *safe*, i.e. does not produce an infinite number of results. If a variable is not bound, the R-tree is joined with the extension of the type of the variable. Of course, this is only possible for types with finite extensions, e.g. unbound integer variables cause an error. Finally, a project node is prefixed to the R-tree to guarantee that the result variables of the `Select` appear in the correct order in the result tuples.

The initial R-tree is then optimized to remove unnecessary joins and to push project and filter operations as far as possible down the R-tree (i.e. into the Storage Manager, if possible). The R-tree is then returned to the Executive which passes it on to the Query Interpreter for processing. QI proceeds to fill the result buffer with the result objects of the R-tree.

As mentioned before, if the result size is unknown and the client cannot tolerate truncation of the result bag, a scan must be opened on the result. This can be accomplished in one of two ways. The call to `Select` may be enclosed inside a call to the `ScanOpen` system function[6]. Alternatively, the `iris_open` entry point may be invoked with the with the original request tree.

13.4.3 Discussion

---

[5]FunUpdate updates stored user functions.

[6]ScanOpen is another system function that permits non-constant arguments, in this case, function call nesting.

The first example illustrated several aspects of the current Iris architecture. First, the `TypeCreate` function is a sequence of steps that update some Iris system tables and then calls a foreign function (to create the typing function). Given the update and sequence nodes in an R-tree, there seems to be no reason why the `TypeCreate` function could not be written as an Iris derived function rather than a foreign function. Update nodes would be used to modify the Iris system tables and a foreign function node would be used to invoke `FunctionCreate`. These steps would be ordered by the sequence node.

Second, we notice that the `TypeCreate` function is implemented in terms of the `FunctionCreate` function. Thus, function creation is in some sense a more primitive procedure than type creation. Function creation, in turn, involves system table updates and perhaps calls to other Iris functions. Our goal is to identify the primitive operations needed to implement the Iris semantics and reimplement the current system in terms of those basic functions. This will result in many of the current system functions being reimplemented as derived functions.

The second example illustrates more sophisticated query translation and introduces the notion of intrinsic functions. In the future, we expect to offer the expressive power provided by the `Select` function (e.g. nested function calls, variables) in the Executive module.

13.5 CONCLUSION

We have proposed a new architecture for the Iris database system. The architecture provides a generalized function evaluator. Database requests of any kind, including queries, updates, and data definitions, are presented to the evaluator as functional expressions. The evaluator executes a request by first compiling it into an extended relational algebra and then interpreting it. The extended algebra supports database updates and foreign functions, i.e., invocation and evaluation of user-defined programs.

To provide adequate performance, database functions may be stored in a compiled and optimized form. In that case, the compilation process consists of obtaining the compiled function representation from disk or a special function cache. The process of interpreting the compiled function can be improved by caching the stored database tables being accessed by the function. This mechanism is crucial to the performance of system catalog accesses. The architecture may be extended with a function value cache. Such a cache would simplify the compilation and interpretation steps of function evaluation in cases where the result of the evaluation could be provided by the cache.

The generalized function evaluation mechanism greatly simplifies the system structure as it is used both for external user requests and for internal requests to the cached system dictionary. The system catalog, for example, requires no special implementation, but is provided as a collection of database functions which are queried and updated just like ordinary user functions.

Prototyping new model semantics and operations can be accomplished by writing procedural database functions with the desired functionality. In order to implement new model semantics, the structure of the system catalog may have to be changed. This is easily done by the addition or removal of functions. Procedural functions can be implemented as derived or foreign functions.

Foreign functions are defined by real programs, e.g., C programs, which make calls to the function evaluator and can be hand-optimized for better performance. Derived functions are defined in terms of other functions by an Iris database language expression. Derived functions may be optimized by the database system, but their power is restricted by the current extended relational algebra. Functions that cannot be expressed in the extended algebra must be implemented as foreign functions.

Large parts of a database application can be expressed as foreign functions stored and invoked by the database system. That way, code that is useful to several applications need only be written once. Furthermore, by storing application code in the database, the amount of data transfer between the application space and the database system can be reduced.

13.6 ACKNOWLEDGEMENTS

Many members of the Database Technology Department at HP Labs contributed to and influenced the design of the new architecture. We acknowledge the assistance of Jurgen Annevelink, Tim Connors, Jim Davis, Charles Hoch, Bill Kent, Marie-Anne Neimat, Tore Risch, and Ming-Chien Shan. The implementation was realized with the help of Marie-Anne Neimat and Ming-Chien Shan.

BIBLIOGRAPHY

[Blasgen,77] M. W. Blasgen and K. P. Eswaran., "Storage and Access in Relation Databases"., *IBM Systems Journal*, 16(4):363--377, 1977.

[Beech,88] D. Beech and B. Mahbod., "Generalized Version Control in an Object-Oriented Database", *Proceedings of IEEE Data Engineering Conference*, February 1988.

[Connors,88] T. Connors and P. Lyngbaek., "Providing Uninform Access to Heterogeneous Information Bases", In Klaus Dittrich, editor, *Lecture Notes in Computer Science 334*, *Advances in Object-Oriented Database Systems*. Springer-Verlag, September 1988.

[Dewitt,87] D. J. Dewitt and G. Graefe., "The EXODUS Optimizer Generator", *Proceedings of ACM-SIGMOD International Conference on Management of Data*, pages 160--172, 1987.

[Derrett,89] N.Derrett and M.C. Shan., "Rule-Based Query Optimization in Iris", *Proceedings of ACM Annual Computer Science Conference,* Louisville, Kentucky, February 1989.

[Fishman,87] D.H. Fishman, D.Beech, H.P. Cate, E.C. Chow, T.Connors, J.W. Davis, N.Derrett, C.G. Hoch, W.Kent, P.Lyngbaek, B.Mahbod, M.A. Neimat, T.A. Ryan, and M.C. Shan., "Iris: An Object-Oriented Database Management System", *ACM Transactions on Office Information Systems*, 5(1), January 1987.

[HP] Hewlett-Packard Company., HP-SQL Reference Manual., Part Number 36217-

90001.

[Heiler,88] S. Heiler and S. Zdonik., "Views, Data Abstraction, and Inheritance in the FUGUE Data Model.", In Klaus Dittrich, editor, *Lecture Notes in Computer Science 334, Advances in Object-Oriented Database Systems*. Springer-Verlag, September 1988.

[Lyngbaek,87b] Peter Lyngbaek, Nigel Derrett, Dan Fishman, William Kent, and Thomas Ryan., "Design and Implementation of the Iris Object Manager", *Proceedings of A Workshop on Persistent Object Systems: Their Design, Implementation and Use*, Appin, Scotland, August 1987.

[Lyngbaek,86] P. Lyngbaek and W. Kent., "A Data Modeling Methodology for the Design and Implementation of Information Systems", *Proceedings of 1986 International Workshop on Object-Oriented Database Systems*, Pacific Grove, California, September 1986.

[Lyngbaek,87a] P. Lyngbaek and V. Vianu., "Mapping a Semantic Data Model to the Relational Model", *Proceedings of ACM-SIGMOD International Conference on Management of Data*, San Francisco, California, May 1987.

[Lyngbaek,89] P. Lyngbaek and W. K. Wilkinson., "The Architecture of a Persistent Object System", *Proceedings of an International Workshop on Persistent Object Systems*, Newcastle, Australia, January 1989.

[Mylopoulos,80] J. Mylopoulos, P. A. Bernstein, and H. K. T. Wong., "A Language Facility for Designing Database-Intensive Applications", *ACM Transactions on Database Systems*, 5(2), June 1980.

[Manola,86] F. Manola and U. Dayal., "PDM: An Object-Oriented Data Model", *Proceedings of 1986 International Workshop on Object-Oriented Database Systems*, Pacific Grove, California, September 1986.

[Shipman,81] D. Shipman., "The Functional Data Model and the Data Language DAPLEX", *ACM Transactions on Database Systems*, 6(1), March 1981.

Chapter 14

Future Directions in Object-Oriented Computing

Gordon Blair, John Gallagher, David Hutchison and Doug Shepherd
Lancaster University

ABSTRACT *This chapter discusses future directions of object-oriented computing. The chapter starts by suggesting that object-oriented computing requires a period of consolidation and experimentation in large scale projects. The discussion then continues with an examination of a number of key areas, namely software engineering methodologies, formal methods, sharing and distribution, open distributed processing and finally multimedia objects. In each case, a number of topics are identified as being worthy of further study.*

14.1 INTRODUCTION

Object-oriented computing has come a long way in its relatively short history. There is now a considerable body of knowledge and expertise in object-oriented tools and techniques. However, more work is required before object-oriented computing can claim to be a mature discipline. This is evident in the abundance of research projects looking at various aspects of object-orientation. This chapter concludes the book by looking at the future directions of the subject. More specifically, the chapter highlights certain key areas as being particularly interesting or relevant. The areas are:-

- consolidation,
- software engineering methodologies,
- formal methods,
- sharing and distribution,
- open distributed processing, and
- multimedia objects.

This list is not intended to be complete. Rather, it reflects the views of the editors on the most important areas of research in object-oriented computing. In most cases, the discussions focus on short to medium term research (as opposed to long term research).

Indeed, in many of the areas identified, significant results are already emerging. The chapter should therefore be used as guidance for ongoing areas of study rather than as a crystal ball on the long term future of object-oriented computing.

14.2 CONSOLIDATION

Historically, most emerging technologies can be seen to follow various stages of development as shown in figure 14.1.

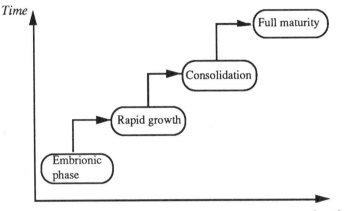

Figure 14.1: Stages of development

Object-oriented computing is no exception. The early seeds of the subject were sown in the late sixties and early seventies with the emergence of languages such as Simula and Smalltalk. This was followed by a period of rapid growth leading to the full range of techniques available today. In our view, the subject is now entering a period of consolidation. This is a critical stage if object-oriented computing is to reach a level of maturity.

At this stage in development it is therefore not so important for new techniques to emerge. It is much more important for existing technologies to be applied in large scale industrial and commercial projects. There is evidence that this is starting to happen:-
- i)   the European Space Agency have recently adopted the HOOD methodology as a standard for object-oriented design,
- ii) Chorus Systemes have re-written their UNIX-like distributed operating system in C++,
- iii) many of the European funded ESPRIT, RACE and DELTA projects regularly use object-oriented languages and concepts, and
- iv) perhaps most importantly, standardization activity such as ODA and ODP are applying object-oriented concepts as a basis for their work.

Similarly, many software houses are starting to recommend the use of object-oriented design and object-oriented programming languages in their contract work. This will inevitably lead to a proliferation of commercial systems constructed using object-oriented principles.

The importance of these developments is that they will provide a number of substantial case studies to test the various claims made about object-oriented computing. At present there are many theoretical arguments why object-oriented computing should help with issues such as maintainability, software re-use and correctness. However, these ideas can only be tested fully when applied to substantial systems. This period of consolidation will therefore lead to a much better understanding of the benefits and drawbacks of object-oriented techniques.

The practical experience will also provide valuable feedback on the current models and vocabulary of object-oriented computing. This will result in a more consistent use of terminology and a more informed level of debate on the semantics of various techniques. This is important as much of the research effort in recent years has focussed on the meaning of concepts such as class and inheritance or on the relative merits of inheritance and delegation, etc.

The other aspect of consolidation is between the traditional levels of a computer architecture. As witnessed in earlier chapters of this book, object-oriented techniques have been adopted in many areas of computing such as operating systems, programming languages, databases and user interface design. This would suggest that a more complete model of computing is emerging. In theory, a single object model could span all layers of a system from the underlying support environment through to the user interface. There are several significant steps in this direction. For example, operating systems are being designed to support object-oriented languages. Similarly, there is a considerable body of work on user interfaces for object-oriented languages. It can be predicted that this trend towards integration will continue. It is unlikely, however, that full integration will be achieved. The main problem is that there will inevitably be different tools to solve different problems; there will always be "horses for courses". This raises fundamental questions about the common semantics across a range of tools. At present such questions cannot be answered. There will also be the need for object-oriented techniques to co-exist with other approaches such as functional and logic programming languages. It is predicted therefore that the future direction of the subject lies in the inter-working (or inter-operability) of different object-oriented tools rather than on the complete integration of all aspects of a computer system around the object model.

Predictions
- attention will switch from the theory and models of object-oriented computing to practical experience
- this practical experience will lead to a better understanding of the benefits and drawbacks of the object-oriented approach
- this feedback will also lead to a more consistent understanding of object-oriented concepts
- there will be steps towards inter-operability between different object-oriented tools

14.3 SOFTWARE ENGINEERING METHODOLOGIES

Many claims have been made about object-oriented computing as a methodology to support the software engineering process. However, at present very few of the claims can be validated. One of the biggest problems is that attention has been focussed on one particular aspect of the software engineering process, namely the development of code. Much less work has been carried out on other aspects of software engineering. This section reviews the state of the art in the application of object-oriented concepts to software engineering and suggests directions for future research.

The key concept in software engineering is that the software process consists of a number of phases covering the whole *lifecycle* of a project. Various lifecycle models have been proposed in the software engineering literature. However, most have the following components:-

- Specification phase
- Design phase
- Implementation phase
- Testing phase
- Maintenance phase

Software engineering is concerned with supporting a coherent approach to the various phases of this lifecycle through the provision of a range of tools and techniques.

One of the arguments of object-oriented computing is that an extra investment at the earlier stages of the lifecycle leads to significant savings at later stages of the project. For example, well-structured, modular code can greatly simplify the task of system testing. Similarly, the evolutionary style of object-oriented programming is a useful approach to system maintenance. There has therefore been great interest in providing object-oriented tools to support specification, design and implementation of software. Progress in each of these areas is discussed below:-

i) Object-oriented specification

Relatively little work has been done in the area of object-oriented specification or on the related areas of requirements capture and enterprise modelling. Perhaps the most significant work is being carried out in the Open Distributed Processing community where a range of object-oriented techniques have been developed. For example, research has been carried out in producing an object-oriented version of the LOTOS specification language [Black,89]. Further details of the work on Open Distributed Processing can be found in section 14.6.

ii) Object-oriented design

This topic was discussed in depth in chapter 8. This chapter concluded that object-oriented design is at a relatively early stage of development. However, a number of object-oriented design methods are starting to appear and more importantly are starting to be used in large scale projects. For example, as mentioned in section 14.2, the HOOD design method has been adopted by the European Space Agency. One of the most significant developments in recent years has been the emergence of CASE (Computer-Aided Software Engineering) tools. Such tools provide sophisticated support for the design process and often provide user-friendly graphical interfaces. For example, an interesting CASE tool is now available based on an Object-Oriented Structured Design (OOSD) notation [Wasserman,90]. This is likely to be a major growth area in the future.

iii) Object-oriented implementation

There is now considerable experience in the use of object-oriented techniques at the implementation phase of the software lifecycle. There is also a generally held belief that the use of an object-oriented implementation strategy can greatly improve productivity. Although many strong arguments may be made to support this position, there is still no empirical evidence to prove or disprove the claims.

This is particularly true in the area of *software re-use*. The arguments for improved re-use of components in an object-oriented language are strong. However, there are no specific metrics to justify this position. Most of the research in this area has concentrated on the provision of tools to support re-use (for example, the ESPRIT DRAGON project produced a number of tools for re-use including a software components catalogue and a designer's notepad [Di Maio,89]). It is therefore an important area of future research to study the success of object-oriented languages in encouraging component re-use.

It can safely be predicted that many object-oriented tools will emerge to support specification, design and implementation. However, at present, the conclusion must be that a coherent, object-oriented approach to software engineering is a distant goal. This has caused some concern in the object-oriented community. However, in the opinion of the authors, this concern is unnecessary and actually reflects two common misconceptions about object-oriented computing:-

i)   that object-oriented techniques are equally applicable in all phases of the lifecycle, and

ii) that object-orientation should have the same interpretation in the different phases.

The first misconception is a consequence of the view that object-oriented computing is a panacea for all problems. While object-oriented computing is proving to be very successful for certain classes of problem, there are areas where other techniques are more suitable. This applies equally to the various phases of the software lifecycle. Object-oriented approaches have had some success in software engineering, particularly at the design and implementation stages. However, this does not imply that the one approach should pervade the entire lifecycle. For example, alternative approaches such as functional decomposition might be more appropriate for large classes of application.

A more pragmatic approach of mixing techniques from different areas is slowly emerging in software engineering. A good example of this is that many CASE tools (such as the OOSD tool mentioned above) use an object-oriented design approach but map on to the language Ada. This highlights the fact that object-oriented design does not necessarily imply the use of an object-oriented programming language[1]. Similarly, an object-oriented approach to design does not imply an object-oriented approach to specification. Alternative techniques such as Z could equally well be used.

The second misconception is apparent from questions such as:-

•   how does inheritance fit into object-oriented design?

•   do the concepts of class or inheritance have any meaning at the specification stage?

This is a result of the narrow view of object-oriented computing which was rejected in part 1 of the book. Many of these issues become clearer if object-oriented computing is placed in a wider perspective, i.e. object-oriented computing is an attempt to exploit abstraction more consistently through such concepts as data abstraction and behaviour sharing (see chapters 1 and 5). In this context, mechanisms such as class and inheritance are vehicles to achieve these aims and may be useful in certain phases of the lifecycle but not at others. For example, inheritance is very much a technique for sharing implementations between objects and as such is not applicable at more abstract stages of the lifecycle.

---

[1] for discussion on the extent to which Ada is object-oriented see Chapter 5.

This drive towards a unified object-oriented view of software engineering is related to the *transformational* approach to software engineering. Transformation (or refinement) is an attractive goal for software engineers as it eliminates many of the potential errors in the engineering process. The subject has therefore attracted considerable interest over the years [Balzer,85][Cheatham,81]. However, research on transformation is still in its infancy. This is especially true in the object-oriented community where experience of transformation techniques is minimal.

One of the biggest problems of transformation is that it is too *prescriptive*, i.e. it enforces a particular approach to the entire software engineering process. The future of object-orientation in software engineering might well be to accept the hybrid approach described above and concentrate on providing *traceability* between the various phases of the lifecycle. The concept of traceability is concerned with maintaining mappings between, for example, the specification and the design phases. The mappings provide lines of accountability between the different phases and can be important in determining the rationale for a particular approach or for analysing the effect of changes to a specification or design, etc.

Predictions
- tools will emerge to support both object-oriented design and object-oriented specification
- transformation techniques for object-oriented software engineering will remain elusive
- a hybrid approach to software engineering will be accepted by the object-oriented community
- accountability between specification, design and implementation will become increasingly important

14.4 FORMAL METHODS

Object-oriented computing has come a long way as a practical subject with many commercial systems and languages emerging over the past ten years. However, in many ways the practical developments have been too fast. At present there is little or no formal basis for most of this work. It is important for the future of object-oriented computing that such a basis is established. There are two reasons why formal methods are likely to be important:-

i) to provide a more solid basis for object-oriented language designs,
ii) to enforce a correct use of terminology across subject areas.

The first reason is important in that it enables many of the difficult semantic issues to be resolved. There is still considerable confusion about many of the issues in object-oriented computing, e.g. what is meant by class and type. There is a strong analogy here with developments in programming languages. At one time, programming languages were developed in a rather ad hoc manner. However, advances in type theory and the semantics of programs have enabled more consistent designs to emerge. For example, the language ML [Gordon,79] is closely related to the typed lambda calculus (as presented in chapter 5) and hence has a very elegant semantics. The second reason is also important. The variation in use of terminology in object-oriented computing is serious and leads to much confusion in the literature. For example, there is a considerable difference in terminology usage between the programming language and database communities.

It is predicted that formal methods will have an important role to play in both these areas. There is already considerable research in this area and results are starting to emerge. In this section, we highlight some of the more significant developments. The discussion centres on two areas of research, namely formal semantics and type theory. The section concludes with some successful applications of theoretical ideas.

Semantics of object-oriented languages In order to understand fully object-oriented languages, semantic models are now emerging. These models usually fall into one of the following categories:-

i) Operational Semantics

> With respect to object-oriented languages, operational semantics describe the *effect* of the application of a given programming construct. This is usually done by considering an abstract machine and observing the change in state of the machine when various constructs are invoked. This is the mechanism used in the Vienna Development Method (VDM) which has been used in this way to provide a semantics for Smalltalk [Wolczko,87]. Applications of this method to more general languages can be found in [Wolczko,88] and [Barnard,89].

ii) Denotational Semantics

> Based around the lambda calculus (as described in chapter 5), denotational semantics aims to provide a precise mathematical meaning to languages. Language constructs are mapped onto mathematical *functions,* as opposed to observing their effect. Denotational semantics for inheritance mechanisms in object-oriented languages can be found in [Cook,89a].

Type theory Another promising area is the typed, second order polymorphic lambda calculus. This provides a basis for the FUN language developed by Cardelli and Wegner [Cardelli,85]. FUN provides facilities for the definition of abstract data types and subtype (inclusion) polymorphism, features central to object-oriented programming.

Type theory as a whole has proved extremely useful in the object-oriented domain, even more so since the need for statically typed languages was identified [Meyer,88], [Schaffert,86]. Indeed, the language ML, mentioned above, is simply a syntactic sugaring of the typed lambda calculus. Work on lambda calculus is being taken further by the ABEL project, based at Hewlett-Packard Labs in Palo Alto, California. The ABEL project is aiming to provide a formal basis for subtyping and inheritance in object-oriented languages. Stemming from the thesis of Cook [Cook,89a] the team has identified problems in the recursive specification of object interfaces. They provide a solution to this problem, known as *F-bounded polymorphism*, and go on to show how this may be of use in future languages that employ subtypes and inheritance [Canning,89].

One of the main features of this work is that it has *formally* shown that the inheritance (implementation) and subtype (specification) hierarchies are not necessarily the same (an issue discussed in chapter 5) [Cook,90]

Applying formal methods Formal methods applied to the object-oriented paradigm is becoming increasingly important. Indeed, some flaws in language design have only been identified and rectified as a result of analysis using formal methods [Cook,89b]. The following describes research which is proving important in the area of object-oriented programming.

i) Goguen's work

Joseph Goguen was originally part of the ADJ group which helped provide a formal mathematical basis for abstract data types using algebras [Goguen,77]. Since then Goguen has used algebraic techniques as the basis of the object-oriented formal specification language OBJ [Futatsugi,85]. OBJ is the specification language for the language FOOPs [Goguen,87] which encapsulates both functional and object-oriented programming. In addition to this, Goguen has worked on applying various formal methods (mostly based around category theory) to produce an object model, the most recent being the theory of sheaf semantics [Goguen,90].

ii) The POOL language

POOL (Parallel Object Oriented Language) is currently being developed at Philips Research Labs at Eindhoven in the Netherlands [America,88] and aims to provide concurrency in an object-based environment. Formal methods have been an integral part of the design strategy for POOL. Operational and denotational semantics have been provided and the construction of an equivalence relation between the two has proved them to be consistent. POOL also incorporates inheritance and subtyping as part of the language. The formal specification of objects has produced a flexible subtyping policy [America,89].

Significant work on formal methods is also being carried out in the context of Open Distributed Processing standardization activities. For example, the work of Cusack on the semantics of class and type was featured in chapter 5. This work is continuing and is providing a formal basis for the object-oriented specification of distributed systems [Cusack,90]. The area of Open Distributed Processing is discussed in depth in section 14.6.

Predictions
- formal methods will have an important role in the future of object-oriented computing
- formal methods will help to resolve some of the difficult semantic issues in object-oriented computing
- the same process will lead to a more consistent use of terminology
- more well-founded languages will emerge in the near future

14.5 SHARING AND DISTRIBUTION

One of the biggest problems with many object-oriented systems is that they are targeted towards providing sophisticated single user environments running on a single machine. For the purpose of this discussion, such systems are referred to as Single User, Single Machine (or SUSM) systems. It is inevitable however that this class of system will prove to be inadequate for many users of object-oriented technology. For example, most computer projects tend to involve groups of people cooperating on a given task. Similarly, a typical computer environment now consists of a number of workstations interconnected by a computer network. It is therefore envisaged that object-oriented systems will evolve from single user to multiple user and from single machine to multiple machine. This leads to the following extended classification of object-oriented systems:-

355

i)   Single User, Single Machine (SUSM)
ii)   Multiple User, Single Machine (MUSM)
iii) Single User, Multiple Machine (SUMM)
iv) Multiple User, Multiple Machine (MUMM)

Considerable technical problems are faced in providing the latter three categories of system. In particular, moving from single user to multiple user introduces problems of sharing whereas moving from single machine to multiple machine adds problems of distribution. This is shown in figure 14.2.

Distribution

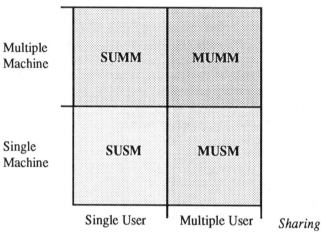

Figure 14.2: Sharing and distribution in object-oriented systems

The problems associated with sharing and distribution are briefly described below.

Sharing The problems associated with sharing can be sub-divided into two categories:-
i)   persistence of objects, and
ii) maintaining consistency across objects.

The move from single user to multi-user systems demands a sophisticated treatment of persistence. Persistent objects provide the unit of sharing in multi-user environments. The issue of persistence is now relatively well understood. There is a substantial research community working on this problem and significant progress has been made. In particular, there are a number of persistent object-oriented programming languages in existence, e.g. Arjuna [Dixon,89], SOS [Shapiro,89] and Galileo [Albano,85] The most interesting work in this field is the work that treats persistence and data type as orthogonal dimensions of a value (or object) [Morrison,87]. This concept is often referred to as *orthogonal persistence* and was discussed in chapter 7. It is likely that orthogonal persistence will increase in importance in the object-oriented community and will be adopted by more and more language developers. Many current implementations of object-oriented languages are naive in their treatment of persistence and hence are not suitable for shared, multi-user environments. For example, persistence in Smalltalk is modelled by taking complete snapshots of the system state to be stored in a filing system.

One of the main repercussions of persistence is that it becomes possible to integrate two previously separate concepts, namely the programming language and the system environment. Traditionally, programming languages provide facilities to manipulate transient data and the filing system provides facilities for manipulating persistent data. A number of routines would then be provided to explicitly map from one environment to the other. In persistent environments, this separation is not necessary. Persistent copies of objects are automatically maintained by the system. This has the advantage that the user of the system need learn only one interface in dealing with objects. In addition, the programmer is relieved of the task of converting between stored and transient forms of data. This area of research is extremely promising and brings together the previously separate areas of system design, programming languages and database languages [Dearle,88], [Atkinson,87]. However, much work remains before full integration can be achieved. Issues such as the modelling of complex objects, inter-relationships, versioning and inheritance all have to be brought into a common framework. The issue of typing is emerging as an important area of study in this context. In particular, polymorphic type systems are receiving much attention and have been successfully adopted in several projects, e.g. [Turner,85], [Demers,80].

The second important problem introduced by sharing is that of maintaining consistency of objects. In multi-user systems, there is a danger of simultaneous updates to objects resulting in corrupted data or inconsistent results. This problem has traditionally been solved by incorporating atomic transaction mechanisms in systems or languages [Bernstein,81]. Atomic transactions guarantee that simultaneous updates will have exactly the same effect as if the updates were carried out serially (*serializability*). Serializability is achieved by imposing constraints on the relative orderings of events in the system.

Most work on transactions has been carried out in the database community and a wide body of knowledge now exists. A range of techniques, generally based on locking or timestamps, are described in the literature. Many of the techniques have also been adopted in the object-oriented community. For example, both IRIS (see chapter 13) and Gemstone [Maier,86] support the use of transactions to maintain the consistency of objects. However, experience is now showing that traditional models of transactions may not be completely suitable for object-oriented environments. There are many reasons for this. For example, the granularity of objects is very different from database environments. Similarly, the patterns of access to objects can be completely different. For that reason, researchers are looking at new approaches to consistency which are more suitable for the object-oriented model of computation. This is likely to be a major area of future research in the subject. The most promising work is looking at more *flexible* approaches to transactions. One of the problems with transactions is that they are very rigid and conservative and do not take into account the semantics of data types. However, object-oriented environments often have much more knowledge of the semantics of individual objects. This ought to be exploited.

Early steps in this work was carried out in the Argus project [Liskov,84]. Argus allows types to be created out of in-built atomic types. Atomic types provide fairly traditional mechanisms for maintaining consistency of the data. This is then enhanced by allowing users to define their own data types with their own semantics of consistency. Other projects are extending this work by taking into account the characteristics of different objects. For example, work on the ANSA project [ANSA,89] is investigating the use of path expressions to specify constraints on the concurrent execution of operations on an object. Other systems looking at flexible transaction mechanisms include Arjuna [Dixon,89] and Avalon [Dtlefs,88]. Researchers at Tromso University in North Norway are taking an interesting approach of determining consistency constraints from the formal semantics of data types [Eliassen,89]. The semantics are written in the algebraic notation of ACT-ONE [Ehrig,85]. Similar research is also being carried out by Weihl at MIT [Weihl,88].

Another interesting area for future research is to weaken the requirement for strict serializability and hence to allow a greater level of concurrent activity in the system. Several approaches to non-serializable transactions have been proposed [Walpole,88], [Skarra,89]. Many object-oriented applications require weak forms of consistency and hence non-serializable transactions are likely to receive much more attention in the near future.

Distribution The move from single machine to multiple machine configurations has an even bigger impact on object-oriented systems. The issue of distributed object-oriented systems is still one of the least understood areas of work. Many of the issues associated with distribution have been introduced in chapter 9. For example, the problems of object location, distribution transparency and remote invocation of methods were all discussed in depth. A certain amount of progress has been made on these issues. However, more work is required before distributed object-oriented systems become viable. One of the main problems is that the required expertise is split between two separate communities. On the one hand, the distributed systems community have been investigating issues such as naming, location, migration and load balancing for many years. On the other hand, the object-oriented community have considerable expertise in the semantics of object-oriented systems, dynamic binding and type checking. A relatively small number of projects combine expertise from both camps, e.g. Comandos [Horn,87], Emerald [Black,86] and ANSA. A further synthesis of ideas is required before distributed object-oriented systems can be fully realized. This situation is shown in figure 14.3.

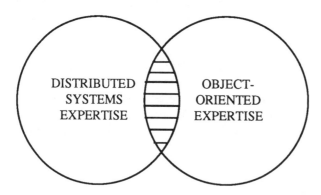

Figure 14.3: State of the art in distributed object-oriented systems

One of the biggest problems to resolve is that of performance. With the current state of the art, it is difficult to implement an efficient distributed object-oriented system successfully. This often reduces to one reason: the conflict between the object model and the facilities provided by the underlying system. More specifically, the process based models of most operating systems are not suitable for object-oriented environments. Practically all operating systems support distribution by providing processes supplemented by an inter-process communication service. All management decisions are then made on the basis of processes. For example, migration is carried out at the level of processes. This is not sufficient for object-oriented environments. One of the main characteristics of object-oriented environments is the wide variation in the granularity of objects. Therefore, it is too simplistic to map objects on to the abstraction of processes. A more flexible approach is required in order that management can be carried out at the object level. Decisions can thus be made to optimize the performance of objects (rather than optimized process behaviour). This area is likely to spawn further research in the future. At present various projects are developing operating system kernels which are tailored towards the abstraction of an object [Bernabeu,88], [Campbell,89].

One of the most interesting areas is the provision of support for object-oriented environments at the lowest levels of a computer architecture, including the hardware design of the system. An interesting approach to hardware support - the REKURSIV machine - was described in chapter 11 of this book. This work has not, however, considered support for distribution. Research at Lancaster University has investigated the use of a front-end board to provide low level support for object management in a distributed system [Lea,89].

Finally, the issue of distributed inheritance has not yet been fully resolved. It is now recognized that in the general case of large, heterogeneous distributed systems it is not feasible to support inheritance. Indeed, Wegner has stated categorically that distribution is inconsistent with inheritance [Wegner,87]. It should be stressed though that the real difficulty is implementing dynamic binding in a distributed environment. The overhead of binding to methods in a distributed system is too great to be carried out at run-time. However, there is no great difficulty in implementing inheritance if static binding is adopted. Further research could well alter the conventional wisdom in this area. For example, greater support for object-oriented systems could well lead to the situation where dynamic binding becomes feasible in a distributed system. Interesting work in this area is being carried out by the Jade project at Washington University [Raj,89].

Predictions
- importance of persistence in multi-user environments
- further integration of programming language and system environment
- importance of flexible transaction mechanisms in object-oriented computing
- synthesis of experience from distributed systems and object-oriented communities
- a move from process based to object based systems
- need for low level support for object management in a distributed system

14.6 OPEN DISTRIBUTED PROCESSING

The Open Distributed Processing (ODP) standardization initiative was introduced in chapter 9, including the contribution made by the ANSA and ISA projects. This present section outlines further the role of objects in the emerging ODP architecture, and in particular looks at the work being done on object-oriented specification.

The five viewpoints of the ODP architecture that were first introduced by the ANSA project have provided a valuable basis for discussion of the modelling of distributed systems, where by modelling we mean a description of a system from a particular point of view. For example, from the enterprise viewpoint, a system model will describe the system as seen by the user; this model will describe what the system is to do (i.e. its functionality) and not how this will be achieved (i.e. not its mechanisms). This is a perfectly good model, and one that is a necessary precursor to a satisfactory design. It is not a functional model in the sense that the details of the system functions are not described.

Although the ODP work is intended to apply to distributed computing systems, many of the results emerging on modelling and specification will apply also to non-distributed systems given that these do not have the additional properties and constraints of distribution. In ODP, modelling is a technique for supporting a specification that will be expressed using some language. A specification language expresses requirements or properties of the system being modelled, as opposed to mechanisms that will be expressed by an implementation language.

In the work of ODP, object-oriented specification describes a system as a collection of objects that have the usual properties of encapsulation and method access. Each object belongs to a class, and the classes belong to a class and type hierarchy. The system designer will specify class templates and objects appropriate to the required level of abstraction. Much then depends on how, or whether, object modelling concepts are used in the specification language to be used. The choice of appropriate modelling languages is the subject of much investigation, for example in the RACE ROSA project [RACE,89].

RACE is a programme of research on advanced communications for Europe, concentrating principally on the provision of a broadband integrated services digital network (B-ISDN) by 1995. Part of the research is aimed at developing tools and techniques for the description of network-independent telecommunications services in an attempt to minimise the lifetime software cost of telecommunications systems; this is the particular concern of the ROSA project. The basic premise of ROSA (RACE Open Services Architecture) is that the description of the services must provide a close match between each real-world service and its representation at the design stage. Object-oriented methods, it was felt, offered the route to success. In this choice, the ROSA project was heavily influenced by the ANSA/ISA work.

The ROSA approach is intended to apply to the entire lifecycle of a distributed system. In the first part of the project, many tools were studied to discover their applicability in describing the behaviour of ROSA objects; these included finite state machines (SDL and Estelle), temporal ordering (LOTOS), abstract data types (ACT-ONE) and predicate logic. It was decided to adopt an algebraic approach based on ACT-ONE to specify the semantics of objects. However, language support is recognized as important so that the designer does not need to deal directly with the algebraic specification technique, and so it has been agreed to develop a conceptual object-oriented linguistic (COOL) support system in the subsequent phases of the project. The ROSA approach is consistent with the work being undertaken on requirements capture and specification in the BEST project and on reusable software in the ARISE project, both of these being companion projects in the RACE programme.

The essence of the specification work in ROSA is that designers need tools that allow the structure of an object to be altered separately from its semantics. Structure may be changed by means of refinements and abstractions while the semantics of the service object remain unaltered. On the other hand, semantics may be changed by using extensions and reductions without necessarily affecting the object structure. The term *refinement* is familiar in software engineering as the process of manipulating a specification repeatedly to produce an implementation, thus adding more detail to the structure, while *abstraction* refers to the process of removing unnecessary detail from the specification. In ROSA, the terms *specification* and *implementation* are used as labels for two different specifications on which the relations *abstraction, refinement, extension and reduction* are defined. Thus an implementation is a transformation of a base specification in which the structure or semantics have been changed.

The ROSA project demonstrates the power of ACT-ONE as a specification tool that adequately represents the properties of objects, conceding that the primitive object-oriented model presented is only the starting point for a much more in-depth study of the role of an object-oriented specification approach for distributed systems.

Predictions
- The ODP standardization work will act as a highly effective promoter of object-oriented research and development techniques into the software industry
- A variety of object-oriented tools will be developed for use in the different viewpoints and for different stages of the software lifecycle
- The work under way in ODP will influence the software engineering community in their way of thinking about systems development
- There will be a closer link between algebraic and object-oriented techniques, because of the high level of abstraction in both approaches

14.7 MULTIMEDIA OBJECTS

Multimedia computing is emerging as one of the growth areas of technology in the 1990s. The reasons for this emergence are twofold. Firstly, there have been dramatic improvements in areas such as computer networks, workstation technology and compression hardware thus enabling more complex data sources to be handled. Secondly, there are increasing demands from industry and commerce for more sophisticated and integrated communications infrastructures to support working between remote sites. With this interest, it is inevitable that multimedia will become a major issue in the design of future object-oriented environments. More specifically, future object-oriented environments will support a range of different data types including:-
- alphabetic and numeric data,
- voice,
- hi-fidelity audio,
- vector graphics,
- raster graphics,
- animation,
- slow scan video,
- full motion video.

This will have a profound impact on the design of object-oriented systems. The effect of moving to multimedia objects can be considered at two levels:-

i) Engineering level
   Multimedia will have a considerable impact on the engineering decisions required to implement object-oriented systems (both at the hardware and software levels).

ii) Conceptual level

    Multimedia computing will also have a major impact on the conceptual view of object models as perceived by the user.

In terms of engineering, multimedia imposes considerable requirements on the hardware and system infrastructure. This area is receiving considerable attention at present and progress is being made. For example, multimedia workstations are now becoming available. Similarly, high density storage devices together with compression hardware are making the storage of multimedia objects a possibility.

Technologically, one of the biggest steps is to move towards distributed, multimedia systems. Again, progress is being made. Multiservice network technologies such as FDDI (for local and metropolitan area communication) and ISDN (for wide area communication) are now becoming commercially available. In addition, research is being directed towards the design and implementation of high performance protocols capable of carrying multimedia traffic[2]. System infrastructures such as the one shown in figure 14.4 are thus becoming feasible.

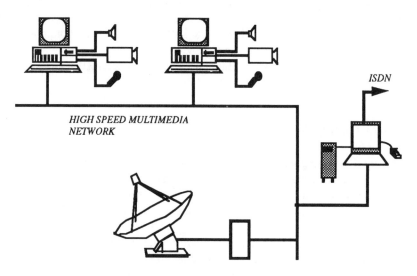

Figure 14.4: Typical multimedia environment

    Considerable progress is therefore being made on the enabling technologies required to support multimedia objects. However, on its own, this is not enough. The introduction of multimedia adds considerable complexity to the management of objects in a system. This is particularly true if the system is distributed. One of the main problems to be overcome is the issue of granularity. It has proved difficult in the past to manage object-oriented systems because of the variation in object size. This problem becomes much worse when multimedia objects are considered. In multimedia systems, an object can be anything from a simple integer to a section of moving video footage. The other problem faced by designers of multimedia systems is the requirement for real-time performance. Certain media types (in particular voice and video) make very stringent demands on the underlying system. If the demands cannot be met, then the service provided will be

---

[2]A full discussion of multimedia computing can be found in [Davies,90]

unacceptable. This places great pressure on the underlying system to make optimal or near optimal decisions. Engineering support for multimedia objects is therefore likely to be a major area of research in the future.

At the conceptual level, multimedia is likely to make an even bigger impact. Object-oriented systems are essentially about modelling concepts in the real world. To date, this process has been restricted by the limited nature of base objects available in a system. In particular, the building blocks of an object-oriented system have been restricted to simple mathematical or character based representations of information. Multimedia can thus be seen as a natural extension to object-oriented systems where the range of information types is greatly expanded. It is equally possible to capture a real world concept using pictorial or audio information as with textual data. In many cases, the greater range of information sources can considerably enhance the utility of a system.

It is likely that the introduction of multimedia will have an impact on object models. Modifications and enhancements will be required to cater for the new styles of information. One of the biggest areas of interest is in the description of complex object structures where an object can be composed of a variety of media types in a hierarchical or networked arrangement. Multimedia document architectures are currently receiving much attention with most of the work adopting an object-oriented approach to describing document contents and structure. Document architectures are complicated by the need to consider a wide variety of relationship types between component objects, including:-

i)   logical relationships between components (e.g. a cross reference),
ii)   temporal relationships (e.g. synchronization constraints), and
iii) spatial relationships describing the structure to be displayed.

A typical document structure is shown in figure 14.5.

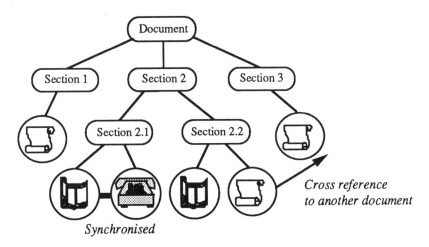

Figure 14.5: Typical document structure

The other major impact of the introduction of multimedia objects will be to open up new areas of application for the technology. The main advantage of multimedia is that a range of different information services can be integrated around the computer workstation. For example, a workstation can have the capability to show a section of video, can be used to manage telephone links to other users and can store and retrieve

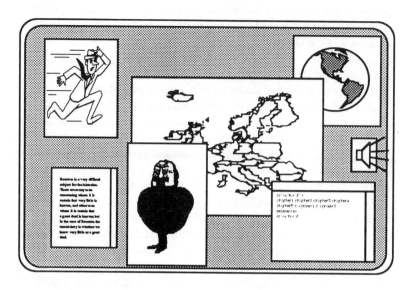

Figure 14.6: Possible multimedia environment

images in parallel with more normal computer operations (a possible scenario is shown in figure 14.6).

This style of working has great potential for many fields of application. Potential applications of multimedia technology are listed below:-

- design environments
- distance learning
- computer mediated conferencing
- medical systems
- office information systems

One of the most significant developments in recent years has been the emergence of the new field of Computer Supported Cooperative Work (or CSCW) [EC-CSCW,89]. CSCW draws on many of the strands discussed in this chapter and indeed in this book. The topic is concerned with providing computer support for a group of users interacting on a specific task (e.g. authoring, designing or management). Much of the work in this field has adopted an object-oriented approach to the problem. In addition, CSCW brings in aspects of multimedia computing, distributed computing, user interface design and databases. CSCW is likely to have a significant impact on object-oriented computing in the 1990s.

Predictions
- multimedia computing will have a profound effect on object-oriented systems
- more refined object management techniques will be required for the storage and transmission of multimedia information
- a wider perception of information will be required
- more sophisticated object models will emerge to cope with the requirements of multimedia systems
- an extensive range of application areas will open up with multimedia systems

14.8 CLOSING REMARKS

Object-oriented computing has made a significant impact in the past decade. However, it is clear that further work remains to be done before the technology can claim to be mature. This chapter has focussed on potential future directions for the subject. From this discussion, one consistent theme emerges, that the subject must enter a period of reflection and evaluation. This is emphasized in the following statements taken from the various sections of the chapter:-

i)   there is a need for a consolidation of object-oriented concepts and terms,
ii) experience will lead to a better understanding of the benefits and drawbacks of the object-oriented approach,
iii) object-oriented computing is not a panacea for all problems,
iv) a more pragmatic view is required of the role of object-oriented computing in the software lifecycle, and
v)   there is a need for a more formal understanding of the semantics of object-orientation.

Object-oriented computing is approaching a watershed. The 1980s have witnessed a period of intense activity, of innovation and to a certain extent of confusion and chaos. This phase is coming to an end. The subject is moving into a period of experimentation and collection of empirical evidence. This in turn will lead to a re-evaluation of the many claims made for the subject in recent years. This will be an interesting stage in the development of object-oriented computing and will inevitably lead to a more sober assessment of the subject. The authors are confident, though, that object-orientation will emerge from this process as a more mature discipline with a leading role to play in the future of computing.

It would be a mistake to give the impression that no more research is needed in object-oriented computing. The period of consolidation referred to above will provide a range of object-oriented tools and techniques to support traditional areas such as programming, databases, etc. This is a very worthwhile goal for the subject. However, this is not the ultimate goal of object-oriented computing and indeed would be a false summit. Object-oriented computing therefore remains an area of active research. The vision for the *next* generation of object-oriented tools can be captured by the three 'i's:-

i) interaction

There is a need for techniques to support a number of end users interacting view an object-oriented environment to achieve a common goal. This introduces many research issues concerned with the sharing and distribution of objects (see section 14.5).

ii) integration

There is a need for object-oriented tools (and possibly other tools) to work together in a common framework. Integration is a very demanding topic for object-oriented computing, involving such areas as inter-operability and standards. The section on Open Distributed Processing (section 14.6) touched on some of the issues raised by integration.

iii) information

A wider view is required of information to encompass the range of media types now available in a modern computing environment (e.g. image and audio). The move towards multimedia in object-oriented systems was discussed in depth in section 14.7.

Collectively, the three areas raise fundamental questions which may have a significant impact on the long-term future of object-oriented computing.

In conclusion, it can be anticipated that the subject will mature through the experience gained in applying object-oriented techniques in industry and commerce. Of equal importance, research will continue with a view to producing a new generation of object-oriented languages, systems and applications.

ACKNOWLEDGEMENTS

Many thanks to our colleagues at Lancaster University who helped formulate the ideas for the section of software engineering (in particular John Mariani and Tom Rodden). Thanks also to Neil Williams for unravelling some of the mysteries of the word processing environment and Alastair Macartney for contributions to the formal methods section of this chapter.

REFERENCES

[Albano,85] Albano, A., L. Cardelli, and R. Orsini. "Galileo: A Strongly-Typed, Interactive Conceptual Language." *Trans. Database Systems Vol:* 10 No.: 2, June 1985, Pages: 230-260.

[America,89] America, P. "A Behavioural Approach to Subtyping in Object Oriented Programming Languages", *ESPRIT Project 415* document 443, Philips Research Labs, Eindhoven, The Netherlands. 1989.

[America,88] America, P. "Definition of POOL2 - a parallel object oriented language", *ESPRIT Project 415* document 364, Philips Research Labs, Eindhoven, The Netherlands. 1988.

[ANSA,89] ANSA. "ANSA Reference Manual, Release 01.00", APM Cambridge Ltd. March 1989.

[Atkinson,87] Atkinson, M.P., and O.P. Buneman. "Types and Persistence in Database Programming Languages." *ACM Computing Surveys Vol:* 19 No.: 2, June 1987, Pages: 105-190.

[Balzer,85] Balzer, R. "A 15-Year Perspective on Automatic Programming." *IEEE Transactions on Software Engineering Vol:* SE-11 No.: 11, Nov 1985, Pages: 1257-1268.

[Barnard,89] Barnard, A.J. "On Introducing a Type System to an Object Oriented Language", *MSc Thesis*, University of Manchester, U.K. 1989.

[Bernabeu,88] Bernabeu, J., Y.A. Khalidi, M. Ahamad, W.F. Appelbe, P. Dasgupta, R.J. LeBlanc, and U. Ramachandran. "Clouds - A Distributed Object Oriented Operating System: Architecture and Kernel Implementation." *Proceedings of the 88'EUUG Conference, Casais, Portugal,*

[**Bernstein,81**] Bernstein, P.A., and N. Goodman. "Concurrency Control in Distributed Database Systems." *Computer Surveys Vol:* 13 No.: 2, June 1981, Pages: 185-221.

[**Black,86**] Black, A., N. Hutchinson, E. Jul, and H. Levy. "Object Structure in the Emerald System." *Proceedings of the Conference on Object-Oriented Programming Systems, Languages and Applications (OOPSLA '86), Portland, Oregon,* Editor: N. Meyrowitz, Special Issue of ACM SIGPLAN Notices, Vol: 21, Pages: 78-86.

[**Black,89**] Black, S. "Objects and LOTOS", *Internal report* Hewlett-Packhard Research Laboratories, Bristol, U.K. May 1989.

[**Campbell,89**] Campbell, R.H., and P.W. Madany. "Consideration for Peristence and Security in Choices, an Object-Oriented Operating System", *Internal Report* University of Illinois at Urbana-Champaign.

[**Canning,89**] Canning, P.S., W.R. Cook, W.L. Hill, and W.G. Olthoff. "Interfaces for Strongly-Typed Object-Oriented Programming." *Proceedings of OOPSLA '89, New Orleans,* Pages: 457-467.

[**Cardelli,85**] Cardelli, L., and P. Wegner. "On Understanding Types, Data Abstraction, and Polymorphism." *Computing Surveys Vol:* 17 No.: 4, Pages: 471-522.

[**Cheatham,81**] Cheatham, T.E. "Program Refinement by Transformation." *IEEE 5th International Conference on Software Engineering, San Diego, CA,* March 1981.

[**Cook,89a**] Cook, W. A Denotational Semantics of Inheritance, *PhD*, Brown University, Providence, Rhode Island. May 1989.

[**Cook,89b**] Cook, W. "A Proposal for making Eiffel Type Safe." *Proceedings of the Third European Conference on Object-Oriented Programming (ECOOP '89), Nottingham, UK.,* Cambridge University Press, UK.,

[**Cook,90**] Cook, W., W. Hill, and P. Canning. "Inheritance is not Subtyping." *Proceedings ACM Symposium on the Principles of Programming Languages (POPL),* January 1990.

[**Cusack,90**] Cusack, E., and M. Lai. "Object Oriented Specification in LOTOS and Z or, My Cat Really is Object-Oriented!" *presented at the REX/FOOL Workshop on the Foundations of Object Oriented Programming, Noordwijkerhout, The Netherlands,* May 28th - June 1st, 1990.

[**Davies,90**] Davies, N.A., and J.R. Nicol. "A Technological Perspective on Multimedia Computing", *Internal report* Lancaster University. July 1990.

[**Dearle,88**] Dearle, A. On the Construction of Persistent Programming Environments, *Ph.D. Thesis,* Universi y of St. Andrews, Scotland. March 1988.

[Demers,80] Demers, A.J., Donahue, J.E. "Data Types, Parameters and Type Checking." *Conference Record of the 7th Annual ACM Symposium on Principles of Programming Languages,* Pages: 12-23.

[Di Maio,89] Di Maio, A., F. Bott, I. Sommerville, R. Bayan, and M. Wirsing. "The DRAGON Project." *The ESPRIT Conference 1989,*

[Dixon,89] Dixon, G.N., G.D. Parrington, S.K. Shrivastava, and S.M. Wheater. "The Treatment of Persistent Objects in Arjuna." *The Computer Journal Vol:* 32 No.: 4, 1989, Pages: 323-332.

[Dtlefs,88] Dtlefs, D.L., M.P. Herlihy, and J.M. Wing. "Inheritance of Synchronization and Recovery Properties in Avalon/C++." *IEEE Computer* December 1988, Pages: 57-69.

[EC-CSCW,89] EC-CSCW. "various papers." *The First European Conference on CSCW, Gatwick Hilton Hotel, UK,* September 1989.

[Ehrig,85] Ehrig, H., Mahr, B. *Fundamentals of Algebraic Specification.* Springer-Verlag. 1985.

[Eliassen,89] Eliassen, F. "FRIL Linguistic Support for Interoperable Information Systems", *Technical Report* University of Tromsoe, Norway. March 1989.

[Futatsugi,85] Futatsugi, K., J. Goguen, and et al. "Principles of OBJ2." *Proceedings ACM Symposium on Principles of Programming Languages (POPL),* Pages: 52-66. 1985.

[Goguen, 77] Goguen, J. "Initial Algebra Semantics and Continuous Algebras." *Journal of the ACM Vol:* 24 No.: 1, January 1977, Pages: 68-95.

[Goguen, 90] Goguen, J. "Sheaf Semantics for Concurrent Interacting Objects." *presented at the REX/FOOL Workshop on the Foundations of Object Oriented Programming, Noordwijkerhout, The Netherlands,* May 28th - June 1st 1990.

[Goguen,87] Goguen, J., and J. Meseguer. "Unifying Functional, Relational and Object Oriented Programming." *Research Directions in Object Oriented Programming.* Editor: B. Shriver and P. Wegner. MIT Press, 1987. Pages: 417-477.

[Gordon, 79] Gordon, M.J., A.J. Milner, and C.P. Wadsworth. *Edinburgh LCF.* Springer-Verlag.

[Horn,87] Horn, C., Krakowiak, S. "Object-Oriented Architecture for Distributed Office Systems." *Proceedings of ESPRIT '87.* North-Holland,

[Lea,89] Lea, R. Network Support for Distributed Objects: Coping with Heterogeneity in Models and Architectures, *Ph.D.,* Lancaster University. March 1989.

[Liskov,84] Liskov, B.H. "Overview of the Argus Language and System", Programming Methodology Group Memo 40,, M. I. T. Laboratory for Computer Science. February

1984.

[**Maier,86**] Maier, D., J. Stein, A. Otis, and A. Purdy. "Development of an Object-Oriented DBMS." *Proceedings of the Conference on Object-Oriented Programming Systems, Languages and Applications (OOPSLA '86), Portland, Oregon,* Editor: N. Meyrowitz, Special Issue of SIGPLAN Notices, Vol: 21, Pages: 472-482.

[**Meyer,88**] Meyer, B. *Object-Oriented Software Construction.* Prentice-Hall.

[**Morrison,87**] Morrison, R., A.L. Brown, R. Carrick, R.C. Connor, A. Dearle, and M.P. Atkinson. "Polymorphism, Persistence and Software Reuse in a Strongly Typed Object-Oriented Environment." *IEE and BCS Journal on Software Engineering* December 1987,

[**RACE,89**] RACE. "RACE Open Services Architecture project deliverable on object-oriented techniques", *Report* RACE Directorate, European Commission, Brussels. July 1989.

[**Raj,89**] Raj, R.K., and H.M. Levy. "A Compositional Model for Software Reuse." *Proceedings of the Third European Conference on Object-Oriented Programming (ECOOP '89), Nottingham, England,* Editor: S. Cook, Cambridge University Press, UK., Pages: 3-24.

[**Schaffert,86**] Schaffert, C., T. Cooper, B. Bullis, M. Kilian, and C. Wilpolt. "An Introduction to Trellis/Owl." *Proceedings of the Conference on Object-oriented Programming Systems, Languages and Applications (OOPSLA '86), Portland, Ore.; Sept 1986,* Editor: N. Meyrowitz, Special Issue of SIGPLAN Notices, Vol: 21, Pages: 9-16.

[**Shapiro,89**] Shapiro, M., P. Gautron, and L. Mosseri. "Persistence and Migration for C++ Objects." *Proceedings of the Third European Conference on Object-Oriented Programming (ECOOP '89), Nottingham, England,* 1989.

[**Skarra,89**] Skarra, A.H., and S.B. Zdonik. "Concurrency Control and Object-Oriented Databases." *Object-Oriented Concepts, Databases and Applications.* Editor: W. Kim and F.H. Lochovsky. New York: ACM Press, Pages: 395-422.

[**Turner,85**] Turner, D.A. "Miranda: A Non-strict Functional Language with Polymorphic Types'." *Proceedings of the IFIP International Conference on Functional Programming Languages and Computer Architecture, Nancy, France,*

[**Walpole,88**] Walpole, J., G.S. Blair, J. Malik, and J.R. Nicol. "A Unifying Model for Consistent Distributed Software Development Environments." *Proc. ACM SIGSOFT/SIGPLAN Software Engineering Symposium on Practical Software Development Environments, Boston, MA,* Pages: 183-190. November 1988.

[**Wasserman,90**] Wasserman, A.I., P.A. Pircher, and R.J. Muller. "The Object-Oriented Structured Design Notation for Software Design Representation." *IEEE Computer Vol:* 23 No.: 3, March 1990, Pages: 50-63.

[**Wegner,87**] Wegner, P. "Dimensions of Object-Based Language Design."
*Proceedings of the Conference on Object-Oriented Programming Systems, Languages,
and Applications (OOPSLA '87), Orlando, FL,* Editor: N. Meyrowitz, Special Issue of
ACM SIGPLAN Notices, Vol: 22, 1987, Pages: 168-182.

[**Weihl,88**] Weihl, W.E. "Commutativity-based Concurrency Control for Abstract Data
Types." *IEEE Transactions on Computers Vol:* 37 No.: 12, December 1988,

[**Wolczko,88**] Wolczko, M. "Semantics of Object Oriented Programming Languages",
Technical Report UMCS-88-6-1, University of Manchester UK. 1988.

[**Wolczko,87**] Wolczko, M. "Semantics of Smalltalk-80." *Proceedings European
Conference on Object-Oriented Programming, Paris,* 1987.

Index

373

375

377